A MANUAL OF ETHNOLOGY

A MANUAL OF ETHNOLOGY

OR THE RACES OF THE OLD WORLD

CHARLES LORING BRACE

Published by

Isha Books
B-63, Ist Floor
New Gupta Colony
Near DDA Market
Delhi - 110009

Distribution Network
gyanbooks.com
India, USA, Canada, UK, Australia

ISBN: 978-93-3316-951-6 (HB)
First Published, 1869

2nd Impression 2025

Printed at: Gyan Press, Delhi.

A MANUAL OF ETHNOLOGY
Author: CHARLES LORING BRACE

THE

RACES OF THE OLD WORLD.

A

MANUAL OF ETHNOLOGY:

OR,

THE RACES

OF

THE OLD WORLD.

By CHARLES L. BRACE,

AUTHOR OF "HOME-LIFE IN GERMANY," "NORSE-FOLK," ETC.

SECOND EDITION.

LONDON:
JOHN MURRAY, ALBEMARLE STREET.
1869.

PREFACE.

THE subject of Human Races has exceedingly interested the public mind, both in England and America, for a number of years, and yet it has been very difficult to obtain trustworthy information upon it in any compact form. The facts in the science are scattered through such a number of varied works, such as the descriptions of travellers, the journals of missionaries, the contributions of army officers to foreign magazines, the papers on particular tribes written by students of races, or the examination of single languages made by students of language, that it is impossible to take a thorough survey of the subject without a vast deal of labour.

The vice of the science, too, has been the substitution of theory and hypothesis for facts, and the little distinction made to the student's mind between the careful results of investigation, and the fancies, whether in physiology or philology, of the author. It seems to be so difficult for any writer upon the subject of Human Races to confess anything uncertain, or to admit any want of classification.

There has appeared to be a need for a compact and careful work upon Ethnology. It is true, PRICHARD still remains the master of the science, and a patient study of his works will give a comprehensive view of the subject. But his various treatises are too voluminous for the common reader, and beside, do not contain the latest results attained by scholars bearing on the subject.

The present Manual of the Ethnology of the Old World is designed, not so much for the learned as for the large number of persons who are interested in the study of History, whether in academies and colleges, or among the people of business and professions. Such often desire to ascertain readily the position of a certain people or tribe among the races of men, or, at least, to know the latest conclusions of scholars in regard to them.

To them history is usually a mere diary of facts, and they want some link of connection, something which will unravel the confused web of human events. This treatise is intended to fill these wants—to present in brief and clear form the latest and most trustworthy results of scholarship and scientific investigation bearing on the question of races, and to furnish a Guide—imperfect though it may be—to the study of history. History is not merely a journal of battles and the reigns of kings: it is a description of the Life of Man, and in no way can this be made so clear as by following down the different lines of descent among the various tribes of the human family. Events, institutions, forms of government, revolutions and changes, which before appeared isolated and arbitrary, become under this investigation the natural and normal developments of the qualities of certain races, and history is made a clear and philosophical record. Many of our narrow prejudices and false theories in regard to Race—ideas which have been at the base of ancient abuses and long-established institutions of oppression—are removed by this study.

The aim in this Treatise has been as much as possible to separate the theoretical and the fanciful from the scientifically true; accordingly the reader must not be surprised that we are often obliged to say "We do not know." The scholar, in examining this work, will meet with many seeming deficiencies. He will naturally expect to find fuller accounts of certain favourite races or nations; much will be omitted which he would wish to see, and sometimes more will be given than he thinks necessary. His own theory or opinion on a particular question may not be adopted, or doubt may be expressed where he would see certainty. But we bespeak his kind judgment, from the consideration of the nature of the work: that it is an attempt to make popular a difficult science, and to present a vast subject in a duodecimo. Many things must be omitted which ought to be said, and the degree of prominence given to each race must be governed by the general scale of the work.

The manual is divided into eight Divisions: the First treats of the leading Races in the earliest historical period; the Second, of the primitive Races in Europe; the Third, of the leading Races of Asia in the middle ages; the Fourth, of the modern Ethnology of Asia; the Fifth, of Oceanic Ethnography; the Sixth, of the Ethnology of Africa; the Seventh, of the Races of modern Europe; and the Eighth, of the Antiquity of Man, and the question of Unity or Diversity of Origin.

It will be observed that we have not touched upon the history of mankind immediately succeeding Creation, the subject leading into such an endless chain of fancies and theories. This book is confined to Races as they appear in History.

If the present Treatise shall be favourably received,

we trust to follow it by another upon the "Races of the New World."

We must beg leave to express especial obligations to the New York libraries for many courtesies shown in the progress of this work. The librarians and assistants of the "Astor Library" have been especially kind and hospitable. The "Mercantile Library," too, is stored with valuable works of History and Ethnology, which are liberally loaned. The "Society Library," of this city, and the "Oriental Society Library," of New Haven, have supplied indispensable assistance.

CHARLES LORING BRACE.

HASTINGS-ON-THE-HUDSON, *April*, 1863.

CONTENTS.

CHAPTER I.

INTRODUCTORY.

PART FIRST.

FIRST HISTORICAL RACES.

CHAPTER II.

THE TURANIANS AND HAMITES.

CHAPTER III.

THE CHRONOLOGY OF EGYPT.

CHAPTER IV.

THE SEMITES.

CHAPTER V.

THE ARYANS.

CHAPTER VI.

THE RULING RACES—1300-500 B.C.

PART SECOND.

THE PRIMITIVE RACES OF EUROPE.

CHAPTER VII.

THE TURANIANS.

CHAPTER VIII.

THE ARYAN RACES OF EUROPE.

CHAPTER IX.

EARLY TEUTONIC TRIBES.

CHAPTER X.

THE EARLY SLAVONIANS.

CHAPTER XI.

TURANIAN RACES IN EUROPE.

PART THIRD.

LEADING RACES OF ASIA IN THE MIDDLE AGES.

CHAPTER XII.

THE SEMITES.

PART FOURTH.

MODERN ETHNOLOGY OF ASIA.

CHAPTER XIII.

THE RACES OF INDIA.

CHAPTER XIV.

RACES OF CHINA AND COCHIN-CHINA.

CHAPTER XV.

THE TIBETANS, TUNGUSIANS, MONGOLS, AND SAMOIEDS.

CHAPTER XVI.

TURKISH RACES.

CHAPTER XVII.

RACES OF PERSIA, AFGHANISTAN, AND BILUCHISTAN.

CHAPTER XVIII.

RACES OF GEORGIA, THE CAUCASUS, AND ARMENIA.

PART FIFTH.

OCEANIC ETHNOGRAPHY.

CHAPTER XIX.

RACES OF OCEANICA.

PART SIXTH.

ETHNOLOGY OF AFRICA.

CHAPTER XX.

THE SEMITIC TRIBES.

CHAPTER XXI.

HAMITIC TRIBES OF AFRICA.

CHAPTER XXII.

RACES OF WESTERN AFRICA.

CHAPTER XXIII.

RACES OF SOUTHERN AFRICA.

CHAPTER XXIV.

DAMARAS AND OVAMPOS.

CHAPTER XXV.

HOTTENTOTS.

PART SEVENTH.

ETHNOLOGY OF MODERN EUROPE.

CHAPTER XXVI.

TURANIANS.

CHAPTER XXVII.

ARYANS OF EUROPE.

CHAPTER XXVIII.

THE ALBANIANS.

CHAPTER XXIX.

THE ROMANIC OR LATIN RACES.

CHAPTER XXX.

THE KELTS.

CHAPTER XXXI.

WANDERING RACES.

PART EIGHTH.

GENERAL QUESTIONS IN ETHNOLOGY.

CHAPTER XXXII.

THE ANTIQUITY OF MAN.

CHAPTER XXXIII.

UNITY OR DIVERSITY OF ORIGIN.

THE

RACES OF THE OLD WORLD.

A MANUAL OF ETHNOLOGY.

CHAPTER I.

INTRODUCTORY.

Definition of Ethnology.

ETHNOLOGY, according to its literal derivation, means the Science of Nations; but in the more comprehensive modern classification, nations have been divided according to descent or race, and the word has come to mean the *Science of Races*. Perhaps, for a treatise like the present, if the word were not strange to common usage, *Ethnography*, or a Description of Races, would be a more appropriate title. The term "Race" has been chosen by writers on this subject because it leaves unsettled the great question at the basis of the Science—the Unity or Diversity of Origin of Mankind; the word designating groups of individuals who are united by the bond of Community of Descent, but not determining whether the races themselves are *Varieties*, that is, branches from one stock, or *Species*, which are distinct in origin.

The mysterious and far-reaching property of blood—of Race, is becoming more and more recognized in modern Science. That power, whereby the most dis-

Race.

tant ancestor shall influence his remotest descendant, and—still more wonderful—that accumulated effect of a line of ancestors on the final progeny, so that a clear stream of inherited physical and mental peculiarities can flow unmingled through human history in every variety of external circumstances and internal influences—is something not to be lightly weighed in the philosophy of man or in the history of his actions.

Whether races have always been distinct from one another, or whether they are to remain distinct and permanent, is not here in question. In the existence of mankind, so far as it is known to us, Human Races evidently play separate and powerful parts, disentangling for us something of the confusion of historic annals, and each contributing its share toward the progress and the final perfection of humanity. In contemplating them, the mind rises above the arbitrary divisions of name and locality and forms of government to the truer classification of common descent and mutual brotherhood; and each group becomes in this aspect, like each individual, an expression of the wonderful variety in the Divine works, and a separate manifestation of moral powers or qualities, and of the ever-acting Spirit of God.

We do not propose, however, in this treatise so much to examine the philosophy of Race—its influence upon the world and human development—as to describe briefly the prominent races classified in some cases on a new basis. Modern scholarship has been gradually approaching the conclusion that among all the tests of

Basis of classification.

community of descent in a given group of human beings, the best is the evidence of *Language*, connecting with it also the testimony of history.

Physical resemblances, or diversities are not found to present so ultimate a ground of classification as those of the human speech. The Word is the highest outward expression for the soul; and the properties of the immaterial part of man—his unconscious instincts, his hopes, his passions, his imaginings, his tendency of thought, his general habit of nature, appearing in language and its forms—are transmitted more entirely from generation to generation, and are less liable to be changed by external influences than any features of the face or the body. It is well known that time and external circumstances, and the mingling with other stocks, can change to a considerable degree (how far, is not here in consideration) the colour, the hair, the shape of the skull, and the size of the body. Yet, after many generations, when the physicist could scarcely, by external signs, recognize the bonds of common blood binding different peoples together, the student of language discerns the clearest and most irrefutable proofs of their common descent. What scholar doubts now the brotherhood of descent, at a remote period, between the Hindoo and the Englishman? and yet how few physical ethnologists could discover it by any bodily features! It is as if the more intangible properties of man's nature were those most acted on by the principle of inheritance, and the last to be changed or destroyed by external physical influences.

Language the best mark of race.

A distinguished naturalist, Professor Agassiz, has thus remarked on the evidence from language, in a preface to the work of Messrs. Gliddon and Nott, upon "Indigenous Races:"

Agassiz's objections.

"Let any one follow upon a map exhibiting the geographical distribution of the bears, the cats, the hollow-horned ruminants, the gallinaceous birds, the ducks, or of any other families, and he may trace, as satisfactorily as any philological evidence can prove it for the human language, and upon a much larger scale, that the brumming of the bears of Kamtchatka is akin to that of the bears of Thibet, of the East Indies, of the Sunda Islands, of Nepaul, of Syria, of Europe, of Siberia, of the United States, of the Rocky Mountains, and of the Andes, though all these bears are considered as distinct species, who have not any more inherited their voice one from the other than the different races of men. The same may be said of the roaring and miawing of the cats of Europe, Asia, Africa, and America; or of the lowing of the bulls, the species of which are so widely distributed nearly over the whole globe. The same is true of the gackeling of the gallinaceous birds, and of the quacking of the ducks, as well as of the song of the thrushes, all of which pour forth their gay and harmonious notes in a distinct and independent dialect, neither derived nor inherited one from the other, even though all sing thrushish. Let any philologist study these facts, and learn at the same time how independent the animals are one from the other, which utter such closely-allied systems of intonations, and if he be not altogether blind to the significance of the analogies in nature, he must begin himself to question the reliability of philological evidence as proving genetic derivation" (p. 15).

These criticisms—and we quote them as best embodying the popular objections to this source of evidence—show such an extraordinary want of appreciation of the very nature of the evidence on this subject, that we could hardly reply to them seriously but for their source. If the students of language derived their conclusions of the common bonds of different forms of speech from the similar articulate sounds uttered by different nations, if they class together all those, for instance, who gave a like sound to their vowels or their consonants, there might be some force in these objections; but so far is this from being the case, that even the like words in different tongues, caught from the sounds of nature, or which are the natural and almost necessary expressions of human feeling, are not considered at all in the evidence of a common descent. It is first, the ***Primitive Words and Roots*** of a language; and secondly, and of more importance, the *Grammatical Structure*, which are the especial proofs of the relation of two tongues. Take the numerals, for instance. How immense the chances are—millions to one—with a score of different tribes, such as the Indo-European, that they would not accidentally hit upon even one numeral which should be alike in all their different tongues; but if it was discovered that most of their numerals were alike, and if it were remembered that, of all words, numerals are the least likely to be lost by an ignorant people, or borrowed by a cultivated one, how great the probability would be of a common origin to these various peoples!

Answer.

Sources of Evidence.

We append as an illustration the following tables of numerals, taken from Max Müller's excellent work, "Languages at the Seat of War:"

NUMERALS.

Latin.	Spanish.	Portuguese.	Italian.	Wallachian.	French.
1. Unus	uno	hum	uno	unu	un
2. Duo	dos	dois	due	doi	deux
3. Tres	tres	tres	tré	trei	trois
4. Quatuor	quatro	quatro	quattro	patru	quatre
5. Quinque	cinco	cinco	cinque	quinqué	cinq
6. Sex	seis	seis	sei	sése	six
7. Septem	siete	sete	sette	sépte	sept
8. Octo	ocho	oito	otto	optu	huit
9. Novem	nueve	nove	nove	nové	neuf
10. Decem	*diez*	*dez*	*dieci*	dece	dix

	Latin.	Sanskrit.	Persian.	Old Slavonic.	Anglo-Saxon.	Welsh.
1.	Unus	eka	yek	yedinŏ	ân	un
2.	Duo	dvau	du	dŏva	tva	dau
3.	Tres	tri	sih	tri	þri	tri
4.	Quatuor	*k*atvar	*k*ehâr	*k*etŏïriye	feover	pedwar
5.	Quinque	pan*k*an	pen*g*	pa*m*tĕ	fif	pump
6.	Sex	shash	ses	sestĕ	six	chwech
7.	Septem	saptan	heft	sedmĕ	seofon	saith
8.	Octo	ash*t*an	hest	osmĕ	eahta	wyth
9.	Novem	navan	nuh	deva*m*tĕ	nigon	naw
10.	Decem	dasan	deh	desa*m*te	tyn	deg

But when, still farther, we find such primitive words as *Father*, *Fadar* (Germ.), *Pater* (Lat.), *Pitar* (Sansk.); or *Widow*, *Viduvô* (Germ.), *Vidua* (Lat.), *Vidhavâ* (Sansk.), as well as many others, so similar; or when we see the names of animals, such as *Sow*, *Sû* (Germ.), *Sus* (Lat.), *Sû-karas* (Sansk.), or *Mouse*, *Mûs* (Germ.), *Mus* (Lat.), *Mûsh* (Sansk.), with innumerable similar, so nearly alike, the probability of a common source to these tribes is still farther strengthened. This evidence is still more increased by the similarity of roots, underlying many words, apparently different; and it may be raised as nearly to complete demonstration as the case will admit, by the more refined resemblances in *grammatical structure.*

Common Indo-European words.

I do not propose at this point to give illustrations of the latter, or full examples of the former, as my object is merely to show the nature of the evidence on which classification of races is based in this treatise.

Grammar is no doubt the most subtile and enduring token of race. We cannot, at this point, of course, present full illustrations of this; yet the existence, for example, of such a people as the *Basques*, in Spain, preserving themselves separate in habits, institutions, and costume, for so many centuries, on a soil where innumerable tribes of Kelts and *Romans* and Teutons have become mingled in almost

Grammar as a token of race.

inextricable confusion, and marking their external separation by a language and grammar which are world-wide in their form from almost any European tongue, is too striking a case in point to be passed over.

Or again, such a fact as the Lithuanian peasant in Prussia, after a separation of unknown centuries from the ancestors of the Hindoos, still declining his verb like the Sanskrit and the Greek, and almost able now to understand a simple Sanskrit expression. What external physical peculiarity is transmitted like this? These grammatical forms seem more enduring even than words. The Osmanlee Turk can hardly speak a sentence without words from the Arabic and the Persian, and his conversation may scarcely contain a pure Turkish word; yet the grammatical structure is as entirely different from that of all the tribes in contact with or subjection to him, as the Turkish character and habits are different. And so permanent is this indication of race, that, says M. Maury, "a coarse Siberian *Yakut* can even now, after ages of ancestral separation, communicate his simple ideas to the intelligence of a Constantinopolitan Turko-Sybarite."

Illustrations.

So the Persian, though conveying his thought in a whole sentence of Arabic words, never loses his ancestral grammar.

It is, perhaps, an advantage of the Science of Ethnology, as based on Language, that it requires ***historical evidence*** for its completeness. No doubt, in many of our natural sciences, the classifications would be much sounder, if it were possible to go back to the exact history of the material world.

Historical evidence needed.

There are certain facts which apparently weaken the evidence of language in regard to race, such as history alone can explain. With human races, as distinguished by language, we find that certain peoples, related to each other, have the power of absorbing one another, until the language disappears—as, for instance, the Romans, in Italy, owing to their greater culture, absorbed the conquering Teutons and merged their tongue in their own, or the Teutons and Normans of England swallowed up the Kelts.

Objections.

Here, it should be remembered, that with men, as with the world of animal and vegetable life, related varieties may run into one another until it becomes difficult to classify them. But, even in these unions, there will always remain tokens of the different tongues, fused together; as, for instance, in all the modern Romanic languages, such as French, Spanish, and Italian, analysis shows the various languages which have contributed their proportions. No tongue is utterly obliterated by another; and history teaches us the conditions on which one language is merged into a second. We find that very divergent languages, such as those of the three great families we shall hereafter describe, do not fuse with one another, and that when they meet, as they did (2400 B.C.) on the plains of the Euphrates, they are almost as distinct and separate as they are now in the same regions. The Persian, the Arab, and the Tâtâr, are as diverse in language as they are in habits, character, and physique. One tongue may drive another out of use, by the one race wholly exterminating the other; but even then, as with the Indians on this continent, or the Kelts in England, the conquered will have left its monuments, never to be destroyed, in the names of innumerable mountains and rivers and lakes.

Answers to Objections.

If two related tongues meet, the one of the higher

cultivation and containing the greater treasures of literature, will usually prevail, and history must teach us which blood predominates in the union. In some cases, the greater power of one race may give even the lower language the victory, as the Roman over the Greek in the colonies of Italy. Small bodies of men may be indeed transported, or forcibly expelled to other countries, until they or their descendants lose their language—as the African slaves in this country, or the negroes of the West Indies—and thus this mark of race disappear. But such occurrences are comparatively rare in the great movements of mankind; while voluntary emigration, in mass, seldom obliterates language. And, even with these, History must aid us in the classification; and no doubt careful investigation would disclose in such instances many definite race-marks in words of popular usage.

This, then, is the basis of our divisions of mankind into Races—that is—*Language interpreted by History.*

Basis of Classification.

To the objection, so frequently made to this method of classification, that Ethnology is thus an incomplete Science, we reply, first, that it is even more so under any physical system of division. And, secondly, that very many natural sciences labour under this reproach. Who supposes that the theories or systems of Geology are at all settled; or the classification of Mineralogy and Chemistry complete; or the divisions and classes of Natural History unchangeable? Study is yearly changing classification in almost every Science, founded on observation. But the advantages of system and division are none the less. They enable us to analyze and group, and to reach general principles. So with Ethnology. Our divisions of races may be hereafter somewhat enlarged. This, for instance, which

Objection of incompleteness.

we shall hereafter call the Turanian Family, may be re-divided and sub-classified. The African races may, by more thorough investigation, be grouped in larger families. The Oceanican may be united with more certainty to Asiatic and continental races. Still there is now classification, well-based enough, to assist much the student of history and of human nature. Even the few threads, which we can now with confidence offer, of the connections of races through human annals, may serve to disentangle to many an earnest student the confused web of human actions, and to clear up to his mind the progress of humanity, and the Divine ideas expressed therein.

Possible changes in the Science.

PART FIRST.

THE EARLIEST HISTORICAL RACES.

CHAPTER II.

THE TURANIANS AND HAMITES.

As we grope far back in the past, we discover three prominent Families of nations, appearing on the field of history. The farther we penetrate, the more they seem to mingle with one another, and the less distinguishable they become. Still, from the earliest records which describe the human race in its divisions as peoples, and under the earliest evidences of language, they stand forth as separate families. From them have flown down through history, three broad streams of Language and Family, covering most of the ancient continents, and possibly embracing all the various rivulets of speech and race which interlace with one another in such apparent confusion along the whole course of human progress. They are the Turanian, the Semitic, and the Aryan Families. The *Turanian* receives its name from Tûrân, the barbarous countries, "outside" or beyond Irân and the Aryans; the *Semitic* from Shem or Sem, the eldest son of Noah; and the *Aryan* from the most ancient name which the ancestors of this family gave themselves,

Three great families.

Turanian.

Arya.[1] This latter is also sometimes called *Japhetic*, from the third son of Noah, and *Indo-European*, from the languages which it embraces.

To these three families may be added a fourth, which, though probably only the earliest appearance of crystallization of the Semitic, cannot, with the evidence yet obtained, be thoroughly identified with either of the others, the *Hamitic*, so called from *Ham*, the second son of Noah, a name referring in its derivation to the *dark colour* of these tribes. It only plays an important part in ancient history.

The most ancient of these great families is the Turanian, while at the same time it is the one the least distinctly defined. It embraces what are called the Nomadic languages, that is, languages less settled into a system and more liable to changes than those of other branches of the human race, and, at the same time, marked by certain similarities of form, which are common to them and to no other.

Turanian characteristics.

One of the most characteristic features of these languages is *agglutination*. This means, strictly, the glueing of the pronoun to the verb, to form a conjugation, or of the pronoun to the noun for a declension, as if in English, "I strike thee" were all one word, "*Istrikethou;*" or "thy son" were written "*Sonthou,*" or "my, thy, and his father" were "*fatheri, fatherthou, fatherhe.*" This, however, alone would not distinguish the Turanian languages, but the great peculiarity is that this syllable, thus glued on, is not identified with the main word, but is felt and contemplated as a distinct word. Another great peculiarity is the *integrity of the roots*, so that by simply adding terminations, we can, in Turkish, for instance, from a single root, *love*, form twenty-four different modifications of the idea to love, the last of which shall

Agglutination.

be as cumbrous a word as this: "nottobebroughttoloveoneanother" (not to be brought to love one another), and yet every one of these shall show the root *love* distinctly.

The Turanian languages are also marked by their *facility in producing new forms*; their *want of irregular forms*, and *the rapid divergence of their dialects*.

Further, the root-meaning of words is so free and general, that many words can be *used as nouns, adjectives, or verbs*, almost indiscriminately.

Other minor features can be adduced, which characterize the common origin of these tongues, such as the *community of words and roots*, though naturally in the languages of such barbarous and roving races, this is not true to so great an extent as in the two other great Families; the *identity of pronominal roots*, and the peculiar *phonetic character* or "harmony of vowels," of the speech of Turanian tribes.

On the continent of Asia, the Turanians were, probably, the first who figured as nations in the ante-historical period. Their emigrations began long before the wanderings of the Aryans and Semites who, wherever they went, always discovered a previous population, apparently of Turanian origin, which they either expelled or subdued.

Probably from one of the first of these migrations arose the Chinese people, whose language may be called the *infantile* language among nations, which, though it cannot be classed distinctly with the Turanian, seems yet the preparation and first formation of it.

Turanian migrations.

According to Müller's hypothesis,[2] which is based solely on the evidence of grammatical structure and gradation, and which may be accepted merely as a supposition, there were two directions for the Turanian migrations, one northern and one southern; that in the latter settling on the rivers Meikong, Meinam, Irrawaddy, and Brahmapootra, and forming the *Täi* tribes; the other following the courses of the rivers Amoor and Lena, and founding the *Tungusic* tribes.

A second one to the south, finding the country occupied, pushes on to the islands and the sea, and lays the foundation for the Malay tribes.

A second to the north is supposed to have originated the numerous Mongol tribes, and to have pressed westward along the chain of the Altai mountains.

Still a third to the north produces the Turkish peoples, and proceeds even as far west as Ural, and the frontier of Europe.

A third to the south is believed to tend toward Thibet and India, and in later times pours its hordes through the Himàlaya, and forms the original native population of India. The last Turanian wanderers to the south, are, in this theory, the forefathers of the Tamuls, afterward crushed by the Aryans; and the last to the north are ancestors of the Finns, and probably of the Basques in Spain, and the Samoieds in Siberia. All these ever-moving streams of people, it should be remembered, flowed from the mountain plateaus of Central Asia, long before the historical period. The only evidence of them lies in the structure and terms of their languages. Neither tradition, nor song, nor monument, nor historical record, has preserved any mention of these primeval wanderings of the first races of Turanian men and women. When they left their hills and mountains, they had no sacred songs, or popular poetry, or system of laws, or common possession of thought.[3] Their intellectual and moral position was probably lower than that of the lowest

Supposed currents of population.

No historical evidence.

American Indians. All that we can probably conclude is, that in those dim, ante-historic times, the successive emigrations of Turanian tribes, spread abroad over Asia and Europe, what is believed to be the underlying stratum of primeval population—a population nearly always crushed or eradicated by the advancing Aryans.[4] The traditions of the latter represent these original inhabitants as giants or dwarfs, or evil spirits and as speaking an unintelligible language. In Northern Europe, the most distinct remains of these early races are preserved in the names of their heroes, and the traditional songs which celebrated their deeds—the Finnish poems of Kalewala and Wainamoinen.[5]

The first historical appearance of the Turanians, is probably to be found in the Scythian Empire of Babylonia, of which mention only was made by the earliest Greek historians,[6] but whose existence has been rendered probable through the laborious researches of Rawlinson[7] in the ruined cities of the Euphrates. There, on the site of the great city of Lower Chaldæa, was the capital of an Empire—called the "Median Empire"—which flourished and fell before Nineveh became known to the world as a great city. Its duration is supposed to have been from 2458 B.C., to 2234 B.C.[8] Not enough, however, is known of it, to attach much importance to its history. Its Turanian character is derived from the inscriptions, which are in Turanian grammar, though with Hamitic vocabulary, indicating a great mixture with Hamitic population. (Rawlinson's Anct. Mon., 1—69.)

Scythian Empire of Babylonia.

Its date.

At the same period, a great Turanian Empire—admitting the Chinese to be the earliest crystallization of this family—was flourishing in China, for we have one date in a Chinese inscription, showing a settled government and society 2000 years before Christ.

In later times, when Aryan and Semitic races also held dominion over Central Asia, the antiquary discovers that every monumental cuneiform inscription must have its three languages, of which one must be of the Turanian family; and it is known that the Persian kings, in the historical period, when giving forth an order to the people, were obliged then, as now, to publish it in each of the three great branches of human language.[9]

The Turanian family still embraces the greater proportion of the Asiatic peoples, and of some in Europe.

Extent of Turanian family.

Its languages include those of the Finns and Laps, the Magyars and Turks, the Tartars, Mongols, Thibetians, Tamulians, and aboriginal Indian peoples, as well as numerous other tribes and nations. It is possible that the dialects of the Eastern Archipelago may come within its limits.

What was the religion of this great family of nations at this early period, is not sufficiently known. They were generally wandering tribes, who depended much on hunting for subsistence, and it is probable that the most of them worshipped only the lowest powers of the elements. Whether the adoration of one God was preserved among them from early traditions, is not certain.

Early Religion.

The supposition of Rawlinson[10] that the *magism* of the ancient Persians, or their worship of the elements, was derived from the Scythians—a generic name, including many Turanian Tribes—does not seem sufficiently supported by evidence.

The Turanian physical type, so far as it is distinctive, will be described hereafter.

It should be remembered by the younger scholar that the Turanian classification is more general and more uncertain than any of our other groupings of races. It includes a vast number of peoples, whose languages show the resemblances, detailed above, which similarities seem sufficient foundation for classing them as one immense group. In this view, practical scholars in Asiatic tongues, such as Caldwell (author of a Comparative Grammar of the Dravidian Languages), and B. H. Hodgson, who has investigated with such success the non-Aryan dialects of India, seem to agree. Max Müller and Bunsen are its great advocates.

Uncertainty of Turanian classification.

It is fair to state, however, that on the other side are the eminent linguist, Professor Pott, of Germany, as well as several distinguished scholars of this country. The most, however, that these latter would claim, we suppose, would be that the Mongol, Turkic, and Finnic languages make a separate group from the Tamulian and non-Aryan dialects of India and the Himàlaya, as well as from the Malay.

THE HAMITIC TRIBES.*

Even before the historical appearance of the Turanians (though probably the result of a later emigra-

* Both in regard to these and the Semitic Assyrian tribes, we would remind the reader that almost the only authority for the new historical results is Col. Rawlinson. His interpretations of the inscriptions have been subjected as yet to but little strict criticism : he apparently confuses at times the Hamitic and Turanian families ; and it is very evident that his mind is not in historical investigation of a close, scientific cast, so that the conclusions as yet are not perfectly satisfactory. Still no one has thus far ventured to oppose them, and Hincks is said to have arrived independently at similar results, while Dr. Brandis confirms, to a certain extent, even the historical conclusions. Oppert, too, attempts in elaborat arguments to prove the connection of the second class of the cuneiform (or the Turanian) both in structure and vocabulary with the modern Turanian, as, for instance, the Finno-Magyar tongues. See his "Expedition Scientif. au Mesop. etc.—Paris, 1858–'59."

tion from Central Asia), was the existence of the most mysterious, the most ancient organized State of antiquity—the Egyptian—founded by tribes who are as yet classed as Hamitic or Khamitic (from *Khami*—"the Black"—the ancient name of Egypt).

They are, in the opinion of the best ethnologists, to be considered as the source or rather the earliest crystallization of the Semitic races; still the evidence thus far obtained is not sufficient to establish this, and they may accordingly, at present, be classed as a separate family.[11]

The Hamites.

It should be understood by the reader that by the term *Hamite*, we do not necessarily mean people of black complexion, but those tribes whose language is represented by the ancient Egyptian, a people undoubtedly of brown and swarthy, and sometimes black colour, with European or Aryan features.

The roots of the Hamitic language are pronounced by Bunsen[12] to be mostly of one syllable, and to correspond with the roots of both the two great classes of language.

Others again describe it as a much less developed language than either the Semitic or Aryan languages; and yet admitting certain principles of inflexion and formation from roots which are exhibited by each of those.

Hamitic characteristics.

The following are its resemblances, according to Renan, with the Semitic. The identity of the pronouns, as well as the similar manner of treating them; the agglutination of accessory words; the assimilation of consonants; the secondary part played by the vowel, and its instability which makes it omitted in writing; certain resemblances of conjugation and of the theory of particles and the analogy of numerals.

Its dissemblances are in the conjugation or formation of noun and verb, and in its older form approaching more the monosyllabic, with little grammar, for which picture-writing was naturally a more appropriate expression than the alphabet. Each word is looked at separately and is not glued to the root. The absence of the tri-literal character to the roots is also a marked difference from the Semitic.

The most received opinion at present in regard to the ancient Egyptian is that it probably represents the ancient Asiatic stock, from which the Aryan and Semitic tongues proceeded. But whether the Hamitic peoples be considered a separate family, or as representing only the original stock, of which the Semitic family was a branch, there is little doubt that they are all derived from Asia. The condensed Biblical narrative which represents Egypt as inhabited by the grandsons (or the tribes following them) of Noah; the shape of many of the skulls found in the tombs; the traditions reported by Pliny,[13] and above all the evidence of language, point to an Asiatic origin of the venerable Egyptian State.

Asiatic origin of Hamites.

There has been much discussion as to the existence of Asiatic Hamites, but there are many arguments in favour of it. The Greek traditions clearly imply their belief in two divisions of the Hamites or Æthiopians—Asiatic and African. The allusion by Homer (Od. 1—23, 24); the traditions which connected Memnon, King of Æthiopia, with Susa, and the region of the Persian Gulf; the ordinary genealogies of Belus; the expressions of Herodotus; the traditions of the Armenians—all point to the existence of Asiatic Kushites, or Hamites. (See Rawlinson's Anct. Mon., vol. 1,—60, 61, etc.) The account in the Bible (Gen. x. 8) would indicate that a primitive Babylonian Empire was erected by a great Cushite (Hamitic) chieftain (Nimrod) whose people were related to those of Egypt, Africa, and Palestine.

This is rendered more probable by the investigations

of Rawlinson among the monumental inscriptions of Central Asia, and by linguistic discoveries. It is believed now, that Hamitic or Cushite tribes, of dark complexion, extended along the whole southern coast of Asia.[14] They settled in Arabia, and Beloochistan, and Kerman; the cities on the northern shore of the Persian Gulf are proved by the inscriptions to have belonged to them; they ruled for a time in Babylonia and Susiana, and relics of their language exist yet in Abyssinia, Nubia, and among various[15] African tribes.[16] Even as late as the century of Nebuchadnezzar (600 B.C.), the Hamitic population, says the same authority, is shown by the monuments to have been a powerful element in the population of Babylonia.

Their settlements.

In what direction or at what date the Hamitic emigration flowed from Asia into Africa, cannot be determined. If it came from Lower Babylonia, as seems most probable, it would have entered through Arabia and by the Isthmus of Suez, and thence spread over the valley of the Nile as far as Syene.[17]

CHAPTER III.

THE CHRONOLOGY OF EGYPT.[1]

In a work of this nature, we had, at first, thought it undesirable to enter upon a subject so difficult and so much discussed as the duration of mankind upon the earth. But following our original plan, we must treat of each race in its first historical appearance, and accordingly are forced to the question, "When did each family first stand forth as an organized nation on the earth?" This question, as regards the Hamitic races, has become of deep interest to the world, from the light their records throw on the duration of the whole life of man. It is not well that this great and interesting problem, so long in the hands of the learned, should be hidden from the common student of history. The apparent mystery of the subject may do more injury than the most extreme publicity, and faith may be shaken by ignorance, which would never be by competent knowledge.

For a number of years, there has been a growing opinion among candid scholars, that *more time* was needed for human history than the received Chronology allowed. Empires are seen at a remote date in the past, in full power and brilliancy; nations of the same family, and in different stages of civilization, are beheld scattered over the most widely separated districts; the most marked physical characteristics of race—such as the colour and facial outline of the Æthiopian and the Mongol—in tribes believed

Need of a longer Chronology.

by the majority of scholars to have emigrated from the Asiatic centre, are discovered on monuments of the most remote and unquestioned antiquity; and the conclusion inevitably forced on the mind has been, that to prepare all this, to organize men in civilized societies, to found empires, to create Art, to scatter similar tribes over such vast extents of territory, and to create and perpetuate accidental peculiarities or climatic effects on such a great scale, an immense Past is needed, of which human records say little. This conviction has been strengthened in many minds by a peculiar class of investigations during the last quarter of a century, namely, the investigations into the nature of Language. In the earliest periods of history, philologists discover languages of completed and mature growth, bearing, to the eye of the student, tokens of a long and gradual development, through patient ages of the growth of the human mind. They claim to detect in the structure, the forms, and the processes of a speech, marks of time as plain and irrefutable as those which the naturalist sees in the inner structure of a tree.*

Growth of Language.

In regard to all such presumptions or evidences of antiquity, though taken together they are undoubtedly calculated to influence reflecting minds, still every one must feel that they are in their very nature somewhat vague and uncertain. No one can presume to say how long it shall take a body of nomadic families to form a settled government and a state; the growth necessary

* So strongly have these evidences affected the mind of an ingenious though theoretic scholar, Chevalier Bunsen, that he computes[3] the time necessary for the formation of the Chinese language as 5000 years, and places this supposed event at 20,000 B.C. The growth of the Turanian languages he dates at probably from 15,000 to 12,000 B.C., and our own family of languages, the Indo-European, he supposes gradually forming from 7250 to 4000 B.C.

for the maturity of art or of literature is equally indefinite; and as for the duration needful for the ripening of human speech—for the growth of richer forms, or more complicated constructions in language—who that considers the wonderful creative power of a single human genius, can ever venture to affirm or deny! The subject, at least, in the present state of our knowledge, would, if this were all the evidence, have remained in doubt.

Weakness of the arguments.

But to these many vague indications of a greater antiquity of mankind than had been previously supposed, were gradually added important scientific and practical discoveries in Egypt. These discoveries are destined to have a permanent effect on the received views of chronology, and it becomes important to know the sources of the evidence upon this question. These are principally three. I. The ancient Egyptian writings. II. The monuments of contemporaneous events. III. The records of Egyptian historians. Each of these witnesses gives us, without collusion, a record of the reigning princes of Egypt, and the durations, both of individual reigns, and of the collective reigns of a dynasty. They testify at different periods of Egyptian history, and with different objects, so that the judgment which shall be formed on their evidence (when well sifted) must be of some value.

Sources of evidence for Egyptian Chronology.

It is the sum of these successive reigns, which gives us the age of Egyptian civilization.

To make the subject still clearer, we will restate the points of evidence in an abridged form, from Bunsen's and Lepsius' statement.

1. Writing is found from the earliest period on the Egyptian monuments.

2. The Sacred Books are the earliest books, and contain historical lists of the kings in succession.

3. Ballads also existed in regard to these kings.

Re-statement.

4. There were three periods in Egyptian history which may be called—(*a*) The Old Empire; (*b*) The Middle or Hyksos Empire; and (*c*) The New from the 18th Dynasty.

5. From the times of the New Empire, we have three great records of Egyptian history, namely: two monumental tablets and one written list of the kings of the two Empires, the tablet of Tuthmōsis, and the tablet of Ramesses, and the Turin Papyrus. The tablet of Tuthmōsis gives us lists of thirty kings of the Middle Empire, and thirty-one of the Old; that of Ramesses gives the 18th Dynasty, and thirty-nine kings of the Old Empire. The Turin Papyrus contained more than 250 names of kings, of which 139 are preserved.

7. Some of the kings are reigning princes, and some are collateral princes who never reigned.

8. Besides these lists, we have the imperfect but generally trustworthy lists of two historians. One, Manetho, an Egyptian priest, who lived in the third century before Christ, under Ptolemy I., and who wrote a history of Egypt, which has perished, though extracts survive in Josephus. His lists of kings, in an abridged form, we undoubtedly possess. The other Eratosthenes, was a celebrated historian and director of the Alexandrian Library—born about 276 B.C.—who carried on researches in this very subject under the royal patronage, and who has transmitted the lists which he has discovered, of the princes and their reigns, in early Egyptian history.

It will be observed that the evidence in regard to the antiquity of the nation, is unusually varied in source, such as probably no other country has possessed of its primeval chronology.

The weak points.

The weak points in the evidence, and those which have divided the opinions of scholars upon the subject, are: (1) the imperfections and corruptions of the lists of Manetho, and the possibility that this Chronology may have had an artificial character; (2) the want of agreement between Manetho and Eratosthenes; (3) the *possibility* that the monuments themselves may merely contain the inscriptions by the priests of the popular, mythical history of Egypt, and so Manetho's and Eratosthenes' lists be but the copy of a myth; and (4) the doubt how far certain of the kings were contemporaneous or successive.

Two Schools.

On this subject two schools may be said to exist at this time. One represented by Seyffarth, Uhlemann, Poole, de Rougè, Nolan, and others, giving more modern dates to Egyptian History; and the other, containing by far the most eminent names in science, such as Bunsen, Lepsius, and Brugsch, claiming for that History at least a duration of 3500 years before the time of Alexander. The earliest historical date, according to Lepsius (in a work issued in 1858, the result of twenty years of laborious effort and research), is that of *Menes*, the supposed founder of the united Egyptian Kingdoms, 3892 B.C., or 112 years after the Creation in Usher's system. Bunsen puts the date of Menes at 3623 B.C. Uhlemann and Seyffarth place it at 2781–2 B.C., and Poole as low as 2717 B.C.

Lepsius' dates.

Lepsius, a most careful investigator, dates the marvellous invasion of the Hyksos or "Shepherd Kings"—probably some of the Semitic wandering tribes, who conquered and held Egypt in subjection at least 511 years—at about 2167 B.C.

Chronology by different authors.

The following, then, are the dates of Egyptian History, according to these various systems:—

Historical Events.	Lepsius.	Brugsch.	Bunsen.	Seyffarth.	Poole.
	B.C.	B.C.	B.C.	B.C.	B.C.
Menes . . .	3892	4455	3623	2781	2717
Invasion of Hyksos .	about 2167	2115	2547	2296	about 2082
Expulsion of Hyksos .	1591	1604	1626	1866	about 1525
Entrance of Abram into Egypt . .	1514	...	2877	2297	2081
Exodus . . .	1314	1327–21	1320	1866	...

It should be observed that the latest of the above dates for Menes falls before the Flood, as given in Usher's system, and only some 438 years after the Flood, in Hale's system, while the most carefully attained and reliable date—that of Lepsius—takes us back within 112 years of the Creation, in Usher's system, and more than 700 years before the Flood, in Hale's system.

In the present state of our knowledge of the Egyptian records of their kings—the uncertainty whether more names may not yet be discovered to be contemporaneous, and in a work of this scope and plan, nothing more is necessary than thus to present the results, hitherto attained by scholars, leaving the final settling of our Chronology to future investigation. Enough is given to show that in a very remote antiquity—possibly nearly 4000 years before Christ, certainly not less than 2600 or 2700 years—the Hamitic tribes had consolidated two kingdoms into one in Egypt, and under a king whose name may or may not be historical, *Menes*, had built up a civilization and art whose ruins even yet astonish the world. When these tribes first penetrated into the region of the Nile from Asia, and how long was the preparation which formed the massive and matured system of Egyptian art and science and mythology, who shall measure?

Results not fully settled.

Antiquity uncertain.

Our province is alone with the historical appearance of these races.

Their language is transmitted in its descendant—the Coptic—a living language till after the seventeenth century.

It is to be observed, that even in the remote period to which the history of this family dates back, the language, according to the opinion of scholars, shows traces of African influences, while the face and features of the negro are as distinctly pictured on the earliest monuments as they could be in any work on physical Ethnology at the present day.

In physique, there seem to have been three distinct types among the Egyptians. One, probably Æthiopian, with prominent cheek bones, swelling lips, broad flat nose, protruding eye-balls, and frizzly hair, and, it is supposed, of dark colour. Another, with long narrow nose, receding forehead, long thin eyelids, short and thin body, long legs and flowing hair: the colour probably red. This may have arisen from the Asiatic mixture. Still another type, the most common, is characterized by short chin, full voluptuous lips, large prominent eyes, slightly-curved nose, with thick nostrils, and full cheeks; the hair usually thick and braided. This may have come from the mingling of the Asiatic and African blood.

Three physical types.

THE HAMITIC CHALDEES.

The most diverse authorities now recognize the intimate connection, at a very early date, between the Chaldees and the African Hamitic tribes. It is supposed that, previous to the historic period, the Hamites from Africa invaded the region of the Southern Euphrates, drove out the Turanian rulers from

Hamitic Chaldees.

Babylonia, and took possession of the government. The system of writing, the language, and the traditions of Babylonia and Assyria, as well as the Scripture allusions to the ancestors of these tribes, all indicate this Hamitic influence. Rawlinson[3] supposes that the Hamites founded an Empire, of which the capitals were at Mugheir, Warka, Senkereh and Niffer, and that they introduced the worship of the heavenly bodies, in place of the elemental worship of the Turanians. In his opinion, they brought with them a system of picture-writing from Egypt, which at that time had not ripened into an alphabet. The first historical date of this Hamite (or Cushite) Empire may be put at 2234 B.C.;* and in the recent investigations in the ruined cities of Babylonia and Assyria, a line of Hamite kings is supposed to have been discovered down to 1976 B.C., in substantial agreement with the dates from Greek historians.

Hamite Empire 2234 B.C.

One in this line of kings, *Kudur-Lagamer* (or Chedor-Laomer), a Hamitic prince of Elam, is believed to have built up a vast empire of conquest like those established later by Semitic and Aryan despots. He marched an army 1200 miles from the Persian Gulf to the Dead Sea, and held Palestine and Syria in subjection for twelve years.† This at a period, as Prof. Rawlinson remarks, when the kings of Egypt had never ventured beyond their borders, and when no monarch in Asia held dominion over more than a few petty tribes, and a few hundred miles of territory. His dominions are supposed to have extended for nearly a thousand miles from east to west, and from north to south, almost five hundred.

A Hamitic Emperor.

* Viv. de St. Martin obtains this date (2234 B.C.) from still another calculation.—See Rev. Germ. 1re Janv. 1862.

† Gen. xiv., 1. Five Anct. Mon., 1, p. 219.

In 1976, another Hamite tribe from Susiana is supposed to have invaded Babylonia, and to have established the second great Chaldean Empire, which lasted till 1518 B.C. Second Hamite Empire.

The theory that the Chaldeans emigrated from the mountains of Armenia to the Lower Euphrates, seems now generally abandoned by the best authorities.* The tribe of that name in the former country were probably either an offshoot of the great Hamitic stock, or emigrants from the Babylonian Chaldees.

The peculiar language on which these ethnic differences are based—the Hamitic—is found with the arrow-headed (cuneiform) alphabet, on vast numbers of bricks and monuments through all the region of the Euphrates. As before observed, it seems to form almost the connecting link, on one side, between the Aryan and Semitic, which developed themselves later, and on the other, the bond between these languages and the Turanian and Nomadic languages of Upper Asia.

Still, the whole subject must be received with great caution, until further and more careful investigation shall make certain the nature of the Hamitic languages, and the early history of Lower Babylonia. Nor is it time, as yet, to accept the newly-published remains of old Babylonian Literature, which Dr. Chowlson is bringing forth; writings which claim an antiquity of 700 years before the era of Nebuchadnezzar. If these should ever be established as historically true, then it would appear that a Semitic population, since called the *Nabathæans*, filled the country of the Lower Euphrates from an early date, and carried Nabathæans. the pursuits of agriculture to a high degree of perfection. They would indicate, also, an early foreign dynasty, which may correspond to the first Hamitic

* Oppert, however, takes this view.

dynasty mentioned above, and they describe a Canaanitish line of kings in the sixteenth century, which would correspond with the Arab dynasty to be hereafter mentioned. The Chaldees—if these records be proved authentic—would then be Nabathæans or Semitic. The probable truth, however, is much more with Rawlinson's conclusions.

After the Hamitic Chaldæan dynasty, there followed, according to Berosus, a dynasty of nine Arab kings, who reigned for 245 years. That is, the Hamites were apparently overwhelmed by a Semitic invasion from Arabia. "The ancient Chaldæans sank," says G. Rawlinson, "about B.C. 1500, into comparative obscurity." They became gradually absorbed into the Semitic stock.

THE FOLLOWING IS THE BABYLONIAN CHRONOLOGY, AS RESTORED BY GUTSCHMID AND RAWLINSON.

				YEARS.	B.C.	B.C.
DYNASTIES OF BEROSUS.	MYTHIC.	I.	86. Chaldæans .	34,080		
	HISTORICAL.	II.	8. Medes. . .	224	2458	2234
		III.	11. (Chaldæans) .	(258)	2234	1976
		IV.	49. Chaldæans .	458	1976	1518
		V.	9. Arabians . .	245	1518	1773
		VI.	45. (Assyrians) .	526	1273	747
		VII.	8. (Assyrians) .	(122)	747	625
		VIII.	6. Chaldæans .	87	625	538
				36,000		

This language—the Hamitic—through the two Chaldee dynasties, and for seven centuries after under the Semitic rule, was the sacred and scientific language of these great Empires. All the mythological, astronomical, and scientific tablets found in the ruins of Nineveh, are in this tongue.[4] Its alphabet was employed both by the Semitic and Aryan races, who succeeded this ancient family in the government of the countries on the Euphrates.[5]

The Hamitic race has disappeared from human families, and has only left the ruins of two mighty civilizations to tell of its former grandeur. To it belong the colossal and gloomy art of Egypt, her severe and materialistic mythology, her elaborate society, and her system of picture-writing, the precursor and suggestive of European alphabets, as well as those teachings of immortality and Divine justice which afterward so deeply influenced the Greek mind; to it also belong the art of writing, the science, the star-worship, and the early sculpture of Chaldæa and Assyria.

Hamitic contributions to history.

During the succeeding ages, the Semitic and Aryan races have led the progress of mankind, but in the earliest times, when Turanian, Semite and Aryan were nomadic tribes, the Hamitic race was the instructor and leader of the human family. "Alphabetic writing, astronomy," says Professor Rawlinson, "history, chronology, architecture, plastic art, sculpture, navigation, agriculture, and textile industry seem, all of them, to have had their origin from Egypt and Babylon, Mizraim and Nimrod, both descendants of Ham." (Anct. Mon., i. 75.)

CHAPTER IV.

THE SEMITES.

THE great family of nations which appears next on the theatre of history is the Semitic. Though occupying a narrower space and numbering fewer members than either of the two other leading classes of peoples, the Aryan and Turanian, it has been the vehicle of grander ideas and more permanent results, for good and for evil,

Semitic achievements.

upon the world than have been produced by all the other families of man. It originated commerce; it produced that great invention which, more than any other one intellectual cause, has tended to elevate the mind of man—the formation of the alphabet. Through it have come forth the most sensual and debased conceptions in mythology which have ever cursed mankind; while from its deep sense of Divinity have sprung all the religions of the civilized world; from one branch, Mohammedanism, with its later train of evils, and from another, under the Divine guidance which acts through the whole course of history, the spiritual and inspired conceptions of Judaism and the Divine Revelation in Christianity.

This family of the human race is distinguished by the peculiar character of the language which it spoke.

Semitic languages.

Those languages, in fact, constitute a group clearly separated from the other leading forms of human speech. The great peculiarity of the group lies in the very structure of its roots, which consist mostly of three consonants, while those of the Aryan and Turanian groups have only one or two.[1] Out of these tri-literal roots, the mass of their words were coined by merely varying the vowels, and in some cases by adding a syllable; on the other hand, words formed by composition are almost unknown. The verb has but two tenses, the noun but two genders, and the relations of cases are not, in general, expressed by inflected forms.[2] In the structure of the sentence, the Semitic dialects present little more than a process of addition; words and propositions are placed side by side, and are not subject to the involution and subordination of clauses, so striking in many of the Indo-European tongues.

In short, these languages have a kind of poetic power, and express passion and feeling with great intensity; but they are lacking in logical precision, deficient in analytical terms, and imperfectly adapted to embody the grandest results of human thought.

The first migrations of the Semites from Central Asia reached beyond the historical period, though evidences of language, of traditions, and the Bible history indicate two central points from which their tribes spread forth; one in the mountains of Armenia, and the other from the region of the Lower Euphrates. The first historical appearance of the Semitic forms of language in the Babylonian records, is placed at about the twentieth century before Christ.[3]

From the Lower Euphrates, the streams of population would naturally tend toward the Persian Gulf and Arabia, and the Sinaïtic peninsula; while from Armenia they easily flowed into Asia

First historical appearance.

Minor, Syria, and Palestine, and from either centre would readily reach the shores of Africa or cross the isthmus to Egypt.

When Abraham, about 2000 B.C. (according to Poole), went forth from Ur of the Hamitic Chaldees into Canaan, he found Semitic tribes already there. It is probable that long before this period the tribes which ultimately formed the Phœnicians had wandered from the shores of the Persian Gulf to the coasts of the Mediterranean, and the Joktanian Arabs had spread over the Arabian peninsula.

Semitic Territory.

The proper Semitic territory in antiquity was Syria, Phœnicia, Palestine, Mesopotamia, Chaldæa, Assyria, Susiâna, and the immense deserts of Arabia.

Some of the most ancient names of localities in Assyria and Babylonia are Semitic, as well as the names of the Assyrian and Babylonian divinities.

The Semitic family may be divided into three great branches: the *Aramæans*, the *Arabians*, and the *Hebrews*.

Aramæans.

The Aramæans held possession of Babylonia after the Hamite dynasties, while a colony had at a very ancient date occupied Syria. Their language is continued in the modern Chaldee. In the times of the New Testament, their dialect was the language of common life over all the vast country, from the Mediterranean to the Tigris, and perhaps farther.

Arabians.

The Arabians, supposed by some philologists to be older in language than the Hebrews, occupied the great peninsula of Arabia. The ancient inscriptions, the Himyaritic, show how early their language was spoken there, though we may well believe, with Renan, that there was a Hamitic population there still earlier. To the Amalekites, an Arabian pagan tribe, may be traced, with much probability, the most of the Sinaïtic inscriptions which so long have puzzled scholars.

One colony, at an unknown date, was sent forth by the Arabians to the coast south of Egypt and Nubia, opposite Yemen, and has maintained itself there to the present day.[4] Their language, the Abyssinian or Gees language, is still preserved in purity in the sacred writings of the nation. Probably from Arabia came the Semitic colonies which have everywhere either mingled with the tribes of Northern Africa, or have themselves laid the foundation of Ethiopian states. To such a degree is this the fact, that philologists claim that the groundwork of all the African dialects from Egypt and Æthiopia to the Atlantic Ocean—the Berber, the Haussa, and numerous others even southward as far as Mozambique—is Semitic.

African Semites.

The *Hebrew* branch of this family embraces the Jews, and their kindred, the Canaanites and Phœnicians.* It is probably from the Canaanites, that the wandering Semitic tribes (the Hyksos, or "Shepherd-kings,") came, who long before the entrance of the Jews (about 2167 B.C., according to Lepsius), conquered Egypt, and held it in possession for at least 500 years.

Hebrews.

* The theory of M. Renan—all whose judgments on Semitic matters must be received with the greatest respect—that the Phœnicians and Assyrians could not be pure Semites, the former, because of their remarkable enterprise and mechanical skill, the latter, from their powerful and centralized government, and both, from their impure mythology—seems too much an *à priori* conception of the Semitic character. The modern Jew is equal to the Phœnician in commercial enterprise, and the ancient was fully as sensuous, though his imagination was tempered by his monotheism. The modern empires of the followers of Mohammed were as centralized and powerful as the Assyrian.

D 2

With these various branches, the Semitic family subsequently penetrated to Cyprus, Cilicia, Pisidia, Lycia, and to Carthage, Spain, Sicily, and Western Africa. The Carthaginian State—rival of Rome—was a Semitic colony.

The Semitic physical type is very distinctly presented, both on the Egyptian and Assyrian monuments, and corresponds in a wonderful manner to its general features, as shown among the Jews of the present day.

Prof. Rawlinson has thus described the Semitic type on the Assyrian monuments: "The forehead straight but not high, the full brow, the eye large, and almond-shaped, the aquiline nose, a little coarse at the end and unduly depressed, the strong, firm mouth, with lips somewhat over thick, the well-formed chin, the abundant hair and ample beard, both coloured and black—all these recall the chief peculiarities of the Jew, more especially as he appears in southern countries." (Five Anct. Mon., i. p. 297.)

Of all the families of man, the Semitic has preserved the most distinct and homogeneous mental characteristics.

Always, in all its branches, tenacious of the past, conservative, not inclined to change or reform, sensual and strong of passion, yet deeply reverent and religious in temperament, capable of the most sublime acts, either of heroism or fanaticism, it was, from the first, a fit medium for some of the grandest truths and principles which can inspire the human soul. Its very peculiarities — its tenacity and sensuousness and reverence—adapted it to feel and retain and convey Divine inspirations. The Semitic mind was never capable of artistic effort, but has made its great contributions to human knowledge in the invention of the alphabet, and in the exact sciences.

Semitic traits.

In poetry, it has given to the world the most sublime lyrics which human language can present; though in the drama, it has produced only as it were the type or introduction, and in the epic, it has contributed nothing. The Semitic races have never shown themselves skilled in colonization—even the Phœnician colonies formed no permanent States—and they seemed almost as little capable of organizing enduring governments. Individuality has been too strong with them for permanent associated effort.

In one of their earliest branches—the Phœnicians—and in the modern Jew, they have manifested a wonderful capacity for traffic and commerce. In the primeval ages, probably no one influence tended so much to unite and civilize mankind, as the Semitic commerce and ingenuity, under the Phœnicians. The sensuousness and the religious reverence of the race—so vividly shown in the Bible history—united in the heathen Semites, the tribes of Syria and Asia Minor, to produce a mythology, debasing and corrupt beyond what the human imagination has anywhere else brought forth; a mythology which transplanted to Greece and refined by the Grecian sense of beauty, has poured through all ages a flood of sensual and licentious imaginations, corrupting art and literature almost to the present day.

Three Semitic religions.

Three of the great Religions of history—Mohammedanism, Judaism, and CHRISTIANITY—have come forth from the Semitic races, and through future time it will be their glory that with all their former vices, and their subsequent degradation, one of their humblest tribes was fitted to receive and was appointed to convey, the purest oracles of God to all succeeding generations.

CHAPTER V.

THE ARYAN FAMILY.

One of the greatest discoveries of modern time, as affecting the question of races, is that conclusion from comparison of languages, which has defined what is called the Aryan or Indo-European family of nations.

Indo-European Classification.

By a simple examination of the roots and structure of various languages, and their comparison especially with those of the Sanskrit, it has been ascertained, on evidence clear and unassailable, that certain nations, the most widely separated and the most diverse in physical characteristics, have a common origin. The blonde Norwegian and the dark-eyed Spaniard, the mercurial Kelt and the steady Anglo-Saxon, the Slavonic Russian and the Frenchman, the practical Anglo-American and the dreamy Hindoo, the German and the Persian, the Greek and the Roman, are proved to be all emigrants from one home and to have spoken once a common tongue.

History traced by language.

We can see also in the words they have all preserved, how far their common forefathers had progressed in thought and in civilization, before the remarkable causes arose which scattered them in various tribes over the face of the earth.

The words which all, or nearly all, their descendants have in common are those which convey the simplest ideas of existence and action; those which describe the nearest family relations, such as *father*, and *mother*, *son* and *daughter;* those for domestic animals, such as *dog*, *pig*, *sow*, *boar*, *goose* and *duck;* those for the simplest articles of food, for certain metals, for the great luminaries of the sky, and "the objects of religious worship, derived from these great phenomena,"[1] and words of feeling, like *heart* and *tears*.

Early Aryan progress.

Language shows conclusively that the Aryan tribes had passed beyond the lowest barbaric stage before they separated. There is no certain evidence that they were agricultural, but they were probably nomadic or occupied with the care of flocks; they had built houses and worked in metals; they had constructed boats and had fastened animals to vehicles for domestic labour, and were acquainted with the art of sewing if not of weaving. Words present to us as clearly as a historical record that even in that distant antiquity, certain great features common to Indo-European nations, whether for good or evil, still existed.

The relation of husband and wife, the position of the sexes, the absence of caste, and the priestly authority of the Father, were characteristics of our earliest ancestors.[2] It is an additional evidence of their early, peaceful life, that the words which are different in the many branches of their descendants are, with a few exceptions, the names of wild animals and those for the instruments of war. The common parent tongue of our ancestors has perished, and in all the various languages of their descendants—whether Sanskrit, Latin, Greek, Keltic, or English—we only see traces of the primeval tongue.

The centre from which these various races first migrated is hid in the mists of a distant antiquity; but both language and the traditions of two races designate the high plateau of Asia lying east of the Caspian, as their common home.

The Persian tradition, in the most ancient sacred writings, the *Vendidad*,[3] places the original habitation of the Aryan fathers near the Belurtag and Samarkand, on the plateau of Pamer, in what is now Eastern Toorkestan, at the sources of the Oxus and the Jaxartes. The Indian Aryans have no definite traditions as to origin, though their earliest songs and many indications, point toward the northwest from India, as their starting-point.

Eastern Asia original home of Aryans.

We may suppose, with Lassen, that the vast table-land, stretching from the mountains of Armenia to the Hindoo Kush, was the original centre for both the Semitic and Aryan races. From this elevated region, successive tribes poured forth toward the north, and the west, and the east.

Through the Caucasus, spreading over Upper Asia, and driving out from Northern Europe the original Turanian population, poured the tribes which became afterward Kelts, Teutonians, Slavonians, Lithuanians, and others.[4] Toward the west, reaching finally Greece and Italy, wandered the Pelasgi, the Phrygians, the Lydians, and numerous other tribes, who subsequently occupied Asia Minor.[5]

Of all these mighty floods of emigration, we have scarcely a historical trace. We only conclude, as probable from language, that the Eastern Aryans, the Hindoos, must have left the common fatherland at a later period than most of the other tribes.

Indian migrations.

The earliest Vedic hymns show the Indian Aryans on the upper branches of the Indus, contending with the native tribes (of Turanian affinity), whom they successively vanquish and enslave, or drive to the mountains, until within the historical period they reach the Ganges. The earliest traditions of their brethren, the Iran or Persic Aryans, contained in the Zend-Avesta, and fully interpreted within a few years, describe what were probably the countries neighbouring on their own districts in Eastern Turkestan, and through which they may have wandered, namely: the south of Turkestan, the north of Persia, Afghanistan, and Cabul, India, and the region of the "Seven Rivers" (the Indus, the five streams of the Penjáb, and the Sarasvatî). Even to this day, the ruling language of those countries is Aryan, while, from their settlements near the Caspian, arose subsequently the great Aryan Empire of Media.

Zend traditions.

From the Indian Aryans have come the great people of the Brahmanic Hindoos; and from the Iran or Persic Aryans, have descended the Persians, the Medes, the Carmanians, the Bactrians, the Sogdians, the Hyrcanians, the Sagartians, and others of minor importance.

In regard to the dates of these migrations, everything is obscure. Bunsen supposes that the Aryans were in the land of the Indus, from 4000 to 3000 B.C. Duncker dates the probable formation of the Vedas, in the earliest ages of the Aryan life in India, from 1800 to 1500 B.C. Rawlinson places the emigrations from the Aryan settlements south of the Caspian, which founded the Empire of the Medes, somewhere between 1160 and 640 B.C. However early may have been the original dispersion of the Aryan tribes, the historical appearance of this powerful family is comparatively late. The Turanian, the Hamitic, and the Semitic peoples, had successively erected powerful empires, ere the vigorous Aryan family came forward upon the field of history. Since that

Supposed dates.

period, with the exception of the Assyrian Empire, and the Semitic conquests under Mohammed, and occasional Turanian invasions, the Aryan races have held dominion of the world; bearing with them Art and Law and Science and Civilization; exercising the singular philosophic and intellectual power of this family; manifesting especially to the world, the principle of public spirit (or individual sacrifice for the good of a community); and becoming the universal instruments through which the Semitic conceptions of Deity, and the Semitic inspirations of Christianity, have been spread through all nations.

Aryan gifts to the world.

Their two great streams of population—the European and the Asiatic Aryans, the practical races and the meditative races—after unknown ages of separation, modified by incomprehensible and countless influences of climate and of nature, as apparently diverse as any two branches of the human family, have, during the past two centuries, met again in the valleys of India, and the last few years have witnessed what is perhaps the final prostration of the Asiatic Aryan beneath the ingenuity and vigour of the European Aryan.

CHAPTER VI.

ASIA.

The Ruling Races—1300 *to* 500 B.C.

EVEN before 1300, the Hamitic kingdom of Egypt had ceased to be the leading power of the world, and the Semitic States of Asia were commencing a career of conquest and commerce, such as the world has witnessed but once since among Semitic races—in the Mohammedan conquests of the Arabian tribes. In the 14th century,[1] the Phœnicians, pressed on one side by the attacks of the Egyptians, and on the other by the immigration of the Jews, had been driven to the sea—to colonization and commerce. In 1000, though insignificant in a political point of view, they had become the great manufacturing and commercial power of the old world. They had traversed the whole length of the Mediterranean—a journey then of 70 or 80 days—and had sprinkled the coasts with colonies and factories and mercantile stations. Their ships were freighted with tin from England, and tropical productions from the mouths of the Indus. Their commercial cities were dotted over the interior of Asia, forming links in the vast exchange and commerce which they established between points as distant as Babylon and Cadiz, Arabia, and Armenia, Sicily and India.[2] [3] Their own manufactures or those from the countries of the Euphrates, which were called by their name, became famous over the world.

Phœnicians.

Weakened finally by their own inordinate luxury and the system of slavery, and assailed by both the Græcian naval forces and the Assyrians, they lost their high position, until at length the commerce of the world was turned into new channels, and they were overthrown by the power of Alexander.

During this period of the glory of Tyre and Sidon and the Phœnician colonies, the Semitic* peoples on the Upper Tigris had been establishing one of the great empires of the past, the Assyrian Empire. The Arabian dynasty, which had held temporary possession of the throne of Babylonia (from 1518 to 1273 B.C.), fell under the assaults of the kings of Nineveh; and with that great city as a centre, the new conquering kingdom was extended over an immense territory in interior and western Asia. From the Persian Gulf and Arabia[4] on the south, the Assyrian rule reached to the northern frontier of Armenia, and from the Mediterranean and Cilicia on the west, to the Caspian and the great Persian desert on the east.

Assyrian Empire.

During the six and a half centuries in which it existed (from 1273 to 625 B.C.), it held subject Susiana, Chaldæa, Babylonia, Media, Armenia, Mesopotamia, parts of Cappadocia and Cilicia, Syria, Phœnicia, Palestine, Idumæa, and Lower Egypt.[5]

The turning point for Semitic rule on the Asiatic continent was the destruction of Senacherib's host (691 B.C.)† by the pestilence. After this the Assyrian power gradually declined.

The architecture and the history of this great empire

* The Semitic character of the Assyrian language is clearly and briefly shown in the lists of words taken from Oppert, quoted in Rawlinson's Five Mon., vol. i., p. 342, &c.

† Lepsius.

have been wonderfully restored to the world, during the last few years, by the researches in the ruins of Nineveh. Like all the Semitic tribes, the Assyrians have shown much more aptitude for architecture than for painting or sculpture. Their art was probably borrowed mostly from the Hamitic Chaldees of Babylonia, and their literature and science were, no doubt, cramped by the necessity of using the learned language of the Chaldees; still the bold Semitic art of Assyria is a grand advance on the conventional and gloomy Hamitic art of Egypt; while the manufactures show a still more remarkable progress over similar Egyptian products.

Assyrian art.

In 625 B.C., the great Semitic city—Nineveh—fell before an Aryan king, Cyaxares, the Mede. By this war, Babylon was freed from the Assyrian rule, and the second Babylonian Empire began, lasting scarcely a century (625 to 538 B.C.), but whose brief history is filled with the last warlike exploits of the Semitic family in antiquity. It reached its height of conquest and splendour under Nebuchadnezzar (604 B.C.).

The Aryan emigration which entered Media from the east, and had driven out or subjected the Turanian population, had now formed a powerful Median kingdom. Another Aryan kingdom existed in Lydia, and in the latter part of the sixth century, these two Governments, in unison with the Babylonian Empire, held possession of most of Asia. But the divided rule between the Semitic and Aryan nations, which had so long existed in Asia, was now to be terminated by a new Aryan Empire of unsurpassed power and extent.

Second Babylonian Empire.

The PERSIAN EMPIRE is the beginning of a new era in the history of races—the end of the Semitic, and the opening of the Aryan period; the transition from Asia to Europe as the ruling power in the world.

In 558, Astyages, king of Media, was deposed by CYRUS the Persian; in the few following years the alliance of Egypt, Lydia, and Babylonia was broken by him; in 538, the great city of Babylon was taken, and the Persian Empire extended over the countries of the Medes, the Lydians and the Babylonians, the Ionians, and Lycians, and Phœnicians, reaching on the north to the Kardusians, the Sakians, the Chorasmians, and even to the Jaxartes, in what is now Kurdestan.

Persian Empire.

Cambyses brought Egypt (525 B.C.) within its limits, and Darius (512) could boast, that, from the greatest cold on the north to the greatest heat in the south, and from the Himàlaya and Indus on the east to the coasts of Europe on the west, he held an undisputed and well-organized empire.

The only cloud of opposition to this mighty despotism arose from some petty self-governing states, inhabited by Aryan tribes, descended from the common ancestors of the Pelasgi, on the islands and coasts of the Ægæan.

The Minor Tribes of Asia—1300 *to* 500 B.C.

The Turanians. Among these are to be classed the Parthians with an Aryan mixture, the Moschi, the probable ancestors of the Muscovites, the Tibareni, and the early inhabitants of Armenia and of Cilicia, together with numerous other lesser tribes.[6]

The Semites. To this family belong, beside the more important tribes already mentioned, the later Canaanites, the Ishmaelites, the Cyprians, the later

Cilicians, the Solymi, and the Carthaginians of Africa.

The Aryans. Under this great branch come the Mysians, (probably) the Lycians, and the Caunians; the Carmanians, the Bactrians, the Sogdians, the Arians, the Sagartians, the Sarangians, the Gandarians,[7] and others.

During the latter half of the seventh century before Christ, the more civilized Aryan and Semitic peoples of Southern Asia were overwhelmed by vast hordes of nomadic tribes, from the northern and north-eastern districts—probably in the main of Tâtâr, or Turanian origin. Among these were the *Cimmerians*,* the *Treres* and *Scythians*.[8] The former lived from 800 to 600 B.C., between the Danube and Don, on the north of the Black Sea, but were driven by the advancing tribes of the Scythians (650 to 600 B.C.) into Europe. They occupied, for a time, the Crimea, and are supposed by many writers of both ancient and modern times, to be identical with the Cimbri, probably a Keltic tribe, who lived on the coasts of Northern Europe, and thus the ancestors of the whole Keltic race. But there is no sufficient evidence of this, though it is not improbable that they are the same with the *Gomer*, mentioned by Ezekiel (xxxviii. 6), and a tribe with strong Aryan mixture.

The Cimmerians.

The *Scythians*, whose marauding expeditions desolated the whole of Northern Asia, and who, according to Herodotus, overthrew the empire of the Medes, and threatened the kingdom of Judah,† and Egypt, have always been considered in their principal tribes a Tura-

* Dieffenbach, on the contrary, considers the Cimmerians as Iranian.

† Jeremiah iv. 13; v. 12; vi. 22, 23; iv. 17, 20, 27; vi. 1, 2, 9, 26; ii. 14, 15, &c.

nian (Tâtâr) people, with all the characteristics of that family. Prof. Rawlinson has endeavoured recently to prove, from some twenty roots which survive of their language, that they belong to the Indo-European family, but forming a distinct branch, as separate from the others, as the Kelts or the Teutons. Dieffenbach concludes from their proper names, that they belonged to the Iranian branch of the Aryans.

The Scythians.

Probably, many of the difficulties about this much-disputed people would be solved by the simple explanation, that the name "Scythian" was geographical rather than ethnological, and embraced tribes of Aryan, as well as Turanian origin.

The Pelasgians.[9]

In the western extremity of Asia Minor, in Phrygia, near the Mæander and the Hermus, lived, during some part of the period of which we have been treating, a people of whom less is known than of almost any other leading Aryan tribe of Asia and Europe—the common ancestors of the Greeks and Italians. We only know from the Greek and Latin languages, that, at a period later than the time in which the European Aryan separated from the Indo-Aryan tribes, these two tongues were one, and spoken by a common people—a people who understood the care of animals, the cultivation of the ground, the culture of the vine, and some of the pursuits of the sea.

Græco-Italian Race.

The Aryan tribes were undoubtedly before their separation not an agricultural race, and language proves that they had never beheld the sea. The European Aryans, in distinction from the Indo-Aryans, all possess common words for the sea, and the Græco-Italians many common names for agricultural pursuits.

From this ancestral family—as yet unnamed—of the Greeks and Romans, came different emigrations, under the pressure of the Phrygians and Lydians, toward Europe. From various indications, some are believed to have passed the Hellespont and the Bosphorus, and thus to have entered Greece; others to have crossed the islands of the Archipelago, and still others to have approached gradually by Rhodes, Carpathus, Crete, and Cythera.

Two streams are supposed to have entered Italy—one from Greece, flowing into Iapygia; the other skirting the Adriatic and passing over the plain of the Po, is thought to have flowed south into Italy. One of the earliest currents of this Græco-Italian race is believed to have been the emigration of that mysterious people, the *Pelasgi;* a tribe so far remote in history that they seemed to the Greek imagination the very "children of the black earth."

Early migrations.

All records respecting this early people are exceedingly uncertain and inconsistent, so that scholars are yet much divided in their views in regard to them. There is reason to believe that they settled early as a peaceful race in the islands of the Archipelago, in Thessaly, Epirus, and Peloponnesus; in Arcadia and Attica, and Ionia and Macedonia. The massive structures of rude stone, called the Cyclopean, scattered over parts of Asia and Europe, are attributed to them. Whether they ever entered Italy is very doubtful—if they did, they were swallowed up afterward by the succeeding conquering tribes. In Greece they are supposed to have been crushed by their more vigorous brothers, who emigrated after them—the Hellenes or Greeks—and perhaps to have formed, in later times, some portion of the multitude of slaves which existed in the Hellenic commonwealths. In Asia

Uncertainty about the Pelasgi.

they must have been, in like manner, merged into the Phrygians and Lydians.

They were, apparently, a weak and peaceful tribe, devoted to agriculture, with a feeling for beauty, shown even in their rude structures. They were nowhere able to resist the more powerful tribes of the same stock, who succeeded them.

We should not do justice to this topic without saying that, in the view of many scholars, the whole people and subject of the Pelasgi, are considered as belonging to the regions of myth. Grote says, "The traditional image of the Pelasgic race, everywhere driven out, nowhere settling themselves for good—of the race which is everywhere and nowhere, always reappearing, and vanishing again without leaving any trace; the image of this gipsy nation is, to me, so strange that we must entertain doubts as to its historic existence."

Geographical Considerations.

The early distinctions of Races, as well as the formation of the first civilized States, were no doubt determined by geographical and climatic conditions.

River-valleys first habitations.

The rich soil and open ground of the river-valleys were probably the first natural causes which tended to change the nomad or hunting tribe to an agricultural, and thus laid the foundation for a future civilization. Accordingly, we find the earliest indications of a settled mode of life in the rich valley of the Nile; then, still later, in the fertile plains between or on the banks of the Euphrates and Tigris; and, later yet, in the country of the Indus and the "Five Rivers." The mountain tribes, or those on the steppes of the interior, were at that period the barbarous and nomadic tribes, doing little for the advancement of mankind. As civilization progressed in Western Asia, the little tribe between the ranges of Lebanon and the sea, their country provided with excellent harbours and inexhaustible stores of the best timber, naturally became the marine and commercial power of the ancient world.

Though a race will frequently pass over the most formidable natural barrier, yet the earliest séparation of families of peoples will be usually denoted by the nature of the surface. Thus in the brief description we have given of the earliest historical races, it will be observed that the Hamitic family hold the valley of the Nile, with branches along the coasts of the Persian Gulf. Its related family—the Semitic—occupy the Mesopotamian valley, formed by the streams of the Tigris and Euphrates, together with a narrow strip of cultivable land between the Euphrates and the desert, and a broad district between the Tigris and the chain of Zagros. Their branches also extend over the Peninsula of Arabia, and over the Continent to the Mediterranean.

Geographical influence.

The peculiar home of the Aryan family is the Iranian plateau and the mountains bordering it. This plateau is a high table-land of oblong shape, broken by many irregularities, but possessing an average elevation of over 4000 feet. It is bounded on the north, says Rawlinson, "by the mountain-chain called, sometimes, the *Elburz*, which runs eastward from Armenia, and passing south of the Caspian joins the *Hindoo Koosh*, above Cabul," on the east by the mountain-ranges bordering the valley of the Indus, on the west by Mt. Zagros, and on the south "by a lower line of hills, running nearly parallel with the coast, along the entire length of Persia and Beloochistan;" the whole containing about 600,000 square miles.

Iranian plateau.

Here and in the beautiful mountain-valleys bordering the plateau dwelt the various branches of the great Aryan family—the Medes and Persians, the Sagortians and Sarangians; the Sattagydians and Arachotians, the Arians, the Bactrians and Sogdians—here also were the fathers of the Indians.

Of the original habitations of the Turanian races, we can speak with less certainty, as they were probably nomadic tribes, and seem to have been covered over or absorbed by the later Semitic and Aryan nations in Western Asia. Their homes were, no doubt, the steppes of Eastern Asia, while they wandered over all Northern Asia, and penetrated through the mountain defiles into the region south of the Caspian.

PART SECOND.

THE PRIMITIVE RACES OF EUROPE.[1]

CHAPTER VII.

TURANIANS.

The Basques and Finns.

ALL over the continent of Europe, and even on the British Islands, are scattered remains and structures, singularly resembling similar relics of a primeval people found on the soil of America. *Tumuli*, vast in size and of incredible number; holes dug in the ground for huts; pottery of rude shape; primitive implements for the chase or for war; knives of bone, flint arrow-heads, stone hammers, necklaces of teeth, and ornaments of amber or of coal of barbaric form; canoes burnt out of trunks of trees;—all indicating, as do the American remains, a people ignorant of agriculture, unacquainted with the use of the metals, and living upon the products of fishing and hunting. The contents of the European sepulchral mounds give evidence, sometimes, even of peoples who devoured human flesh. They were evidently nations constantly pressed and attacked by more powerful tribes, for one of their most original customs is the the building huts—like some of the South-American Indians—on piles in the water, for defence;[2] or, as in

Early European remains.

one memorable instance in France, upon masses of dried clay, thrown into a morass,[3] to be approached only by a narrow and dangerous entrance.* They appear, judging from their remains, to have entered Europe on the north and east, following the courses of rivers and the shores of lakes and oceans, roaming in hordes over southern Sweden and Denmark, penetrating the vast forests of Germany and France, some tribes settling in the northern portions of Spain, and others, perhaps, passing over the channels to the British Isles. Whether any of this primeval people ever crossed the Alps to Italy, is uncertain; though the remains of water habitations found in the Lago Maggiore, and d'Isco, would render it probable. The earthen mounds are not their only structures; they mark their path everywhere with strange monuments of massive stones, placed carefully one on another, but never with any work of masonry upon them. No historical records reveal the immense antiquity of these European savages. We only know that some of the mighty animals of the last geologic period the gigantic ox, the bear, the beaver, the elk, and the tiger—had survived the convulsions and the gradual changes which had altered the face of the world, and still roamed the woods at the same time with these primitive tribes.[3a] The human remains in their burial

Lake habitations.

* Remains of these water-habitations or villages, are found in the lakes and morasses of almost every part of Europe. In some cases, they were probably intended for defence against the wild animals; in others, they may have been used as sacred places by the priests; but more often, they were, without doubt, merely houses of security against hostile tribes. Sometimes they seem to have been floating habitations. The implements found in them, belong both to the flint, bronze, and iron "ages," but it is not improbable that various races may have used them in succession. (See an interesting article by M. L. Valliemin, in the *Bibliothèque Universelle*—Août, 1861: "Des Habitations Lacustres en Suisse."

mounds are pronounced, by physiologists, to be different from those of the races who succeeded them, the skulls being marked especially by their round shape, in distinction from the long skulls of the Indo-European peoples. The type in general of the head is low and barbarous. Who, then, were these early tribes of Europe?

Physical type.

Before attempting to answer this difficult question we must advert to another class of evidence.

Among all the Teutonic and Keltic races, especially in Northern Europe, there exist certain common superstitions; beliefs which, in their origin, may have been historical traditions, but which, gradually coloured by imagination and fear, have lost their first character and seem now pure fruits of the fancy. These have for their object a dwarfed race of beings, living far in the North, much skilled in mining or in works under ground, powerful in magical arts, cunning and malignant, lecherous in the extreme, useful to the husbandman or cattle-tender when well treated—a people ugly, yellow or dark in complexion, who long even by stealth for a union with their superiors, the fair race, and who are always persecuted and destroyed when no longer profitable to their masters. As has been ingeniously suggested by various students of European mythology, why may not these universal superstitions in Germany, Scandinavia, and England, be the faint echoes of early historical facts—of the existence of a primeval race in Europe, corresponding somewhat to these superstitious fancies, and afterward extirpated or driven north by the conquering Keltic and Teutonic races?

Early superstitions.

No family of man would so nearly correspond to these pictures of European superstition, as the *Finnish* family, especially in one of its branches.

In Northern Europe, the precursor of the Teutons and Kelts, it has been for unknown ages the inferior race; the dwarfed, dark, cunning, and supposedly malignant people, the race in all its branches given to magical arts and in some skilled in mining, holding a union with the Teuton its greatest honour, and addicted to extreme sexual vices. Whether any satisfactory historical conclusion can be drawn from this, we are not prepared to say. It is at least certain, that the skull found in the ancient *tumuli* is the Finnish skull; and the Turanian dialects, of which the Finnish is one, are discovered now protruding—like primitive cliffs under a wide deposit of succeeding and different strata—from peoples as separated and different as the Spanish and the Swedish. It is now believed by many philologists that the Basque, the Finnish, and the Lap dialects all belong to a great family, which extended in historical times from the Baltic to the Obi, and which in all probability covered the continent of Europe.

Finnish race.

The ancient Basques, or *Iberians*,[4] occupied the northern provinces of Spain, near the Pyrenees, and Southern France, or Aquitaine, from the Rhone on one side to the Garonne on the other. They even colonized in Sardinia, Corsica, and Sicily. They were a people, especially known to the ancients, as miners. The description of them given by classical historians, shows how much the modern Spaniard has derived from his Turanian ancestors.[5] They are spoken of as singularly grave in dress, and temperate and sober in habits; a people of unyielding spirit; not distinguished in open warfare, but unconquerable in guerilla combats and famed for their defence of walled cities; fond of brigandage; cunning and subtle; remarkable for their great respect for

Basques.

women and for their courteous and gallant manners.

The *Finnish* race,[6] of which we shall speak more particularly hereafter, includes a great number of tribes and nations, of which the best known are the *Magyars*, the *Finns*, and *Laps*, and *Samoieds*.

Finnish nations.

Their language belongs to that great division or family at present distinguished as the *Turanian*. So that language may prove to us that in Europe as in India and on the Euphrates, the first tribes who struggled with the wilderness and the savage beasts were of a similar stage in progress and belonged to the same vast brotherhood of nations.

Students of antiquity[7] have made a very valuable classification of the most ancient European history, according to the material of the instruments and ornaments found in the primeval tumuli, or scattered at various points beneath the soil. They have constructed from these relics—what they have called—the *Bone* or *Stone Age*, the *Bronze Age*, and the *Iron Age*. The first, in the evidences of its mode of life, and in its physical peculiarities, corresponds to the period in which we have supposed the Finnish or Turanian races to have roamed through the forests of Europe. The second belongs more to the Keltic period, and the third to the Teutonic. Though interesting as an archæological division, the classification has but little value for Ethnology.

The three ages.

The correspondence of bone and flint implements at a certain low stage of human development is true of all parts of the world,* and proves nothing but

* See Wilson's "Pre-Historic Man," where the remarkable resemblances in primitive arts, between the earliest inhabitants of America and Europe, are clearly exhibited.

common wants, and a like degree of barbarism. The similarity of design and the like tastes manifested in higher works of beauty, such as are made in bronze might be more distinctive of race, but here it is found that, at least in Great Britain, the works of bone and of bronze mingle at the same period, and there is no evidence that the aboriginal Turanian inhabitants of Europe might not have advanced sufficiently in intelligence to copy designs in bronze from other races. Neither can we say that the earliest Kelts might not have used bone or flint materials, or the later Kelts, iron implements, even as much as the Teütons.

The division not ethnological.

To the archæological division above described, the recent discoveries, which we shall describe in a future chapter, of a still more primeval race, must add yet another era—the *Flint Age.*

CHAPTER VIII.

THE ARYAN RACES OF EUROPE.

I. The Kelts.[1 2]

THE second great stream of population which flowed over Europe from Central Asia, was probably the Keltic. The entrance of this people—the oldest of the Aryan races—on the soil of Europe dates back far beyond historical records, to an unknown antiquity. The first information which history gives of them shows them firmly settled in the centre and west of Europe, and even sending out streams of emigration toward the east. There is scarcely a tradition even of their eastern origin, and they are commonly considered by the earliest historians, as natives of the soil. But language—which is the most unerring record—proves them a member of the great Indo-European family, and that they, too, must have wandered in far remote ages from the great mountain-plateau east of the Caspian. The language is considered by many scholars, to be earlier in its development and formation, even than the Sanskrit.[3] Scarcely any Aryan race has spread itself so widely over Europe, or has so distinguished itself by conquest, as the Keltic. From the Danube, and Asia Minor, over Sweden, Germany, France, Italy, Spain, to the western coasts of Ireland and the highlands of

First appearance of Kelts.

Distinguished for conquests.

Scotland, traces of their residence and their conquests are preserved. If we follow the hypothesis of Dr. C. Meyer, we may suppose that their tribes entered Europe in two streams; one proceeding in a south-western direction, through Syria and Egypt, and along the northern coast of Africa, reached Europe at the Straits of Gibraltar. After passing through Spain to France, it divided itself into three branches; one of which crossed to Great Britain, another entered Italy, and still another, following the Alps and the Danube, ended near the Black Sea.

Supposed migrations.

The second great emigration he supposes to have passed over the north of Europe—Sweden, and Prussia—until it finally (about 600 B.C.) reached Scotland and the neighbouring islands through the German Ocean. To the first migration, he ascribes the Kelts and the Gauls of classic historians; to the second, the Picts and Scots.

Whatever exact value may attach—and certainly there is very little historical basis—to this hypothesis, the first authentic history shows the Kelts in struggle with the Iberians in Spain. They are supposed, before this period, to have lived between the Seine and the Garonne, and the geographical names of the Peninsula of Italy, as well as the Keltic element of the Latin, show that they were among the earliest inhabitants there. At a remote period—when, is uncertain—they are believed to have crossed the Alps, and occupied the plain of the Po. There are indications of their early presence, even in the extreme south of Italy. In the north, at least in the fourth century before Christ, they had wrested both banks of the Po from the Etruscans, and founded the State, known afterward as Cisalpine Gaul; in 390, they captured Rome. In 280, vast hordes of Kelts passed over the centre of Europe, and arousing the Kelts of Illyria who had been settled there at least a century before, they attacked Greece, Macedonia, and Thessaly: others crossed the Dardanelles, and ravaged Asia Minor for a long time. Even the Scythians were assaulted on their own plains. A Keltic State, Galatia, was founded in Asia. Switzerland was mainly Keltic, as was the southwestern part of Hungary.

Early invasions.

Whether the Cimbri, who, in 113 B.C., from some unknown cause, emigrated in mass from the north of Europe and poured themselves on Italy, were Kelts, cannot be determined with certainty. The probability seems to be that they were Keltic tribes, living in close proximity to Teutonic.

The ancient Kelts are divided into two great classes, the Gaelic and the Kymric. The Gaels, according to M. Thierry's supposition, entered France first, and settled in the south and east of that country, up to the line of the Marne. The Kymric Belgians, who came from the countries on the North Sea, occupied, on this theory, the provinces north and west as far as the Seine or the Loire. The Gaels extended over parts of Spain, Italy, and Illyria; the Kymri over the British Isles, and in the opposite direction, to Asia, founding the Empire of Galatia. There is great reason, however, to doubt whether the Belgians were Kelts, and if they were, they were probably much mingled with German tribes. Whether this classification corresponds with the divisions of the modern Keltic tongue is also doubtful, as so little is known of the ancient Keltic. The exact ethnological position and the authentic history of the supposed Keltic tribes is—like that of the Pelasgians—one of the knottiest questions for the ethnologist. We are only certain that a numerous and

Thierry's classification.

Uncertainty about Kelts.

warlike people, the undoubted ancestors of some portion of the modern Kelts, spread themselves over every part of Europe in the earliest historical times, enslaving the original inhabitants (probably of Finnish origin), and carrying terror to all organized Governments. We see that in many of their moral traits they corresponded well with the modern Kelts. A race—according to the oldest authorities—brave, quick to quarrel, vain and fond of display, with little pertinacity, but capable of extraordinary efforts, liable to excessive discouragement and unreasonable elation, never attached, like the Teuton, to the soil, but preferring the associated life of large towns, intelligent and apt, but seeking wealth by plunder rather than by slow gains, a people who fill the history of the past with the glory of their conquests, but who found no permanent State and who are never willing to submit long to their own constituted authorities.

They seem in the earliest periods, to excel in valour and individual genius, but never possess the deep moral qualities which are needed for the foundation of enduring Governments.

Keltic traits.

From the first they are represented as credulous and easily ruled by their priesthood.

They were the freebooters and mercenary soldiers of antiquity, until, at length, their undisciplined valour sank under the steady organized military power of Rome, and their tribes became absorbed first into the Roman people, and then into the Teutonic conquerors.

Though the moral traits of the Kelt have so little changed to our day, his physical have been exceedingly modified by the influences of climate and of nourishment. In the times of Cæsar, the Kelt is described as tall, with ruddy complexion, blonde temperament, light hair, and blue eyes—a picture

Physique.

to which the Highlander alone of modern Kelts would correspond. His dress was a garment like the modern tartans; he wore little armour, and for ornament usually a gold ring round his neck.

The Keltic remains, scattered over Europe, show that this people early understood the art of working in metals. Bronze, iron, and gold; ivory, glass, and wood were all turned by them into articles of use or beauty. They possessed an endless quantity of vases and glass vessels. Coins also were in use by them; and garments of the most costly materials. They constructed ships and houses of a peculiar shape, and bridges and well-laid roads. Their round brick towers are well known in various parts of Europe. In the tumuli and sepulchres of the Kelts, their remains show that they burned their dead, in distinction from the Finns, who buried them.

Arts.

The Kelts possessed the art of writing, and are supposed to have had an alphabet, related to the Greek. All the evidence from these sources shows that though a roving and warlike people, the continental Kelts manifested thus early much of the ingenuity and sense of beauty and order of their descendants.

The British Kelts, if one may trust the accounts of the Latin historians, were in the lowest state of barbarism—scarcely beyond the present condition of the South Sea Islanders.

Of the Keltic religions, little is known. It is probable that they worshipped the personification of the powers of Nature, and according to Roman authority, they believed in a future life and in the removal of the soul after death into other bodies or animals. They are known to have followed the revolting custom of human sacrifice. The whole race seems, even in the earliest times, to have been under the rule of a powerful and privileged Hierarchy—the Druids.

The modern Keltic language is divided into two great branches: the *Kymric* and *Gaelic* (or Gadhelic).

Keltic language.

The *Kymric* embraces the Welsh, the extinct Cornish, and the Armorican, of Brittany (*Bas Breton*), in France. The *Gaelic*, or *Erse*, comprises the Irish, the Gaelic of the Scotch Highlands, and the dialect of the Isle of Man.[4]

The leading characteristics of the Keltic language are given as *flexibility*, *elasticity*, and *analytical distinctness*. Its structure proves a great antiquity to it.

The Etruscans.[5]

Among the fragments of Aryan tribes may probably be reckoned the ancient people of the *Etruscans*, or *Rasena*, as they called themselves—Tyrrhenians, as they were called by the Greeks. There is reason to suppose that they emigrated into Italy through the passes of the Tyrolean Alps, where relics of their language still survive, and first established themselves on

Early abodes.

the north of the Po, until their power was overthrown by the invading Keltic tribes. Their peculiar abodes were on the western coast of Italy, between the Arno and the Tiber, and west of the Apennines. Here they founded a State which was one of the leading naval powers of antiquity, and which reached its height of greatness in the sixth and seventh centuries before Christ. Their population, even under Roman rule, remained somewhat distinct till the time of the Emperors.

Though the Etruscans are now considered by the best ethnologists to belong to the Indo-European family,

Probably Indo-European.

the evidence for it is very slight indeed. The few words known of their language are mostly found in sepulchral inscriptions and consist in great part of proper names. These show an element of ancient Latin (or Umbrian); of ancient Greek, and a third mixture not known, which, if it has any affinities distinguishable, has them with the Indo-European tongues. One theory, accordingly, is that the Etruscans are a mixed people; the basis being some portion of that ancient and unknown Græco-Italian race, the fathers of the Greeks and Romans, and the other portions made up of conquering barbarous tribes from the north of Italy, probably of the great Aryan family. Still another theory is that they are a foreign tribe, probably of Aryan descent, who conquered the ancient Latin tribes and assimilated to a degree their language.

The most prominent influence in history of the Etruscans was exercised upon the Romans in the direction of their mythology and superstitions, to which this ancient people had so peculiar a tendency as to lead one to suspect a Turanian or Finnish element in their race, while their remarkable skill in mining may remind us of the Ibero-Finnic tribes, who colonized so near them, on the islands of the Mediterranean. Their custom, too, of employing women as diviners, was peculiarly Finnish. The Etruscan civilization was essentially practical and useful—even materialistic—and no doubt affected the Roman civilization also, in this direction. At present the question of their ethnological position must be considered at best as only probably settled.

Other Primitive Italian Peoples.

The other primeval races of Italy may be divided into two great branches, which are probably older in Italy than the Etruscans—the *Iapygians* and the

Italicans.[6] The former, moving probably from the north, occupied the south-east of Italy, and were a barbarous tribe. Their language, though different from the other Italian languages, is thought to belong to the Pelasgic, or Græco-Italian family, while other historical indications make this conclusion the more probable.

Iapygians.

The *Italicans* may be subdivided into two important branches: the *Latins* and the *Umbrians*; the latter embracing the Volskians, Marsians, and Samnites.

Of the "Italican" peoples, there is no doubt of their being members of the Aryan family, and closely related to the Greek, much more nearly connected than, for instance, the Teutonic to the Keltic. From these Latin tribes in the centre of Italy—removed fortunately from the overpowering influence of Greek civilization—have come forth the original influences in law and language and civilization, which acting on the more uncultivated Teutonic and Keltic tribes, have tended to form the character of all the leading nations of Europe, and which will shape and direct the advance of mankind for many centuries to come.

Italicans.

CHAPTER IX.

II. THE EARLY TEUTONIC TRIBES.[1]

In attempting to penetrate the early ethnological relations of Europe, one is at first utterly confused by the appearance of the Teutonic tribes. To an observer, who could have overlooked the Continent during the few centuries immediately preceding the introduction of Christianity, there would have seemed an almost indistinguishable medley of marches and emigrations of warlike peoples; here, a nation slowly advancing with women and children and property, to take possession of forests and rivers abandoned; there, multitudes of armed men ravaging and plundering peaceful territories; here, a people entering the Roman Empire as mercenaries, or, in another place, transplanted as agriculturists and tributaries—waves on waves of population—currents intermingling with currents of peoples, all at first flowing from the east, all composed of half-barbarous tribes of a common stock, and all surging and beating against the outworks of the great civilized State of antiquity—the Roman Empire. The world has never witnessed such a movement of nations as convulsed Europe for seven hundred years—beginning at least in the second century before Christ. From north to south, and from south to north, from east to west, and again toward the northwest, are constant migrations of German tribes during all these centuries, so that the

Teutonic wanderings.

F 2

same names appear in the most opposite quarters, and every conceivable mingling of race would seem the result. Some of these nations uttterly disappear, others become partly absorbed into the older and more civilized Latin populations, and others are blended with the Keltic and Slavonic tribes whom they subdue.

The great family, of whom these various nations are tribes, is even then the most powerful race which has appeared. The old Roman Empire goes down under their shock; the corrupted civilization of Europe is in many quarters trampled under foot; and the effete and worn-out Græcian or Italian Aryans, are vivified with the fresh, vigorous blood of the Teutonic Aryans. From this family has come most of the energy and civilization of modern Europe, and the Teutonic tribes have formed the most powerful element in the leading nations of Europe and America.

What cause originally impelled this movement of population from Asia into Europe is hid in obscurity. Causes of migrations. There are, indeed, certain coincidences in Asiatic annals and names, with the migrations and familiar words of European history, which might fix a date and cause of the Teutonic wanderings —such as the contests of the Chinese with the fair-haired Scyths, the *Hakas*, who are supposed to be the *Sakas* of the Hindoos, the *Sacæ* of Bactria, the *Saka-sonnas* of Armenia, a name corresponding to the *Khetas*, or Khouti (Gothi), of both Asia and Europe, which is thought to have given its origin to the name of the supposed cradle of the Teutonic race, *Scanzia* (Scandinavia), and their most vigorous tribe, *Sakasunas* or Saxons. But all this, though presenting data for future interesting investigation, cannot be regarded as historical evidence.

We may only suppose as probable, that about 1200

B.C.,[2] some great internal popular movement, or some change in the physical conditions in Asia, pressed the neighbouring tribes upon the Teutonic races, and drove them to the country on the north of the Black Sea. From these provinces, three great currents are believed to have flowed, in the fourth century B.C., into Europe; one up the Dnieper or Dniester, to the countries on the Baltic, and to Scandinavia, another to the Lower Danube, and still another up the Danube to the valley of the Rhine. From Scandinavia, it is believed by some,[3] that in the third century B.C., two streams flowed toward the south, one of which, mingling with the Kelts, formed the nation of *Belgæ*, and the other near 113, forced out the whole nation of the Cimbri from Northern Europe, upon the Roman Empire.

Earliest probable date.

This, however, is again only probable theory. History begins for the Teutons, with their appearance in Eastern Europe, in the third and fourth centuries after Christ, though some tribes are mentioned, even before the Christian Era; the immediate pressure for their migrations being the encroachments and attacks of a warlike Finnic (or Tschudic) people of Asia, the Huns.

First historical appearance.

An ancient division of these tribes can be made into the pure Germans, or *Saxons*, and the *Sueves*, who were somewhat tinctured with Slavonic blood. The latter included fifty-four peoples, as the Goths, Longobards, Vandals, Burgundians, Rugians, Herulians, and others. They are distinguished, in general, from the other great branch of the German family, as being more nomadic and warlike, less inclined to agriculture, and with constitutions of government of a more monarchical nature. The Saxons are more democratic, and with less unity of national feeling.

In general, it may be said, that there were *four* conspicuous and leading nations, or confederations of tribes, among them—the *Goths*, who tended mostly to the east of Europe; the *Franks*, who wandered to the west; the *Saxons*, toward the north; and the *Alemanns*, to the south.

Under the Goths, may be included the Gepidæ, Danes, Swedes, and Herulians; under the Franks, the Chatti; under the Saxons, the Angles, Jutes, and the Frisians; with the Alemanns, the Suevians. Besides these, there were the Vandals, Burgundians, Longobards, and many other tribes, more or less important.

Goths.

Goths. Of these we hear, in very ancient times, as occupying the southern part of Sweden. In 375 A.D. they appear as West Goths, on the Lower Danube, and penetrate to Thrace; pressing on, they finally reach Gaul, where, in the fifth century, they found the West Gothic Kingdom. Remains of this branch are found in the Crimea, even up to the present day.

As *East Goths*, in the latter part of the fourth century, they pass over the Lower Danube to Bulgaria; forced from these provinces they finally (480) reach Italy, where they rule for nearly one hundred years, until their kingdom is overthrown by the Byzantine army. Another division have possession of Eastern and Northern Germany.

Vandals.

The *Gepidæ*, probably of Gothic origin, appear in Hungary about 400, and are conquered by the Longobards in the latter half of the sixth century. The *Vandals** are spoken of in Hungary as early as 166 A.D., and (406 to 409) in company with other peoples, they march through Gaul to Spain, and thence their invasions reach Africa (429 A.D.), conquering the Roman armies, and one division

* The Vandals are supposed by Latham to be *Slavonian*, partly from their name, and partly from their localities. He divides them into two branches, one living on the Daco-Pannonian frontier, in confederation with the Goths; and the other, on the south-western frontier, were the Sorabians of Saxony and Silesia, the ancestors of the present Sorbs of those countries.

returning, burns Rome (455 A.D.). In 534, they are overpowered, and finally disappear.

Alemanns. These are seen about 214, in Central Germany, between the Danube and the Maine, in the land of the Sueves. They wage constant wars with the Romans, with much success. Their progress is finally checked by the advancing Franks (496). The German Swiss and Suabians are their descendants.

Alemanns.

Franks. In the third century we hear of this people, or confederation of peoples, on the Lower Rhine; they advance slowly through Germany, toward the Rhine. In 355, they are in Gaul, and have formed several small kingdoms; in 487, Clodwig has destroyed the last vestige of Roman power in what is now France, and overpowers the Alemanns, the West Goths, the Thuringians, and Burgundians, preparing for the great empire of Charlemagne, and the final division of Europe into many of its present States.

Franks.

Saxons. This name first appears in the middle of the second century. The Saxons are then neighbours of the Frisians, and their territory extends from the Weser, over the Elbe to Holstein and Denmark. They were the pirates and marine freebooters of those early ages. They conquered most of England, in union with the Angles, in 450, and their relatives, the Norwegian and Danish Normans, after plundering and laying waste most of the countries of Europe, subdued and settled Normandy (911), and furnished the martial population which again (1066) conquered England under William the Conqueror.

Saxons.

From the sixth century on, they are in uninterrupted struggle with the Franks, which only ends with their incorporation into the Frankish monarchy, in 803. From this time, the name describes all North Germany. Besides these, the *Burgundians* founded on the Rhone (414) a Burgundian kingdom, which was subdued by the Franks (523 to 534). Their prominent cities were Geneva, Besançon, Châlons, Vienne (on the Rhone), and Avignon.

Burgundians.

In Upper Italy the *Longobards* laid the foundation (574) of a Lombard State, which was destroyed in 774 by the Franks. It included Piedmont, Tuscany, Milan, Genoa, and other provinces.

Lombards.

Thuringians. This tribe is supposed to be the same as the Hermunduri, mentioned by Tacitus. From the fifth century, they occupy the lands on the left bank of the Danube, northward of the Alemanns and Suabians, as far as the Elbe and the Harz, which separates them from the Saxons. In the sixth century they lost great districts on the east, through the attacks of the Slavonians, at the same time that they were exposed to the assaults of the Franks, by whom they were finally subjected. After this period, their name disappears as one of the leading German nations.

Thuringians.

The *Bavarians* (*Baiovarii*) are first mentioned in the early part of the sixth century. They held, then, the eastern part of that great South German territory known as Suevia. Their country stretched over the Rhætian plain to the Alps, and northward to the Danube, between the Sueves on the west, and the sources of the Drave and the Enns on the east. They were probably made up of small Suevic tribes, and were especially related to the Thuringians, Alemanns, and Longobards. Various other German tribes, without doubt, united themselves to the Bavarian confederation. They became subject to the Frankish monarchy under Charlemagne.

Bavarians.

To sum up these brief sketches of the early Teutonic races, it may be said that the following was their position in Germany in the third century. In the north, from the Rhine to the Elbe, and even reaching to Schleswig, was the *Saxon* confederation. West of this, all the tribes related to the *Franks* had settled, and pushed further westward, they had occupied Northern Gaul. The *Alemanns* held the south-west of Germany—the districts on the Upper Rhine. To the north of them were the *Burgundians*, to the east the *Suabians.* All the east of Germany was held by the many tribes who ranked under the *Goths.*

Teutonic races in third century.

The first of the Teutonic tribes in antiquity was undoubtedly the Gothic people. All the various branches were proud of their descent from, or alliance with, this nation; and even yet, in Spain, the mingling of the "blue blood"—the Gothic—is considered a mark of nobility. Their power was greatly weakened by the overwhelming attacks of the Huns, and from their position in the Roman Empire, they received much more of the weakening and corrupting influences of the more civilized races, so that they finally utterly disappeared as a distinct nation.

Goths.

The *Vandals* are supposed[4] to have received much mixture of Slavonic blood. In Africa they accepted the old Semitic civilization and perished under its influences. The *Longobards*, originally from Jutland, who were nearer the source of the race, preserved their purity of blood much longer than the other tribes. In the Middle Rhine and on the Upper Danube, they were thought to have been much mingled with Kelts.

The *Burgundians* preserved their original stock even longer than the Longobards, though finally taking into themselves many Keltic and Slavonic elements. The *Franks*—the purest in Teutonic blood of nearly all the tribes—survived most of them, and for a long time, ruling over kindred tribes, escaped the enervating influences of the corrupt Latin races. Of all the Teutonic peoples, the one which was least exposed to the effects of Roman civilization, and which did least to regenerate the world by its infusion of new blood, were the fierce and warlike *Saxons*. Living at the extreme north of Europe, their attacks were not much directed against the Roman Empire, but fell more upon the east of Germany or the British Isles; they experienced in consequence little of the influence which a semi-barbarous people feel in contact with a highly civilized. The Saxons preserve the pure Teutonic force, and finally develope a race which, of all others, has most deeply impressed modern civilization.

Saxons.

In the middle of the third century the Teutonic element first enters into public affairs in the Roman

Empire; in 476 the Western Empire is overthrown by this power; and in 800 a new Teutonic empire under a Frank King (Charlemagne) is erected, which extended over most of Spain, Germany, France, and Italy.

In regard to the geographical position of the Teutonic tribes, it may be said, in general, that the fierce assaults of the Huns in Eastern Europe crushed many of these in that quarter, and tended to mass the others in the west and northwest of Europe, leaving the east to Slavonic and Finnic populations—a condition which has endured to the present day.

Gegraphical position.

After the destruction of the Roman Empire (476), the Teutonic tribes were distributed somewhat as follows: In Illyria and Italy were a mixture of Herulians, Rugians, and afterward of East Goths; in Spain remains of Sueves and Vandals, and West Goths in the north; in Southern France West Goths, in Eastern France Burgundians and Alemanns; and in the north, in Belgium and on the Lower Rhine, Franks. In Holland were the Frisians; in Westphalia the Saxons; and south of these the Thuringians. On the left bank of the Danube, near Vienna, the Longobards; in Bohemia and Suabia, the Sueves and the Bavarians, and Markomanns; in Hungary and Moldavia, the Gepidæ.

Teutons in the fifth century.

The Teutons had thus lost all the provinces to the east of the Elbe, which were occupied by Slavonians.

Many of the Teutonic nations were in no way affected by that great event—the overthrow of the Roman Empire. But the East and West Goths were delivered up through it to the influences of a corrupt civilization, and the Franks finally felt its effect in the merging of their German population into the Keltic and Latin elements, which were in contact with them, till in the tenth century a new people, the *French*, were the result.

At the time of Charlemagne, the ethnic relations of Europe were somewhat as follows:*[5] In South Italy there were great minglings and crossings of races—Semites from Saracenic conquests, ancient tribes of Aryan, or possibly, Turanian origin, and Greek or ancient Græco-Italian remains. In North Italy the Teutonic Lombards were preponderant, and not yet much assimilated to the Roman and Keltic populations. In Spain the south and centre were under the Semitic conquests of the Arabs, while in the northwest were descendants of Sueves and Visigoths, with minglings of the Iberian race. In the south of France were ancient deposits of Keltic and Roman population with Gothic mixtures. From Provence and Languedoc, the West-Goths had mostly disappeared while the Roman influences were very strong, with some Semitic remains from the Saracenic invasions. In the east of France, the Franks are the leading race over a Burgundian population. In Burgundy, West Switzerland, Savoy, and Piedmont are many traces of the Keltic and Slavonic races. In central France, the Franks predominate over a Gallo-Roman population, and Brittany shows a decidedly Keltic population.

European races in Charlemagne's era.

From the Seine to the Rhine, and on the other side to the Maine and the Danube, the Teutons or Germans are the leading race, though mingled much with Keltic and Slavonic races.

Denmark, Sweden, and Norway, and the northern coasts of Europe, are covered with unmixed Teutonic peoples. Even Russia soon received from this powerful race her ruling family, who, in 862, laid the foundation of the Russian Empire, and held possession of the

* De Gobineau.

Government for more than 700 years. England, with a Keltic population, had received continual mixtures of German blood, until, at length, the Teutons in the Saxon conquest, and again in that of the Northmen, held undisputed rule, and infused the masses of the people with their vigorous blood.

The description of the German races, from the classical historians, and in their own Sagas, gives us a consistent impression of their characteristics, both physical and moral.

They are pictured as a tall, powerful race, with light hair, and blue eyes, and clear blonde complexion. Their hands and feet were small. The especial mark of high rank was the brightness of the eye, and long hair was considered a beauty.

Teutonic traits.

They were a race remarkable for personal dignity, which became easily corrupted into excessive pride, and for a boundless spirit of individual enterprise. With these traits, they united a simplicity and trustfulness, which were observed by strangers. They were notoriously reckless of their own lives, and cruel to enemies; fond of adventure, especially on the sea; preferring whatever involved peril and hardship; greedy for booty, and given to the pleasures of the table and gaming. In regard to sexual virtue, and the respect paid to woman, they stand forth far above all other races of the past. It is an evidence of Teutonic virtue in this direction, that the ancient Teutonic dialects have no word to express the idea of *prostitute*—Slavic and Keltic words being applied for this purpose. To the old German influence, even before the introduction of Christianity, and still more to that influence refined by it—woman, in all modern society, owes something of her high position.

Purity of morals.

The Teutonic character was arbitrary, and therefore

delighted in slavery and difference of classes, but it always supported self-government in the ruling race. In distinction from the Kelt's love for cities, the Teuton preferred the life on "farms;" each landholder calling his farm his "court," and even carrying his independence so far as often to fortify his property; yet with all this, he is seldom found with any very deep attachment for his native soil, changing it readily where ambition or profit would tempt.

The old German nature was not pre-eminently religious, though not deficient in reverence. It shows much fire of imagination in its semi-barbarous days, yet even then, its predominant mental tendency was either toward the subtleties of law and government, or to a mythology which seems more scientific than religious. The Teutonic mind, however, was always peculiarly moral in its directions.

The Teuton's respect for woman, their morality, and their belief in one God, as well as their associated self-governments, prepared them for the reception of Christianity, and gave them great power in spreading its truths.

Influence on the world.

Language.

Max Müller's division is probablythe most scientific, into: (1.) The *Low-German*, including Gothic, Old Saxon, Saxon, Friesic, Dutch, Flemish, and Platt-Deutsch. (2.) The *High-German*, including Old High-German, from the seventh to the twelfth century, Middle High-German, from the twelfth century to Luther, and the New High-German, the present literary language of Germany. (3.) The *Scandinavian*, represented by the Old Norse and its three dialects, Danish, Norwegian, and Swedish, and embracing two branches, the East and West Scandinavian.

Language.

CHAPTER X.

III. THE EARLY SLAVONIANS.[1]

It cannot certainly be decided whether this important family settled in its European possessions before or after the migration of the Teutonic nations from Asia. The most probable conclusion is, that, pressed by the Turkish hordes who were devastating Asia, the Slavonians moved on toward the west, in the track of the Teutons, and settled on the lands which these had abandoned. They seem seldom to have been a conquering and purely military race; and their possessions were mostly gained by them as colonists and tillers of the ground. The great peculiarity of their early history is the tenacity with which they retained both their national character and their own habitations under wave after wave of successive conquests.

Their tenacity.

They had the misfortune to be settled near the outworks of European civilization, where the first attacks of the fiery and cruel Asiatic tribes always fell. Forced on the west upon the rear tribes of the advancing Teutons, and in continual struggle with them, on the east they were submerged by the irresistible onsets of Huns, Avars, Bulgars, Chazars, and Turks, and yet they seem never to be exterminated as were certain Teutonic tribes, but they appear again after the storm is over as peaceful cultivators of the soil, and in many cases, as with the Teutonic *Rossi* and the Bulgarians, they denationalize their conquerors and merge them into the Slavonic family. The origin of the Slavonians, even within the historic period, is unknown.

The connection of the early Slaves with the tribes of ancient Sarmatia, is not sufficiently certain for historic statement, yet admitting of much probable conjecture.

Ancient writers divide the Slavonians, or *Wendes*, into two great classes, which correspond with modern divisions—the *Antes* and the *Sclavens*,[1a] or the East Russians and the West Russians. The Sclavens lived between the Danube and the Dniester, and extended northward to the Vistula; the Antes inhabited the vast countries east of the Dniester. The European home of the whole family is undoubtedly the country on the Upper Volga, and around the Valdai mountains.

Ancient division.

It is believed that for four centuries before Christ, and for two hundred years after, the movements of the Slavonians were mostly toward the north and east; the vast steppes of Eastern Europe being especially attractive to their agricultural habits. From the third century to the seventh, the overcrowded population in the eastern provinces, and the constant attacks of the Asiatic nomad tribes, pressed them toward the south and west.

The destruction of the Huns (about 469), and the overthrow of the Roman Empire (476), undoubtedly first laid open Western Europe to them.

In the sixth century we have some of the first historical accounts of their tribes. The Longobards have abandoned Pannonia, or Hungary, and the Avars, a Turkish tribe, have taken possession of this fertile country, and assigned

First historical accounts.

lands to their allies, the Slavonic tribes. The Antes are spoken of as ravaging Thrace in 546. The Sclavens have occupied the country beyond the Danube, and their military expeditions, or their migrations, cover Illyria, Thrace, and Dalmatia, and reach even to the walls of Constantinople (552). After the invasion of the Avars, they begin to make settlements in these countries. In the sixth and seventh centuries great internal revolutions occur among the Slavonic peoples, and the *Wendes* spread from the Dniester and the Danube, to the shores of the German Ocean and the banks of the Elbe, occupying the districts which the Burgundians, Herulians, Suevians, and other Teutonic tribes had abandoned.

Sclavens.

Of the Eastern Slaves, some are designated as allies of the Romans in Bulgaria, in 594. Servia and Dalmatia are gained by the Servians and Croats of this branch in the first part of the seventh century, and Illyrian Slaves of this division are spoken of in the seventh century, and heavy masses of Eastern Slaves have settled on the south-eastern declivity of the Alps, toward the Adriatic, in the sixth and seventh centuries. The Russians, or Muscovites, belong to this branch of the Slavonic family, though their name is derived from a Scandinavian tribe—Rossi—who gave them their governing family for some centuries.

The *Western Slaves* are heard of as invading Greece in 582, which, together with the neighbouring districts of Thessaly, Epirus, and Asia Minor, they plundered and occupied for several centuries, until, in the eighth century, Greece seemed about to become Slavonic.

West Slaves.

They appear first in Germany, on the Elbe, in 623; they settle Moravia; as Tchechs, they furnish the population to Bohemia which has endured to the present day;

they colonize and build cities on the Northern Sea, between the Vistula and the Elbe. From them come the Dalmatians, the Frankic Slaves, the Slaves between the Elbe and the Oder, the Saxon Slavonic population, the Poles, or Laechs, the Pomeranians, and the Slovaks of Hungary.

The divisions of the language at the present day, correspond to these ancient divisions of the people. The *Eastern*[2] (or South-Eastern) comprises the Russian, the Bulgarian, and the Illyrian; the latter including the Servian, Croatian, and Slovenian. The *Western* includes the Polish, the Bohemian, the Wendian and the Polabian. Of these, we shall speak more particularly in treating of the modern Slavonians.

Divisions of dialects.

The ancient Slavonic tribes do not equal the Teutons in the spirit of bold adventure, nor are they as conspicuous for purity of morals. They show, however, even greater tenacity of character and a toughness of nature, which causes them to survive all the conquests of which they were the victims. Their instinct of race, or of nationality, was as strong in the earliest times as it is now. In the peaceful arts, they were undoubtedly in advance of the Teutons, and there is reason to believe that the word *plough*, as well as the knowledge of some portions of agriculture, came to the Germans from the Slavonians. From the fifth to the ninth centuries, while the Teutons held Western Germany, and the Slaves Eastern, it was observed that the latter country was by far the more peaceful and prosperous. The Slavonians showed no lack of courage and patient endurance, when called on to fight, or to suffer for their rights, but their inclinations were always toward commerce and agriculture. It is their high honour,[3] that, in an age of servitude, they possessed no

A peaceful race.

slaves, and developed, even in that early time, an instructive example of *communal* self-government.

They were always a populous family, and apparently in ancient times more remarkable for the general well-being of the people, than for any conspicuous individuals. The Slavonic family showed in antiquity the rare faculty of submission, without the tendency to degeneracy or slavishness. Their religion, with many superstitions and poetic pagan accompaniments, which only several centuries of Christianity could eradicate, contained a pure monotheism.

Traits.

In general, the Slavonic family of ancient times, may be characterized as one of the most tough and enduring races that ever appeared; with qualities, whose vigour and solid worth only the slow progress of many ages could fairly develop.

The Lithuanians.

On the eastern coast of the Baltic, from the Vistula to the Memel, and reaching south as far as the Bug and the Narew, a branch of the Slavonic race lived from the most ancient times, whose language still interests the scholar from its remarkable approach to the Sanskrit—the ancient Lithuanians.

They are described by classical historians even as early as the fourth century before Christ, as a peaceful agricultural race, with different habits from those of the Sarmatians, who adjoined them, as trafficking much in amber, collected on their coasts. They were divided into the *Aestui* and the *Venedi*. Schaffarik supposes that the attacks of the Gothic nations separated the two tribes, and that the Venedi retreated to Russia, while the Aestuans remained as serfs, or subjects, to the Teutonic conquerors. They

Aestui and Venedi.

were subdued again by Ermanrich (332 to 350 A.D.). No tribe in Europe showed such desperate opposition to the approaches of Christianity, as did the ancient Lithuanians and Prussians. This may have been in part owing to a remarkable system of hierarchy, established among them by their own priests. They were only finally conquered by the Teutonic Knights, in the thirteenth century.

Resistance to Christianity.

There were three distinct branches of this family: the West Aestuans, or the ancient Prussians; the East Aestuans, near Memel, or the Lithuanians; and the Lettic tribes, the inhabitants of Kurland and Livonia.

The language of all these branches was formerly supposed to be a distinct and original tongue—that of another race in the Aryan family, who had survived between the Finns and Slavonians on one side, and the Teutons on the other. It is now, however, classed as a sister tongue with the Slavonic, under the same family, distinguished by some as the *Windic*. Of its three divisions, the Lithuanian, the Old Prussian, and the Lettish—only the first and last have survived. The Lithuanian has transmitted but little literature; yet is deeply interesting to the student of language, from having preserved the most primitive features of the original Aryan tongue.[4]

Language.

CHAPTER XI.

TURANIAN RACES IN EUROPE.[1]

THE last of the waves of the Indo-European emigration is supposed to have been the movement of the Alans—a tribe, probably, of Medo-Persian origin, yet resembling, in many respects, the Finnish and Turkish nations that followed it, and which, finally, utterly disappeared. From the third century to the ninth, a new movement of peoples began—stirred up, probably, by wars and struggles as far away as on the borders of China—a rapid inroad of nomad tribes, carrying desolation and terror over Asia and Europe, destroying kingdoms, overthrowing the most valiant Aryan nations, bearing the wild Asiatic horseman as far within the limits of civilization as the territory of France, yet leaving scarce any permanent fruits behind, except works of destruction, and founding but one permanent Government—the Hungarian.

Alans.

The cradle of these races seemed to be the cold region between the Volga and the Obi, on both sides of the Ural, and even as far away as in the midst of the Altai Mountains. The Finnish, or the mingled Finno-Turkic tribes settled after the third century on the plains of Southern Russia, between the Volga and the Lower Danube. In the ninth century the more undoubted Turkic races inundated all the plains north of the Caspian and the Black Sea, while other tribes of the same family

Turanian invasions of Europe.

passed south of the Caspian and the Caucasus, invaded Persia and the valley of the Euphrates, and Asia Minor, undermined the Byzantine Empire, and finally erected the powerful Empire of the Ottoman Turks. The first of these invaders, so terrible to Europe, were the Huns and the last of the Finnish tribes—the Khazars; the last of the early Turkic tribes—the Cumanians.

We shall treat of them but briefly, as they do not bear with importance on the course of history.

THE HUNS.

It is still a matter of dispute to what branch of the Turanian family the Huns belonged—whether they were Mongol, Turkic, or Finnish, though the best authorities incline to the belief that they were Turkic.

Uncertain origin.

The description of them—no doubt exaggerated by the imagination of the Teutonic tribes whom they conquered—is as of the most hideous and cruel nomadic tribe—desolating and plundering all the countries over which they pass. The allusions to them in early Asiatic annals are not sufficiently authentic for history. It seems probable that they left their steppes near the Ural Mountains, somewhere near 350 A.D.; in 375, they had passed the Volga and Don, and were attacking the Gothic tribes. The kingdom of the East-Goths was destroyed in a single battle; the Alans were overthrown, and the Teutonic tribes, even as they had been driven from the regions of the Black Sea, are again forced from the country of the Lower Danube, into the interior provinces of Europe. The Huns held possession of the immense country from the Theiss far into the wilds of Siberia.

Hunnic invasions.

The reign of Attila, their terrible chief, lasted from 433 A.D. to 453, and extended over Pannonia and Dacia, as far west as the eastern frontier of Bohemia, including certain provinces south of the Danube:[2] his expeditions reaching even to France. His kingdom dissolved at his death, almost as soon as it had risen, under the attacks of the Teutonic tribes, whom he had subjected; and after the middle of the sixth century no mention is any more made of the Huns as a distinct nation.

Another Turanian tribe are the *Khazars*, probably Finnic,[3] though with Turkic mixtures. They appear in Europe between the seventh and tenth century, and rule over the country between the Caspian and the Dnieper. They are followed by the *Pechenegs*, a Turkic tribe, who occupy Bessarabia, Cherson, and part of Taurida, in the tenth and eleventh centuries. The *Komanes* (or *Cumani*), another Turkic tribe of Europe, gained a foothold in Hungary in the eleventh century, and have transmitted descendants.

Turkic tribes.

The Avars. The first historical notice of this nation, which, for two centuries, desolated Eastern Europe, is in the middle of the fifth century. They are probably also a Turkic nomad tribe. In 558 A.D., they come in contact with the Alans, in the districts near the Caucasus. In 560, they appear on the Danube. Slavia, Eastern Germany, and Bavaria, Saxony, and Lausitz were overrun and plundered by them. They finally occupied Hungary, and founded an empire which lasted till 803. Their conquering expeditions extended over Dalmatia, Croatia, Thuringia, and parts of Gaul, and their rule reached from the Volga to the Elbe. Their power was broken by the Frankic nations and the Slavonians of Bohemia, and they were at length overthrown and destroyed by Charlemagne (803 A.D.).

On the ruins of the Empire of the Avars was founded the great *Bulgarian Empire*. The Bulgarians were a Finnic tribe, from the Ural Mountains, who had invaded the country near the Don, the Dniester, and Pruth, and were subdued by the Avars. They recovered their independence (634 to 641), and after the overthrow of the Avars by Charlemagne, established an empire which extended from the Theiss to the frontiers of Greece, and lasted till the beginning of the tenth century. The Bulgarians became eventually absorbed by the Slavonic tribes whom they had conquered, even adopting the Slavonic language. They were all brought under Turkish sway in 1392.

Bulgarians.

The Magyars. This is the only Turanian tribe, except the Ottoman Turks, which has retained a foothold in Europe as a nation. It is a Finnish people, probably originating from the regions near the Ural Mountains, and is called *Ugri* or *Hungri* by ancient historians. In the ninth century, they are heard of as a fierce nomad race, in alliance with the Khazars, on the wide plains between the Dnieper and the mouth of the Danube. They enter Hungary through Transylvania, in 889; and after plundering and overrunning Europe for at least a century, threatening Constantinople, and invading France, Germany and Italy, they settle down in the country which has taken their name. Their sense of nationality was so strong, that various tribes who were probably remaining on the soil of Hungary, of Turkish origin—Cumanians, Pechenegs, and Bulgars—were absorbed into their race, and only the Slavic tribes could resist their influence. Their force and vigour are shown in the proud sense of their nationality, and the self-governing institutions which they have preserved for a thousand years,

Invasions of Magyars.

Their vigour.

under every variety of disaster and success. The Finns of Sweden are their only near relatives in Europe, and the Turks of Europe form another branch of the same family.

It remains to be seen, whether the Turanian family is to be entirely expelled from the Continent of Europe, or whether here is a branch which shall equal the glories of the Asiatic Turanians.

PART THIRD.

LEADING RACES OF ASIA IN THE MIDDLE AGES.

CHAPTER XII.

I. THE SEMITES.[1]

SINCE the ancient Semitic Empire of the Assyrians, under the Aryan Empires of the Persians, and of Alexander, and under the rule of the Aryan Romans and Byzantines, the Semites had been mostly subject or inferior tribes.

With the tenacity peculiar to the race, they had still retained, under all the conquests, their national characteristics, and after centuries of submission and quiet, they rose again at the call of religious fanaticism, with the same fire and passion which they had shown as Jews, under the Maccabees or against Titus. The foundations for their remarkable conquests were laid by the constant emigration of Arab tribes to Persia and various countries of Asia, whose population became thus gradually much mingled with Semitic elements.

In 622, Mohammed proclaimed the Semitic doctrine of the unity of God and the peculiar tenets of the Islam faith. Within twenty years vast countries of Europe and Asia were overrun and

Semitic uprising.

conquered by his fiery disciples. Syria was subdued from 632 to 638; Persia from 632 to 640; Egypt in 638; Cyprus and Rhodes in 649.

Conquests.

Within a century, the Semitic Moslems had conquered Asia from Mt. Taurus to the Himàlaya and the Indus, and from the Indian Ocean to Mt. Caucasus and the Iaxertes on the north; they held the north of Africa, and after defeating the Teutonic Goths in Spain, took possession of most of that country. They had even invaded France, and seemed about over-running all Europe, when they were defeated at Tours, in 732, by Charles the Hammer.

Certain tribes of them in the ninth century ravaged North Italy, and held possession of passes in the Alps.

Arabian Empire.

At the time of the division of the empire, by the formation of the Emirate of Cordova (756), the Arabian rule extended from the coasts of Spain to the country beyond the Indus, and from middle Africa and the Indian Ocean to Mount Caucasus, the Caspian, the deserts beyond the Iaxartes and the borders of China—an empire greater than that of Alexander. It reached its height of civilization, power, and commerce, under Haroun-al-Raschid (786 to 809).

Since this brilliant period of conquest, the Semitic family of nations has never again attained to a leading place among the races of men.

Semitic art and science.

Even as in the ancient days of Semitic glory in Assyria, this race again distinguished itself in the exact sciences and in architecture. Geometry, astronomy, anatomy, and chemistry, all witnessed a revival under the new Arabian civilization; and the Moorish architecture, a product of the sensuous Semitic mind, under the more graceful influences of Byzantine taste, covered Spain with its gorgeous and fantastic structures.

Many nations felt a new infusion of life from the Arabian energy, and the Aryan Persia, after frightful disasters, received from the Semites an impulse to a fresh career in intellectual activity.

During this modern period of civilization the Semitic mind showed, as of old, the lack of tempered imagination, and produced in all this time no orator or dramatist. Even its lyrics, without the grand ideas of the Jewish faith, became tame and spiritless, or mere plays of luxuriant fancy.

II. THE TURANIANS.[2]

Of the five prominent branches of the Turanian family—the *Tungusic*, *Mongolic*, *Turkic*, *Samoiedic*, and *Finnic*, we find only the Turks and the Mongols among the leading races of Asia in the Middle Ages. The name *Tartar* or *Tâtár*, which issome times applied erroneously to Turkic tribes, and which is also used by German scholars somewhat as Turanian is used in this treatise, we shall limit solely to Mongolic tribes.

Turks and Mongols.

If we consider Eastern Asia geographically, we shall find that the desert of Gobi was the separating country of the different races of Turanian origin. On the north and east, were the Mongol or Tâtâr tribes, as well as the Tungusian; on the southwest the Tibetians of the Bhotiya class, and on the north and northwest, from Lake Baikal to the sources of the Irtish on the whole northwestern declivity of the great plateau, the Turks.

The Turks can now, from evidence of language and tradition, be distinctly traced to a tribe living on the northern borders of China, near the northern bend of the Hoang-ho, mentioned in the Chinese annals—the *Hiung-nu*.

Origin of Turks.

This tribe was known as early as the middle of the third century before Christ. There were two important migrations from them—one in the first or second century after Christ, caused by one portion of the nation, which had been subdued by the Chinese, attacking the other part and forcing them toward the west; and the second, in the beginning of the third century, of the remaining portion of the tribe forced out themselves by the attacks of Mongolic and Tungusic hordes. The second great home of the Turkish tribes was thus near the sources of the Irtish.

Turkish tribes.

One tribe of this family, called by the Chinese, *Tukiu*, succeeded in founding a State in the sixth century, between the Altai Mountains and the Caspian Sea, which was finally destroyed by another Turkic tribe. In 568 Turks were settled even as far west as the Volga, and the Sea of Azof.

Still another tribe, the *Oighours*, descended from their mountains and gained possessions in Chinese Turkestan, and at length founded a kingdom. From their descendants come the West Turks. A related tribe, the *Seljuks*, first obtained a foothold in Eastern Turkestan; then they are found on the northern banks of the Iaxartes, then on the plains of Bokhara, and they appear at length on the vast pastures of Khorasin. There they master another Turkic tribe, the Ghazneoides (1034 to 1037), and push their incursions into all Iran, Armenia, Georgia, and even to the Euphrates. The chief of this tribe soon obtained supreme power in Persia. In the eleventh century there were five branches of Seljuks, one of which held the sovereignty of Iconium. In 1067 they had passed the Euphrates, and before the end of the eleventh century nearly all Asia Minor was in possession of the Turks.

The *Osmanlis*, who are the ruling portion of the

modern Turks, and the tribe best known to history, left their homes in East Persia, forced out by the attacks of the Mongols in 1224 A.D., and entered the territory of the Seljuks in Asia Minor. Their chief, Ertoghrul, received as reward for warlike services, done for the Seljuk Sultan of Iconium, a part of Phrygia. The tribe became finally independent, and their chief, Othman, from whom the nation has received its name, attained to the sovereignty of Iconium. In 1327, his descendant, Soliman, became master of the Dardanelles; in 1362, Murad I. took Adrianople, and defeated the Bulgarians and their allies in a great battle (1389). Bayazeth, his successor, overran Thessaly, the Peloponnesus, and Bosnia, defeating the Emperor of Germany, and would, without doubt, have erected a Turkish Empire equal to the more modern one, with Constantinople for its capital, but for a new attack of its old enemies, the Mongols. These fierce hordes, under Tschingis-khan, were sweeping irresistibly over Asia. Even the higher discipline, and the more complete armament of the Othman or Osman Turks, could not withstand the fiery assaults of the nomad Tâtârs, and in the battle of Angora (1402), the Turkish Empire was overturned. The Mongol Empire did not long endure, and within twenty years, the Turks had regained their power. In 1453, Constantinople itself was taken by Mohammed II., and became henceforth the capital of the Turkish Empire.

Osmanlis.

Turkish conquests.

Mongol conquests.

The Turkish blood, wherever it became intermingled with the worn-out Greek population, was no doubt of much present benefit, and gave a new vigour to Western Asia. The weakness of the original Greek population in Asia Minor is measured by one geographical writer (De St. Martin), by the feeble life preserved in the ancient names of mountains, rivers, and localities. Through other European countries, the earlier races, if possessed of any power of imagination or feeling, have retained their own geographical names under foreign conquerors; in Western Asia, to a vast extent, these have entirely disappeared.

The Turkish physical type in those countries became soon much mingled, and the prominent result has been the cross between the Turk and the Greek, or Circassian.

Language.

Of the Turkish language, it has been remarked by an eminent scholar, "We might imagine it to be the result of the deliberations of some distinguished society of learned men." The ingenuity and transparency and perfect regularity of the structure, are much commented on by scholars. In a work of this design we cannot go into detail on this subject, and we will merely illustrate the nature of the language by quoting Max Müller's description of the formation of new roots in the Turkish verb. (Lang. at Seat of War, p. 111.)

Sev-mek, for instance, as a simple root, means to love. By adding *in*, we obtain a reflexive verb, *sev-in-mek*, which means, to love one's self, or rather, to rejoice, to be happy. This may now be conjugated through all moods and tenses, *sev-in*, being in every respect equal to a new root. By adding *ish* we form a reciprocal verb, *sev-ish-mek*, to love one another.

To each of these three forms a causative sense may be imparted by the addition of the syllable *dir*. Thus,

1. *Sev-mek*, to love, becomes iv., *Sev-dir-mek*, to cause to love.

2. *Sev-in-mek*, to rejoice, becomes v., *Sev-in-der-mek*, to cause to rejoice.

3. *Sev-ish-mek*, to love one another, becomes vi., *Sev-ish-der-mek*, to cause ourselves to love one another.

Each of these six forms may again be turned into a passive by the addition of *il*. Thus,

1. *Sev-mek*, to love, becomes vii., *Sev-il-mek*, to be loved.

2. *Sev-in-mek*, to rejoice, becomes viii., *Sev-in-il-mek*, to be rejoiced at.

3. *Sev-ish-mek*, to love one another, becomes ix., *Sev-ish-il-mek*, not translatable.

4. *Sev-dir-mek*, to cause one to love, becomes x., *Sev-dir-il-mek*, to be brought to love.

5. *Sev-in-der-mek*, to cause to rejoice, becomes xi., *Sev-in-dir-il-mek*, to be made to rejoice.

6. *Sev-ish-dir-mek*, to cause to love one another, becomes xii., *Sev-ish-dir-il-mek*, to be brought to love one another.

This, however, is by no means the whole verbal contingent at the command of a Turkish grammarian. Every one of these twelve secondary or tertiary roots may again be turned into a negative, by the mere addition of *me*. Thus, *sev-mek*, to love, becomes *sev-me-mek*, not to love. And if it is necessary to express the impossibility of loving, the Turk has a lesser root at hand, to convey even that idea. Thus, while *sev-me-mek* denies only the fact of loving, *sev-eme-mek* denies its possibility, and means, not to be able to love. By the addition of these two modificatory syllables, the number of derivative roots is at once raised to thirty-six. Thus,

1. *Sev-mek*, to love, becomes xiii., *Sev-me-mek*, not to love.

2. *Sev-in-mek*, to rejoice, becomes xiv., *Sev-in-me-mek*, not to rejoice.

3. *Sev-ish-mek*, to love one another, becomes xv., *Sev-ish-me-mek*, not to love one another.

4. *Sev-dir-mek*, to cause to love, becomes xvi., *Sev-dir-me-mek*, not to cause to love.

5. *Sev-in-der-mek*, to cause to rejoice, becomes xvii., *Sev-in-der-me-mek*, not to cause one to rejoice.

6. *Sev-ish-dir-mek*, to cause ourselves to love one another, becomes xviii., *Sev-ish-dir-me-mek*, not to cause ourselves to love another.

7. *Sev-il-mek*, to be loved, becomes xix., *Sev-il-me-mek*, not to be loved; and so on to twenty-four forms.

Some of these forms are, of course, of rare occurrence, and with many verbs these derivative roots, though possible grammatically, would be logically impossible. Even a verb like "to love," perhaps the most pliant of all, resists some of the modifications to which a Turkish grammarian is fain to subject it. It is clear, however, that wherever a negation can be formed, the idea of impossibility also can be superadded, so that by substituting *eme* for *me*, we should raise the number of derivative roots to thirty-six. The very last of these, xxxvi., *Sev-ish-dir-il-eme-mek*, would be perfectly intelligible, and might be used, for instance, if, in speaking of the Sultan and the Czar, we wished to say, that it was impossible that they should be brought to love one another.

II. The Mongols.[1]

Of all the nomad tribes from Eastern Asia, who have carried desolation over the world, the Mongols are probably those who have done the most evil with the smallest number of men. They are comparatively a modern tribe in history. From intimations in the Chinese annals, it is believed that they are vaguely alluded to in the ninth century, as occupying the country near the sources of the Amur.

Mongols in ninth century.

Their first historical appearance is in the thirteenth century, when the different tribes were united by their great leader, Tschingis-khan into one nation. Their country then was to the southeast of Lake Baikal, near the Onon and Kerlon; and Karakorum, their central point was in Mongolistan, on the southern slope of the Altai, about 600 miles northwest of Pekin. The nation included many Tungusic as well as Mongolic tribes, and afterward, as the Mongol conquests spread, great numbers of Turkish hordes were embraced in the conquering army. To this fact and to the natural pride of each race, as it became dominant in Asia, is to be ascribed the confusion respecting the names Tâtâr or Mongol, and Turkish, as applied to certain tribes. It is possible also that the

Confusion of Tâtâr and Turkish.

chiefs of a tribe may have been sometimes of different race from the people.

The term "Mongolian type," describing the pyramidal skull, projecting cheek-bones, oblique eyebrows, and flat nose, with other features peculiar to many peoples in Eastern and Northern Asia, has been a source of wide-spread error, as will be hereafter shown, since this type is by no means confined to the Mongols.

Tschingis-khan and his descendants conquered one of the greatest empires the world has ever seen. China was subdued on the east, and the Mongol dynasty of Yuan placed on the throne. On the west, Tangut, Tibet, Persia, and even Russia were overrun and subdued. In 1240-41 the Tâtâr hordes invaded Poland and Silesia. At the close of the thirteenth century, the Mongol Empire embraced all the independent States and vast populations from China to Poland, from India to Siberia. It broke up speedily from its very extent; and new and independent Mongol Kingdoms arose in China, Turkestan, Siberia, Southern Russia, and Persia.

Mongol Empire.

It arose again in the fourteenth century under another mighty Mongol conqueror, Tamerlane, whose conquests desolated every country from the Ganges to the Mediterranean. The hitherto invincible Turkish power fell before these fierce nomad hordes, and on the death of Tamerlane (1405) his empire extended from Smyrna on one side, to Delhi on the other, and from the Don to the Nile. It gradually fell to pieces as did the first, while the Turkish Empire, which it had crushed, rose again to new power. A descendant of Tamerlane founded a dynasty in India, which endured to our own times as the great Moguls of Delhi.[2] The last of his line—for a long

Tamerlane.

time a titled pensioner of England—was captured after the Rebellion of 1857, and, in 1858, banished to the Cape of Good Hope.

Language poor.

The Mongol language is pronounced the poorest, next to the Tungusic, of the Turanian family, "and the scantiness of grammatical terminations accounts for the fact that as a language it has remained very much unchanged" (M. Müller).

PART FOURTH.

MODERN ETHNOLOGY OF ASIA.

CHAPTER XIII.

THE RACES OF INDIA.

Turanians—The Hill Tribes.

Earliest races.

THE leading race of India, the Hindus, as is well known, is Aryan. But beside this powerful and numerous people, tribes of a different stock and language had earlier settled in various parts of the country, and had finally been driven by their invaders to the mountains and to the southern portion of the Peninsula—the Dekkan. Here, in regions defended by impenetrable swamps and forests, traversed by wild beasts, and subject to the most deadly diseases, these earliest settlers of India still survive. In some districts, their language and nationality have been swallowed up by the more vigorous Aryan race; in others, the language exists either pure or mingled with Hindu words and forms.

In all, both language and physical structure prove them entirely different races from the Aryan tribes, who subdued them. Their physical type is pronounced generally to be Turanian (Mongolian), and their language places them with this same family. From early ages, they are

Physique.

described as resembling negroes in colour, though unlike them in other features. According to their climatic position, they are more or less black, with straight hair.

Turanian type.

The *Turanian type* which they present, and which prevails over a large part of Asia, the Pacific and South Sea Islands, and portions of America, is thus distinguished.[1a] The skull is pyramidal or conoidal; the oval of basis cranii is laterally expanded and compressed at the ends, especially in front; the lower jaw is long, and the cheek bones prominent and angular, so that the outer extension of both produces a great breadth of face across the cheek-bones, and a narrowness of forehead, giving the contour a lozenge shape. The nasal bones are flat and broad, so that the cheek bones, and the space between the eyes, are nearly on the same plane; the lower part of the nose is rounded and not flat, as in the negro; the nostrils are open and broad. The eyes are small, deep-set, and wide apart, with the line of the eyelids inclined upward; the eyebrows are thin, beard scanty, hair dark and thick. The complexion is usually yellow, lightest in the Chinese, and blackest in the Indian tribes, but varying much; the height is below the middle size, and the limbs are thick.

The mass of the Indo-Turanian tribes live in a poor condition, and are little developed; some jungle tribes being unable even to protect themselves from the tigers.

Wherever the traveller proceeds in India, he meets with or hears of these aborigines—the "Hill tribes," as they are often called. He finds, them, when dwelling in the low-lands, despised and outlawed by the Hindus, living outside of their villages in little thatched cottages, owning no property but asses and dogs, occupying land tax free, which they seldom cultivate, but underlet, and receiving a minimum portion of produce from each field through the Hindu municipality. They are everywhere proverbially honest, and with their experience as hunters, become the best police detectives. They are employed to convey revenue from one province to another, and to protect and serve travellers.

The Hill tribes.

Their customs and institutions are utterly different from those of the Hindus. They have no castes; their widows are allowed to marry again, even with the younger brother of the deceased husband; they have no objection to any kind of flesh, and do not care by whom it has been prepared; they feel no horror at the spilling of blood, even in their sacrifices. In entire opposition to the rules and habits of the Aryan Indians they indulge freely in intoxicating drinks; they do not venerate the Brahmans; they bury without burning their dead; their institutions are patriarchal, not municipal; and their courts of justice are made up of heads of tribes, and not equals. Their religion is often fetishism, and they occasionally practise cannibalism.

Differ entirely from Hindus.

If language were not decisive, these customs alone would establish the different origin of these races from the Hindus.

That they belong to the Turanian family in their language, has been rendered probable by B. H. Hodgson, R. Caldwell, and various other scholars.

The points of evidence, showing the relationship between the non-Aryan races of India and the Turanian, are thus grouped by Mr. Webb. 1. The agreement between their languages and the Turanian (Scythic) portion of the ancient tablets at Behistun. 2. The analogy in *laws of sound*, with the modern Turanian

Evidences of Turanian origin.

languages, such as "the harmonic sequence of vowels," and "the convertibility of words and consonants," and "the dialectic interchange of consonants." 3. The method of treating *roots*, which has already been mentioned as a leading peculiarity of the Turanian. 4. The *want of gender* in all nouns, and the indefiniteness of number—this being determined by the connection. 5. The separate existence of the auxiliary words, denoting case-endings, and their identity, both in the singular and plural. 6. The *analogy of the numerals* with the Ugrian and Finnish, while there is not the smallest resemblance to be found to those of the Aryan family. 7. Analogies of pronouns, of structure of the verb, and the use of the "relative participle." 8. Resemblance of words, especially with those of the Finnish family.

These conclusions, it is but fair to say, are doubted by an eminent scholar of this country, Prof. W. D. Whitney, who, in his note on Mr. Webb's article in the Journal of the Amer. Oriental Soc., vol. vii.—1862, suggests that the terms of the comparison are not sufficiently known, to justify a scientific result, and that the analogies established *may be* the effects of a similar grade of culture and capacity.

With reference to this great class—the Turanian—so much questioned by scholars, B. H. Hodgson, a high authority, says, "The ampler stock of Caucasian and Mongolian vocables thus placed within my reach, has needed only to be compared with my own larger stores from the Himàlaya, Tibet, Sifan, Indo-China, and Tamulian India, to satisfy me that the widest assumed scope of Allophylian (Turanian) affinities might be placed on a reasonable basis." (Mongol. Aff. of Caucas., p. 62.)

Whether all these tribes belong to one branch of the Turanian family is not certain. They are called "Dravidians," from Dravida, the name of the country of their principal tribe, the Tamils. Thus far they may be distinguished into two great divisions,[2] from the regions which they occupy, (1.) the tribes of the *Vindhya Mountains*, and (2.) the tribes of the *Dekkan*.

The Vindhya and Dekkan tribes.

The proper boundaries of the Aryans in India are the

Indus on the west, the Ganges or the Brahmaputra on the east, the Himàlaya on the north, and the Vindhya on the south. It is the latter mountains which, from ancient times, have been the barrier to Aryan civilization. On either coast, especially on the west, the Aryan tribes have advanced more to the south. But in the main, we may say that all the vast country, south of the Nerbudda, and all the inaccessible regions of the Vindhya are occupied by the Turanians—the Dekkan, and the Vindhya tribes.

Aryan boundaries.

Still another large division of this family exists in the north-east of India, on the Himàlaya and the Ganges —the *Bhotîya* tribes.[3]

(1.) *The Vindhya Races.*

(*a*) The *Bhilla* or *Bhills*. This wild tribe live on the Vindhya, near the rivers Tapti and Nerbudda, and on the northern extremity of the Eastern Ghats. They are found least mingled with other tribes on the left bank of the Nerbudda, from Nemar to Guzerat, and in the western Ghats up to Puna. They are described as of short stature, with curly hair, thick lips, very dark complexion, and more masculine in form than the Hindus. They must have been one of the earliest peoples who entered India. Their original dialects have been much superseded by the Hindu forms of speech, yet enough remains to identify them as of the Turanian family. (*b*) The *Mina* and *Mera* are tribes resembling the Bhills, living in the mountains of Kalikho, from Agmir to the Jumna.[4] (*c*) The *Kôla* or *Koles*. The name of these nations is liable to confusion, from its being applied promiscuously in India to uncivilized peoples, and also to porters (Coolies) by the English. There

The Bhills.

Koles.

are two great branches of Koles, one of the Dekkan or Tamulic races, and the other an aboriginal people of the Vindhya races.

The latter is sometimes called *Munda*. The *Hos*, in Singbhúm, are closely allied with these. The *Sontal*, near Chuta Nagpúr, are Koles. The Kole language Max Müller supposes to have been spoken in India, before the Tamulic conquest.

The Koles live on the western side of the West Ghats, to the northward of Bombay; others dwell in the mountains of Guzerat, and still others further in the east, near Singbhúm and Gangpur. They are described as a bold, manly-looking people, and the Mundus of Holesun are said to be men pre-eminent for physical beauty. This people is, on the whole, in advance of the Bhills, and has been much influenced by Brahmanic civilization.

(*d*) The *Pahária*. This Vindhya tribe have kept their habitations in the Rajmahál Mountains, through all the Aryan and Tamulic invasions from the earliest times. Their language shows the strong influence of the Tamulic tribes.

Pahária.

They were formerly very troublesome and dangerous as robbers and murderers to the subjects of the India Company, but have been civilized by the kindness and patience especially of one English official. In appearance they are of dark complexion, small eyes, broad face, and lips thicker than those of the men of the plains.

(*e*) The *Kanda* or *Khonds* occupy a district about 200 miles long, by 170 broad, in Ranapur, in the district of Ganjam, to the east of Lake Chilka, and touching on the Bay of Bengal. They are succeeded in the south by the *Saura*, who hold the country up to the Godavery.

(2.) *The Dekkan or Tamulic Races.*

The Tamulian type is thus described by Mr. Hodgson:—[4]

"In the Tamulian form there is less height, less symmetry, more dumpiness and flesh than in the Aryan; in the Tamulian face a somewhat lozenge contour, caused by the large cheek bones; less perpendicularity in the features to the front, occasioned not so much by defect of forehead or chin as by excess of jaws and mouth; a larger proportion of face to head, and less roundness in the latter; a broader, flatter face, with features less symmetrical but, perhaps, more expressive, at least, of individuality; a shorter, wider nose, often clubbed at the end and furnished with round nostrils; eyes less, and less fully opened, and less evenly crossing the face by their line of aperture; ears larger; lips thicker; beard deficient; colour brunette, as in the last, but darker on the whole, and, as in it, very various."

Tamulian type.

Nearly all the tribes of the Dekkan are superior to the Vindhya peoples, though often closely resembling them. The principal exception to this, *the Gonds*, were formerly classed with the non-Tamulic races; but late investigations in language bring them within the Dekkan races. (*a*) The *Gonds* occupy the immense district, covered with forests, contained within the Vindhya on the north, the Eastern Ghats, and a line connecting these, drawn from the mouth of the Godavery to the centre of the valley of the Nerbudda.

The Ghonds.

They are in a condition of the lowest barbarism. In appearance they are of black skin, forehead low and broad; eyes small, deep-set, and reddish; with thick lips, dirty black teeth, and long black hair—though the latter is sometimes red and woolly.

(*b*) The *Tuluva* (or Tulava) inhabit the thick forests which skirt the West Ghats in Conara. Their language has a close affinity with the Malabar.

(*c*) The *Malabars*, who, like the Tuluvas, are a black tribe, dwell in the dense hot forests, between the Kandragiri and Cape Comorin. Some who live higher upon the hills are of fairer colour.

Tamuls.

(*d*) The people from whom these races are often called, the *Tamuls*, are found on the east coast, from Palikat to Bangalor, and thence in Ragakotta and Palghat.

(*e*) Still other tribes, the Telinga (or Telugu), the Karnata, and the Malabars of Ceylon, belong to this family. The former hold the country to the eastward of the Mahrattas, and west of the Bay of Bengal. The Karnata table-land was anciently all the high land north of the Ghats, but the name Carnatic and Carnara has been transferred to a province below the Ghats. The language of this people, the Karnataka, is spoken by the natives of all the countries, from Coimbatore, north, to Bida, and between the Western and Eastern Ghats.

Beside these, are the *Toda* in the Nilghiri hills, who are remarkable both for having been untouched by Sanskrit influences, and for their fine personal appearance. Some of them are said to present strikingly the Roman cast of features; their figures are tall and athletic; complexion brown, and beards bushy. The women have long black hair, and beautiful teeth, and are fairer than the men.

The Brahui, on the mountains of Sindh, are related to the Toda. The people of Ceylon belong also to the Dekkan tribes.

The *Tamulians* are considered by M. Müller, judging from their language, to be the last tribe who separated from the Turanian centre to migrate southward, just as the Finns are thought to be the last who wandered toward the north. The language has reached a certain degree of grammatical growth, and is much in advance of some other Turanian languages, such as the Tungusic, or the Bhotiya, or the Chinese. The people had evidently reached a considerable degree of unity and civilization before they were exposed to Aryan influences, so that their language has been able to resist the Sanskrit, though adopting many of its words and expressions.

Tamul language.

(3.) *The Bhotîya Races.*

In the northeastern countries of India, on the Himàlaya, and in the valleys of the Brahmaputra and the Ganges, is still another race of Turanian stock, allied with the Tamulians of India, and with the inhabitants of Tibet. A line from north to south, cutting across the Brahmaputra, and following along the Dhansri, is the line which separates these monosyllabic people from the Tamulic. They are on a much lower stage of social condition than these latter; they have not so many of the restrictions of religious customs, especially in eating, and are more fierce, and depend more on the chase. Their religion is a worship of natural objects, without any use of temples or idols. Many resemblances are discovered between them and the Polynesian tribes; among others, the custom of exposing the dead for four days on a scaffold, before finally burning them. These tribes on the northeast of India have preserved their independence much longer than those on the northwest, who met the tide of Aryan and Tamulic emigra-

Differ from Tamulic races.

tion earlier; one of their States, that of the Kocchs, having existed even down to the eighteenth century. They are probably among the oldest and first settlers of India.

Their physique is not materially different from that of the Tamuls. They are of a pale brown complexion, and Turanian type of features. Some individuals show a high degree of personal beauty, almost Aryan in type; others, again, are excessively degraded in features. The upper region of the Himàlaya, a plateau, some 10,000 feet above the level of the sea, bordering on Tibet, is especially inhabited by the Bhotîyas.[5]

Other tribes of similar stock, dwell in the temperate region on the declivity of these mountains, in the basins of the large rivers—the Brahmaputra, the Tistâ, Gandakî, and others—which flow into India. These are the ***Mishmis***, ***Lepcha***, ***Butanese***, ***Kirantins***, and numerous others.

The lowest region at the foot of these mountains is occupied by peoples of this family, who live in pestilential swamps, and breathe the most deadly miasmata, without any apparent injury to their health. Among these are the Kocchs, Chepangs, Bodos, Tharus, and many others. This capacity for breathing malaria is a remarkable physiological fact, and, Hodgson states, characterizes all the Tamulian inhabitants of India. They are generally fine healthy races of men, though dwelling where no other human beings can exist. It is one of the strongest evidences, as Mr. Hodgson observes, of the great antiquity of these tribes on Indian soil.

Swamp tribes.

Though most probably descended from the inhabitants of Tibet, these various tribes show much more physical resemblance to their neighbours, the Tamuls, than to the Tibetians—climate in this, as in innumerable other cases, having modified or changed the bodily type of a race.

The Tibetic language is much less advanced grammatically than the Tamulic. Müller observes that in the Tibetic (or Bhotîyan), there are no verbal terminations to express the different persons of the verb, while many of the Tamul dialects have a regular system of verbal affixes.

Tibetic language.

Beyond the regions of which we have been speaking, the Bhotîya emigration spread toward the east into *Burmah.* In the mountainous district adjoining the Brahmaputra, and from the Tistâ, the boundary of Bhutan to the Irawady (Irâvâti), are found a vast number of wild tribes belonging to the Bhotîyan races—the ***Miris***, the *Nagas*, *Khyengs*, *Karens*, and many others. According to the testimony of Mr. Kincaid and Mr. Cross, the Karens possess well-defined traditions of their origin from Tibet.

Karens.

Mr. Cross[6] states that they are scattered over a territory between 28° and 10° N. latitude, and 99°—93° E. longitude. The Kakhyens and Karens seem to be identical, and taking all the tribes coming under their names, sprinkled over various territories, they are supposed to number about five millions.

The Karens are remarkable for preserving religious traditions which bear a great analogy to the Biblical history, and for the simple and faithful spirit with which they have received Christianity.

The Taï Tribes.

Still another branch of the Tibetic races exists farther toward the east, between Eastern India and Western China—the *Taï* tribes. They occupy the country extending over 14 degrees of latitude along the Menam, Salwen, Irawady, and Kyen-

Geographical position.

dwen rivers, up to the source of the Irawady.[7] They are the *Siamese*, *Ahom* (Shyan), *Laos*, *Khamti*, and *Kassia* (Khyi) peoples. The country which they inhabit, in fertility, salubrity of climate, advantages for mining, agriculture and commerce, is unsurpassed in Asia, yet, held by these tribes, it has almost run to waste. The Ahoms—who are nearly identical with the Siamese—no longer speak their own language, but have adopted both the language and faith of the Hindus.

Physique.

In physical traits, these nations present the same Turanian type, except that bad nourishment has caused, with some of the Karens, a tendency to protuberant bellies and thin limbs; their complexion is yellow; the skull ovoid, with a great expansion of forehead, so that they show more "Mongolian" traits than the Mongols themselves. The Anamese head presents the most delicate Turanian type—a perfect ovoid and globular form. Though pressed on every side by various races: on the east by the Chinese people; on the north by the Tibetans; on the west by their related tribes, as well as the Aryan races, they have preserved their individuality, while receiving influences in religion and civilization from every source. The language of the Taï tribes belongs, like the Chinese, to the monosyllabic, and is marked by a somewhat similar system of musical accents or intonations.

There seems no doubt that one family inhabit Indo-China, the Himàlayas and Tibet.

The Aryans of India.

The modern Indo-Aryan is thus vividly described by a careful observer.[4]

"In the Aryan form there is height, symmetry, lightness, and flexibility; in the Aryan face, an oval contour with ample forehead and moderate jaws and mouth, a round chin, perpendicular with the forehead, a regular set of distinct and fine features; a well-raised and unexpanded nose with elliptic nares; a well-sized and freely-opened eye, running directly across the face; no want of eye-brows, eye-lash, or beard; and, lastly, a clear brunette complexion, often not darker than that of the most southern Europeans." Aryan type.

The only exception to be taken to this description is in regard to the complexion of the Hindus. It is true that the original word for caste in India, means *colour*, and that the Aryans are usually lighter in complexion than the Turanians. Yet all this depends on geographical position, climate, and circumstances of birth. There are tribes of Brahmans in the Himàlaya, who have the blonde colour and blue eyes;[5] and there are pure Brahmans in Southern India who are as black as many tribes of negroes. Black Aryans.

The Aryans of India may be divided into *five* great divisions according to lanlanguage:— Five Divisions.

(1.) The *Eastern* or *Bengals*. These are found north and south of the Ganges, in the province of Bengal, east of Mahananda; they have invaded the valley of Assam, and mingled in the south with the people of the Odra. They number at least thirty millions. (2.) The *Middle* Hindus, who speak *Hindi*. These inhabit mostly the districts of Middle India; their language is spoken by the Rajputs in Udajapur and Haravatî. They also hold the country north of the Vindhya, and on both sides of the Jumna and Ganges up to the Himàlaya, and all the vast provinces of Sinde and the Penjáb.

The *Hindi* is not to be looked upon as one language, like Latin or French, but as a general name for various dialects. One of these dialects which has been much enriched with Persian and Arabic words, and is the speech of the Mohammedans in North India, is the *Hindustani*, or Urdu.

(3.) The *Southern*, or *Mahrattas*. Of all the Aryan tribes, these have penetrated farthest to the south, and are the only tribe which has passed the West-Ghats. Their northern limits are the Kolwan hills near Daman and the Saptura chain. Their eastern boundaries are not strictly defined. The Mahratti is spoken in all Berar and in a part of the district of Nagpur. In the valley of the Tapti, it is mingled with the Gudjerati. It extends south-westerly to the neighbourhood of Bider, and mingled with Tulu and Canara dialects, reaches nearly to Udapu on the western coast. (4.) The *Western*, or *Gudjerats*. These occupy the province of Gudjerat and Guicowar, and a portion of the valleys of the Nerbudda and Tapti, and the coast of the Gulf of Cambay as far as Daman. They are an agricultural people. and press on the Mahrattas, who are rather a mountaineer and pastoral tribe, wherever the nature of the soil favours their pursuit. (5.) The *Orissá* tribes speaking Urija, holding the eastern coast south of Bengal, from Hoogly to forty-five miles south of Gandjam. Here the Telinga begins to be spoken, and at Vizigapatam this is the ruling language. (6.) The *Northern* in Kamaon, Sirmor, and in Kashmir.

The locality of the Aryan dialects and tribes shows —even if other proof were wanting—that the direction in which the Aryans entered India was from west to east.

In the Penjáb and the valley of the Ganges, these dialects are spoken even to the tops of the mountains; in West Nepal, Turanian dialects appear; in Bhutan we find an Aryan religion (Buddhism), but the language of another family; and still farther east, on the west entrance of Assam, and to the south of the mountains, the Aryan languages entirely disappear.

One thing must be evident in this condensed account of the prominent races of India, that colour and physical traits are not, in that country, distinctive marks of race. Nowhere in the world has blood been preserved so pure, and yet complexion and a high physical type are found to

Colour not decisive of origin.

vary endlessly, according to position and climate and food.

The Turanians, though generally Mongol in features, are sometimes found closely resembling negroes, and at others almost Aryan in physical beauty. In general the mountain tribes, of whatever race, are fairer than those of the jungles.

The Brahmans differ equally in colour, and sometimes in physical development.

It is climate more than any other one cause which has tended to make the Aryan of India so different from the Aryan of Persia, both in appearance and in his moral and spiritual development.

Effects of climate.

CHAPTER XIV.

RACES OF CHINA AND COCHIN-CHINA.[1]

IT is remarkable that the largest family of mankind, the Chinese, numbering nearly four hundred millions of human beings, cannot be certainly connected with the other great families of races. The physical type is decidedly Turanian; but this, on the principles which lie at the basis of this ethnology, is not decisive of race.

Uncertain connection with other races.

Of the language, we can only say that it most probably is the *inorganic* condition of human speech, from which we should naturally expect other growths, such as the Turanian, to spring. Some scholars claim to discover clear links of connection between the Chinese and the Turanian. Enough is not known, however, as yet, to prove the certain unity of origin of these two great bodies of language; it is only most probable that the former represented that early condition of speech from which the latter grew.

The Chinese physical traits belong exactly to the Turanian type, stamped on so many nations of Asia and America.[2] The complexion is the lightest shown by any of the Turanians; the cheek bones are less prominent than those of the Mongols; and the

Physique.

prominence in the head is anterior, rather than lateral, as in the American Indians and the Tungusic tribes. The peculiar distinguishing characteristics are the smallness of the eyes, and the obliquity of the eye-lids. The nose is usually small and depressed, though sometimes, in favourable physical conditions, natives are found with a slightly aquiline nose, giving the face a close resemblance to that of the American Indians, or New Zealanders.

The Chinese differ from the Tibetans or Indo-Tibetans, in the strength of these peculiarities, and in the oblong form of the skull. The Cochin-Chinese are distinguished from their relatives, by a more delicately oval type of skull. The Mandchus, who form the governing race in China, are said to show quite a superior type of feature to the Chinese. Some of them have blue eyes, florid complexion, aquiline nose, and brown beard; in general, they are heavier than the Chinese, with more beard, and a more intelligent face, and sometimes a lighter complexion.

Chinese language.

But it is *language*, which, more than anything else, distinguishes the Chinese from the rest of mankind, and which has, perhaps, most of all, checked their progress. If our readers will call to mind the first utterances of children, or the expressions of people of reserved and sententious habits, and long intimacy, where each word or each syllable is a sentence; where the tone and gesture indicate whether the single sound emitted is a noun or adjective or verb, or all three together; where grammar and copula, cases and inflexions, are all dropped as unnecessary, so perfect is the understanding by the subtile tone and manner; and if he will suppose this, through some unexplainable cause, petrified and transmitted as an enduring mode of speech, he will have an appreciation of the nature of the Chinese language.

Its distinction is, not merely that it is monosyllabic, but that each syllable is a substantial thing; a sentence in itself; as if the minds who used it, never grew to the idea of a *sentence*—of making various words, in their modifications, subservient to one logical expression. The Chinese has substantially no grammar; the arrangement of the words, and the musical tone, indicating whether a syllable is noun, verb, adjective or particle.

No grammar. There is an average of eight words spelt and pronounced exactly alike, for every sound which they possess.

We are told[3] that there are 212 characters, each of which is pronounced *che;* 113 pronounced *ching;* 138 pronounced *foo;* and 1165 which are all read *e.* The difficulty of distinguishing these is obviated in part, by placing synonyms together which differ in sound, to explain one another, and by arbitrary connections of words. Picture writing, and a phonetic system, have also been employed to a limited degree; but in practice, the Chinese know nothing of any phonetic system or alphabet. They may be said to have as many letters in their alphabet, as words in their language. Morrison's Dictionary gives 12,674 characters, with forms and meanings distinct from each other.[4]

Writing, as M. Maury well observes, has not emerged with the Chinese language from the *ideographic* period; that is, ideas are represented by images, or by signs which are the abridged form of images. These twelve thousand signs or letters above spoken of, were, in early times, the material pictures of objects, and are now the altered, or abridged, or compounded forms of these pictures. Out of these sensible representations of metaphysical ideas would naturally arise *figurative signs.* Next, the sound given to the ear by the word representing the sign, has become attached to the sign itself, and the sign has finally become the written expression of the sound, or a *phonetic sign;* so that, as before intimated, the Chinese will employ two signs, side by side, one to indicate the pronunciation, and the other to determine the sense.

Defects in the language.

It will be seen what a fearful barrier to advancement in learning, or science, or general knowledge, such a language must be. Oratory could scarcely exist with it, or poetry, or any popular literature. For humour and wit, and the most abstract reflection, we might suppose such sententious, algebraic speech peculiarly adapted.

Some scholars believe that they discover in all Aryan and Turanian language, traces of just such an early condition through which these have passed. Of the Chinese, we can only say, with the evidence thus far obtained, that it is most probable, but not certain, that it connects with the early Turanian.

There are but slight distinctions in the great family which inhabits China. A Tungusic tribe—the *Mandchus*—one of the most vigorous races of the Turanian family, have given for some two centuries its rulers. There are, beside, what are called aboriginal tribes, especially in the west and south-western districts, which are supposed to have been conquered by the Chinese and driven to the mountains, but which seem to be of the same, or a related race. The Chinese authorities describe them often as "black," or dark, but it is uncertain whether they refer to their complexion or character. They are pictured as very low and brutal in habits, living often in caves, or holes in the ground, or working as slaves and servants.[5] Their religion and language are said to be different from those of the Chinese; but with regard to their speech, this may mean only that it is a dialect of the Chinese language.

In physique they are said to be smaller in size, with shorter necks, and more angular features than the Chinese. The northern and western of these tribes resemble the Tibetans, while the southern bear a strong likeness to Malays and Birmese.[6] Little, however, is known of them. They are the *Si-fan*, a mountainous Tibetan tribe, to the west of the provinces Shensi and Su-chuan, near the sources of the Yellow and Blue rivers;[7] the *Miáu Tsž*, scattered through the provinces of Hirk-wáng, Sž-chuen, Yunnán, Kweichan, and Kwángsé; the *Lolos*, in the south-eastern part of the empire; and the *Khiang*, or Tibetans. There is, beside, a class of people, treated by the Chinese as a separate race, who are employed on the sea-coast, and who closely resemble Esquimaux. They are called *Tankia*.

Aboriginal tribes.

Of the Mandchu, Mongol, and Turkish races, who come under the Chinese rule, we shall speak hereafter.

The *Miáu Tsž* (or "children of the soil") are said to show many points of resemblance with the *Karens*. They are a mountain tribe, very brave, and mostly independent of the Chinese.

The inhabitants of Cochin-China—the *Anamese*—are nearly related to the Chinese, speaking a dialect of the same language.

II. Japan and its Dependencies.

Though independent of China, the empire of Japan shows the wide-reaching effect of Chinese culture, and without doubt, emigration from China has much modified the original Japanese race. It is difficult as yet to obtain trustworthy accounts of the races in the various islands which make up this empire, and no sufficient comparison of dialects has been made to pronounce with certainty on the position of these peoples in the

Turanian family. The opinion now prevails among historical scholars,[8] that from the Lew-Chew islands over the whole Japanese kingdom to Jesso, and thence opposite to the coasts of the Asiatic continent and on the other side, through the Kuriles, Aleutians, and Kamschatka, one barbarous race originally held possession — the *Ainos*. The evidence of this is derived from remains found in tombs, and from customs and fragments of language still existing.

The Ainos.

The Ainos on the Kurile islands are described in the narrative of the American Expedition (1852–54) as a tribe of fishermen, with short figures, not ill-favoured, and with well-proportioned features. Their colour is dark, and their hair coarse, falling in clusters over their face till it mingles with their beards; their legs were covered with a rather remarkable growth of coarse hair.

Their language proves them to be of the North Turanian family, but does not precisely determine the race to which they belong—though it is not improbably the Tungusian.

Probably Tungusian.

The Lew-Chew islanders and the Japanese speak a somewhat different language from one another, but are, without doubt, of one origin.[9] What was the graft on the Ainos which produced the modern Japanese, we are not certain. It seems most probable that it was a mixture with Chinese, as this nation is known to have colonized these neighbouring islands, and many words of its language are found in the Japanese tongue. The physical type prevailing in the Japanese islands, is thus described by the latest scientific observers.[10] The head is oval, and like the European—the frontal bones rounded, and the forehead high. The face is oval, with a mild expression; the eyes large, with heavy arched eyebrows; the nose hand-

Japanese physique.

some, and the root not depressed, nor the nostrils dilated, as in the Chinese. The cheek bones are not prominent, but the mouth is large, with teeth broad and white; the chin is covered with a strong black beard. The women of the higher classes are fair and pretty. There appear to be great varieties in colour, from a dark copper-colour to almost a pure white.

The language is entirely different from the Chinese, though using the letters and many words of that tongue, and is polysyllabic.

The following are its grammatical peculiarities, which make certain its classification as a Turanian language.

(1.) There is no radical difference between the words for substances, quality, and action; no declination, no conjugation, or grammar; every grammatical form is a complex term formed by the juxta-position of two substantives. Given a radical, you can make of it, verb, adjective, adverb, or noun. In Hungarian, there are twenty cases; in Japanese, as many cases as there are prepositions.

Turanian peculiarities of language.

(2.) The radical is often separated from its termination, by several words; so that a long sentence may be given in a single word. (3.) The *formation by breakage*—that is, the leaving out all but a syllable or letter of the primitive radical. (4.) The faculty of marking by numerous and particular endings, the relations of inferiority or superiority to the persons addressed. This peculiarity is also found in some of the American languages. (5.) The adjective, as in so many of the Turanian languages, is unchangeable, and does not follow the gender and number of the noun. (6.) The degree of comparison is expressed by adding particles. (7.) The numeral adjectives can be employed as nouns or adjectives, according as the termination is annexed. (8.) The pronouns are identical with those of the Turanian languages, in form. (9.) The auxiliary verb is formed from the pronoun of the third person. (10.) The verb, as in Finnish, never takes a personal termination. (11.) The formation of tenses is similar to that in the Turanian. (12.) Post-positions are declined by means of other post-positions. (13.) The syntax, the phonetic harmony, and many words, are Turanian. (De Charency.)

Of what particular branch this language is a member, cannot, as yet, be satisfactorily determined. Pott[11] says that its structure would make it allied to both the Mongol and Mandchu, but would not prove a community of descent with those tongues.

Of course the question is still in dispute and perhaps may long be, how far the similarities—such as are sketched above, are the effects of a common origin, and how far they are merely the results of a like stage of intellectual progress. It is certainly no solid objection to the Turanian classification to urge that languages in the interior of Africa—such as the Vey and the Bornú—show some similar features; or that the American dialects present many. The objector must prove the impossibility of migration by any of the Turanian branches to distant regions.

Pott's objections.

CHAPTER XV.

THE TIBETANS,[1] TUNGUSIANS, MONGOLS, AND SAMOYEDS.

It will be remembered, according to Max Müller's classification,[2] that the Turanian family is divided into two great divisions—the *Northern* and *Southern*—the Northern comprehending the Tungusic, Mongolic, Tâtâric, and Finnic branches, and the Southern including the Taïc, Malaïc, Bhotîya, and Tamulic races.

Two great Turanian divisions.

In this latter branch we have considered the Tamulic, Taïc, and Indo-Bhotîyan tribes. We will now take a brief view of the original Bhotîyans (or Tibetans), as well as of the Mongolic, Tungusic, and Samoiedic peoples.

I. The Tibetans.

The language of the Bhotîyans—not considering its relatives the Indo-Tibetan dialects—is confined to the valleys of Tsangpo and the Indus, the upper Sutlej, and Sarpi, and Chenáb.[3] In Kanawar, the Hindu and Tibetan meet. The country of Tibet is remarkable as being now the centre of Buddhism. The singular custom of *polyandry* also exists among the people—that is, one woman can have several brothers for husbands. In general, however, Hindu customs, ideas and literature prevail among the people, having been introduced by the Buddhist missionaries in the seventh century.

Polyandry.

The people are nomadic cultivators, and only a few tribes have become stationary. The barrier of caste is unknown, and on the other hand, says Hodgson, "there exists not in any tribe or race, any notion of a common human progenitor, or of a Deity" by name.

In appearance, the Tibetans resemble the Chinese and the Mongols, but are more athletic and powerful.

Many of the mountaineers, according to Hodgson, differ entirely from the Turanian type, and approach the highest Aryan. No absolutely white skins are seen, but often a very pale brown complexion, with red hair and gray eyes, and a good deal of bloom on the faces of children.

Their language has many strong resemblances to the Chinese. The simple nouns are generally monosyllabic, whether substantives or adjectives.[4] The words are mostly indeclinable, and their relations are expressed by their position in the sentence, and by suffixes which indicate declension, or conjugation, or the relation expressed by prepositions. There are no genders to the nouns, and the sex, as well as plurality, is distinguished by an additional or separate word.

Tibetan language.

Besides the native Tibetans, great numbers of Mongols are found in Tibet, supposed to have been settled there since the time of Tschingis-Khan.

II. The Tungusians.

The Tungusic language is considered the lowest in the Turanian family; its grammar not being richer than the Chinese, and not having the advantage which that language possesses, of an "architectonic order."[5] In Mandchu, the dialect of the most powerful tribe of this race, there are a number of words with no distinctive terminations, and the same words can be used as nouns, verbs, adverbs, and particles.[6] The Tungusic dialects of Siberia are said to be richer, however, than the Mandchu.

The area occupied by this race is very extensive. One tribe, a people of remarkable intelligence and energy, and the only Tungusians who are not nomadic—the Mandchus—hold the government of the immense Empire of China, which they conquered in 1644. They fill many of the offices, and form the military power of the kingdom—the Mandchus occupying the garrisons and being the soldiers of China.

Tungusic area.

They possess a literature of their own, and an alphabet was invented for them from the Mongolian language, at the command of an intelligent emperor in 1599. They are described as in appearance, of lighter complexion than the Chinese, and heavier form, with more beard and a more intelligent face. Their expression is said to indicate more haughtiness than that of the Mongols, and more "determination and largeness of plan" than that of the Chinese.[7] Many are found with blonde complexion, brown beard, aquiline nose, and blue eyes.

Mandchus.

The other tribes of this race extend over Chinese Mandchuria, and above into the Russian provinces of Asia—roving over the immense steppes, or through the wild mountain-defiles of the almost unexplored country from the Yenesey to the Pacific, and from the frontiers of China to the Arctic Ocean.

They present, in general, the extreme Turanian type of features, though modified by climate and habits of life. Their religion in China is mostly Buddhism; in Siberia, either Christianity (of the Greek Church) or Paganism.

The different divisions are the Tungusians of *Dauria*, to the north and north-west of Mandchuria and east of Lake Baikal; the *Lamuts*, or those between the Aldan and the Pacific; those at Ochotsk and near Yakutsk; and those on the *Yenesey*, between the two Tonngouska rivers. The latter tribes depend on the bow and arrow for subsistence, and resemble in their habits and their religious ideas the North-American Indians.

One tribe of Tungus—the *Tshapodzhir*—tattoo themselves. The whole number of the Russian Tungus is only between 35,000[8] and 40,000.

In the late explorations of the Amour river much interesting information is given of the nomadic and pagan Tungusian tribes on its banks. The *Orotchones*, *Manegrians*, *Daourians*, and *Birars* occupy the territory on the Upper Amour; the *Gholdes* and *Ssamghers* on the middle, and the *Mangounes* and *Ghiliaks* on the lower. The Manegrians are described as the superior tribe in physique, wearing often the Mandchu costume. (See Bull. de Geog. Avril-Janvier, 1861.)

Tungus of the Amour.

III. The Mongols.

The type of features and head, which we have called the Turanian, has been usually named the Mongolian, but for no good apparent reason, as the Mongols do not show these peculiar traits as purely as several other races of this family.

The Mongolians are, with a few exceptions, a nomadic people, and inhabit especially the great deserts and steppes lying in the north of the Chinese Empire, called Mongolia. Scattered tribes, however, of this race are found in various parts of Asia and Eastern Europe; in Siberia, on the Don and the Volga, and even in Persia. The prominent tribes are the

Mongol territory.

Kalkas, the *Sunid*, the *Buriats*, the *Hazara*, *Olöt*, and *Kalmucks*.

The Kalkas are described[10] as short, squat, with high and broad shoulders; their nose short and broad, and chin prominent and pointed; the teeth large and distant from one another; eyes black, elliptical and unsteady; the neck short and thick, with the extremities bony and nervous. Their legs are short, with muscular thighs, and their stature is nearly equal to the average European.

They inhabit Mongolia, and have spread into the Russian Empire, where they are found, especially in the province of Irkutsk, and on the banks of the rivers which empty into Lake Baikal.

The *Sunid*, or *Souniats*, live to the east and south of the Kalkas, ranging over the desert country. They were formerly a very numerous tribe.

Mongol tribes.

North of the Great Wall, and to the west of the Mandchu country,[11] between the 120th and 116th degrees of east longitude, are a number of Mongol tribes, the *Tumet*, who are in part agricultural, the *Orat* (or Urad) the *Ortú* and various others.

The *Buriats*, numbering, according to Castrén, about 190,000, live in Siberia, from the borders of China to the Upper Lena, and are more civilized than the other Siberians.

The *Songarians*, formerly a powerful Mongol nation, but conquered and dispersed by the Chinese, are found in various parts of Asiatic Russia, or among the Turks of Bokharia, or on the banks of the Kho-kho-nor.

The *Olöt*, and *Kalmucks*, are considered as substantially the same. Their centre is the mountainous country on the frontier of Turkestan and China, south of Lake Balkash. Colonies of these tribes, especially from the clans Dürbet and Torgod, have settled since the seventeenth century on the Don and the Volga. In the valley of the Ili, they have been much mingled with the Turkish hordes. Other Kalmuck tribes have penetrated into Siberia, where they formed in 1832 nearly four per cent. of the Cossack army, and have scattered themselves over many of the countries of Asia.

Kalmucks.

The Mongols of Cabul and Persia are called *Aimâk*, (or Eimauks*) and *Hazára* (Hazaureh). They l ve mostly in the Paropamisan mountains, between Cabul and Herat.[12]

The Mongols are now everywhere the subjects of the powers which they once overthrew—the Russian—Turkish, and Chinese governments.

Of the Mongol, M. Huc says:—

He is full of gentleness and *bonhommie;* he passes suddenly from the wildest and most extravagant gaiety, to a melancholy that has nothing repulsive. Timid to excess in general, when excited by fanaticism, or the desire for vengeance, he displays an impetuous courage that nothing can arrest; he is simple and credulous as a child, and is passionately fond of stories and marvellous recitals.

The vices generally attributed to the Mongol Tartars are, aversion to labour, love of pillage, and rapine, cruelty, and debauchery. . . . We have always found them generous, frank, hospitable; inclined, it is true, like ill-brought-up children, to appropriate little objects of curiosity, but in no manner addicted to what may be called robbery. As for their aversion to labour and a sedentary life, they are much the same as they always were; it must also be admitted that their morals, in some points, are very lax; but their conduct, in this respect, proceeds more from thoughtlessness than corruption, and we rarely find among them the hideous and brutal excesses to which the

Huc's description.

* Strangford states that only one tribe of the *Eimauks* are Mongol; the rest being probably Iranian.

Chinese are so violently addicted. . . . The Mongols are strangers to every species of industry; their felt carpets, skins coarsely tanned, and some few articles of sewing and embroidery, are not worth mentioning; but, on the other hand, they possess in high perfection, the qualities of a pastoral and nomadic people, in the prodigious development of the senses of sight, hearing, and smell. Many attempts have been made to convert the Mongols to Christianity, but hitherto they have all proved fruitless.

The Mongol language is interesting to the scholar, as instancing growth in language, even at the present day. Castrén states that while the literary language shows no pronominal affixes,* whether subjective or predicative, this feature has just begun to appear in the spoken dialect of the Buriats, and in the Tungusic idiom spoken near Nyertshinsk, in Siberia.

Growth of Mongol language.

IV. [1]*The Samoiedes.*

Among the detached branches of the northern division of the Turanian family, is a small and barbarous people, widely scattered over the most northern provinces of Asia—the *Samoiedes*,† or "Swamp-dwellers."

* To illustrate this roughly in the English tongue, suppose our language only so far developed that we could express *I love*, or *have loved*, or *will love*, or *thou lovest*, &c., but by one word, *loving*, and the pronoun must be expressed by gesture or accent, and the time by some word like *day*, placed near it; or suppose that having attained the pronoun, we could only say *loving-I*, and the position would indicate whether we meant *my love*, or *I love*, or *lovely me;* and so *my father*, must be *father-I*. This would correspond in a general way to the low grammatical condition of the Mongolian language. The Buriats would be so far advanced as to say *love-did-I* (I loved), or as in French, "j'aimer-ai," *I have to love* (I will love), keeping the affixes separate, and not melted into the word as in English. They could also say, "*Fatheri*," that is "my father."

† The derivation of this word from the root of the Finnic, *Suomelaiset* (men of a swamp), seems, on the whole, the most probable. See Latham.

Their especial habitations are on the bleak, mossy, swamps or plains, beyond the line within which trees will grow, near the borders of the Icy Sea. Here they pasture their reindeer and wander about during the summer. They are Russian subjects, and before they were conquered, some of their tribes were powerful and warlike. They are now weak and savage nomads, living in the bleakest and most inhospitable regions of the earth. A few of the Samoiedes are nominally Christian, but the most are pagan. In race, as has been said, they are of the Turanian family, especially allied with the Finns, the Tungus, Mongols and Turks.

Samoiedes.

The extent of territory on which they live is very considerable; their tribes reaching from the Ubsa Nor in Chinese Mongolia, to the North Cape of Asia, and for 80 degrees from the river Mesene and the White Sea, to the Lena. They are divided into the North and South Samoiedes. The Northern, embrace (1.) the *Yurak*, (2.) the *Tawgi*, and (3.) the *Ostiak*.

The Yurak dwell near the Mesene, and the White Sea, and between the latter and the Yenesey; the Tawgi, from the Yenesey to the Chatunga; and the Ostiaks, who are to be distinguished from the Ugro-Ostiaks of the Obi, on the heights between the Obi and the Yenesey, near their sources. The southernmost point of these tribes is Tomsk. The Southern Samoiedes include the *Soiot* and *Kamas*, and *Koibal*, with other tribes on the high land of the East Altai range, near the sources of the Yenesey, and among the Sayan Mountains. The Soiot occupy in part Chinese territory, while some are found in Siberia near Lake Baikal. The Koibal are a nominally Christian tribe.

Divisions.

The Samoiedes have been forced from the country on

the Middle Yenesey, and the Finnik Ostiaks hold their place; but they are found again on the Icy Sea, and in West Siberia, on the Obi.

There is less known of this miserable people than of almost any other in Asia.

Prof. Müller's division of these tribes is somewhat different. He divides the Northern Samoiedes into the *Yurazes*, the *Tawgi*, and the *Yenisei*; and the Southern, into the *Ostiako-Samoiedes* and *Kamas*.

Physique.

The physical characteristics of the Samoiedes are the broad face and pyramidal skull of the Turanian family. They exceed the Lap in average height.

Related to Finns.

There has been much question as to where the Samoiedes should be placed in the ethnological classification, but Castrén's investigations have put beyond a doubt their near relation to the Finns. The languages of both peoples, he says, are distinguished from the Tungusian and Turkish, by the far greater development of the principle of *agglutination*; so much so, that it approaches to the *flexion* of the Aryan languages, and may almost form the means by which the one family of languages can be connected to the other.

CHAPTER XVI.

TURKISH RACES.[1]

THE Turkish race is a very extensive and widely-scattered family; its members being found from the banks of the Lena and the shores of the Arctic Ocean to the frontiers of Hungary and the northern and eastern provinces of Africa.

The Yakuts. This tribe are the most remote of any of this family, and at the same time they preserve in language the Turkic type the most purely. They live on both sides of the river Lena, in its lower part, and they have scattered themselves over one of the most desolate and inclement countries in the world—the north of Siberia. Their pasturages in summer are the beds of dried-up lakes (*albuty*),[2] which at that season yield a rich vegetation, though the mean temperature of Yakutsk is 6°, Reaumur, below freezing-point, and quicksilver is a solid body there during one-sixth of the year. The original habitations of this tribe were northwest of Lake Baikal.

Yakuts.

In religion they were, till recently, Pagan, holding fetisse superstitions, though recognizing a Great Spirit. Christianity, through the Greek Church, is gradually gaining an influence on them. Their male population is given by Müller as 100,000. Their language can be used as a key to the grammatical forms of the Osmanli and other Turkic dialects.[3] The Yakuts present the pure Turanian physical type.

The Turks of Siberia. After the dismemberment of the Empire of Tschingis-Khan, several Tartar (or Turkic) Khanates were formed in Siberia. They were conquered by the Russians in the sixteenth century. The principal towns are Tobolsk, Yeniseisk, and Tomsk. The Barabas, between the Irtish and the Obi, and the Urañhat, on the Chulym, are separate tribes.[4]

The Kazan Turks (called Tartars). These are distributed over Permia, Viatka, Simbirsk, and Orenburg, in European Russia. They are in greatest numbers in Kazan, and their whole population amounts to more than 700,000.

Kazan Turks.

They are interesting to the student as being now in process of change from the nomadic to a settled agricultural life, and are described as an honest, industrious, frank, peaceable people, who are fast progressing in the arts of civilized life. Their faith is a zealous Mohammedanism. Two very different physical types are said to exist among them—one, that of the European Turk, with oval contour of face, prominent features, arched nose, not inexpressive eyes, and full beard; the other, of the extreme Turanian, with broad flattened nose, prominent cheek-bones and glabrous skin.[5]

There seems to be no doubt that a portion of the population, by favourable circumstances, have become changed from the type of the Chinese Mongolian, or Turkic Yakuts, to something near that of the European.

The Kirgis. The country between the Yenisey and the Tom, in Southern Siberia, was the mother-country of this tribe. In the beginning of the eighteenth century they were forced out of

Kirgis.

Siberia by the Songurian Mongols, and they now occupy the northern and eastern portions of Turkestan, whence they rove over a vast extent of country. They are divided into the *Great* Horde and the *Little* and *Middle* Hordes. The Great Horde is not the most numerous, but is pronounced the most dangerous and savage of the Kirgis. Their district lies to the east, near the frontiers of Chinese Turkestan and Mongolia, though their chiefs were met by Mr. Atkinson far to the north and east in Siberia and Mongolia. The tribe is subject to Russia.

The Little Horde is found between the rivers Yemba and Ural, and in Oremburg, wandering from the Aral to the Caspian; and the most powerful—the Middle Horde (or Kirgis-Kasak)—holds the country between the Sarasu and Yemba, and since 1854 occupies the district of Ssemipalatinsk. This Horde is partly independent and partly tributary to Russia and China. The whole number of these Hordes, with other Kirgis tribes, is estimated at 1,251,000.

They are generally described by travellers as an idle, roving, uncertain, and dishonest people, but with one virtue of a nomadic race—hospitality. They are in constant border warfare with China and Tibet, and are only kept in control by the strong hand of Russia. The type of head and feature is decidedly Turanian.

Turkomans.

The Turkomans (or Turkmans). This tribe of nomadic robbers occupies the country in the north of Persia, in the west of Armenia, and south of Georgia, and in Shirwan and Dagestan. East of the Caspian, they are under the command of the Usbeks, and, still more to the east, they are under the Chinese sway. In Khorasan there are Turkoman tribes subject to the Persians.[6]

The independent Turkomans boast that they neither

rest under the shadow of a tree nor the authority of a king. They are a race of roving plunderers. The type of feature again is the extreme Turanian. They are more wiry and lithe in form than the Osmanli Turks, with less tendency to fulness; their complexion is more copperish and swart.

Usbeks.

A closely-related tribe, the *Usbeks*, differ from the Turkomans, in being in part agricultural and dwelling in towns. They possess Bukhára, a large city, and the provinces of Balkh, Khokan, Khiva, and Ferganah. The Usbeks are descendants of the 'Huy-'he and Uigurs, and live side by side with the ancient Aryan inhabitants, whom they have subdued—the Persians. Their religion is the most bigoted Mohammedanism.

Nogais.

The Nogais, another tribe of this family, live to the west of the Caspian and north of the Black Sea. One tribe, which are remarkable as being excellent agriculturists, have settled in the Crimea. The main body rove about with their herds near the Kuban and Kuma. One horde on the Volga—the Kundur—is subject to the Kalmucks.

Russia is now removing the Nogais in great numbers, and substituting the Bulgarians. They are a brave race, and many have volunteered under the Circassians. In physique they are tall and athletic, with the oblique Turanian eyelids.

Turkic tribes.

Still other Turkic tribes are the *Bazianes*, near the sources of the Kuban; the *Kumüks*, on the river Sunga (or Zundzha), Aksai, and Koisu, subjects of Russia; the *Karakalpaks* near the sea of Aral, subject partly to Russia and partly to the Khans of Khiva; and the *Baskirs*, in Orenburg and the adjacent provinces. These latter are somewhat mingled with Mongolic blood, and are Mohammedan in faith;

they are subject to Russia. Their number is about 392,000.

The *Osmanlis* or *Ottoman Turks*. This, the leading Turkish tribe, has held Constantinople since 1453. Though possessing large provinces in Europe, at the south of the Danube, the number of pure Turks in Europe is said by Shafarik to be not more than 700,000, though it is probably nearer 1,000,000. In Asia Minor, the Turkish race has been much mingled with Græcian and Armenian blood.

Osmanlis.

The Osmanlis are the ruling class through all the Turkish possessions in Europe, Asia, and Africa. They number between eleven and twelve millions; and form the nobility and gentry of Turkey. Their language is the speech of persons of rank and education, and is the official language in Syria, Egypt, Tunis, and Tripoli. It is spoken in the southern provinces of Asiatic Russia, on the borders of the Caspian, and through the whole of Turkestan.[7]

The language of the whole Turkish race can be understood by any of its members, provided no foreign words be used. The speech of the upper classes has a large infusion of Persian and Arabic words, so that a well-educated Turk, says M. Müller, can speak a whole sentence without a word of Turkish origin. The three great dialects of the Turkish are: (1.) the *Chagatai*, spoken in Turkestan; (2.) the *Tataric*, spoken in the Kipchak and Siberia; and (3.) the *Osmanli*.

Turkish dialects.

It will be gathered from these brief notices of the Turkic tribes that the general type of feature is what is called Mongolian or Turanian. This type, however, changes when the Turk becomes mingled with foreign blood, and when he assumes a

Physique.

more stationary and civilized life in the low lands or cities, as, for instance, in European Turkey, or Crimea, or the Russian provinces of Kazan, Orembu Oufa, and the districts on the Volga. *[8]

* We were at first inclined to accept Prichard's view, that this a manifest instance of the change of a race-type under new phy influences. But closer investigations—especially in Dr. Rigler's cellent medical statistics of Turkey—show the great extent to w intermarriage is carried by the Turks, and leave the question sti doubt.

CHAPTER XVII.

RACES[1] OF PERSIA, AFGHANISTAN, AND BILUCHISTAN.

PERSIA, the ancient home of one important branch of the Aryan family, the Iranian Aryans, who separated at some remote period from the Hindu Aryans, has been subject for ages to the inroads of invading tribes. Its steppes and mountains show remnants of nations from all the three great families of man which have been described in this Treatise, and the physical type varies from the extreme Turanian, and that of the black Hindu-gipsy, to the most noble, classic type of the pure Aryan. Out of the various tribes, two distinct and broad divisions present themselves—the population of native Persian descent, the *Tájiks*, who are Aryan, and the wandering hordes who are usually either Semitic or Turanian, called *Iliyáhs*.

Two divisions of Persian tribes.

The Tájiks are agricultural, as opposed to nomadic; they are the inhabitants of the towns, and they hold usually the low lands, while the Iliyáhs occupy especially the mountains. They form the principal population near the cities Kabul, Kandahar, Ghazna, Herat, and Balkh.[2] Their traders wander over great part of Central Asia, and their tribes furnish the language, and a large portion of the population of Bokhara, where they are mingled with the Uzbeks. In Afghanistan, Biluchistan, Turkestan, and Eastern Bokhara, and in districts still farther to the east, these

Tájiks.

native Persians, or Tájiks, are the agricultural and the commercial classes. Their creed is Mohammedan, of the Shiite sect, in opposition to the Iliyáhs who are Sunnites.

The native Persian, in his purest type, is very handsome, with a long oval face, regular features, long black eyebrows, and large black eyes; his stature is not tall; the complexion is usually brown, though in the southern provinces, as in Seistaun, it becomes entirely black under the influence of climate,[3] and other physical causes. The Parsees, of India, who are of Persian descent, are much darker than the native Persians, though still very handsome men.

The native Persian tongue has passed through various stages in the history of the past. It was the language of the Zendavesta, the sacred books of the Persians; it was preserved in the inscriptions of Cyrus, Darius, and Xerxes; in the Pehlevi (226 A.D.); in the Parsi, the language of the epic poem of Firdusi (1000 A.D.); and it appears in the present much mingled tongue[4] of modern Persia.

Persian language.

The Iliyáhs (or Iliats). This term, it should be remembered, is not so much the designation of a race, as of a large division of tribes, whose habits are entirely different from those of the Tájiks. Some of the Iliyáhs are of Persian descent though nomadic. Of these, the *Biluchs* (or Bâluchs) are the most important. They occupy a district of some 600 miles in extent, to the south of Afghanistan, near the borders of India, called Biluchistan. They are a tribe of nomadic robbers, under the nominal leadership of the Khan of Kelaut. The Baluchs were originally from the mountains east of Kerman. They occupy especially the lower districts of the west and east of Biluchistan, from which they appear to have dispossessed the Brahui, whom they drove to the mountains. A portion of them have made conquests and settlements in Sindh, where they are in constant hostility with the English. They are described, by one writer, as so unfortunately placed, as to receive the vices of both barbarism and civilization, without the virtues of either. This nation is said to resemble the Jews strongly in features, as well as in certain institutions, and for that reason has been called Semitic, or Arabian, by some, but there seems little doubt of its Aryan (Iranian) origin. Capt. Postans estimates the number of fighting men of this people, on the Indus, as about 40,000.

The *Feilí* are another nomadic tribe, of the old Persian stock, inhabiting the western side of the mountains of Lúristan. Besides these, are the *Bakhtiyári*, in the neighbourhood of Lúr, and on the southern border of the plateau of Iran; and the *Laks* scattered over Persia, but chiefly found in the regions of Kazwín, and Fars, and Mazanderan.[5]

Iliyáhs.

The great body, however, of the Iliyáhs are not Aryan, but Semitic and Turanian; that is, they are Arab, or Turkish, or Mongol. Among those of the Turkish race are the Kajárs, in the northern part of the country, and the Afshárs. The Aimâk (Eimauks), and Hazára (Hazaureh), have been already mentioned * under the Mongol tribes.

The *Arabian Iliyáhs* are said to have emigrated from Nejd, in Arabia.

There are beside nomadic *Kurdish Iliyáhs*, who are of race allied to the native Persians.

The contrast between the two classes of inhabitants in Persia is said to be the most striking in Khorasan—the Iliyáhs usually showing the broad face and flat nose of the Turanians, and the Tájiks presenting the hand-

* Page 127.

some Persian type. There are, however, certain of the Turkish Iliyáhs who possess a very noble type of features.

Beside these various races, the Indian peoples have several off-shoots in the Persian Empire: the *Karaschi* (Keredji) or Gipsies, the same Hindu tribe who have wandered over Europe, and the *Brahui*, in Biluchistan, a dark people of Tamul origin.

Gipsies.

The name *Keredji* is a term of contempt from their colour, and might be translated "niggers." This tribe is much despised by the native Persians, and seems even more worthless and unprincipled than in most countries. Like all the Iliats, they have a representative in every city, who collects their taxes for the Persian government.

The *Brahui* form a very marked contrast to the Baluchs by whom they are surrounded. Instead of the lank form, long face and prominent features which characterize these latter, they present a round face, flat features and short thick bones, and often have brown hair and beard. They are a much more peaceful, industrious and honest race than the robbing Baluchs, from whom they secure themselves in the heights of the mountains. Large numbers of these also are found near Kelat, and in Sakavaran and Ghalavan.

The interesting circumstance in regard to them is, that a relic of the early Tamul immigration into India should be found so far from the present habitations of the race.

The Afghans.

This people are directly descended from an ancient Aryan race, and are allied to the Iranians or Persians. They call themselves Pushtun, which has been corrupted into *Patan*. Their language—the Pushtu—is spoken from the valley of Pishin, south of Kandahar to Kaffaristan on the north; and from the banks of the Helmand on the west to the Indus on the east, in a district, says Capt. Raverty, as large as the Spanish peninsula.

Afghan language.

In physical development, the Afghans are an instance of an unmixed race, presenting nearly all gradations of colour according to the position they occupy and the climate of their respective districts. The Western Afghans on the high table-land are said by Prichard to be fair as Europeans, while those on the Indus are nearly black.

Of the many wild hordes of this people, the *Duranis* or Western Afghans, are the most civilized and honest. Their creed is Sunnite. The higher classes are somewhat educated in Persian literature. They are very much attached to their native country, and especially to their sacred city, Kandahar. Herat is another of their cities.

To the eastward of the Duranis, is the country of the *Ghilzyes*, another leading Afghan tribe. It stretches to the northwest of the Paropamisan Mountains, and eastward to the mountains of Solimán.[6] The Ghilzyes hold Cabul. They differ from the Duranis in having a less arbitrary government. The *Berduranis* are still another important division in Eastern Afghanistan. Beside these are various independent fierce tribes, the *Khyberis*, a black people, of the famous Khyber Pass; the *Afridis*, on the borders of India, and the *Ensof-ze*, or "children of Joseph," who touch the Indus on the east.

Afghan tribes.

It is this Afghan people, it should be remembered, who in the twelfth century, conquered India and inflicted unknown evils upon that unhappy land, until the fierce tide of Mongolian conquest under Tamerlane and his descendants swept away the last of the Afghan dynasties.

The Kurds.[7]

The country whence the many roving tribes of this people come is on the western frontier of Persia. It is bounded on the north by Armenia; on the east by Aserbeijan and the Persian Irak; on the south by Khusistan and the district of Bagdad; and on the west by the Tigris. The Kurds are found, however, in Loristan on the Persian Gulf, in the pashaliks of Haleb and Damascus in Asia Minor, in the Russian Empire and the southern parts of Georgia. Their province is divided into two parts by the Zagros Mountains, the portion west being under the Turkish rule and that on the east under Persian. The whole number of Kurds is estimated at from two to three millions, and, perhaps, will reach four. They are considered to be direct descendants from the ancient Karduchians mentioned by Xenophon.

Kurdish territory.

The nation is divided into two great classes of peasants and nobles, who are even to be distinguished in features —the former having a softer and more regular countenance, with almost a Græcian type, and the latter being more hard-featured, with eyes deep-sunk and abrupt lines of face. The peasant-class is in a state of great misery and oppression.

Kurdish features.

The Kurds are a high-spirited people, much given to plunder and war, and are exceedingly rude in manner; they profess, with the exception of the *Yezidis*, the Moslem creed. The Kurdish language is Iranian, though having a strong mixture of Arabic and Turkish elements, and being without literary cultivation. The upper classes speak, beside their own language, Persian and Turkish. The Kurdish is never taught in their schools, and has no written form.

*The Yezidis.** It has been a long time doubtful whether this remarkable people were a religious sect or a separate race. They are widely scattered throughout Assyria, Mesopotamia, North Syria, Kurdistan, Asia Minor and Armenia. Their principal habitation is in Mesopotamia, within a circuit of two days' journey around Mosul. Their number is about 50,000.

Dr. Grant, in his work on the Nestorians, supposes them to be Semitic, from their Jewish customs of circumcision and the passover-feast. Mr. W. F. Ainsworth argues with much ingenuity, that they are the direct descendants of the ancient Semitic Assyrians.

Dr. Grant's theory.

The points of resemblance are the following: In physique, they are described by Haxthausen, as well-formed, large and muscular, with finely-arched eyebrows, black eyes, aquiline nose and a rather broad countenance; features which correspond almost exactly to those seen on the Assyrian monuments. Other analogies are, their place of residence on the plains near Nineveh, the architecture of their tombs, preserving the peculiar terraced form of Assyrian architecture, the use of the cylinders and other relics of the ancient Assyrians; the worship of the cock, the adoration of the sun, the traces of fire-worship in their annual festival, and the dedication of a bull to the sun.

Resemblance to ancient Assyrians.

The more received conclusion is that the Yezidis are

* This name may be derived from *Yezed*, meaning the good God, as the Guebres still use it for the good Principle; or it may be derived from *Yezd*, which is now the head-quarters, and always has been the chief holy city, of the Fire-worshippers; or it may come from the ancient name of an Arabic tribe, *Azd*. (Rev. H. Homes, Bib. Repos. 1842.)

a Kurdish tribe, of Persian stock, not converted to Mohammedanism, who retained their ancient worship of the Sun, and of the Evil Principle, or Shaitan. Others assert that they do not worship Shaitan, but only seek to conciliate him, because of his power, and that they offer sacrifices to him much more than to the Good Spirit, because they are less certain of his kind wishes. The sacred bird, whose image they worship, presents another analogy to the ancient Magian adoration of the sacred birds representing evil spirits.

Probably Persian.

It is held by some scholars—and there are strong reasons for this opinion—that the Yezidis were originally Christians, and afterwards converted to Manichæism.*

The important divisions of the *Kurds*, are the *Dschelali*, numbering 5000 tents; the *Mela*, 2500 tents; the *Schakaki*, 50,000; the *Haideranly*, of whom the eastern branch has 4000 tents, and the western, which wanders from Lake Van to the Euphrates, about 2000; and the *Selăly*.

Nearly all these tribes live by plundering caravans, and then escape either the Persian or Turkish Government, by fleeing from the territory of the one to that of the other, or by retiring to their inaccessible mountains. Some are said to be tribes of settled habitations; but even these change their whole residence twice or thrice in the year.

The vices of the two first divisions of tribes we have mentioned, seem gradually destroying them; and the others, the Turkish Government is seeking deliberately to denationalize, by trans-

Gradual extinction.

* Haxthausen maintains that their doctrine of Satan is the Gnostic doctrine of Demiurgus.

planting large bodies of them. It is thought by investigators,[8] that the Kurdish nation will soon utterly disappear.

The numerous division of the *Schakaki* have been greatly improved in condition and morals, through the efforts of the American missionaries.

Nestorians.[10]

Amid the mountains of Kurdistan, and in the northwest province of Persia, Aserbeijan, are the relics of a branch of the great Semitic family, and of the oldest Christian sect—the Nestorians.

As a sect, they date from the fifth century, and they are without doubt a branch of the Aramæans, early converted to Christainity, and retaining many Jewish customs. Their ancient language and literature were Syriac, probably the same tongue as that which Christ used in Judæa. The modern tongue is a version of Syriac, with Kurdish, Persian, and Turkish words intermingled. The missionaries of this devoted sect once traversed Asia from Palestine to China, and it is supposed that many of the Christians now known to be living in the interior of China, are the descendants of their converts.

Probably Aramæan.

Beside the mountains, the Nestorians hold the broad plain of Oroomiah, and the Roman Catholic division of the people, called Chaldees, occupy a portion of Mesopotamia. The range of the tribe is from 36° to 39° north latitude, and from 43° to 46° east longitude. Their least populous districts are subject to the Kurds, while others, as the valley of the Zab, occupied by the *Tiaree*, numbering some 50,000, are quite independent. This latter tribe choose their own rulers, and are as brave or ferocious as the Kurds themselves.

Nestorian territory.

It is probable that ultimately the whole people will come under Turkish authority. The Nestorians are a pastoral people, rarely proprietors of the soil, and sometimes suffering much from poverty. Many in the plains live as serfs under their Mohammedan masters; these latter Nestorians are said to show much more of the Persian urbanity than those in the mountains.

In appearance, the Nestorians are represented as generally handsome, with regular features, blonde complexion, and light beard. Dr. Grant thinks they bear a strong resemblance to the Jews.

Much interest has been excited in this people by the efforts of Dr. Grant to prove their descent from the ten lost tribes of Israel. It is generally thought by scholars, however, that his argument proves too much; and only establishes the Oriental, or at most, Semitic character of the race, not their connection with those particular tribes.

Dr. Grant's theory.

The whole number of Nestorians was estimated, in 1843, at about 140,000.

CHAPTER XVIII.

THE RACES OF GEORGIA, THE CAUCASUS, AND ARMENIA.[1]

THE Caucasus, Müller tells us, has been called by the Persians the "mountain of languages," such is the mixture of races and tongues that prevails among its valleys.

Even in the times of Herodotus, each caravan of Greek merchants passing through this region was accompanied by seven interpreters, speaking seven different languages. Through the Caucasian isthmus flowed one of the three great streams of early Aryan and Turanian migration from Asia into Europe; and among these mountains there may be supposed to have been eddies or deposits from all the various streams of race which poured into Europe. Georgia, for instance, presents an Aryan language and race, entirely different from any others surrounding it, and puzzling to the ethnologist from its position—the *Ossetian: Os* being the name by which this people is known to its neighbours, and *Iron* the name they call themselves. They occupy the country to the north of Tiflis, near the sources of the Rion, and in the valley of the Terek. They are nominally under Russian rule. According to Georgian traditions, they extended formerly from the Cau-

Mixture of languages in the Caucasus.

The Ossetians.

casus to the Don; and are supposed by Klaproth to have been the descendants of a Median colony, transplanted by the Scythians into Sarmatia in the seventh century B.C., and related to the Alans and Roxolans of the Middle Ages. This theory of their origin is not held to be proved.

A marked resemblance is observed between many of the customs and practices of the Ossetes and those of the German peasantry; so much so, as to lead to the theory that they are connected in race with the ancient Teutons. Their language, however, proves them to belong to the Persian side of the Aryan family. In physique, the men are short, thick-set, with broad, haggard features, blue eyes, red or light-brown hair. The women are short, stout, with flat noses, but having small and well-shaped feet.

Aryan in race.

The Turanian tribes in this region are much the more numerous. Among these are the *Georgians*, the boundaries of whose country are the river Alazan on the east; the Black Sea on the west; the Caucasian Mountains on the north, and the Kur on the south, with some adjacent mountains. They are divided into: (1.) the Georgians or *Grusians;* (2.) the inhabitants of *Mingrelia* and *Guria;* (3.) the *Suans* (or Swan); and (4.) the *Lazi.*

Turanian tribes.

The Suans are in part independent and in part subject to Mongolian princes; the Lazi are under Turkish rule and are Mohammedans. Of the Suan language Berger says that only one-third of its roots are Georgian, and the others have no connection with the other Caucasian dialects. Though the language of these tribes is probably Turanian it is not distinctly connected with that of any of the great Turanian races, and the physical type is like the purest Aryan development. The

Georgian women, according to some authorities, are more beautiful than the Circassian.

The testimony of travellers, however, does not confirm the general impression in regard to the remarkable personal beauty of the Georgians and Circassians. They state that the slaves sold to the Turks are the best samples of the population, but that the mass of the people, though well-looking, are by no means conspicuous for beauty. Reinegg says rather spitefully: "a short leg, a small foot, and glaring red hair constitute a Circassian beauty." Haxthausen, on the other hand, describes the Georgians as tall, slender, of noble bearing, with regular features, aquiline nose, finely-formed mouth, dark complexion, dark eyes and hair.

Beauty of Georgians and Circassians.

The Caucasian Races

May be divided into three branches. (1.) The Eastern, or *Lesghi;* (2.) the Middle, or *Mizjeghi;* (3.) the Western, or *Circassian* and *Abasian.*

In Lesghistan, the country of the Lesghi, there are four different languages spoken: the Avarian, that of the Kasikumüks, of Akuska, and Kura. With the Lesghi are mingled many Turkic tribes, who have in some degree caused this variety of tongues. The Lesghians are Mohammedans, and their faith has during late years been stimulated by the Porte for the sake of opposing Russian influence.

Lesghians.

The Lesghic language is thought to show affinities with both African and American dialects, but cannot be certainly classified.

Of the *Mizjeghi* (or *Tshetsh*), without going into a minute classification of the tribes, it is only necessary to say that, with the exception of the Ingush, they are all Mohammedans, and bitterly opposed to Russia. Their language has many Turanian features, and was supposed to have belonged to the Samoiedic class; but doubts are thrown on this, and its position is yet uncertain.

The *Circassians*, who occupy the coast of the Black Sea, to the north-west of the Caucasian Mountains, have become known to the world, especially through their heroic resistance of the Russians. These call themselves Adighé, while those of the interior, in the Kabardah, are called "Cherkessian." They formerly extended even to the Crimea. A portion, only, have been subjected by Russia.

Circassians.

The *Abassians*, says Müller, have held their present districts on the Black Sea, since the Christian era. A part of them on the coast have been conquered by the Russians, but those in the interior are still independent. The ethnological position of these tribes is still doubtful, though probably Turanian. Their physical traits are black hair, blue eyes, a finely-shaped nose, sallow complexion, and small thin forms. The princes and nobles have much larger and more powerful frames than the peasantry.

Abassians.

The population of the Caucasian tribes is thus given by M. Müller, from whom, as well as from Klaproth, these condensed statements are taken:—

Cherkessians	280,000
Abassians	140,000
Ossetes	60,000
Georgians	50,000
Mizjeghians	110,000
Lesghians	400,000
Tâtârs (Turkic)	80,000
	1,120,000

Berger gives a somewhat different estimate, as well as ethnological division. (Peter. Mitt. V., 1860.)

Abassian (or Abchasian) stock . . .	144,346
Suan (or Swanethian), 1639 houses or about	10,000
Circassian (or Adige)	290,549
Ubichian	25,000
Turkish (Tâtâr)	44,989
Tshetsh	117,080
Tuschinian, Pschawians, and Chewssurien	11,456
Lesghian	399,761
Ossetian	27,339

With respect to the political position of these various tribes, the American missionaries, Messrs. Dwight and Smith, state that the limits of Russian sway among them do not at all correspond to the pretended boundaries on Russian maps. "Nearly half of the country of the Abassians," they say, "is marked as subject to Russia, but in fact, their authority is acknowledged no farther than the guns of their garrison reach. *Swaneti*, too, has the same mark of subjection, though it is well known that the Swani (Soanes) confine themselves to the neighbourhood of the perpetual snows of Elburz, in order not to compromise their liberty. Two passes through the mountains, also, are marked as Russian soil; but not even the weekly mail is sent through that of Dariel without an escort, amounting, sometimes, to a hundred soldiers, two field-pieces, and several Cossacks. . . . To the territory of the Lesghies, Russia has a more plausible claim."

Political relations.

Of the religions of these tribes, the same writers state, that "with the exception of about 200 families of Armenians among the Cherkés, a considerable body of Jews around Andrera, on the borders of Daghistán, and the Lesghies, who are known as bigoted Sünny Moslems, the religion of the mountains is a nondescript mixture of Mohammedanism, Christianity, and Paganism. In the superstitions of some of the tribes, as the Abkhâz and Cherkés, the features of the Moslem faith are predominant; in others, as the Swani, Christianity forms the largest ingredient; and in others still, as the Ossetians and Ingoosh, we find little but Paganism, associated with a strong predilection for Christianity over Mohammedanism. History, tradition, and monuments, in their country, unite with various parts of their superstitions, to testify that nearly all of them once professed the faith of Christ."

Religions.

The following vivid description of the costumes in Tiflis, by the same authorities, will give an idea of the mingling of nationalities in those provinces.

Costumes.

The Russian soldier stands sentry at the corners of the streets, in a coarse great-coat, concealing the want of a better uniform, and even of decent clothing. The Russian subaltern jostles carelessly along in a little cloth cap, narrow-skirted coat, and tight pantaloons, with epaulettes dangling in front of naturally round shoulders. In perfect contrast to him stands the stately Turk, if not in person, yet represented by some emigrant Armenian, with turbanned head, and bagging shalwár. The Georgian priest appears, cane in hand, with a green gown, long hair, and broad-brimmed hat, while black, flowing robes, and a cylindrical lambskin cap. mark his clerical brother of the Armenian Church. The dark *Lesgy*, with the two-edged *kama* (short-sword), the most deadly of all instruments of death, dangling at his side, seems prowling for his victim as an avenger of blood. The city-bred Armenian merchant waits upon his customers, snugly dressed in an embroidered frock coat, gay calico frock, red silk shirt, and ample green trousers, also of silk. The tall lank Georgian peasant, with an upright, conical, sheepskin cap, and scantily clothed, looks as independent in his cloak of felt, as Diogenes in his tub. His old oppressor, the Persian, is known by more flowing robes, smoothly-combed beard, and nicely-dinted cap. In the midst of his swine appears the half-clad Mingrelian, with bonnet like a tortoise-shell, tied loosely upon his head. And in a drove of spirited horses is a hardy mountaineer, whose round cap, with a shaggy flounce of sheepskin dangling over his eyes, and the breast of his coat wrought into a cartridge-box, show him to be a Circassian.

The Armenians.

This people, though inhabiting a territory which has been the battle-ground of the world, always oppressed and conquered, even by far inferior races, has yet through many ages preserved its rich physical and mental endowments, and has retained its language, customs, ritual, and religion.

From various causes, by conquest, forcible removal and voluntary emigration, the Armenians have been remarkably scattered over Eastern Europe and Asia. They are found in Anatolia, the north of Syria, Mesopotamia, Georgia, Circassia, Persia, and in Russia and European Turkey. Systematic and successful efforts have been made by the Russian Government to induce them to emigrate from their own provinces to the Russian territory. They are a people especially devoted to mercantile pursuits, and Armenian merchants may be met with in St. Petersburg, Vienna, Venice, Constantinople, Cairo, Bombay, Calcutta, and many other cities. Yet in all countries, they look back with unchanging affection to the Patriarchate and their native land.

Dispersion.

Armenia Proper consists of the valley of the Aras, the country between the Kur and the Aras, the valley of Murad-chai, or Eastern Euphrates, and the basins of Lake Van and Lake Oroomiah. The boundaries on the side of Kurdistan and Aserbeijan are more uncertain. Its extent is 430 miles in longitude, and 300 miles in latitude. It contains

Boundaries of Armenia.

politically the Russian governments of Eriván, Shoosha, and Tiflis; the chieftainships of various Kurdish chiefs; the Persian government of Tabriz, and the Ottoman pashaliks of Kars, Erzroom, and others. Armenia Minor embraces the pashalik of Cesarea, with other minor Turkish pashaliks.

The people are spoken of with commendation by travellers, as showing far more honesty and intelligence than their Turkish masters or neighbours. They are far superior to any Oriental race in agriculture. Their religion is Christian, though often much corrupted, and they have held to it with great faithfulness in persecution and exile. Their nature seems more open to spiritual ideas than that of any other Eastern people.

The Armenians are a member of the great Aryan family, though their language differs, both from the Indian and Iranian type. It has preserved a rich literature, dating from the fourth century A.D. The ancient tongue is a dead language; the modern, according to Dwight and Smith, is divided into two dialects: one, that of Constantinople, which has spread through Asia Minor and Erzroom, and has borrowed many forms* from the Turkish; the other, the dialect of Mount Ararat, or Armenia, which has a greater resemblance to the ancient tongue, and is spoken in the other parts of Armenia.

Aryan in race.

Prof. Neumann claims the Armenian as belonging to the old Medo-Persian family, "so that most of the

* This fact is adduced by Mr. Marsh, as an evidence that even the grammar of one race may become mingled with that of another (Orig. and Hist. of Eng. Lang., p. 46); but it seems true, here, only to a limited extent in the cities. Dr. W. H. Thompson, who has spent his life among these races, assures the author, that the Armenians only speak Turkish where they are a small minority in the midst of Turks.

Median words preserved by Herodotus can be explained by means of the Armenian." This is questioned, however.

In physique, the Armenians are handsome and well made, with dark complexions. They are a sober, industrious, frugal, and hospitable people.

PART FIFTH.

OCEANIC ETHNOGRAPHY.

CHAPTER XIX.

THE RACES OF OCEANICA.

WE shall use the term OCEANICA, in the sense in which it is applied by many writers on ethnography, as describing all the land comprised between the coasts of Asia and America, including the East Indian Archipelago, the many smaller clusters of the Pacific, and the continent of New Holland.

Uncertainty of race.

The whole subject, of the distinctions in race among the wild inhabitants who have settled on these countless islands—the "nomads of the sea," as Prof. Müller calls them, is even more intricate and involved than the differences among the nomads of the land. The languages of many of the tribes have never even been compared, and some of them are scarcely known at all, so that all conclusions must necessarily, as yet, be very doubtful and liable to much change hereafter.

There are at least two very different schools on this subject, each represented by high authority. One, led by the celebrated William Von Humboldt, assigns but two, or at most three, races of men to this immense range of inhabitable land, namely the Malay, the Polynesian and a race of Oriental negroes.

Humboldt and Crawfurd.

The other, represented by a scholar of great ability, Mr. J. Crawfurd, divides the inhabitants of Oceanica into five brown races, with lank hair, distinguished by varieties of language; and eight races of Oriental negroes. The tendency, however, of all late investigation is toward the unity of these varieties, and modern conclusions approach those of Humboldt much more than those of Crawfurd.

General divisions.

OCEANICA may be divided into five great divisions: (1.) *Malaisia*, or the East Indian Islands, together with the peninsula of Malacca, inhabited by the Malay race. Of these islands the most prominent are Sumatra, Java, Borneo, Celebes, Molucca, Sooloo, and the Philippines. (2.) *Melanesia*, or the islands inhabited by a dark race, with woolly or frizzled hair, comprising New Guinea, Arroo, Mysol, and others, together with New Britain, New Ireland, the Solomon Isles, and New Hebrides. (3.) *Australia*, or New Holland, a vast island sparsely peopled by a black race, with straight, smooth hair. (4.) *Micronesia*, a long range of little groups of islands and strips of coral rock in the North Pacific, east of the Philippines, including the Pelew, Ladrone, Bānabē, and numerous other islands from 132° E. longitude to 178° W.; and from 21° N. latitude to 5° S. (5.) *Polynesia*, or the islands in the East Pacific, occupied by a race kindred to the Malay, of which the best known are the Navigators, the Friendly, Society and Sandwich islands, together with New Zealand.

Malaisia.

Melanesia.

Australia.

Micronesia.

Polynesia.

The great natural peculiarities of this quarter of the globe which have determined the divisions of race and family, have been its insular character, the periodicity of its winds and the malarious climate of some of the islands; while the existence of a people on its western border, with a highly-flexible and euphonious language, and gifted with much enterprise—the Malay race—has affected the ruling stock through all this wide region. These nomads of the sea, whenever desiring adventure, or seeking commerce or plunder, or driven forth by defeat or by hunger, had only to put themselves and their wives, with their few utensils into their light canoes, and trust themselves to the prevailing trade winds, and they were certain, finally, to land on some new island, where they could either intermingle with the old inhabitants, or form a new community. It is thus that the almost countless islands, from the Philippines to Easter Island, through 8000 miles of ocean, were peopled by a similar race.

Determining causes of race.

There were certain of the islands, which only admitted of the habitation of the black tribes, owing to the highly malarious character of the climate, and upon them especially these tribes are found.

The climate has probably protected them against the assaults of the more organized nations. Whether they were the original settlers, it is impossible to determine. Their usual position on the mountains, in the interior of an island, would indicate an earlier habitation. Possibly, as is supposed by some ethnologists, their appearance here may date back to an immense antiquity, before all the islands were separated from one another or from the Asiatic Continent;* while their colour and

* Both Dana and Hale notice evidences of a gradual subsidence of the land, even in the historic period; the ruins of temples on Bānabē for instance, being found partly submerged by the sea.

their power of resisting malarious influences may be due to the gradual accumulation and transmission of advantageous changes, adapting them to their circumstances, through vastly-extended periods of time.

Judging from the gradual change in language and customs as well as from other indications, the great movement of the Oceanican peoples must have been from west to east, against the prevailing trade wind; and investigations show that even now, at peculiar seasons of the year, there are regular winds blowing from the west, which drift the natives hundreds and thousands of miles.

Principal migration eastward.

One great link has, perhaps, been discovered by Prof. Müller and others, showing the connection between the nomads of the sea and the nomads of the lands, in their investigations into the Taï and Malay languages. It appears from these, that these two bodies of language resemble each other in the following particulars:—

Links between Taï and Malay languages.

(1.) In the want of inflections. (2.) In the fact that particles expressing grammatical inflections, which, in certain languages, must always be placed after the root, in these languages can be either pre- or post-positions. (3.) The genitive is expressed by juxtaposition, and the governed word is last—the reverse of the Chinese. (4.) The accusative takes no preposition. (5.) Other cases are formed by prepositions. (6.) The plural is expressed by an adjective, and the singular often by the addition of the numeral *one*. (7.) Gender is not expressed except by the addition of a word. (8.) The adjective fellows the noun. (9.) Comparison is expressed by a proposition. (10.) Malay numerals resemble the Taï and the Turanian method, in forming the number 8 by writing 10 – 2, and 9 by 10 – 1. (11.) These languages, together with the Burmese and the Chinese, have a common peculiarity in the use of a word, corresponding to our word, *head* or *sail*. As, for instance, they describe beasts, birds, fish, or reptiles, as so many "*tail;*" or trees, logs, spars, or javelins, as so many "*stems;*" or cannon, guns, candles, torches, and letters, as so many "*tops.*"

These generic exponents or numerical affixes are entirely peculiar to those languages. Many other evidences are adduced of the relation between the languages of the islands and the Asiatic continent, so that if this connection be fairly established, the language of a vast portion of Oceanica may be included in the great Turanian family.

The Malays.

Malay area.

Besides the large islands, which have already been spoken of as occupied by this family, they hold also the small islands south of the Philippines up to the west coast of New Guinea, and those on the east point of Java, as well as those between Java and Sumatra, up to the straits of Malacca. Their language, which is found purest on the Philippines, is one of the most widely extended of Asia, traces of it being discovered from Madagascar to Easter Island, and from Formosa to New Zealand, over 70 degrees of latitude and 200 of longitude. This race has for ages possessed the knowledge of letters, worked metals and domesticated useful animals, and has led the commerce and enterprise of the Pacific Ocean. The flexibility of its tongue has made it everywhere the medium of communication, and even in Madagascar, at 3000 miles distance, Malay words form one fifty-seventh of the vocabulary of the islanders. The Malay conquests and settlements, after the remote emigration from the continent, are supposed by Crawfurd to have begun from the centre of Sumatra, and to have first extended to the Malay Peninsula and the coasts of Borneo. Their influence was only excluded from two quarters by different causes—from the Asiatic shores by the superior

Chinese civilization already prevailing there, and from Australia by the great degradation of the inhabitants. Physical obstacles alone prevented their reaching the coasts of America. The Malay language shows that it has been acted upon by both Indian and Chinese influences.

The Malay bodily type is described by Prichard as Indo-Chinese. The nose is short, but not flat, the mouth large and lips thin, cheek-bones high, and face broadest at that point; the complexion yellowish. The form is squat, and height only about five feet three or four inches.

Physique.

The Polynesians.

The second great race, of similar physical structure and language with the Malays and undoubtedly of the same origin, are the Polynesians. The islands especially occupied by this people are those lying between New Zealand and Easter Isle, north up to the Sandwich Islands, and west as far as the Fejee and New Hebrides. Mixtures of this with other races are found all over the islands of the Pacific. They were for centuries a half-civilized people, and have possessed a well-established government, together with religious doctrines and usages, and a sacred language unintelligible to the people, as well as a system of ecclesiastical authority. They exhibited skill in various arts, and were bold and experienced as sailors. They had no writing, but possessed many legends and traditional poetry. Yet they and their kindred, the Malay race, have the infamy of being the principal and almost the only race indulging habitually in cannibalism.

History obtained from language.

Physically, the Polynesians are placed among the class of light-brown complexion, verging to white.

They are described by Hale, as above the middle height, well formed, with thick strong black hair, slightly curled, and scanty beard; the head short and broad, and higher than most races in their stage of development, with a remarkably flat posterior head, like that of the American Indians. In disposition, they are represented as good-humoured and fickle, and very ready to adopt new usages.

The Polynesian language, Hale supposes to have spread especially from Bouro, the easternmost of the Malay islands.

The whole number of the Polynesians proper is less than 500,000.

From the evidence of language, Mr. Crawfurd concludes that there was, in the ante-historic times, a great Polynesian nation, whose speech lies at the basis of all the various Malay and Polynesian languages at the present day. This people—judging from the records preserved in the words they have transmitted—had made some progress in agriculture and understood the use of gold and iron; were clothed "with a fabric made of the fibrous bark of plants, which they wove in the loom," while knowing nothing of the manufacture of cotton, which they acquired afterwards from India. They had tamed the cow and the buffalo, and possessed and fed upon the hog, the domestic fowl and the duck.

Crawfurd's theory.

The massive ruins and remains of pyramidal structures and terraced buildings on the Pacific Islands, are probably from this primeval race.

The Micronesians.

Micronesia, as was before stated, embraces a long range of small islands in the North Pacific, east of the Philippines, including the Pelew, Ladrone, Bānabē, and others, from 132° east longitude to 178° west; and from 21° north latitude to 5° south.

Owing to the peculiar position of these islands, they are exposed to winds blowing from various quarters, so that the emigration which settled them, would naturally be from many different sources. In physical type, the people are of reddish-brown complexion, rough skin and high bold features; the head is high, compared with its breadth, hair black and curled. They show skill in various arts, and, in Hale's view, give indications of having descended from a higher to a lower civilization. In advance of the Polynesians, they possess the art of varnishing and of weaving; they also understand steering by the stars. The practice of tattooing is observed, not only for decency or ornament, as with other tribes, but for the purpose of distinguishing clans and memorizing events. Their government is more intricate than that of the Polynesians, and their religion is different, resembling more that of Eastern Asia, and recognizing the worship of parents. *Taboo* is not in use. On some of the islands, as Bānabē and others, architectural ruins of a remarkable appearance are found. The language of Tarawa contains a mixture of Polynesian and Melanesian or Papuan, but, on the whole, it is uncertain if there is a distinct Micronesian race.

Physique.

Arts.

Remarkable ruins.

The Melanesians.

The black tribes of Oceanica present a difficult subject to the student of races. Not enough is known of their languages to affirm either as to their origin or their divisions.

They are found first in the west, on the Andaman Islands, between 10° and 14° north latitude. These

Melanesians, or Negrillos, are considered by Professor Owen as the lowest of mankind. They have no tradition or history; no inventions, except door-mats, and bows and arrows; no agriculture, and their habitations are the rudest and most primitive. Both sexes go naked without shame, and families and wives are in common. According to the same authority, the Andamans have no notion of Deity, or spiritual beings, or a future state; an assertion which does not seem easily proved. They are not cannibals, but show a great hostility to strangers. Neither skull nor teeth present the characteristics of the lowest African tribes. Prognathism is no more common than in most of the South Asiatic peoples; the hair resembles that of the Papuans and Australians, as well as of the lower African negroes. They approach the orangs and chimpanzees in their diminutive stature, but show the well-balanced human proportion of trunk to limbs. Latham states that there is a very evident link of connection between the language of the Andamans and the monosyllabic Burmese.

Andaman blacks.

The black tribes next appear in the Nicobar Islands; then upon the mountains of Malacca, where they are called "Semangs," and in the Philippines, where, under the name of *Negritos*,* they number about 25,000. On Luçon, there are 3000 of them under the Spanish rule.

* The Negritos are said by Bowring to possess a remarkable facility in the use of their *toes*, and their feet are marked by a greater separation of the toes than is usual. They can descend the rigging of a ship, head downward, clinging with their feet.

They are slight in form, agile, small and thin, with handsome face and dark copper complexion. The hair is black and curly; head small and round; forehead narrow; eyes large and penetrating, and veiled by very long eyelids; the nose of medium size, slightly depressed; mouth and lips medium; teeth long. (Sir J. Bowring's Visit to Phil. Islands.)

On Ceram, a tribe of them is found so low, as to live in trees instead of huts. A wild race of blacks is supposed also to occupy the interior of Borneo, though there is not full evidence of it.

Black tribes.

Crawfurd supposes that there is but one race of Oriental negroes, as these blacks are called, north of the equator, and two races south in the Malay Archipelago, and on New Guinea. Of these latter, one has the negro features, but not in the extreme. The hair is frizzled, long and bushy, skin of lighter colour, forehead higher, and the posterior head not "cut off," as it were. The nose projects, the upper lip is longer, and prominent, and the lower very projecting. The other race he distinguishes by its lank hair.

The more general conclusion now is, that there is but one race of Oriental negroes, even including the black Australians and the inhabitants of Van Dieman's Land. Latham doubts even the existence of the negro tribes on the smaller islands of Melanesia.

One race of negroes.

"The Australian languages are more like the Malay and the Polynesian than they are like anything else." There are often, he allows, greater approaches of the black to the brown tribes in language than the received physical divisions would justify.

The black tribes are not considered, by travellers, as inferior in capacity to the brown, but they are peculiarly wild and impatient of control, and thus not easily organized, so that they readily fall under the power of the Malays. It is not found to be true that the blacks disappear before the advance of civilization in the Eastern Ocean. On the contrary, in some islands, even the most civilized, they have increased; but the great cause of their decrease is to be found in the bitter hostility and superior organization of the Malays and Polynesians.

Without the knowledge of their languages, these physical divisions are not sufficient to determine origin or the divisions of race. The probability is, that these black tribes are off-shoots from the ancient black races of India and Asia, scattered widely by the conquest of others, or their own pursuit of plunder, over the Pacific Islands. A black tribe is known still to exist on the mountains between Cochin-China and Cambodia, called the *Moys*, which may be a portion of their ancestral people. On some of the many islands which the black nations settled, they were extirpated, or were driven to the mountains, where they are still found; on others, the malarious climate defended them from foreign encroachment, and on others, they became mingled with a different race. Many of the Melanesian tribes present great mixtures of blood.

Probable connection with Asia.

The Papuas, who are distinguished by spirally-twisted hair, frizzled and dressed by them in a huge mass above the head, are a cross of the dark races with the Malays. The Eastern Islands—as Tanna and others—show Polynesian blood. Timor contains within its limits every variety of colour and hair. The Feejees * are probably a mixture of Papuans and Polynesians. In their mould, they are said by Mr. Williams to be decidedly European, with very large and powerful frames. The face is oval, profile vertical, nose well-shaped, but the hair frizzled and bushy. The complexion is between the black and brown—sometimes

Papuas.

* The Feejee Islands Mr. Williams supposes to be the point where the Asiatic and African elements among the Polynesians unite. (Fiji, &c., p. 12.)

H. C. von der Gabelentz finds evidence of the mixture of Polynesian and Melanesian in the Feejee language. (Die Melan. Spr., Leipzig, 1860.)

almost "purple." The nearest approach to the negro is on the island of Kandavu. The Feejees resemble the blacks in their use of the bow, and the manufacture of their pottery, and the Polynesians in the making of their paper-cloth, the preparation of *Kava*, and the practice of tattooing. The language contains one-fifth of Polynesian words and four-fifths unlike any other tongue. The aborigines of Van Dieman's Land are classed by some among the Papuans. The Melanesians are notoriously sullen of disposition and deficient in enterprise, and manifest a different temperament from either that of the Polynesians or Africans.

Feejees.

The prominent distinction between the languages of the negro and the brown races, Crawfurd states to be, that the first contain more consonants in proportion to vowels, and more harsh combinations of consonants than the latter.

H. C. von der Gabelentz has made a careful investigation of the dialects of many of the Melanesian tribes. Those, for instance, of the inhabitants of the *Feejee Islands*, of *Annatom*, *Erromango*, *Tana*, *Mallikolo*, *Marè*, *Lifu*, *Baladea*, *Bauro*, and *Guadalcanar*.

His deliberate and carefully-formed conclusion is that all the Melanesian languages, though disintegrated and apparently separated from one another, owing to the barbarism and isolation of each of the tribes, do yet belong to one stock. He is also of opinion that both in roots and in many grammatical peculiarities, there are numerous remarkable resemblances between the Polynesian and Melanesian, so that the hypothesis of their common origin is a highly probable one.

Melanesians of one race.

If this be hereafter more fully demonstrated, the whole vast population of brown and black peoples, the

Malays, Polynesians, and Melanesians may be referred to one source, and, in all probability, be joined with the Turanian races of Asia.

Latham makes a separate division of the Oceanican languages into the "Papua class," comprising those of North Britannia, North Hanover, North Ireland, Solomon Islands, &c., Mallicollô, Erromango, Annatom, &c., &c.

The Australians.

Different accounts of their physique.

The inhabitants of Australia and Van Dieman's Land, belonging to the black races, are pronounced to be almost the lowest of mankind. They have no government, and their religion consists only of the most childish or debased superstitions. Their physical type seems a cross of the Malay and the African, the most distinguishing feature being the long, fine, wavy hair, like the hair of a European. The evidence with reference to their physique is quite conflicting. Many of them are said to show a deficiency of *bone* in their structure; and some tribes are represented as so degenerated, physically, as to resemble *crétins*, and to be in process of extinction. On the other hand, Pickering states that one of the finest types of muscular frame and the most classic mould of head he has ever beheld, he saw among the Australian natives. He speaks of them as active, strongly-formed, and stately. Various physical types probably exist among them. In general, the features are as follows: the forehead is narrow, mouth large, with thick lips; the nose depressed, and widened at the base, but often aquiline; the beard thick, the form slight though well-proportioned, and colour black. The number of these blacks in Australia is said to be about 200,000. They are supposed to be all of the same stock, though this conclusion is derived more from a resemblance discovered in a few words than a close comparison of grammar. Not a Malay word is found in their language. Of their character, a competent witness (Rev. William Ridley) says, that they are deficient in forethought and concentrativeness, but that in mental *acumen* and in quickness of sight and hearing, they are superior to the whites. They are generous, honest to one another, and often attentive to the weak and the aged, though cruel to women. Notwithstanding their barbarous condition, there exists among them a very strict division of castes, and a certain kind of priesthood.

It is interesting to know what capacities the lowest tribe or race of the human family may show. We learn, from quotations of a recent report to the English Government on this subject, that the Australian negroes show minds quick and keen—"rather like a treasure sealed up than a vacuum." Their perceptive faculties are remarkable—far superior to those of Europeans, while, as might be expected, they are deficient in the reflective powers. As a consequence, the children are found to learn an external study, as geography, with great readiness, though showing much inaptitude for an abstract study, like arithmetic. Mr. Parker, a Visiting Magistrate of the school in Mount Franklin, says that the native children manifest just as great capacities for improvement as do English children, and that the main obstacle to their elevation is from moral rather than physical causes.

Their capacity.

Favourable accounts.

The numerals of the Australian languages rarely reach *five*, and generally stop at three. Some affinities have been discovered between them and the Tamul.

We have classed the Tasmanian tribes (of Van Dieman's Land) with them, but the basis for classification is, as yet, extremely uncertain.

The great difficulty in determining the races of Oceanica is, that the tendency of a nomadic people to continually form new words and new languages as they found new colonies, is here intensified by the separation which the sea naturally causes. There is something, too, in the disposition of the black races which has, doubtless, increased this tendency to disintegration. Crawfurd, who may have exaggerated in this particular, states that there are forty languages on the little island of Timor, and many hundreds in Borneo.

Tendency to new dialects.

Nearly all writers allow that climate and circumstances have produced the most marked effects here on persons of the same race. Among the Tahitians and Maorians, for instance, the lowest castes are found nearly as black as negroes, and with crisp, woolly hair, while the higher—the chiefs and others—less exposed to the sun and to the influences of the weather, resemble Europeans both in features and complexion, though both, there is every reason to believe, belong to the Polynesian race. Similar differences are observed in New Zealand among the blacks.

Effects of climate.

The Semangs—the blacks of Malacca—are brown where not exposed to the sun, and in language and character have so strong a resemblance to the Malays as to be considered by many a tribe of that race.

The points of resemblance between the Polynesians and the Central American Indians are so striking as to induce many writers to assign the same origin to both peoples.

The Asiatic origin of the Malayo-Polynesian races seems to us clearly indicated, so that these resemblances cannot be considered in this connection.

Asiatic origin.

PART SIXTH.

ETHNOLOGY OF AFRICA.

CHAPTER XX.

I. THE SEMITIC TRIBES.

(a.) *The Berbers.*

LONG before recorded history, perhaps even before the full formation of their distinctive language, that family of mankind from which the Semitic tribes have come, poured forth its hordes from Asia over the northern portion of Africa. Of these, one vigorous tribe, with the tenacity of the Semitic stock, have held possession of the valleys of the Atlas, under all the successive waves of conquest which have passed over Northern Africa. The colonies and conquests of the Phœnicians, the Romans, the Byzantines, the Vandals, and the Arabs, have not destroyed or absorbed this tough and warlike people. Pressed farther to the south by the fierce attacks of the Arabs, in the first half of the eleventh century, they could not be driven from the desert; and they hold, now, a larger extent of territory than is occupied by any other race on African soil. From the Atlantic Ocean, on the west, their tribes extend to the borders of Egypt on the east, and from the Atlas chain on the

Tenacity and antiquity of Berbers.

north over the oases of the Great Desert to the region of the Niger and Sudan on the south.

Their traders form the great media of commerce between Central Africa and the Mediterranean coast, while their wild and nomad hordes are the especial obstacle and danger to the traveller. They are known under the name of Libyans, in the most ancient history; their distinguishing features are beheld even on the pictures of Egyptian monuments,* and, on the other hand, the most warlike and distinguished of modern military corps is formed originally of their soldiers, the *Zouaves.*†

Libyans.

The name by which this race is best known is BERBER, a word much disputed, but whose origin may be naturally traced to the Roman name of these people, *Barbari.* The name which they most habitually give themselves is *Mazigh*, or *Imóshagh* (Freemen), but that which modern travellers usually apply is *Tawárek.* This latter, Dr. Barth supposes derived from an Arabic expression, implying that they had "changed" their religion, having all, in his opinion, been at one time Christians. The Berber language is a direct descendant from the ancient Libyan, and the antique bi-lingual rock-inscriptions in Northern Africa, show that not only the idioms, but many of the letters used by the Numidians are still employed by the modern Berbers.

Tawárek.

The Berbers, like most of the Semites, have inclined to monotheism, and but few have been pagans; the great majority now professing Mohammedanism. This

* Dr. Barth says that they are clearly to be recognized as the *Tămhŭ* of the Egyptian monuments, a people of very light colour, with a peculiar curl on the right side of the head, and ear-rings, similar to those worn at the present day.

† The Berbers are called *Shawi*, or "Nomads," in Algeria, corrupted in Tunis into *Suav*, (French) Zouave. (Prof. Müller.)

race, beside the names already mentioned, receives various titles, according to the countries which it occupies. Those in the northern part of Morocco, are called *Shulu*, and those in the hill-country of Tunis and Algeria, *Kabyls*, or "mountaineers."

Kabyls.

The Kabyls have been interesting to the student of history from the vigorous resistance which they have offered to the French arms, and from their supposed descent from the ancient Teutonic tribe of Vandals. Their long fair hair and blonde appearance, the traditions current among them of their Christian origin, the custom of tattooing the cross on their foreheads, and the high position which woman holds, compared with the little respect paid her among other tribes, all favour this view; but their language shows no trace of Teutonic origin, and the opinion has become general that they belong alone to the Berbers. They were, no doubt, exposed for a considerable time to Vandal influences.

Teutonic peculiarities.

They are described as a savage, liberty-loving, warlike people, inhospitable and faithless. It has been extremely difficult for the French to subdue them, but their want of cavalry and their more settled habitations have exposed them to assaults, from which the nomadic Arabs are delivered. They are not entirely barbarous, but are good agriculturists, and are well versed in some mechanical arts, such as the manufacture of arms and gunpowder, and the building of stone houses. They vary in appearance; in the plains, being more often dark, and short in stature, while those on the mountains are of light complexion and tall form.

Varying physique.

The *Tawárek*, or Berbers of the desert, are described by traders as the tribe of the most beautiful type among all the African races. They are fair, tall, and well-made, with full beard, and of a warlike and even quarrelsome disposition. A servile part of the same race, the *Imghád*, are almost black, though presenting no other negro features, an effect, perhaps, of inferior comfort and additional exposure to the weather. A distinguishing mark in costume of the Tawárek is the custom of wearing a covering over the mouth. In general they are a nomadic people, though some tribes possess villages and settled dwelling places. Their women are freer than among the Arabs, and take more part in public affairs. Precisely the same language is spoken by them over a great extent of territory—the same in Agades as in Ghat or Timbuctoo.

Black Tawárek.

The *Temght*—the dialect of the Southwestern Tawárek—differs from the Shilluh, the Kabyl, or the Ghadami, as the Portuguese differs, for instance, from the Spanish or Italian.

In many cases this people have intermarried with negro races, and the offspring are looked on with contempt by the purer Berber tribes. The inhabitants of the oasis Air or Asben—the *Kelowi*—are a cross of the Berbers and negroes, and unite, says Dr. Barth, "the severe, austere manner and fine figure of the Berber with the playful and cheerful character and darker colour of the African."

Intermarriage with blacks.

The Kelowi are distinguished also by their living in settled habitations.

The Tawárek are divided into numerous tribes who are usually hostile to one another; of these, the purest are the *Hogar* and *Azkar*, between Ghat and Tawat, and the *Awelimmiden* and *Tademekket* on the Niger. The *Tinylkum*, in Fezzan, and the *Busane*, between Asben and Haussa, are much more mingled with other races.

The ruling tribe of the important kingdom of Bornu, lying between Lake Tsád on the east, and Lake Yeou on the west, is Berber; and many Berber tribes have formerly mingled with the people, though the language spoken there—that of the *Kanuri*—is rather of the Turanian.

Of the Kanuri, Mr. Norris says: "Its nouns are fully declined by post-fixed syllables; its roots are not subject to any modifications; it forms its plural by adding a syllable; it has an accusative case; it uses possessive pronominal affixes; it has negative verbs, and its verbs have distinct personal endings, which are however, unconnected with existing pronouns. There appear also some traces of the Tartar vocalic harmony. Arabic words are found in the language, though not many."

The Kanuri people have the usual physical characteristics of what is called the negro. Their religion is Mohammedan.

The *Tibboo*, or *Tébu*, a black people inhabiting the eastern part of the Great Desert, remarkable for their handsome European features, are probably a mixture of African with Semitic races. Their language, Dr. Barth states, is closely related to that of the ruling tribe of Bornu. They are divided into a number of tribes. The principal region of the Tébu is Bilma, some hundred miles north of Lake Tsád.

Tibboo.

(b.) *The Haussa.*

In the centre of the continent, in the finest provinces of Negro-land, a black nation has been met with by travellers, whose origin is traced with great probability, through its language, to the Semitic family. They are the *Gober*, or *Haussa*, speaking the Haussa language, and till this century they

Semitic negroes.

possessed an important Empire in Kátsena, Kano, and other neighbouring provinces. Remains of the nation are found as far north as Asben. The fierce Mohammedan invasion by the Fellatah, of which we shall speak hereafter, overthrew their empire. Their central province, Kátsena, is situated on the water-shed between the basin of the Tsád and that of the Kwára, and is one of the most salubrious and productive districts of Central Africa. Dr. Barth thus describes the contrast between the Haussa and the Kanuri of Bornu: "The former are lively, spirited, and cheerful, the latter melancholic, dejected, and brutal. . . . The same difference is visible in their physiognomies, the former having, in general, very pleasing and regular features, and more graceful forms, while the Kanuri, with his broad face, his wide nostrils, and his large bones, makes a far less agreeable impression." (Vol. i. p. 536.)

Haussa Empire.

Others speak of them as having peculiarly open and noble countenances, with prominent nose and expressive black eyes. The *Haussa*, if not entirely Semitic, are at least the connecting link between the tribes of Central Africa and the Northern Semitic nations. When declared Hamitic, as they are by some, it must be remembered that this view does not differ widely from that which makes them Semitic, as those two families are considered by many to be different stages of growth of the same stock.

Hamitic according to some authorities.

THE SEMITES OF EASTERN AFRICA.

(c.) *The Abyssinians.*[1]

This people contain, without doubt, some of the tribes called by the ancients Æthiopians, who, though black, or dark in colour, were conspicuous for the beauty of their type. They are not, however, to be classed with what are named Hamitic tribes. Their language proves them to be distinctly Semitic, and, probably, a colony from Southern Arabia. The *Gheez*—the ancient Abyssinian language, handed down in the Æthiopic version of the Scriptures—is a dialect of the Arabian,[2] and is the same as the Himyaritic of Southern Arabia.

Semitic Æthiopians.

The modern language of the upper classes — the *Amharic*—which has taken the place of the Gheez, is a Semitic language.

As Professor Ritter has shown, Abyssinia is marked by three great natural divisions, which form bases for the divisions of population. There are three tablelands, rising one above another, in lines nearly parallel with the coast. The tribes in these various divisions, though undoubtedly of the same origin, vary in complexion, according to the height of the district they occupy. The *Danakil*, a barbarous people, who inhabit the low grounds near the coast, are black, and usually with long crisped hair. Their expression is lively and pleasant, their features are regular and even fine, and their forms show remarkable vigour. Those in the neighbourhood of Angote have smooth hair. Their language is Semitic, and their own traditions indicate Arabia as the original source of their tribes.

Colour varying with altitude.

The first table-land is the country ruled by the Baharnegash, or Emperor. In Dixan of this region, the inhabitants are spoken of as still dark—the copper hue not appearing to the traveller until he reaches the people of the highest tracts.

The second table-land is the Kingdom of Tigré, or that part of Abyssinia near the Tacazze. It occupies nearly the site of the ancient Kingdom of Axum. Tigré has been a powerful State, till within a late period, and independent of the Emperor of Abyssinia, but during the recent civil wars it has been subdued.

The third mountain district is the Kingdom of the Amharas, the ruling people of the whole country. It embraces the upper course of the Nile, the high region of Gojam, and the provinces of Begunder, Mena, Belassen, and others.

Both the Tigrani and the Amharas speak Semitic dialects, and are of one origin, though the latter are more civilized now than the former. In complexion, they vary, says the Rev. Mr. Gobat, a missionary, through all hues, from black to copper colour, according to their locality. Their features are generally regular and well-formed, and their bodies exceedingly well-proportioned; the hair is sometimes straight, but often crisped or curled. The Amharas are decribed by a French *savant* (Lefebvre), as having very large heads, eyes of remarkable beauty, bodies well-proportioned, hair crisped (though to this there are exceptions), and colour of a brown olive. On the whole, physiologically speaking, the Abyssinians are considered to belong to the black races.

Physique of Amharas.

M. d'Abbadie, who spent eleven years in Abyssinia and the adjacent countries, has come to the conclusion that the differences in colour of the people are due not merely to elevation, but to diet. The tribes that feed on cereals, he states, are generally dark or black and those that live mostly on animal food are red, or of lighter complexion. Thus the "*Hazzo*," who do not like cereals, and live mostly on milk and meat, are very red. The *Tigray*, though under the same burning climate, and of

Colour dependent on diet.

undoubted Semitic blood, are dark and black; they seldom eat flesh. The *Saho*, again, living on cereals, are darker, and often black; the *Gurage*, on the other hand, who eat much flesh, are nearly always red.

That this cannot be the result of mixture with negro blood, or a lighter blood, is shown by the exact names which are given to the slightest crossing of the blood of different races, whereas these tribes are called perfectly pure. The process also of the *darkening of the skin*, is observed to go on here to such a degree that the Amharas have given it a distinct name—*madyat*. Even foreigners suffer from it.

Darkening of skin.

Among the tribes conspicuous for personal beauty, but of jet-black colour, are mentioned by M. Lefebvre, the *Hababdés*, some of the *Chotos*, the *Taltals*, and the *Danakils;* yet with all these, he holds it impossible there could have been any mixture with native African races.

In disposition, the Abyssinians are described as lively and inconstant, with much vanity and self-love; they are also gifted with a considerable talent for eloquence. They are best known to the world now, as the most degraded and superstitious of Christian nations. Though notoriously debased by superstition and shamefully lax in common morality, no people has ever shown such continuing interest in pure doctrine; and the theological dogma of the exact nature of the person of Christ has torn and rent the nation for centuries, with the most bloody and venomous disputes.

Characteristics of Abyssinians.

They have also suffered severely in late years from the fierce invasions of the *Gallas*, a Hamitic nation on the south, of which we shall speak hereafter.

N 2

Abyssinia offers, in its religious customs, many traces of Jewish influence. It is remarkable as containing a native tribe—the *Falashas*—who are Jews in religion and habits, though their language shows that they are not at all of Hebrew stock. Their conversion must date from a period before the conversion of the other tribes to Christianity—that is, previous to the fourth century. They are a quiet, peaceful people, more industrious than the Amharas, and living among the highest mountains of the country, in Samen. They are as ignorant and superstitious as the Christians.

Falashas not Hebrew.

Other tribes of Abyssinia are the Agows, the Gafats, the Gongas, and Enareans, whose origin is not yet distinctly known. The Saho and the Adaiel are Semitic.

The existence of this Arabian colony and this Semitic Christian people in the heart of Africa, preserving its language and its religious customs pure, though modified in physical traits by unknown climatic influences, until the type approaches in many particulars the African, is one of the most interesting that can be presented to the ethnologist and the historian, and deserves more investigation from scholars than it has yet received.

Besides these Semitic races, are others to the southward — the people of Harar and Hurrar — and the numerous pastoral tribes of Somauli, occupying a large territory to the south of the Arabian Gulf as far as the river Juba, and on the coast to Magadoxo. The latter are remarkable for their fine regular features, and long flowing hair, coloured of an artificial flaxen.

The Somauli.

Many show the influences of the African climate and circumstances, in approximation to negro features—a protruding jaw and broad turned-out lips. The beard also is usually thin. The skin, especially of those living in the hot regions, is smooth, black, and glossy, but, says Burton, "as the altitude increases, it becomes lighter, and about Havar it is generally of a *café au lait* colour." There is an approach with many to the *steatopyge*.*

Their language distinctly proves them to be Semitic, and there is no doubt of their origin from Arabia. It is possible, however, that they may have mingled with native black tribes, though there is no sufficient evidence of this.

Semitic origin.

The language of the people of Harar, according to Burton, is a Semitic dialect grafted on a native stock.

Some branches of the Somauli are no doubt intimately related to the *Gallas*, hereafter to be described.

The *Wakuafi* and *Masai*, inhabiting a great district west of Chaga, stretching between two degrees north and four degrees south of the equator, are thought to be of Arabian, or at least Semitic, origin. They are nomad and robber tribes, accustomed to acts of horrible barbarism. In physique they are remarkable for their beauty of feature and form; their colour is dark brown.

They are Pagan in religion, but with an idea of a Supreme Being. Circumcision is practised among them.

(d.) *The Arabs.*

A Semitic immigration, subsequent to that which laid the foundation of all the African tribes thus far described, was the Arabian. This poured itself over all Northern and Central Africa, founding powerful States, and carrying a degree of civilization and literature, and a higher religious belief among the pagan tribes of Negro-land.

* A remarkable hump or accretion of fat on a portion of the body.

The three prominent divisions of the Arabs of the north are called *Cachin*, *Hillel*, and *Machil*. These Arabs occupy the Barbary States and wander over the Great Desert. On the borders of Negro-land they are often mingled with the native black tribes or the Berbers.

Three divisions.

The mixed tribes in Senegambia are the *Trarzas*, *Darmankours*, *Braknas*, and *Dowiches*.

The Arabs of Northern Africa are mostly descendants of the invading tribes who overran Africa in the seventh century, conquering the Berbers and Moors. Though generally pure, they are occasionally, according to Pulszky, crossed with other tribes. Several tribes of Kabyls in the province of Constantine speak Arabic; the Kabyls in the neighbourhood of Ghelma bear a strong resemblance to the Arabs in dress and language and physique. The tribe of the Amrauahs is half Arabic, half Berber; and large numbers of Moors are known to have intermarried with the Arabians.

Arabian mixtures.

The great natural division of the Arabs is into settled Arabs, and roving Arabs, or Bedouins. The Arab country-population of Algeria resemble the original Bedouin, but the pure Bedouins are found only in the Land of Dates and on the confines of the Desert. The Arabic of Barbary is a dialect, and is understood with difficulty, says the authority above quoted, by the Arab Egyptians, and scarcely at all by the pure Arabs.

In North Africa the inhabitants of the plains are Arabs; of the mountains, Kabyls; and of the cities, Moors. The Arabs are the shepherds and nomad warriors; the Moors the peaceful farmers and towns-people; the Kabyls ferocious and plundering tribes who till the soil. The latter, though Semitic in race, differing much in physical appearance

Arabs and Moors.

from the Arabs, and often resembling the Northern European.

The only tie which unites these various nations is that of religion—Mohammedanism; and though nominally under the rule of France, the mountain tribes of Kabyls and the Arabs of the Land of Dates are as free as they ever were.

Numerous Arab tribes have settled in Egypt. Impelled by the two prominent impulses of the Semitic family—the love of gain and religious fanaticism—they penetrated to the most interior portions of Nubia, and subdued the Hamitic or native races. But despite their conquests, the Arabs have never more than pitched their camps in a hostile country, uniting but little in blood with the neighbouring population. Those on the west of the Nile are the *Magdyeh* and *Ellahonyeh;* those on the east of the White Nile, the *Hetsenat* and the *Mohammedyeh;* those in Nubia, the *Chonkryeh;* with many others, whose names it is useless to mention.

No permanent settlements.

In Egypt it may be said generally that those on the left bank of the Nile come from the Barbary States, and those on the right bank from Arabia. The spoken language of the Egyptians is generally Arabian. Arabian colonies and influence have likewise extended over Kordofan, Darfur, Waday, and Bornu; and even as far south as Zanzibar, a royal dynasty of pure Arabian blood sits on the throne. Madagascar itself shows traces of this Semitic race.

Arabs in Egypt.

Many of the Arabs, it appears from various testimony, have been greatly modified in physical type by their residence in Africa. Those of North Africa are described as a strongly-built, handsome race, as tall as the Scotch Highlanders. Their face is usually sun-burnt, with white and hand-

Change of physique.

some teeth, and black eyes, "of a proud and fearless expression," a short beard and moustache, and head shaved with the exception of a single lock. "Their deportment is daring and commanding," but when riding, they habitually bend the head forward. Many travellers consider them the handsomest race in the world. Some tribes of unmixed blood are described as jet-black, though presenting, in other respects, Arabian features.

Through all their migrations in Africa, the Arabs have preserved much of their old independence and isolation; they have disdained to borrow idioms from the African languages; in the midst often of sedentary nations, they have followed their old nomadic habits, and in the Sudan, for instance, they have never embraced the absurd customs, characteristic of the negro peoples, of the breaking out of teeth, tattooing, and *infibulation*.

The following is a table of the Berber and Arab population in the Barbary States:[3]—

	Arabs.	Berbers.
Morocco . . .	3,000,000	8,000,000
Algiers . . .	1,000,000	3,000,000
Tunis . . .	500,000	800,000
Tripoli . . .	300,000	500,000
	4,800,000	12,300,000

(e.) *The Jews.*

This people is to be found in all the cities of Northern Africa, and even extending into the oases of the Great Desert. Everywhere it is a despised and oppressed race. The Jews of Algeria are said to be superior in bodily strength to those of Europe. Their physiognomy has more of the Oriental type than that of the Turks or Moors; and the women are remarkably beautiful. The great majority of the people, as usual, are traders.

A tribe of Jews is described by Mr. Tristram (quoted by Dr. Beddoe, "Ethnol. Trans.," 1861), living in the oasis Waregla, about 32° north latitude, who are "almost as black as negroes," without the slightest trace of negro features; "their lineaments were as distinctly Jewish as in any clothes-dealer in Houndsditch." "They were as dark as the black Jews of Abyssinia;" the hair was "grizzled, without being woolly." He considers the colour an effect of climate.

Black Jews.

Careful investigation seems to show two physical types among the Jews; one dark, with black hair and eyes, and the well-known hooked nose, another with very regular profile and beautiful features, but blonde, with light hair and blue eyes.* This latter type is seen a great deal in the East, especially in Constantinople and Africa; even red hair being often met with. The blonde type is the one from which the traditional representations of the Saviour are made, and is not improbably very ancient among the Jews. The relation of the Jewish type to climate, of which so much is made by Prichard, does not seem to bear the test of closer investigation. (See Dr. Beddoe, "Ethnol. Trans.," London, 1861.)† A peculiar physiological fact in regard to this people should be noticed here, that they are able to live and multiply in almost all latitudes. Their increase in Sweden is said to be greater than that of the Christian population; in the towns of Algeria they are, according to Boudin, the only race

Two Jewish types.

* This type has been seen by the learned travellers of this city, Dr. E. S. Smith and Dr. W. H. Thompson.

† It has been claimed that the complexion and hair of the Jew vary according to climate, being blonde and light in the northern countries, and dark in the southern; but later researches show that the two types above described are found under all climates.

able to maintain its numbers; and "in Cochin-China and Aden—the latter one of the hottest places in the world—they succeed in rearing children, and in forming permanent communities."—Beddoe.

(f.) *The Moors.*

Of the ancient populations of North Africa the Moors are distinguished by their milder manners and their superior education. From an early period they have dwelt in cities and seaports. They are described by Wagner as well-built, but not so tall as the Arabs, and inclined to corpulence. Their features are noble, but not so energetic as those of the Arabs; the complexion of the children is clear, white, and rosy; the men are more brown. Their hair, which is usually shaved, except a single lock, is jet-black; their eyes are also black. The expression of their faces indicates mildness and melancholy. Their bearing is remarkably imposing and dignified.

Of their origin very exact information cannot be given, but there seems little doubt that they are Semitic tribes, perhaps an early offshoot from Arabia, with whose people they are closely united in language and customs. After their entire subjugation by the Arabs, in the seventh and eighth centuries, and the deportation of large numbers of them into Arabia, the two peoples began to unite in marriage and social life, until at last they formed but one nation.

Semitic origin.

The present Moors are supposed to show traces of the blood of the ancient Semitic Mauretanians, as well as of the modern Arabs and the Spanish Arabs.

Mixed blood.

CHAPTER XXI.

THE HAMITIC (OR CHAMITIC) TRIBES OF AFRICA.

IT should be remembered that by the term *Hamitic* races in this treatise, are not meant necessarily either the black races of men, or the supposed descendants of Ham. The name is used as identical with *Chamitic* (Egyptian), or *Kushitic* (Æthiopian), to designate that family of mankind whose more especial representative in antiquity were the Egyptian people, and whose modern descendants are the Kopts, Nubians, and other nations of dark complexion, but with European features. The distinguishing marks of the race are to be found in the language, though it should be borne in mind, that this presents so many analogies and resemblances with the peculiar features of the Semitic family of language, that farther investigations may demonstrate a unity of origin of these two families. At present the presumption is, that the Hamitic nations broke off from the common stock before the Semitic tribes had been developed into distinct races.

Definition of Hamitic.

For this reason the opinions of scholars differ in regard to certain African nations—such as the Berber, the Ghúber (or Haussa), the Gallas, Danakil and Somauli, and others—whether they are Hamitic or Semitic.

Different theories.

We have endeavoured to give what seemed the most trustworthy conclusion in regard to each, under the present aspect of the evidence. Future research, no doubt, will bring the Hamitic and Semitic races into one great family.

(a.) *The Kopts.*[1]

It is remarkable that the only Christian tribe of any importance in Egypt should be direct descendants of the ancient Egyptians. Their language—the modern Koptic—is the representative and offspring of the ancient Koptic. Their faces are said to correspond wonderfully with the faces painted on the monuments or represented in the ancient sculpture, the same high cheek-bones, large lips, light beard, broad nose, brownish complexion, and ears placed high in the head; presenting the same—as a French writer expresses it—" air de majesté et de puissance,"[2] which so impresses the traveller, on those calm and grand faces of Egyptian sculpture.* The Kopts, like their ancestors, are of a grave and melancholic temperament, and, like them, possess much talent for administration and calculation. They are prudent and industrious, and often very shrewd and cunning. They are employed chiefly as accountants and interpreters.[3] In language they make great use of the Arabic. Their creed resembles in many points that of the Roman Catholic Church, except that they believe that the Holy Spirit proceeds from the Father alone. Their priests are ignorant, rigid and prejudiced, but harmless.

Features correspond with old Egyptians.

Creed.

The Kopts are met with principally in Upper and

* A close examination shows that there were varieties of physical type in ancient Egypt as there are in the modern.

Middle Egypt, and but few comparatively in the Delta.

The agricultural Kopts do not differ in appearance from the Fellahs.

The language in its two dialects—the *Sahid* and *Memphite*—still show the ancient division into Upper and Lower Egypt.

(b.) *The Fellahs*[1] *(or Labourers).*

The unfortunate industrious class of Egypt, that which has produced the wealth, and borne all the burdens for its Turanian masters—the Turks—are the *Fellahs.* They are described as a heavy, coarse-featured people, with an habitual expression of childish simplicity and sometimes of clownish cunning on their faces. One prominent peculiarity, corresponding to a well-known feature in the faces of the ancient sculpture, is a heavy eye-lid, protecting and half closing a very keen eye. The complexion is greyish brown, "as of unburnt brick,"[2] warming sometimes into a dark-red flush, not unlike that portrayed in antique Egyptian wall-painting. The mouth has the old Egyptian placidity of expression; the beard is thin. Beside the resemblance of physical traits, many customs and religious ceremonies are discovered among them bearing a strong similarity to those of the ancient Egyptians. The Fellahs with the Kopts are the only race in Egypt which have had time sufficient to become adapted to the climate, and which have thus gained the power of perpetuating themselves. All other races—the Negro and Nubian on the one side, and the Turk, or Arab, or European on the other—though bearing the climate of the Nile in proportion to the quality and grade of mental and physical organization peculiar to each race, equally fail to transmit de-

Physical traits.

scendants beyond the second or third generation.* It seems probable, therefore, that—though sometimes mingled with Arab blood—this degraded, ignorant, filthy and sorely-oppressed class of Mohammedan Fellahs are among the most direct descendants of the ancient Hamitic people, who conquered Æthiopia and overran Asia, and whose learning was a light even to Grecian philosophers.

Probably very ancient.

The physical history of the Egyptians—if the statements on this subject by Gliddon and Pulszky and others be correct—is an instance of the power of the principle of Inheritance in a given race to preserve the type pure, despite certain mixtures with other races, as well as of the process by which a given tribe becomes adapted to its circumstances.†

The first settlers in Egypt—perhaps Asiatics—after a long course of time became *acclimated;* that is, certain variations in organs, physical habits and temperament, adapted to resist the destructive agencies of the climate and soil, were perpetuated,—the offspring born with fewer of these advantages, perishing, and those endowed with a greater degree of them, surviving; until by transmission and this process of "selection," the line is reached in which the physique is adapted to its place, and a new variety or race is formed. These powers of resistance, or, in other words, this new physical organism is attended—we know not why—by certain features and bodily peculiarities, which form the external Egyptian type.

Acclimation.

During many centuries this type was constantly

* Of eighty-three children of Mehemet Ali only five have survived, and similar facts are found true of others.

† The philosophy of Acclimation and the Formation of Varieties will be explained more fully in the chapter on "Unity or Diversity of Origin."

modified, in the higher classes, by crossings with other races: first with the Semitic, under the Phœnician and Canaanite immigrations and conquests; then with the Aryan, under Macedonian, Greek, and Roman invasions, until at length the country fell under Mohammedan rule, and the Fellahs embraced the faith of the Prophet.[2] Under this new religion, they were forbidden to intermarry with strangers, so that since the seventh century the population of Egypt—with the exception, as before mentioned, of some slight Arabic mixture—has recruited itself by intermarriage within its own limits, and the process has again gone on undisturbed, of adapting the physique to its situation and circumstances, and of bringing back the original type. And now, after great variations of type during past centuries, we have restored, the pure antique Egyptian type, closely corresponding to one prominent type represented in the oldest sculpture and painting: and characterizing a variety of men, which, as was before said, is the only human race out of the many that have temporarily occupied Egyptian soil, that has had time sufficient to perpetuate itself.

Return to original type.

(c.) *The Eastern Nubians.*

In the eastern part of Nubia, in the desert between the Nile and the Red Sea, and among the mountains running parallel with the coast, are three tribes of a very ancient race, probably of Hamitic origin—the *Hadharebe*, the *Ababdeh*, and the *Bishari*, the modern representatives of the old Æthiopians. Renan classes their language as probably of the Hamitic family, which other writers confirm, while their physical type is neither that of the full-blooded negro, nor Semitic like the Arab. They are

Probably Hamitic.

usually of a very dark colour—sometimes black*—with regular European features. The Bishari are the most powerful of these tribes, and their country extends northward from the frontier of Abyssinia[3] to the latitude of Derr, and from Sennaar on the Nile to Dar Berber and the Red Sea. They are a shrewd, active nomad people, not of large stature and with pleasant features.

The Ababdeh, who inhabit a wild country from Kosseir to Nubia, are small and badly made, but full of vigour. Their eyes are large and their teeth fine. They have the black skin, but regular features, with curled hair.

The Eastern Nubian or Bisharine race is thought to be descended from the ancient Blemies, and, like the Kopts and the Fellahs, is without doubt one of the oldest of existing peoples.

(d.) *The Gallas.*[1]

To the south of the Hamitic tribes on the Nile, and encircling Abyssinia, is a warlike, barbarous people, who are ranked among the Hamitic races from the evidence of their language, though this, also, shows more than the usual affinities to the Semitic. This people—the Gallas—have been the terror for more than three centuries of the Abyssinians, upon whose territory they are constantly encroaching. They are divided

Gallas tribes.

into more than twenty tribes, but the prominent divisions are the *Bertuma*, or East-Gallas, and the *Boran*, or West-Gallas. They are described by D'Hericourt as a tall, handsome race, with

* Dr. E. S. Smith, of New York, who has spent three years among the Arabs, speaks of these Nubians as truly remarkable for blackness. The colour is a kind of deep coal-black, quite different from the usual lighter black which we see in the African of the coasts.

large forehead, aquiline nose and well-cut mouth. Their colour is coppery, and the hair curled.

A few profess to be Christians, but the most are Pagans or Mohammedans. Those in the Kingdom of Choa number about a million and a half. They are especially infamous as slave-dealers.

The heathen Gallas extend from the equator to about 4° south latitude. Their number is from eight to ten millions. They are an exceedingly savage and cruel people, and are said to delight in drinking blood from animals still living. The *Ukuafi*, south of the Gallas, are in such a barbarous condition that they do not even bury their dead, but leave them to the wild animals.

(e.) *The People of Sennaar (probably Hamitic).*

To the south of Nubia lies the high mountain-plateau of Sennaar, inhabited by a dark-brown tribe, which Renan classes as probably Hamitic. Nothing certain, however, can as yet be concluded about the origin of this nation. In general, they present frizzled hair and dark complexion, but regular and agreeable features. A considerable variety in colour is seen among them; even the red tint, with reddish hair and eyes.

BLACK RACES OF UNCERTAIN ORIGIN IN EASTERN AFRICA.

The Barábra or Berberins of Nubia.[1]

The reader may see in any book of plates, or in stereoscopic views of Nubia, the representation of the Egyptian Kings carved in the rock at Abu-Simbal. The type here presented, the long oval face, the finely-curved nose, broad at the top, with full nostrils, the voluptuous lips and high cheek-bones, and rich bronze colour, are the characteristics of the modern Nubian, the descendant of the ancient race

Physical type.

of Æthiopians—the Nubæ—who crowded the banks of the Nile with their gigantic works of art.

Many of the modern Nubians, or Berberins, are black, especially as they approach the south, but with fine and even noble features, and hair, though frizzled, never woolly. In character they are distinguished for their independence, their honesty and faithfulness; so much so, as to hold in Egypt something of the position which the Swiss do in Europe, of guards and trusty servants and porters. Like that nation they are greatly attached to their native soil. They are not remarkable for cleanliness, and live nearly naked in Nubia. There are scarcely any upper classes among them, and the masses are much better educated than those of Egypt. Great jealousy and dislike exist between them and the Arabs.

The African nations are remarkable as being almost the only peoples with whom Christianity has entirely died out and been replaced by another belief.

Ancient Christian nations.

We have already seen that the Tawáreks of the Berber race are supposed to have been formerly Christians, though now bigoted Mohammedans or Pagans. Some writers have concluded that the Pagan and Mohammedan Gallas were once a Christian people; whether this be the truth regarding those tribes or not, it is well known that the Nubian Berberins were once Christians, and that Christianity began to decline about 1517 A.D., after the Mohammedan invasion of Sultan Selim. In the year 1673 the Nubian churches were entire, but closed. There are now only a few superstitious relics remaining of the early faith.

Possibly the fire of the Mohammedan conquest and the physical power of the early Arab invasion, may be the causes of this defection among African nations; or possibly there may be something in the Semitic temperament which inclines it to a reverential monotheism and a system of arbitrary law, rather than to the free spiritual life and affectional relations of the Christian system.

The Berberins, notwithstanding their name, have no connection with the Berbers, and though their physical type is almost precisely what may be called the Hamitic type, they are not found to be connected either with the Hamitic or Semitic races. Their language is distinct. It is remarkable as containing no genders, except in personal pronouns, and no numerals above twenty.[2] Arabic words are in constant use by the people. From the evidence of language, Prichard derives the Nubians from a negro tribe, called Noubas, of Kordofan, and supposes that the negro type has changed in the process of centuries, to the present type. Farther investigation will be needed for the settlement of this question.

Origin doubtful.

The present limits of the Nubians are from Assuan on the north, to Sennaar on the south; and their principal divisions are the Kenoos in the north, and the Nouba farther up the Nile.

People of the White Nile. The inhabitants, from the Chillouks to the Baris, are negroes; but with the *Keks*, *Bohrs*, and *Tschers*, and others, a new element appears —the European type of feature with the black skin; resulting, as M. de St. Martin supposes, from a cross of the Gallas with the negroes. The figure is full and handsome, and the face often beautiful in outline, but the spirit is degraded. No belief in a God is discovered among them; they do not even understand agriculture, and they are generally unclothed.

Wild tribes.

The following table will show the proportion of d ferent races in Egypt in 1844:—

Mohammedan Fellahs	1,600,000
Christian Kopts	150,000
(Osmanlis) Turks	12,000
(Bedouin) Arabs	70,000
Negroes (slaves)	10,000
Circassians, Georgians, &c., (slaves)	5,000
Jews	7,000
Syrians	5,000
Greeks and Romans	7,000
Europeans	9,500
Berberins	5,000

CHAPTER XXII.

THE RACES OF WESTERN AFRICA, NORTH OF THE MOUNTAINS OF THE MOON.

A NATURAL division of the continent of Africa is formed by the two great spurs of the Mountains of the Moon, which are thrown off parallel to the western coast, the one north and the other south. These mountains, known as the Kong Mountains, extend along the coast for 2000 miles, and at a distance of only from 100 to 350 miles from the ocean. The narrow strip of country shut up between these high lands and the Atlantic, and reaching from the southern borders of the Great Desert to nearly 16° south latitude, is generally known as WESTERN AFRICA.

Geographical divisions.

Its prominent physical peculiarities, which in part determine the character of its peoples, are the want of good bays and harbours, thus cutting it off from foreign commerce; the wide belt of malarious jungle, which, for a hundred miles within, guards its coast from invasion or settlement, especially by whites, and the mountains on the east which separate the country from the whole interior.

All these obstacles have indeed been overcome, but all have more or less aided in forming the race-characteristics of each family of tribes.

Western Africa is interesting to the student of races, as containing that exceptional type in Africa—the so-called "pure negro type." Its natural divisions, which are at once separations of country and of race, are (1.) *Senegambia;* (2.) *North Guinea;* (3.) *South Guinea.*

I. SENEGAMBIA—the flat country extending from the Great Desert to 10° north latitude, and watered by the Senegal and the Gambia, contains three prominent races, who have by no means confined themselves to the limits of the country—the *Fellatah*, the *Iolofs* (or *Wolofs*), and the *Mandingoes.**

The Fellatah or Fúlbe.[1]

For some time the existence of an important people in the west of Africa has been known, who differed both from the Berbers on the north and the negro tribes immediately surrounding them. They were represented by travellers as conspicuous for their noble bearing, their fine and Aryan features, and for the intelligence and poetic feeling which they displayed. Their colour was a rich brown, often no darker than that of Spaniards or Portuguese: certain portions of the nation were black, with smooth hair, and others of the lowest class were grayish-black. Their disposition contrasted with that of the Africans in being grave and reserved, with the capacity for the most fanatical enthusiasm; their pursuits were pastoral and their mode of life nomadic, in the midst of settled black tribes engaged in agriculture and commerce. Their language, too, had no relation with the dialects of the neighbouring tribes, and if connected at all with the languages of Africa must be traced to those of the Southern provinces. This people—the Fúlbe (sing. Pullo), or Féllatah, or Fullan, or Féllani, are interesting to the student of present history, as having enacted,

A brown tribe.

* Wilson's statement that these three are of one stock is contradicted by Kölle on apparently good evidence.

within this century, on the plains of Africa, something of the part played so formidably by the Arabians in Asia under Mohammed. A nomadic people, scattered in various tribes over the vast basin of the Niger and through the valleys of Senegambia, they have united under the fanatical leadership of a religious reformer, and have conquered a Mohammedan empire, the most powerful in interior Africa. These tribes and their rule extend now from the Atlantic Ocean and Senegambia on the west, to the kingdoms of Bornu and Adamawa on the east, and from the Great Desert on the north to the Mountains of Kong, and even to the Bight of Benin on the south—embracing a territory equal in extent to one-tenth of the whole continent of Africa, and as large as one quarter of Europe. Many of these tribes are tributary to the nations among whom they reside, and others are purely nomadic and independent, connected with no government or settled society.

An African Empire.

The countries held by the Fellatah in Central Africa are the kingdom of Sókoto, the province of Adamawa, the lands in the south of the Lower Benue, the kingdom of Gándó, the lands on the west and south of the Niger, and the kingdom of Mássina.

The districts occupied by them in Western Africa are Futa-Torro, near the Senegal, Futa-Bondu, and Futa-Jallou, whose capital is Timbu.

As the preachers of Islamism, the Fellatahs have undoubtedly advanced the progress of civilization among the pagan tribes of Africa; for Mohammedanism, to a certain degree, restrains brutal passions, does away with human sacrifices, cultivates learning, and substitutes the sense of personal dignity, and the belief in an immovable and beneficent Providence, with the feeling of a mem-

Benefits of Mohammedanism.

bership in a vast community of believers, for the lc habits, the superstitious beliefs and isolated selfishne of pagan tribes.[2] It has aided, too, to a certain exter in checking slavery and the slave trade, for the ci code of the Koran forbids the enslaving of a man bo: of free parents and professing the Mohammedan faitl and in no case can a Mohammedan be reduced slavery. The Fellatahs have made use of this pr clamation of liberty to the slave in their wars with th other African States, with great effect.[3] The Fellata Empire, though holding loosely together at the preser time, is still very formidable, and must be the grea instrument to the Europeans for improving Centra Africa.

The physical traits of the Fellatah have been a gree puzzle to ethnologists. They are found in certai tribes, presenting the darkest colour of the negro wit perfect European features. These people, called *Toródi*

Toróde.

are said by Dr. Barth to be a cross of th Iolof—the handsomest black race of Afric —with the Fúlbe. D'Eichthal states that the Toród have shown more power than the Fúlbe, and have eve driven out the pure race, and that the Toucolors, c cross with the black slaves of Fouta Djallon, hav become masters of the Fúlbe. But it is not ye certain whether the black colour of this portion of th Fúlbe is not due to their circumstances and mode (life. The inferior class of Fellatah—the herdsmen (Adamawa—whose colour is "greyish black," Dr. Bart allows to be pure, and probably coloured by thei habits of life.

The Fellatah have made some progress in domesti manufactures, but they are, in general, pastoral, an skilful in the care of cattle. Though considered th most intelligent of all the African tribes, they have a yet no native alphabet, and make use of the Arabic for writing. The pagan tribes of this race are distinguished from the Mohammedan by their lower morality, and more barbarous habits of life and dress.

Theories of origin.

Of the origin and position of this people among the races of men, nothing can as yet be said with any certainty. The theory of their Malay origin[4] does not seem sufficiently sustained; and we can only at present wait for further evidence. Dr. Barth, and other travellers, are of opinion that they were derived originally from the east, perhaps from Egypt. He adopts the theory of a second migration from the west, back to some of their original seats towards the east.

It is remarkable, and perhaps shows the effect of Mohammedanism, that this warlike race have never participated in the foreign slave-trade, unless in the few instances in which criminals have thus been disposed of, instead of being killed. But few Fúlbe, also, have fallen into the hands of Europeans as slaves, and in some of these cases[5] they have been thought worthy of education, from their remarkable intelligence.*

Language.

The numerals of the Fellatah language only reach five; their nouns have no gender and form their plurals by changes in the beginning, the middle or at the end of the word. Sex is often marked by a different word. There are three forms of the personal pronouns, and there is discovered a euphonic harmony in some of the changes of the

* One instance was that of a Fellatah brought to Maryland as a slave, and ransomed by Oglethorpe, and then sent back to his own country, after receiving a good education in England.

There is yet living a Fellatah in the United States (Wilmington Del.), expelled from his country for crime, and now held as a slave. (Wilson's Africa, p. 80.)

words, which bears a resemblance to the alliteral concord of the Kaffir languages. On the whole, this language has much resemblance, in grammatical structure, to the Yoruba, Ashanti, and Timmanee, though differing in vocabulary.

The Mandingoes and the Iolofs.

These tribes, together with the ***Nones*** and ***Sereres***, are said to be scarcely distinguishable from each other in personal appearance. They have the same general physiognomy, the same deep-black colour, woolly hair, thick lips, broad flat nose, and tall powerful frame, and a similar force of temperament and character.

All these tribes, even when professing Mohammedanism, retain the ancient superstition of the *fetish*, and somewhat of the general African belief in a Deity, namely, the fear of a powerful Being who has become indifferent to the affairs of his creatures and lets the world go on under evil influences. The rite of circumcision is practised by most of them. In the social institutions, *caste* is found to exist among them, and something approaching to a feudal relation of chieftain and retainer.

The Mandingoes have their principal settlement in Manding, in the high land about 600 miles from the sea-coast, and they are found in small communities around all the European settlements, on the Gambia, near Sierra Leone and Cape Mesurado, and on the upper waters of the Senegal.

This tribe are thought by some to show more capacity for improvement than any other negro nation.

Superiority of Mandingoes.

They possess well-ordered governments and good public schools; their leading men can all read and write (the Arabic); agriculture has been carefully pursued by them; and in manufactures, they are very skilful in weaving and dyeing cloth, and tanning leather, and working up iron into various instruments. Their merchants are very enterprising and industrious, and exercise great influence through Northern Africa.

In religion, the Mandingoes are zealous Mohammedans, though a few hold to the old pagan belief. In character and temperament, they are described as cheerful, inquisitive, credulous and fond of flattery. With respect to their origin, they have a tradition that they are derived from Egypt, and M. D'Eichthal has presented many analogies between their language and the Coptic, but there is as yet no certain evidence of their Hamitic origin.

The *Bambarras* are a warlike tribe of the Mandingoes, who emigrated to the Senegal from the banks of the Dhîoliba. Many of the slaves sent to Europe were formerly taken from this tribe. They are polygamists, and sell their wives as slaves.

The *Iolofs* live principally in the Delta of the Gambia and Senegal. Their four principal provinces are Sin, Salem, Cajor, and Brenk. They are mild, hospitable, and trustworthy in character, and of the Mohammedan faith. The population is about one million. Many of the Iolof States have been absorbed by the great Fellatah Empire.

Owing to the dense jungles and swamps lining the West African Coast, for a hundred miles in width, the climate under which these nations reside is excessively malarious, and to Europeans very dangerous. The deep black colour of the races of Senegambia seems to have more connection with this peculiarity of the physical geography, than the degree of heat alone. The mountain tribes, as usual, are the

Colour affected by climate.

more fair, though this does not appear to be an absolute rule.

II. NORTHERN GUINEA extends from Cape Verga, 10° north latitude, to the Kameruns Mountains in the Gulf of Benin, and lies between the Kong chain and the Atlantic. Its length is some 1500 miles, and, according to Wilson, it contains a population of between eight and twelve millions.

The inhabitants are inferior races in civilization to the Fellatah and Iolofs, and are distinguished from them by their professing paganism instead of Mohammedanism, and by the low physical type of the negro which they present.

Among the nations inhabiting this territory there are important general differences in their habits and mode of life. From Sierra Leone to Cape Lahu—says Rev. Mr. Wilson, from whom the most of this information is derived—a distance of seven or eight hundred miles, there is a similar grade of condition. The people live in strongly-built circular huts, with peaked roofs, but poorly lighted and ventilated. Their only clothing is a loose cloth around their bodies. They are active and industrious, and becoming every year more engaged in agriculture and commerce.

North Guinea tribes.

On the Gold and Slave Coasts, on the other hand, a higher grade of civilization prevails. The people live in square houses, two or three stories high; they wear more clothing and cultivate the soil more skilfully, and have made a greater proficiency in the mechanic arts.

The numerous tribes gathered on these coasts have not been able to organize themselves into any important governments, the largest being the small military despotisms of Dahomi and Ashanti, and the others embracing communities of from one to twenty thousand inhabitants.

The important ethnographical divisions of the inhabitants are the *Grebo* races, the *Avekwöm*, the *Ashanti* or *Fanti*, and the *Efik* and *Yebu*. Near Sierra Leone we find the *Timanis* and *Susus*, both probably related to the Mandingoes. These are, in general, pagan tribes (though the Susus have become in part Mohammedans), and are in a low condition, morally and physically. They present the degraded negro type, with which foreign countries are familiar through the slave trade. Yet they are not among the lowest of mankind, as both agriculture and commerce are pursued to some extent by them.

Low type.

The *Grebo* races include the Krumen, the inhabitants of Cape Mesurado, and other tribes between Grand Cape Mount on the north and St. Andrew's on the south.

One of the neighbouring tribes, allied to the Mandingoes—the Veys—has the high intellectual glory of having attained, within a few years, unassisted, that which few of the most gifted races have reached—the invention of an alphabet. Books have even been printed by the missionaries in the Vey language. The Veys are a more highly developed tribe, physically, than the neighbouring peoples, possessing large, well-formed heads, and graceful, slender frames, though all are jet-black in complexion.

The Vey language is remarkable, says Mr. Norris, for the total absence of declension in the noun; for particles affixed to the verb, simulating inflexion without constituting true inflexion, and for the peculiar use of certain pronouns. There are in it, as in many African languages, a number of imported Arabic words. The alphabet contains 200 signs, and shows the originality of its invention by its being an alphabet of syllables, not letters.

The Krus. This people occupy the coast from Cape Mesurado to St. Andrew's, including a number of smaller tribes. They are said to possess less general intelligence than the Fellatahs and Mandingoes, and less wealth and fewer arts than the inhabitants of the Gold Coast, but to be superior to both in *physique* and force of temperament.[6] They are conspicuous for their open frank bearing, and their fine figures, though presenting the usual negro characteristics. Every shade of colour however, from light mulatto to black is seen among them. The Krus are comparatively an intelligent and industrious race, furnishing the most of the "coolies" of Western Africa. They follow commerce and are skilled in the culture of the ground, and have organized governments of a peculiar and democratic form. Land is held in common by their communities. Slavery has never existed among this people, nor have they carried on the slave trade.

Advancement of Krus.

The Krus are classed by Dr. Bleek under the Mandingoes; but they show even a greater resemblance in language to the Ashantis and Fantis.

The Fanti or Ashanti Races. The Fantis on the Gold Coast differ from their neighbours, the Krumen, in being more uniformly black, and in an inferior muscular development, as well as in presenting a less open and manly expression of countenance. They are superior, however, in mental attainment, and show what progress in civilization even low African races can make. A large proportion of the population have learned to read and write in English, and many are employed by Europeans as teachers, or clerks in business houses. They manufacture also, and are skilled in the construction of musical instruments, iron

Progress of Fantis.

tools, and gold ornaments,[7] and even in the making of cotton cloth, which they have prepared with a loom of their own invention. They are also good blacksmiths and carpenters and gardeners.

This nation has had the misfortune to be exposed to two influences from America, which have done more to corrupt it than any other causes—one, the demand for slaves from the Southern States, and the other, the supply of rum from New England.

No doubt, however, their contrast with the Krumen and Fellatahs in the matter of slavery is due, primarily, to a lack of native independence of character.

The Ashantis. Though the Fantis are of the same race with this people, the African coast has been ravaged for years by wars between them. The Ashantis are the only people of Western Africa, with the exception of the Fellatahs, who have had a history; and this reaching but to the beginning of the eighteenth century. Their government is the most absolute military despotism, and included at one time an area of some 300 miles square, lying between the country of the Fantis and the Kong Mountains. The population is supposed to be not less than 3,000,000.

Ashantis.

The Ashantis are inferior to the Fantis in their general cultivation, yet have made some progress in the mechanic arts.

The common language of this race, including the Denkyira and Vasa populations, and the inhabitants of Akim and Akwam, as well as other minor districts, is called the *Otshi.*

The *Avekwöms* reside between St. Andrew's and Dick's Cove, on the Ivory Coast. Their principal tribe is at Cape Lahu.

The *Yebus* occupy the country about the river Lagos, and the *Efiks* or *Callabars* live about 50 miles from a river of that name, not far from the island of Fernando Po. Both peoples are notorious as having engaged much in the foreign slave trade.

The *Ibos* or *Eboes* are interesting as being a tribe of lighter complexion than the other tribes near the coast, though with full negro features. They live on the higher land near the mouth of the Niger. They are supposed to be connected with nations in the interior.

Farther down the coast are the peoples of Benin, Dahomey, and Yoruba, of whom but little can be said as to their ethnographical relation. The effect of slavery and the slave trade has been to disorganize all the governments on this coast. Dahomey may, perhaps, claim the evil fame of being the most savage and cruel organized government on the face of the earth. The tribes of Yoruba seem to present more favourable indications. Of their language, Bowen states that it is rich in abstract terms, and peculiarly favourable for spreading the ideas of Christianity. The people are said to possess a constitutional government and to profess a pure monotheistic religion, though many idolatrous practices are still upheld by them. They are industrious, and peculiarly free from the vice of licentiousness. A considerable progress has been made by them in manufactures, and various mechanic arts. A missionary station among this people—*Abeokuta*—has presented a most striking instance of the capacity of improvement which exists in the African races.

Dahomey.

Throughout Northern and Southern Guinea, various religious and national customs exist, which may hereafter throw some light on the origin of the different tribes—customs which bear a wonderful analogy to many practised among the Jews—such as circumcision; division of tribes into families, and often into the number twelve; the interdiction of marriage between families too nearly related; bloody sacrifices and the sprinkling of blood upon the altars and door-posts; the observance of new moons and weekly festivals; the division of time into seven days; the shaving the head and wearing tattered clothes in sign of mourning; the rights of purification and the belief in demoniacal possession.

Jewish customs.

The legal custom of transmitting inheritance through the female, and through the sister of the deceased, rather than his sons, seems peculiarly African, and prevails also on the eastern coast.

Singular African custom.

CHAPTER XXIII.

RACES OF SOUTHERN AFRICA.

THE Mountains of the Moon form a natural and entire division of the inhabitants of Africa. Leaving the Semitic and Hamitic races and the innumerable smaller tribes, whom the disorganizing process of barbarism has separated into petty communities, until all trace of their class or origin is lost, we come forth in

Great South-African race.

the southern half of Africa on a clear field of research. Here we find that one great family of men, from very remote times, has settled itself on the coasts, and penetrated the difficult jungles which guard the interior, until every known portion of the southern continent, with the exception of the areas occupied by the Hottentot and Bushmen, has been traversed or occupied by them.

From the very fact of their unity, still clearly to be recognized, they are not supposed to be as old inhabitants of the soil, as the black populations of North Africa, whom a longer time has disintegrated into so many apparently separate races. Of their origin or classification among the great families of the human race, nothing can as yet be confidently said. They are only known thus far to be united among themselves, and to be utterly different from the races of North Africa.

The class of languages, on which this broad generalization is confidently based, has been called the "Alliterative Class." Their distinguishing feature is the alliteration or euphonic concord, defined by Bryant as "a peculiar assimilation of initial sounds, produced by prefixing the same letter or letters to several words in the same proposition, related to or connected with one another." The initial letter of the leading noun reappears in the beginning of all the dependent or related words in the sentence. This principle is said to be so strong as to control the distinction of number and to quite subordinate that of gender, and to mould the pronoun after the likeness of the initial letter.* The peculiar mental tendency which could produce this euphonious structure of language, shows a community of origin in these widely-scattered peoples, which no similarity of colour or physique, or likeness of institutions could ever prove.

Alliterative languages.

As usual the lines of language cut right across the differences of physical characteristics, and this great South-African family includes all shades of colour, from light-coffee and copper colour, to jet-black, and hair both straight and woolly, and the facial traits of the negro, as well as of the European. The prominent tribes embraced by it are the Pongo and Congo peoples, or *Bunda* race, of the western coast; the Kaffirs, Zulus, and Bechuanas of the south; and the Swahere and other tribes of the east coast, as well as numerous tribes in the interior, recently explored. We shall denominate this great

Physical type not characteristic of race.

* An instance given by Byrant, is "*izinto zetu zonke ezilungileyo zi vela kŭ Tixo*" (all our good things come from God). Perhaps the following will illustrate the principle. Suppose in English, instead of "Nations arise against nations," we were obliged to say "Nations narise nagainst nations," or, instead of "Man's life is brief," "Lan's life lis lbrief," and we have an analogy to the African alliteration.

family from one of its leading tribes—the KAFFIR FAMILY.

It is supposed that even the aboriginal inhabitants of Madagascar are of the same race.

The only other important division of the races of Southern Africa is the *Hottentot* family, a population more ancient in that continent than the Kaffirs. They include the *Hottentots*, *Namaquas*, *Corannas*, and *Bushmen*, on the north of the Cape Colony and near the Orange River. Their language is described as belonging to the "Click Class." We shall examine them hereafter in detail.

Hottentots.

Southern Guinea.[1]

The contrast between the dialects of North and South Guinea is an illustration of the differences existing between the North-African races and the great South-African family. Those of the former are usually harsh and abrupt, but energetic and direct. Their vocabulary is small: the words have but few inflexions, and express only bold outlines of thought. The dialects of the latter are soft, pliable, and flexible; their grammatical principles, says Wilson, are founded on the most philosophical basis, and their words may be multiplied almost indefinitely. "There are, perhaps, no languages of the world capable of more definiteness and precision of expression."

Of their external characteristics Wilson says:—

If the native of Southern Guinea has not the tall and commanding figure of the Mandingo or the Jolof the athletic frame of the Kruman, the manly and independent gait of the Avêkwom, or the mechanical ingenuity of the Fanti, he has an intelligent and exquisite countenance, a well-formed head, a graceful figure, and is, beyond doubt, superior to them all in the gentleness and urbanity of his manners, and the inimitable ease and readiness

External traits.

with which he accommodates himself to any circumstances in which he may be placed. If he has not the means of making so imposing a show of wealth as the natives of the Gold Coast, he has a much clearer appreciation of what constitutes true civilization, and can much more readily conform himself to the views and feelings of civilized men.

There are two prominent divisions of the tribes of Southern Guinea—the maritime, and the interior, or bushmen. The former feel the influences of intercourse with civilization and are gentle, peaceable, and even polite; cleanly and decent in appearance, and living in comfortable bamboo houses. The latter are often almost in a state of complete barbarism. Those on the high lands are invariably lighter in complexion than those in the low country.

On the Pongo coast, between 4° north latitude and 3° south, there are great numbers of tribes—the Kamerun, Banâkâ, Corisco, Mpongwe, Kama, and others on the seabord, and the Shekanis, Bakēles, and Pangwes, in the interior.

Mpongwes.

The *Mpongwes*, who live on the banks of the Gabun River, are interesting as having shown unusual capacity for improvement. Their language is remarkable for its smoothness and methodical arrangement, the great flexibility of its verbs, and its capability of almost unlimited expansion, as it is required to express new ideas. The Mpongwes are the most imaginative of the negro races of Western Africa, possessing an inexhaustible store of traditions and poetic fables. In disposition they are said to correspond to their language, being wonderfully facile and mild and flexible.

Of the interior barbarous peoples, the *Pangwes* are the most numerous, numbering nearly a million, and the most remarkable. They are independent and warlike, and are rapidly encroaching on the maritime nations.

They are the only people of Western Africa that have a circulating medium. Of their appearance, Wilson says, that of all men he has ever met, they are those of the most noble and imposing bearing. Their complexion is lighter than that of the tribes on the sea-coast, and their features, though African, are regular.

The Pangwes have now taken possession of the head waters of the Gabun.

The peoples of Loango, Congo, Angola, and Benguela, are all of the same race, the *Bunda* race, so called because their language belongs to the same branch with that of the Ambonda, an independent people south-east of Angola. They belong, as has been said, to the great South-African, or Kaffir family.

There are various minor tribes among these nations; of those in Loango, bordering on the mountains, the Dongos, Azinkos, and Ntekas are the principal.

Congos formerly Christian.

The condition of the Congo nation is another African instance of Christianity almost dying out, and becoming replaced by barbarism and heathenism; though, in this instance, the complicity of the Romish Church with the slave-trade may be the cause of its decreasing moral influence.

The *Quisamas*, in Angola, are quite independent of the Portuguese, who have conquered so many of the native tribes. In appearance, they have a strong resemblance to the Hottentots, though probably belonging to the Kaffir family.

Of the inland tribes east of Angola—the Basongs and others—Livingstone says:—

All the inhabitants of this region, as well as those of Londa, may be called true negroes, if the limitations formerly made be borne in mind. The dark colour, thick lips, heads elongated backward and upward and covered with wool, flat noses, with other negro peculiarities, are general; but while these characteristics place them in the true negro family, the reader would imbibe a wrong idea, if he supposed that all these features combined are often met with in one individual. All have a certain thickness and prominence of lip, but many are met with in every village, in whom thickness and projection are not more marked than in Europeans. All are dark, but the colour is shaded off in different individuals, from deep black to light yellow. As we go westward, we observe the light colour predominating over the dark, and then again, when we come within the influence of damp from the sea air, we find the shade deepen into the general blackness of the coast population. The shape of the head, with its woolly crop, though general, is not universal. The tribes on the eastern side of the Continent, as the Caffres, have heads finely developed and strongly European. Instances of this kind are frequently seen, and after I became so familiar with the dark colour as to forget it in viewing the countenance, I was struck by the strong resemblance some natives bore to certain of our own notabilities. The Bushmen and Hottentots are exceptions to these remarks, for both the shape of their heads and growth of wool are peculiar; the latter, for instance, springs from the scalp in tufts, with bare spaces between, and when the crop is short resembles a number of black pepper-corns stuck on the skin, and very unlike the black frizzly masses which cover the heads of the Balonda and Maravi. With every disposition to pay due deference to the opinions of those who have made ethnology their special study, I have felt myself unable to believe that the exaggerated features usually put forth as those of the typical negro, characterize the majority of any nation of South Central Africa. The monuments of the ancient Egyptians seem to me to embody the ideal of the inhabitants of Londa, better than the figures of any work of ethnology I have met with.

Bunda nations.

The Bunda nations extend even into the heart of Africa, as the *Makalala*, including the *Barotse*, *Bayeye*, and others, according to the same authority, are of this race. The *Maschona*, as far east as 31° east longitude, are supposed also to be of the same family.

Among the Congo tribes, two, remarkable for their intelligence, are mentioned by Ladislaus Magyar, a recent Hungarian traveller—the *Kabundas* and *Musso-rongo*. They live on the lower part of the Zaire or Congo River, and are skilful mariners and ship-builders, having even built ships which they have sent as far as Brazil, laden with slaves.

Both tribes are conspicuous for their fine physique. They speak a dialect of the Bunda language.

Congo languages.

M. Maury says of the Congo languages, that like most African tongues, they are poor in distinct verbs, but remarkably rich in the modes of the individual verb. Thus the verb *sala* means, to labour; *salila*, to facilitate labour; *salisia*, to labour with somebody; *salanga*, to be in the habit of labouring; *salisionia*, to labour one for another; *salan-gana*, to be skilful in labour. Yet they have no one word for *living*, but must say "conduct one's soul," or "being in one's heart." They have often no gender, only the division into animate and inanimate; and in animate things the gender is simply *man* (or intelli-gent creature), and *omte* (or animal).

Black Jews.

Albinoes are frequently met with through all these countries. No mention is made by late writers of the black Jews in Loango, of whom Prichard speaks, and the rumour is probably derived from the numerous customs and rites practised by the people, singularly analogous to those of the Jews.

The black tribes under Portuguese rule are said to have greatly deteriorated.

The *Bashinje*, on the river Quango, just east of Angola, show a very low negro type, according to Livingstone.

CHAPTER XXIV.

THE DAMARAS AND OVAMPOS.

FROM near the 17th degree of south latitude to about the 25th on the west coast, these two nations, related branches of the great Kaffir family, wander over a vast extent of territory. The Damaras or *Ovahereros*, who are supposed to have emigrated, within the last hundred years, from the interior of Africa and invaded the country which they occupy, extend as far east from the Atlantic as Lake Ngami; on the west, they border on the *Aunin* or Coast Namaquas; in the north they touch the Ovampo and a desert mountain-land, inhabited by the Hill-Damaras and Bushmen. They are a pastoral people, and live principally on their flocks and herds. Their iron utensils are procured from the Ovampos and the European colony on the coast. The whole people only numbers about 40,000, but is divided into a great number of small tribes, governed by chiefs, dependent on chiefs above them. In religious belief they are said to have no clear idea of a Supreme Being: of the being whom they worship, it is uncertain whether it is to be considered a god or one of their ancestors. They practise circumcision—as do so many of the African tribes—offer sacrifices of animals and pray to the spirits of the dead.[2] They suppose a tree to have been their ancestor. The Damaras are in constant warfare with a Hottentot tribe—the Hill-Damaras—and with the Namaqua-Hottentots on the

Religion.

south, and it is probable, will eventually be entirely exterminated by these more powerful nations.[3] The *Ovumbantieru*, on the east, belong to the same race.

Ovampos.

The *Ovampos* (or Ovambos), who speak a kindred dialect, live to the north of the Damara people, and are much more settled and civilized in mode of life. They are agricultural, and possess well-laid out farms; many are skilled in working metals, and others carry on the trade between the former nation and the Portuguese. The honesty of dealing and hospitality of the Ovampos are much praised by travellers. Their love of country is said to be so great that the Ovampos are not considered by the traders to be profitable slaves, as they sicken and die of home-sickness.

Both nations are black, with handsomely-shaped limbs and body, comparatively regular features, and a facial angle of about 70 degrees. The Ovambos have short, crisped hair.

Their religion, customs, habits, appearance, and especially their language, prove their membership of the South-African or Kaffir family.

To the north-east of the Ovampos, between 16° and 17° south latitude, and 18° and 19° east longitude, is the kingdom of Kamba, near the River Kunene: the inhabitants belong to the considerable race of the *Munyanika*, which includes a number of separate communities. The Hungarian traveller—Ladislaus—who has given almost the only information about these tribes, says but little in regard to their language. They are negroes, and probably belong to the Kaffir family. A remarkable custom existing among them—which is also found among the *Batokas*, in Central Africa—is the breaking out of three teeth from the lower jaw. Their occupation is mostly robbery, and they are on a very low grade of social condition. Their religious belief is a faith in a good and evil spirit, of whom they regard the latter as the more powerful.

Bechuanas.[4] The *Bechuanas* (or Bitshuanas), a name meaning "Equals," or "Fellows," are the most powerful and intelligent of the Kaffir races. They are scattered over a wide extent of country, from 28° south latitude to the region of Lake Ngami, and even as far as 18° south latitude, while one of their tribes—the Makololo have extended to 14° south latitude. They are bounded on the east by the Kaffirs proper, and on the south by the Hottentot Bushmen and Griquas. On the west, they extend into the Kalahari Desert, where they are found to degenerate in physique.

Geographical position.

This people is divided into a great number of tribes, the Batoanas, Bakwains, and others, named each after a certain animal; a custom probably originating from the animal worship, which, as with the Egyptians, formerly prevailed among them. Their customs—such as circumcision, polygamy, the practice of rain-making by the sorcerers, with others of the kind—are the same which we discover among all the Kaffir races. The Bechuanas are an eloquent, quick-witted people, but given to theft, and vindictive in disposition. Gardening and agriculture are much practised by their women, while the men usually occupy themselves in war and the chase. Some of their tribes show a great readiness and capacity for commerce.

Like many of their related tribes, they are said to have no belief in a Supreme Being, but it is not improbable that this impression about them, results from ignorance of their language and customs.

The Bechuanas are not a fully-black tribe—the Makalolo, of whom Livingstone speaks so much, having a lightish-yellow complexion.

Livingstone gives a classification of the Bechuanas which he obtained from one of the Makalolos. 1st The *Bakoni* (or Basuto), embracing, in the south, the Batan, Baputi, and others—wild tribes, some of them even addicted to cannibalism—and including, in the north, numerous tribes, such as the *Batlon*, *Bapo*, &c., who are agricultural, and raise large quantities of grain. On their labour, the distant *Boers* live. 2nd. The *Bakalahari*, the western branch, including many communities and hordes, among them the *Batlapi*, who have felt especially the influences of Christianity. They were filthy and degraded tribes when first known, but have been gradually raised in condition by the influences of civilization and religion.

Livingstone's classification.

The following description of the Bechuana language or the *Sechuana*, is from Rev. L. Grout, the missionary.

The Sechuana language is rich in names for external objects but very deficient in metaphysical terms. It has no words signifying "conscience," "spirit," &c., and none to express the abstractions of mind. Harmony and clearness are its chief qualities. Its words generally have from two to four syllables, each syllable being composed of one consonant and one vowel following it. The noun is composed of a variable prefix and a radical. The plural number is formed from the singular, by changing the prefix *le* into *ma*, as, *legeba*, plural *mageba*; *mo* into *ba*, as *motu*, man, plural *batu*, men; *se* into *li*, and *bo* into *ma*; or else the plural is marked by the prefix *li*. The article is nothing but the prefix of the noun repeated, and is used to bind the adjective to the substantive, as, *sefate se segolu*, great tree, literally, tree the great. The adjectives are few, because of the frequent employment of nouns to express attributes, as *motu oa musa*, "man of amiability," *i. e.* amiable man. The adjective takes the prefix of the substantive to which it belongs and is always placed after the noun, as *selomo se segolu*, "precipice the great." The place of the comparative degree is often supplied by employing the verb, *feta*, to surpass; yet comparison is regularly expressed by the use of the preposition *go*, to

Bechuana language.

towards. The pronoun of the third person accommodates itself to the prefix of the substantive to which it relates. Thus the prefix *se* gives the pronoun *sona* or *sea*, before the verb; *le* gives *lona*, or *lea*; *bo*, *bona* or *boa*; *li*, *chona*, or *lia*. The verb has three forms, the efficient, causative, and relative; and each form has three voices, the active, the passive, and the middle. (Or. Soc. Journ., vol. i. p. 426.)

The Kaffirs.[1]

Kaffirs.

This people, from whom the extended family of nations in South Africa have been named, occupies the country on the southeast coast, extending from the Cape Colony nearly to Delagoa Bay. They are divided into three branches—the *Kaffirs* *Zulus*, and *Fingoes*, each speaking a separate dialect of the Kaffir language. The Kaffirs include the *Amaxosas*, *Abatembus*, and *Amampondos*.

The first tribe are especially the Kaffirs of British Kaffraria.

The Zulus include the inhabitants of Natal; the *Amazulus*, whose country extends from the Utugala River nearly to Delagoa Bay, and inland to the Quathambla Mountains; and the subjects of *Umoselekatsi*, who have been driven out from their former habitations, and are supposed now to be somewhere inland from Inhambane.

The Fingoes include wandering Kaffirs, such as the *Matabele Amafengu* and others, either bordering on Natal, or who have migrated to a distance in the interior. The former tribe have already founded an important kingdom in the centre of Southern Africa.

In person the Kaffirs are remarkable for symmetry and beauty; their height is usually over five feet eight inches, and their carriage is stately and upright. Their heads are large, the forehead being high and well developed. The hair is woolly, the features are fine, and the eyes remarkable for their keen, piercing expression; the nose varying in form, but sometimes of the perfect classic shape. The skin is dark-brown, growing more black in the more northerly tribes. The people are conspicuous for their regular and pearly white teeth.

In pursuits, the Kaffirs are mostly a pastoral people, living under a patriarchal government. Their superstitions and customs correspond to those already mentioned of the other branches of this family.

The whole number of Kaffirs and Zulus, according to Fleming, in 1852, was only 445,000.

The Kaffir language is the representative of the great alliterative family. Its principle of "euphonic concord" leads to a remarkably soft, fluent, and harmonious enunciation, and aids in giving precision and clearness to the expression of ideas. A foreign element in the language is the use of *clicks*, probably derived from the Hottentots, as the Zulus, who are farther from that people, are much more free from them than the Kaffirs proper.

Kaffir dialects.

The divergence of the dialects of the South-African family corresponds with the geographical situation of the tribes; that of the Kaffirs proper passing gradually into the Zulu dialect, and this again into the Bechuana, and this changing into that of the remotest Bechuana peoples. The great distinction between them is, that the eastern dialects are softer than the western.

As we review the position of the Kaffir races in Southern Africa, we find a remarkable movement among the nations similar to that which we observed in Central Africa. The black peoples are the farthest from being stationary or sluggish. Emigration in masses, invasion and conquest are proceeding all the

Remarkable migrations in Africa.

while. Empires are being erected, and nations subjugated or absorbed continually. On the east there is the grand movement of the *Matebele*,[2] under Moselekatse, who have finally founded a great kingdom, reaching from the Schaschi River to the Zambesi. Mingled with the Matebele are fragments of numerous smaller tribes, such as the *Makalaka*, *Badonga*, *Bakurutse*, *Maschona*, and others. A part of the Maschona have preserved their independence in the mountains, eastward of this country.[3]

In the district of the Tschobe and Liambye, the Makololo, after leaving their old habitations on the Orange River, have erected, under Sebituane, a powerful community, conquering all the nations from the Tschobe to 14° south latitude. Among the Bechuana tribes incorporated into this nation are the *Bakwain*, *Batauana*, and others. The Makololo have been much diminished by the African fevers, so that negro tribes, such as the *Barotse*, *Bayeye*, *Batoka*, now form the majority of the subjects of their empire.[4]

Between these two kingdoms, a number of fragments of different nations are found, united in the common desire of preserving their independence.

In the west we have already spoken of the kingdom of the Damaras, a comparatively modern government, as the people is supposed within one hundred years to have emigrated from the highlands of Central Africa; and yet, already overpowered and nearly destroyed by the attacks of the fierce Hottentot nations.

The recently-explored Districts of South Africa.[5]

The most important community in this country, so lately brought into public view by Livingstone, is the empire of Matiamvo. Its capital is situated about 8° 20′ south latitude, and 22° 32′ east longitude. The most southern village under his rule is that of Manenko, about 13° south latitude; many petty chieftains are subject to him, and his command stretches as far west as the Loange, and northward to the upper branches of the Liambai, and the country governed by Cazembe. The great race who occupy most of this territory are the *Balonda*. In physique, Livingstone says they are full-blooded negroes, but seldom with the low negro type, which, from acquaintance with degraded blacks, who have been exported as slaves, we have come to consider the usual type. Their heads are usually very well shaped, though some have long skulls, with thick lips and flat noses. The government of Matiamvo is described as a mild and absolute despotism. He alone possesses all the flocks and herds of the country.

The Balonda.

The soil cultivated by his subjects is generally fruitful and well watered. As the Bechuana language is understood everywhere, they are probably also of the Kaffir family.

Between Londa and Angola are several tribes, such as the *Kasabi*, *Kasan*, *Baschinjé*, and others, in alliance with Matiamvo. The *Bangala* are the easternmost under Portuguese rule; but on the left bank of the Coanza, the *Kissamas*, *Libolo*, and *Kimbonda*, are independent. In the northeast the first independent people is that of the *Jinga*.

On the eastern coast the Portuguese rule extends inland only as far as Tete. North of this point, a number of tribes are met with, known as *Maravi*. Northwesterly again from this people are the *Babisa*, or *Aiza*, who hold mostly in their own hands the trade in ivory, and slaves with the peoples of the Zambesi. West of Zete, on the right bank of the Zambesi, are the numerous villages of the *Bambiri* or *Banyai*.

Of the race immediately south of the Zambesi—the *Landiens*—Livingstone is uncertain whether they are Zulu or Bonda, but they are, without doubt, members of the great Southern family, speaking the alliterative languages.

Of the tribes south of the Zambesi, on the coast, nothing certain as to their race is known, but there is reason to believe that the *Inhambane*, *Sofala*, and *Quilimane* belong to the Kaffirs proper, and that the dense population north and northeast of this river are members of the Bechuana division of the South-African family.

Three classes on Eastern coast.

In general the population of this eastern coast may be divided from its occupations into three classes. The first are wild, nomadic herdsmen, who live on the plunder of war, or the produce of the hunt: these include the *Galla*, the *Masai*, the *Somal*, and the *Kaffir*. The second are the tribes which, like the *Wakamba*—a people belonging to the great Kaffir family—are in part herdsmen and in part cultivators of the soil. They have no settled dwelling-places, and let the tilling of the soil be done by their women. The *Wabembe*—living on the northwestern shore of the Tanganyika Lake—are described by Burton as having "abandoned to wild growth a land of the richest, most prolific soil; too lazy and unenergetic to fish or hunt, they devour all kinds of carrion, grubs, and insects, and, like the Fans, are not disgusted with the worst form of cannibalism—eating the bodies of persons who have died of sickness." (Ethnol. Soc. Trans., 1861, p. 320.) The third class, which have already begun on the first step of improvement—the regular cultivation of the ground—are the tribes, such as the *Wanikas*, *Wasumbaras*, and others dwelling between the coast and the interior lakes.[6]

The *Wanika* are supposed by Burton to be a people who have degenerated from a more civilized condition; he considers them as in stock, negro (probably Bechuana), but mingled with Semitic blood. Their heads are pyramidal and longish round, low in front, and pressed together on the sides. The face is moderately broad and flat; the forehead broad and prominent; the nose and chin of low negro type; colour chocolate.

Wanika.

In their spiritual condition, the same authorities already quoted cannot discover that they have any distinct religion, but merely a religious instinct. The Being whom they regard as highest is at once good and bad. They sacrifice on the graves of their ancestors, but without any idea of a future life. Circumcision and polygamy are common to them with all their related tribes, and, like others of the African races, they delight in the forming of secret associations. They have no organized government.

The following slender information is from the Rev. L. Grout, missionary, and is probably the best that can yet be obtained in regard to the remaining tribes on the coast:—

At some distance from the coast, and about due north from the mouths of the rivers Zambesi and Quilimane, lie the Makoas, to which nation many of the emancipated slaves of the colony belong. They are supposed to extend from about 17° to 9°, or 10° south latitude. Still farther in the interior. and to the northwest of Mozambique, from which place they are thought to be two or three months' journey, dwell the Monjous. From Mozambique to as far as Nombasa and Nelinda, along the coast lie the Sowauli, or, as they are termed by Dr. Krapf, the Sooahelees. Some of these people are also found in the interior of the island of Zanzibar, where they are called Nookhaden. From a statement of Dr. Krapf, in the Missionary Register, it would appear that the Sooahelee language is spoken a considerable distance beyond Nelinda. On his visiting Barawa, about 2° north latitude, he thus writes: "The language of Barawa is Somalee, but most of the inhabitants understand the Sooahelee language, which is spoken from Nukdeesha to Mozambique, but only on the coast, not in the interior. The tribes inland, from Nombasa, are called Wonicas and Wakambas, the former inhabiting the plains, and the latter dwelling in the hills and forests. The language of the Wakambas seems to be similar to that of the Wonicas; and those Wakambas who have much intercourse with the Wonicas, understand and speak the Wonica language perfectly well."

With reference to these different tribes Mr. Boyce observes, in his introduction to Mr. Archbell's Sechuana grammar, that they speak languages only slightly different from the Sechuana spoken near the Cape Colony. An Arab, he adds, who had travelled for commercial purposes, from Nombasa to Mozambique, at some distance from the sea-coast, gave the writer some specimens of the language spoken among the tribes through which he had passed, in which Kaffir and Sechuana words were easily recognizable. Natives conveyed from the interior to Mozambique, and from thence taken to the Bechuana country, have found no difficulty in making themselves understood; sufficient proof, this, of a radical identity of language.

This opinion is supported by that of Dr. Adamson, of Cape Town, who has had the opportunity of inspecting two manuscript grammars, prepared by Dr. Krapf, one of which appears to be that of the Sooahelee tongue referred to in the preceding paragraph, which he found to be a slightly-modified form of the Sechuana.

Some additional light has been thrown upon the language of the interior by a visit of Rev. T. Arbousseh, of the Paris Missionary Society, to some captured negroes near Cape Town, in 1845. He says: "I found the number of captured negroes to amount to 262, belonging to three principal tribes, namely, the Makoas, Mazenas, and Koniunkues. The Koniunkues seemed to be the farthest removed in the interior. One of them assured me he had been three or four months in one Arab gang before they reached the channel of Mozambique. The Mazenas live nearer the coast, probably between the former and the Makoas. The language of the Koniunkues is soft and musical; the words simple and liquid, the vowels distinct and almost always one to every consonant, as in Kaffir and Sechuana, which it much resembles; but it has not the disagreeable click of the former, from what I know of it." (Or. Soc. Journ., vol. i. p. 431.)

The *Sooahelees* (or *Sawáhili*) are subjects of the Sultan of Muscat. They extend certainly along the coast from the river Juba to Zanzibar, and are scattered, it is believed, as far south as Delagoa Bay. The language, though mingled with many Arabian words, proves this nation to belong to the Kaffir stock, with much crossing of Arabian blood.

The people are marked by a great variety of physical type, and their colour ranges from olive to black. Their form is moderately high, and shows good muscular power. Some resemble Arabs, and others the pure negro tribes. The costumes and modes of life are equally varied with the physical appearance. The religion of this people is the Mohammedan, though not a fanatical form of it.

The *Wakamba*—to whom we have already referred—dwell in the neighbourhood of Mombas, in Zanguebar.

Wakamba.

They only number some 70,000. Though situated almost under the equator, they are a remarkably powerful race, with nothing of the low negro type, and only blackish in colour. Their features are thus described by Dr. Krapf: "Their lips are somewhat large, their eyes tolerably large, the chin rather pointed, the beard scanty or altogether wanting, the teeth white and artificially pointed, the skin smooth and blackish; the forms both of men and women slender, and their hair is either shaved or curled with wire." (E. Africa, p. 286.)

Like most of the East-African tribes, they are inferior to the West African in their religious conceptions. Their idea of a Supreme Being is very weak ; they have no idols, and have not even attained to fetichism, and it is supposed that their belief in any Deity has been kept awake by Mohammedan influence. Like all the Kaffir races, they have great faith in witchcraft and rain-making, and practise the rite of circumcision. One great cause of the degradation of all these East African races is the slavery and slave-trade practised by them.

Tribes on eastern coast.

Of the *Wakarima*—a black people—on the eastern coast and the *Wabonga*, *Mukamango*, and other tribes in the interior, little is ascertained as to their origin. It is only known that the most fearful battles are waged among them, resulting in a horrible increase of the supply of slaves for dealers.

The description which Burton gives of the interior tribes west of Zanzibar—the Wajiji, Wurundi, Warori, and many others—is of the most degraded, licentious, and barbarous peoples.

CHAPTER XXV.

THE HOTTENTOT RACE.[1]

A REMARKABLE ethnological problem is presented by the appearance of a single race in the southern portion of Africa, entirely different from the South-African family, both in physique and in language—a race of copper colour and low development amid dark races of noble physical structure, and separated from them both by mental peculiarities, and by a language presenting features exhibited in no other tongue.

This people—the *Hottentots*—are supposed to be the oldest people on the South-African Continent, and among the evidences of this is the fact that the rivers, even in the Bechuana territory, bear Hottentot names. Though found prinpally on the southern point of the promontory of Africa, various fragments of their tribes are met with far in the interior, even north of Lake Ngami, as if the race had been gradually pressed down from the north by more powerful tribes. It is an instance of the vitality of race, that the Bakalahari, the poorest of the Bechuana tribes, living side by side in the desert with the Bushmen, the most degraded of the Hottentots, under precisely the same circumstances, are as different from them as they ever were; the former gladly raising, wherever possible, a few pumpkins, or keeping a few goats, and the latter scorning any culture

Hottentots very ancient.

Power of race.

of the ground or care of cattle, and preferring the wild life and the poor game or vermin which the desert furnishes.[2]

The Hottentot peoples have been gradually disappearing before the attacks of civilization. In the beginning of the last century, a number of tribes were settled on the south-east coast, between the Cape and the river Kai. Some of these have been entirely exterminated; others have become scattered servants of the colonists, or have entered the Hottentot regiment in the colonial army; while a considerable body of emigrants have settled themselves on the Winter Mountain, near the Kat River. The whole number is not thought to exceed 20,000.[3]

Griquas.

On the southwestern coast some of their nations have also disappeared, and others have become intermingled with Europeans, producing a race called *Griquas*, or bastards. The Griquas are a restless race, constantly changing their habitations; they formed two stationary communities for a time at Amandelboom, on the west declivity of the Karree mountains, and at Schietfontyn, on the eastern. From this point their migrations have extended over Lake Ngami, up the Teoge, even to Libebe, the city of the Bawicko. Others of the Griqua wandered toward the north, under the name of *Orlam*, and conquered the country between the 'Aub, the lower 'Garib, the coast, and the Zwachaub. These tribes have retained their independence; they are very wild and rough, and preserve much of the Hottentot type, as well as the ancient customs. They speak the Nama dialect of the Hottentot, while the Griquas speak the Cape-Hollandish. The Orlam are also joining in the great national emigrations, which are so characteristic of interior Africa. A famous chief—Jonker Africaner—has led some of these expeditions, usually directed toward the country in the north, thus far unexplored by Europeans.

The districts on the lower 'Garib are occupied by another Hottentot tribe—the Namaquas—as well as the Griquas. The upper provinces on this river are held by the 'Korannas, who are rapidly disappearing.

The Namaquas are said, in 1859, to have reached as far north as 19° 24′ south latitude, and to have occupied, along with the Hill-Damaras, or *Haukōin*, the mountainous country between the upper course of the Omuramba, and the land of the Ovampos.

Bushmen.

The most remarkable of the Hottentot tribes are the *Saan* or *Bushmen*. They have been sometimes supposed to be merely the lowest of the Cape Hottentots, reduced by a life in the desert to their present degraded condition. But their activity, far surpassing that of the former people, their independent dialect, and the wide distribution of their numbers, make it probable that they are a distinct nation of the Hottentot race—perhaps the first of these peoples who entered Southern Africa from the north, and who afterward were conquered and beaten down by succeeding hordes of the same family.[4] This latter supposition would account for the hatred still existing between the Bushmen and the Hottentots proper, and agrees with the traditions among the Namaquas. The central habitation of the Bushmen, as is well known, is in the Cape Colony. They extend from the borders of Caffraria to the northwest of the colony, generally in the condition of the most savage barbarism, sometimes living in holes in the ground or in the bushes, and yet having resisted for centuries the most incessant persecutions and hostilities, and still reckoned the best herdsmen, huntsmen, and warriors of the native population. Of all the South-African races, they are the only one that has exhibited

Artistic talent.

any degree of artistic talent; their drawings on their caves in the mountains and the decorations of their calabashes, showing considerable beauty and taste. They are, in their wild habits, the Indians of Africa, and the only settled community ever formed of them is the one at Freemanton, on the south-eastern boundaries of the colony.

Beside these provinces, the Namaqua territory has occasional hordes of Bushmen. Recent investigations have disclosed also their existence in the districts east and north of Lake Ngami, and there is no doubt of their extension as far as 17° south latitude. It is not improbable that farther researches will show that Bushmen are scattered over a great part of interior Africa. Galton concludes that they are settled in the latitude of Caconda, or about 13° 30′ south latitude.

From various evidence, it appears that some of their tribes are black. Moffat states that negro slaves have been in the Cairo market, from the interior of Africa, who spoke a dialect resembling the Hottentot. There is reason to think that some of the dark tribes on the coast of Aden and Habash have a *click* in their language, so that the theory which linguistic research is favouring, of the Egyptian origin of the Hottentots, is rendered more probable by these scattered traces of the Hottentot race through the interior of the continent. Nothing definite, however, can as yet be concluded on this difficult question.

Origin of Hottentots.

The moral condition of the Bushmen is exceedingly low; all family ties are disregarded; they have no personal names, and their language recognizes no difference between maiden and wife. In disposition, however, they are cheerful and friendly, good-natured and generous, true to their promise, and quick to feel gratitude.

The notion of the physical type of the Hottentot is, as is common, derived from the most exaggerated cases. Livingstone and Anderson inform us that in many instances, even the Bushmen exhibit good features and a fair bodily type. They are, however, usually badly fed, sometimes living on small ground-animals, or mice and rats, wandering around in most barren and desolate countries, as in the Great Namaqua land, where there are only *four* inhabitants to the square mile, in 148,000 square miles, and the natural result is a low physical type. They are often under-sized, hardly more than four feet high; the limbs are thin, body slight, and abdomen projecting. The eyes are small, black, and oblique—giving the face a Mongol expression—but keen and suspicious; the nose is very broad and flat, the skin yellow, the cheek-bones prominent, and the hair grows in small twisted knots, like the hair of a brush, leaving bare spaces of the skull between. The skull is small, but long from front to back. On some of the females, the *steatopyge* is found — a peculiarity, however, seen on some other African peoples.

Physique of Bushmen.

The chief external characteristics of the Hottentot languages are "deep aspirated gutturals, harsh consonants, and a multitude of ugly inimitable *clicks*."*

Clicks.

"The Namaqua language," says Mr. E. Norris, "is an interesting study of itself, on account of its remarkably simple and yet comprehensive and expressive structure, and from its possessing features, such as the grammatical gender and accusative

* Of the clicks in the Zulu, probably derived from the Hottentot dialects, Rev. Mr. Grout says that there are three general classes—the *dental*, the *palatal*, and the *lateral*. The *dental* is made by placing the tongue firmly upon the front teeth, and withdrawing it suddenly with a suction. The *palatal* is so called from its being made by pressing the tongue closely upon the roof of the mouth, and withdrawing it suddenly, so as to produce a sharp, quick noise. The *lateral* is so called from its being made by the tongue, in conjunction with the side (double) teeth.

case, usually considered as peculiar to the most highly organized languages." Its few affinities are with Coptic and Semitic. The vocabulary is limited, and, as in Chinese, many words appear to have the same sound.

Namaqua language.

The nouns have two real grammatical genders, distinguished by their terminations. There are plural forms, and two dual forms; one appropriated to a pair, like the Semitic, the other to two individuals, as in Greek—advantages of form which even our own language does not possess. There is also a copious declension, formed, as in the Finnish language, by terminations, which may be called post-positions.

The pronouns are very numerous, and have "distinct forms for every conceivable modification of meaning;" the second person as well as the third distinguish the genders. All are completely and regularly declined. The verb is conjugated by the addition of certain syllables. The Namaqua is provided with a considerable number of conjunctions, "a part of speech," says the same authority, "generally very deficient in uncultivated languages."

The Hottentot languages are said by M. Maury, to exhibit one peculiarity, which assimilates them to the Polynesian—a double plural (one common and one particular), and a double form of the first person plural, indicating if the person addressed be comprised in the "we," or not. This form is also found in some of the North-American Indian tongues.

Enough has thus been briefly stated, to show that this language—an implement of wonderful precision and beauty, yet the dialect of, perhaps, the lowest human race on the earth—places this degraded people at an infinite distance above the brute, and even ranks it in capacity and origin with the most highly developed races of men.

With reference to the general physical divisions of South Africa, Livingstone gives it as his opinion that there are *five* longitudinal bands of colour running up the southern continent.

Five physical divisions.

Those on the seaboard, both east and west, are very black; "then two bands of lighter colour lie about 300 miles from each coast, of which the westerly one, bending round, embraces the Kalahari desert and the Bechuana countries; and then the central basin is very dark again."

This can be only a very general appearance, as numerous exceptions are found to it; the Bushmen of lighter colour, being scattered around in the centre of the continent, and the Makololo, who are of light-yellow complexion, having migrated to the central regions. All travellers agree that the colour of the Africans, to a certain degree, changes according to heat and dampness, the same tribe (as the Batoka for instance) being black, or lighter-coloured, as they are exposed in a greater or less degree to these two influences. The lines of language—as, for instance, those of the Kaffir family—cut across the distinctions of colour, and one undoubted race may embrace persons jet-black, and others with unmixed blood of a light copper-colour.

The Semitic races—as the Arab and Berber and Abyssinian — vary endlessly in complexion. Some Arabs are reported to be jet-black; and the Berbers, as shown by Dr. Barth, are sometimes almost black, and at others, fair as North Europeans. The Abyssinians range from black to copper-colour, according to locality.

What is called the "negro type"—that is, the low type of the coast of Guinea—is comparatively the exception—perhaps as much so as the low Irish type in the Keltic race. The negro features are combined in Africa in every possible variety. As Prichard has shown, and as may be seen by referring to descriptions already given of the particular nations in this treatise, there are jet-black negroes with woolly hair, but noble Aryan features—such as the Iolofs, Mandingoes, Guberi, and others; or black people, with frizzled and even straight hair and regular features, such as the Bishari and Danakil, and some of the Fellatah; or blacks with flowing hair in ringlets, as the Somauli and the tribes near the Zambesi; or light-brown people with woolly hair, and European forms and face, as some of the Kaffirs; or light-brown, with negro features, as many east of Angola; or brown, with the lowest negro type and hair in tufts, as the Hottentots.

Minglings of type.

M. d'Abbadie—an eminent *savant*—who has had eleven years of experience among the races of Eastern Africa, states as his conclusion—the more trustworthy as opposed to his previous opinion—that colour is in the main the result of food and climate. Our usual classification and entire separation of the negro from the white, he thinks, are due to our commonly seeing the extremes of the two types—the Guinea negro and European white—in contrast. This scaffolding of classification, he says, fell when he first saw certain tribes—the *Doqqo* and others—in Eastern Africa, and now, with all his experience, if he were to choose among individuals in Æthiopia (excluding all mixture of races), it would be impossible for him to say where the negro begins, and the red man ends.

D'Abbadie's view.

There is nothing in the great source from which evidence of difference and of unity among different peoples has been sought in this treatise—namely, Language—to prove the negro radically different from the other families of man, or even mentally inferior to them.

A large portion of the brown and black tribes of Northern Africa, as has been shown, belong to the same family as that which first originated commerce, which invented the alphabet, produced the sublime Hebrew poetry and Arabian science, and which was, through many ages, in one of its branches, the especial medium fitted by Providence for transmitting the most elevated religious inspirations to mankind, and in which the Divine manifestation of JESUS CHRIST was made. The Semitic negro can certainly never be considered by the worshippers under a Semitic religion as inferior in blood to themselves.

Semitic negro.

Still another group of peoples, both brown and black—many fully black—are descendants of that family which erected the ancient empires on the Euphrates, and which, unknown centuries ago, built the pyramid-tombs on the Nile, and founded the gloomy art, the artificial civilization, and the science of Egypt. Surely the Hamitic black is not, by necessity of race, a being inferior to those races who first learned science of his forefathers; and if it be shown in the investigations of the next few years—as many philologists predict—that the lowest African race—the Hottentot—is a descendant of the highest, the Egyptian, then will be demonstrated that no degradation of physical type or mental condition is a necessary proof of diversity of origin.

Hamitic negro.

The families of Central Africa have not, indeed, all been classified, and no absolute proof can be presented of their identity of origin with the rest of the human race, but their languages show no radically different features. The laws of human speech apply to them as to all other tongues: they are founded on the same principles: they are sometimes conspicuous for their richness and flexibility, and a great scholar of Germany (Pott) has ranked many of them among the noble tongues of more cultivated races.

Achievements of black races.

These races have manifested no want of capacity for commerce, or agriculture, or government. Some have erected in this century great empires; some are the traders through wide deserts; some have organized governments, opened schools, and even accomplished the wonderful feat of inventing a phonetic alphabet.

Many are distinguished for the highest physical type; and others in force and energy, and even ingenuity, are not behind more favoured races.

The great Southern or Kaffir family, including so many nations, presents no inferiority in that highest expression of the human soul—Language—but has a tongue which is remarkable for its melody, richness, and precision of expression.

Their present position.

It is true that, owing to its isolation caused by the malaria of its coasts, the want of navigable waters, and he difficulties of land transit, the continent of Africa has been almost untouched by the great currents of commerce and by the grand movements of Christianity, so that its races stand at this day lower than those of any part of the globe, except Oceanica.

The African peoples—with the exception of the Semitic and Hamitic races—have no literature or history: they are beclouded with the shadow of ignorant minds—the superstitious dread of unseen powers: they are cursed with the vices and wrongs of slavery: and they have not yet produced a man with intellect or moral power sufficient to mould and lead nations. Yet with all this, they are no lower than probably were many of the Aryan races on their first entrance into Europe; they are to be looked upon as young in the immense period necessary for the historical development of races, and there is nothing to show that they may not yet grow, in their own direction, to the full stature of the other families of man.

The future.

Mohammedanism has already begun, in a partial way, the improving process, by solidifying separate tribes and spreading the idea of a community of believers. Still more has Christianity proved on the western coast what order and intelligence, and good morals might spring up under its genial reign. The African disposition is said to show a certain openness to pure religious influences; so that if the Divine working in history shall produce some great African prophet or reformer, inspired by the system which is more congenial to the African nature than either Mohammedanism or Judaism—Christianity—what may we not yet hope for African development and civilization!

PART SEVENTH.

ETHNOLOGY OF MODERN EUROPE.

CHAPTER XXVI.

TURANIANS.

I. The Finnic Races.

THIS family is remarkably scattered over various parts of Europe, extending to the utmost limit in the north of Sweden and Norway which will admit of human life; forming the under-stratum of population in various provinces of Russia; appearing on the bleak declivities of the Ural, and cropping forth again on the rich plains of Hungary. They are a remarkable and undisputed instance of the effect of climate, food, and occupation upon the physical type of a race. We have had the good fortune to see both extremes of this family—the Lapps and the Magyars—and two more utterly different peoples in appearance, size, complexion, and bodily development could hardly anywhere be found among the white races. The Magyars, though not a tall people, show almost the perfection of muscular form; the features are regular, and their faces are often remarkably handsome; the

Effect of circumstances on physique.

R

hair and eyes are dark, with usually a harsh complexion, though occasionally light, and a beard generally full and dark. There is no finer race, physically, in Europe. The only peculiarly Turanian feature that we have observed in them is an occasional obliquity of the eyelids, such as marks some of the Mongols. The Lapps, on the other hand, are often short, poorly formed, with thin legs and prominent abdomen, having common or ugly features, light complexion, high cheek-bones, scanty beard, and protruding chin. Their complexion is sometimes dark. They are in physique the meanest race in Europe. Their head and appearance are decidedly those of the great number of Turanian tribes. The contrast between the Magyars and the Ostiaks, from whom the former are descended, is almost equally great; the latter being of middle stature, with yellowish hair, their faces and noses disagreeably broad, their body weak, and habits disgusting.

Contrast between Magyars and Lapps.

These differences between the branches of one family are due to the long influence of a genial climate and the pursuits of civilization, upon one side, and the want of proper nourishment, together with the severity of the cold, on the other.

The Finnic family is divided into four branches—the *Tchudic*, *Bulgaric*, *Permic*, and *Ugric*.

The *Tchudic* includes the *Finns*, *Lapps*, *Esthonians*, and *Livonians*.

Tchudic tribes.

The Russian Finns, who call themselves *Suomalaïnen*, or inhabitants of fens, are settled in Russian Finnland, and in the provinces of Archangel and Olonetz. They number over a million and a half. Their language is the most advanced of the whole family, and, except the Magyars, they are the only Finnic people which possess a literature. They have the glory of originating and transmitting one of the great Epic poems of the world—the "Kalewala." The country shows at this day, in its schools and universities, a considerable development in civilization.

The Russian Finns are not inferior in physical development to most European peoples. Their complexion is often dusky, and they have a serious, gloomy aspect, but their bodies are strong and well made. Those who are called Finns in Norway are not Finns, but Lapps. The *Quaens* are the Finns of the northwest part of Finnland, along the coast of the Gulf of Bothnia.

One of the most peculiar characteristics of the Finnic races is their tendency to superstition; and, though Finnland is Christian, many of the quaint old pagan superstitions still survive among the people, and few even of the cultivated classes are entirely free from them. The Finns are wilful in disposition, often morose, and do not easily change their old ways, or learn the habits of strangers. They are steady and industrious, and show considerable mechanical skill. Labour in the mines, from the earliest times, seems to have suited the Finnic disposition.

Finnic traits.

The language presents the agglutinative type of the Turanian, and its grammar is said by M. Müller to show a luxuriance of grammatical combination, second only to Turkish and Hungarian. *Kellgren* says, that of all the languages of this family, the Finnish has been preserved the most pure and harmonious; that while the Hungarian and Turkish, in the constant conflict of their peoples with various nations, have admitted into themselves many foreign elements, the Finnish, protected by the deep forests and the savage climate, and transmitted in the songs of the national heroes, has maintained itself rich and consistent in its forms throughout.

The Finnish has the same agglutination, says M. Maury, and the same *post-position*, as the Basque; this post-position being an adjunctive particle, placed at the end of a word to distinguish cases—a structure of language which antecedes the use of cases.

The Lapps.

This branch of the Finnic family is the only nomad population in Europe, and probably the only one attached to heathenish beliefs.

European nomads.

The principal animals employed respectively by the Finns, and their relatives, the Lapps—the cow and the reindeer—are types of their respective social conditions; the one being an evidence of stationary and agricultural life, and the other of wandering and barbarous life. The habitation of the Lapp is determined by the pasture for his deer, on which he almost entirely depends for subsistence. His range is as far north as 71° or 72° north latitude, and, owing in part to the greater mildness of the European-Arctic climate, he is in a far better physical condition than the Arctic tribes of America. His inferiority to his relative, the Finn, is due, Von Buch thinks, to external agencies. The Finns are well fed and warmly clad, and have warm houses. The Lapp, on the contrary, he says, "never keeps himself in a degree of temperature sufficient for physical development."

The language of the Lapps differs from that of the Finns, as much as German from Danish; and the people do not understand one another. It should be remembered by travellers, to avoid confusion, that in Norway the Lapps are called *Finns*, and the Finns of Finnland, *Quaens*.

Though the most degraded European race, and not so far advanced as the majority of African races, they have already felt the improving influences of Christianity and have manifested some remarkable moral results. The whole number of Lapps under Sweden and Russia is said to be only about 28,000.

The proper territory of the Finns and Lapps, says Professor Munck, is bordered toward the east by a semicircle, or third of a circle, from the Gulf of Livonia to the western part of the White Sea, and toward the west, by a similar curved line from Malanger in Finmark, to Umala on the Gulf of Bothnia.

Esthonians.

The *Esthonians* live on the upper part of the river Salis, and border on the Finns. Their language is closely allied to the Finnish. The people are mostly a miserable race of serfs, under Slavonian masters. They number over 633,000. Esthonia, with Livonia and Kurland, form the three Baltic provinces of Russia. The islands in the Gulf of Finnland are mostly Esthonian.

The *Livonians* of pure blood do not number much more than 2000, according to Latham.

The *Bulgaric* branch. This includes the Tsheremissians and Mordvinians in Viatka, Kazan, Orenburg, and other Russian provinces near the Volga—the former numbering about 165,000, and the latter some 480,000. The Tsheremissians are mostly pagan, while the others of this branch are Christian.

The *Permic* branch comprises the *Permians, Sirianes,* and *Votiaks.* The Permians occupy the Russian province of Perm, and the Sirianes that of Vologda. The Votiaks are mostly found in the government of Viatka.

The two former tribes are nominally Christian, and, though descended from a nation famed for its commerce and enterprize in the early Scandinavian history—the

Beormas—they preserve no recollection or tradition of their ancestors, or explanation of their monuments.

The Votiaks resemble the Finns: they are conspicuous physically as a red-haired people. The chase is their principal occupation. Many of their pagan superstitions still survive.

Votiaks.

The *Ugric* branch is made up of the Voguls, Ostiaks, and Hungarians.

The Voguls are a wild hunting tribe living along the ridge of the Northern Ural. In religion they are mostly pagan.

The Ostiaks are found mostly on the river Obi. They are a pagan tribe, living principally by hunting and fishing, and of such filthy habits that they are subject to many cutaneous and scorbutic disorders. Their physical type is quite degraded. The women tattoo themselves. They are the undoubted source of the Magyars.

The Magyars.

The *Magyars* have the glory of being the only Turanian race which has conferred any permanent benefit on Europe. Not merely in literature and science, wherein they have made no contemptible progress; but in what is more distinctively their own, and indeed is a higher gift to civilization, an organized constitutional government, leaving many liberties to the subject and lasting for many centuries, they have proved that the Turanian can take a worthy part in the development of mankind. Differing in blood from nearly all the rest of Europe, they show in their mental characteristics and their modes of life, their Asiatic and Turanian origin. Their dignified courtesy of manners, their lavish hospitality, their fire of feeling and richness of imagination, are not Aryan or European. So, too, their constant use of the saddle and their low houses built like tents, and their fondness for animals, point to a nomadic origin.

The practical talent which they have manifested, and their political skill during so many centuries, together with the sound morality and unshaken patriotism displayed in their individual and national misfortunes, is an evidence that the high qualities of the Aryan races are shared by some of the other families of man. The Turanian genius has the fame of having produced one of the greatest orators of modern times—KOSSUTH.

The Magyars, as has been said, are descended from the Ugric tribe of the Ostiaks, and not from the Huns, as has often been claimed.

The affinity of the Hungarian and Ugro-Finnic dialects, says Müller, was first proved philologically in 1799.

We give a comparative table of numerals in the dialects of this family, drawn up by M. Müller (Lang. of the Seat of War, p. 121).

Branches.	1	2	3	4	5	6	7	8	9	10
Tchudic ...... Finnish.........	yksi	kaksi	kolme	neljä	viisi	kuusi	seitsemän	kahdeksan	yhdeksan	kymmenen
Tchudic ...... Esthonian ...	üts	kats	kolm	nelli	wiis	kuus	seitse	kattesa	üttesa	kümme
Bulgaric ...... Tcheremissian	ik	kok	kum	nil	vis	kut	sim	kändäxe	endexe	lu
Bulgaric ...... Mordvinian ...	vaike	kavto	kolmo	nile	väte	kóto	sisem	kavkso	väikse	kämen
Permic .... Sirianian	ötik	kyk	kujim	njolj	vit	kvait	sizim	kökjâmys	ökmys	das
Ugric .... Ostiakian......	it	kat	chudem	njeda	vet	chut	tabet	nida	arjong	jong
Ugric .... Hungarian ...	egy	ket	harom	negy	öt	hat	het	njolcz	kilencz	tiz

Pulszky, in his able articles on the Hungarian language, shows that it differs from the Aryan tongues much less than many allied Asiatic languages.

Hungarian language.

Thus the "affixes" are not mechanically glued to the roots, but influence them and are influenced by them; though their influence does not usually extend beyond the final syllable. Many of the elements of the pronoun are the same with those of the Aryan pronouns; some of the forms and affixes are identical with those of our family of languages, while the most are altogether different. It is, in many respects, a language far more developed than the most of the Turanian.

II. The Turks.

Another race of the Turanian family settled in Europe are the *Turks*.

Their tribes in Russia—the "Tâtârs" of Kazan, of Astrakan, Siberia, and the Crimea; the Bashkirs, the Kirghiz, and the Nogays have already been spoken of.

There are, besides these, great numbers of minor Turkish tribes in Russia, some extending even beyond the Arctic circle.

European Turk.

"The Asiatic Turk, with his well-formed head," says M. Boué, "his lengthened countenance, his regular features, his black or brown hair, and his handsome figure, becomes, by mixture of blood in Europe, almost too colossal when he is the issue of marriages with Servians; or he takes on an ignoble physiognomy when he is half Bulgarian." The Greek blood produces Mussulmans with aquiline nose, lively and piercing eyes, in whose expression defiance has replaced the nonchalant confidence to which the true Asiatic Turk willingly abandons himself. The eyes, he further remarks, of the genuine Turk have something savage or foreign in them, to which the European cannot at once accustom himself. In the cities his colour is almost lifeless; and his limbs are meagre in the extreme, when accidentally exposed from their voluminous garments.

The women have usually a very pale complexion, with poor figures.*

* Dr. Hamlin.

Dr. W. H. Thompson, on the other hand, describes the Turk as singularly resembling the ancient picture of the Scythian—bow-legged, with heavy, squat figure, in which the trunk is very large, but the legs short, arms long, shoulders rounded, face very broad and heavy, eyes small and very piercing.

The Turks are scattered over all Turkey, holding all the prominent offices and professions.[2] They are divided into (1.) the true Turks or *Osmanli;* (2.) the *Mandjiouk,* and (3.) into Bulgarians, Greeks, Albanians, and others, who are of mixed Turkish blood. The Osmanli are at once to be distinguished by their superior type of feature. It is still a matter of question—as has before been intimated—with ethnologists, how far the changed type of the Osmanli from the original Asiatic type is due to mixture with Greek and Circassian blood, and how far to new circumstances and occupations. We are inclined to the opinion that the same causes which now tend to the rapid and inevitable diminution and destruction of the Turkish race in Europe—a fact well known—also favour the "selection" of the best physical type. Polygamy, of course, diminishes population on the broad scale, and limits the reproduction of a race to the most favoured classes, as it is they who get possession of the women, and are able to marry. *Fatalism*—a rooted peculiarity of the Turk—acts destructively on all classes during the spread of pestilence, or under the usual destructive agencies of human society, especially in the cities, inasmuch as it prevents proper care and foresight, but it of course acts most fatally on the poorest and most degraded. The recruiting system, which draws principally on the Mussulmans of all the races in the Empire, must naturally cut off the lowest of the race first. All these influences, while they certainly diminish the

Changed type of Osmanli.

Selection of best type.

population, are, as it were, "selecting" the best physical types for perpetuation. To these may, no doubt, be added the crossing with Greek, Georgian, and Circassian blood.

The European Turks have illustrated many problems with regard to the mixtures of races. The offspring of the white Turk and the negro mother,* we are told by Dr. Rigler, an experienced medical writer, of long residence in Constantinople, are a vigorous and intelligent race, which need the crossing of several generations with whites, to render them like their white ancestors.

The mixture of the Turks with other races in Europe is pronounced by the same authority to be generally

Turkish crossings.

beneficial. The most common intermarriage is with the Slaves; besides this, with the Greeks, with the Æthiopians, Arabs, Abyssinians, and Berbers; with the Albanians, and occasionally with the Kurds; with Georgians and Circassians; with Græco-Slaves; and sometimes with Wallach and Servian women. A natural result is every variety of physical type.

The greatest number of Turks have always been concentrated in the eastern part of the empire; at Constantinople, Adrianople, and in some of the towns of Thrace.[3] In Eastern Bulgaria, a very compact population of Mussulmans is found in Belgrade, Shumla, and other cities, as well as in most of the towns along the Danube. In the southeast of Macedonia, and the northeast of Thessaly, there are also Turkish villages.

In the rest of European Turkey, there are few exclusively Turkish towns, but Turks are found sprinkled through all the provinces, especially in Western Bul-

* These marriages are so prolific, that Dr. R. says the Turks choose negro wives for the sake of the large families. (Rigler's Die Türkei, &c., Wien, 1852.)

garia, and in Upper and Lower Mœsia. In Bosnia the principal *employés* of Government are of this race.

The relations of the mixed Turks are by no means amicable toward the Osmanli.

This race shows the wonderful power of *governing*, which once characterized it, by the small proportion which still, both in Europe and Africa, form the ruling class over vast multitudes. In European Turkey their number is only estimated to be from 700,000 to 1,000,000, though holding in check a population of about 10,000,000.

Governing power of Turks.

The unnatural vices prevalent among the Turks, and their political weakness, are signs of the absolute decay of the race, and it is probable that before many decades have passed the Turkish nation will cease to be known in Europe, except in past history.*

III. The Basques[1] *(or Euscaldunac).*

This people present the remarkable phenomenon of a race of utterly foreign origin and language, inserted or left behind from previous populations, among the Aryan races of Europe. The theories of their origin have been countless; one of the most modest of these, by Erro and others, urging that the Basque was once the universal language, and spoken by Noah in the ark!

It is certain, at least, that this vigorous and original people occupied substantially the provinces which they now hold in the north of Spain and the south of France, during the Keltic invasions which threatened youthful Rome, through the wars of Car-

Antiquity of Basques.

* Dr. Hamlin remarks on a common phrase of the Turks in Europe, as if they felt themselves intruders, "*We are only guests!*" and yet they have occupied their European possessions twice as long as the Anglo-Americans have been in America. The great cause of this feeling is, no doubt, their being in a minority in the European possessions.

thage and the Roman Republic, under the Empire of the Cæsars, amid the attacks of Vandals and Goths, through the fiery contests with Mussulmans and Arabs, and in the uprising of Spain against Napoleon. There seems no doubt, after the investigations of Wm. von Humboldt, of the connection of the Basques with the ancient Iberians, and of their having once been scattered over Spain. In France they never reached farther than the left bank of the Adour.

The Basque language is Turanian,* and is thought by many philologists to belong to the Finnic family.† It is wonderfully rich in grammatical forms, sonorous in tone and clear in expression. It contains double the number of cases which the Latin possesses for each declination. The article is placed at the end of the word, thus *egun* (day), *eguna* (day-the). Terminations

* The points of evidence for its Turanian affinities are thus stated by De Charencey. (1.) A list of many similar words in Basque, and the Turanian languages, is given. (2.) Itspeculiarity of agglutination. (3.) Its incorporating faculty :—a word is divided, in order to put between its two parts another word—as *aldet* (I can), *albadet* (if I can). (4.) The dative endings in *en*, and *i*, are found in Finnish, Lap, and Tcheremisse. (5.) *La*, or *ra*, indicating the end or direction, is found in Finnish. (6.) The sign of plural is *k*, as in Magyar, and one dialect of the Lap. (7.) Nouns possess, as in Finnish, an active and passive termination. (8.) *Gavren*, an ending for ordinal adjectives, is found in *gar* of the Oelets. (9.) The pronoun of 2nd and 3rd pers. sing. indic. is the same as in Turkish. Thus, Basque *s'era* (thou art), *d'a* (he is) ; Turkish *s'ignis* (thou art), *d'our* (he is). (10.) The conjugation formed of the reunion of the participle and the verb *to be* is like those of the Turkish. (11.) the great number of voices—negative, causative, potential—in the verbs is like the idioms of the Oural peoples ; also the combination of voices resembles the Hungarian. (12.) Other similar features are to be found in the inverse structure of the phrase, the frequent use of the absolute participle, also the confusion of the conjunction with the post-position. (Ann. de la Phil. Chrét. 1860, t. lx. p. 104.)

† All the words for domestic animals are Finnish ; the word for *iron* is similar to that in Ostyak and Vogul. (Charencey.)

will change a noun into a verb, or adverb, or other parts of speech.

The conjugation is very difficult and very rich, there being not only active and passive forms, but many shades which, in other languages, must be expressed by combining several verbs or phrases. Thus, expressions like "a little too great," "a little too good," are given by one word; "good and great," is *ontnoa*, and "good and small," *onttoa;* "one who falls easily" is *erorcorra;* so "one who strikes with blows of a stick," is distinguished by a slight difference of termination from "one who strikes with blows of a stone"; and ideas like the "reason of friendship," the "reason of enmity," and the like, are expressed in a single word.

Language.

The different voices of the verb express either an active or passive state, or repose, or negation, or doubt, or increase, or diminution, as well as many other shades of meaning. Each voice has *eleven* moods, and many of the moods *six* tenses.

The Basque declines almost everything—prepositions, adverbs, interjections, and even alphabetic letters. In its power of expressing a combination of ideas in one word it resembles some of the North-American Indian dialects, as well as in other features.

The numeration is from twenty to twenty.

There are three dialects of the language which are not easily understood in the different provinces. In some villages in Alava the Basque tongue is entirely obliterated, and in several of the French communes the old Basques no longer consider themselves as belonging to that people.

The genius of the Euscara is best seen in the popular poetry transmitted in the mouths of the people, from the most ancient times, and in the extemporized tragedies and comedies exhibited by the peasants.

The provinces occupied by the Basques in Spain are Upper Navarre, Biscay, Guipuzcoa, and Alava; in

Basque provinces.

France, Labourde, and Soule. In physique, the people are tall, straight, muscular, and agile, with black hair and brown complexion; the women are remarkably beautiful, but very large and powerful in frame. In disposition the Basque correspond to the ancient Iberians—proud, impetuous, and irritable, but frank and sincere; faithful friends, but implacable enemies; excellent guerilla-skirmishers, but poor soldiers.

Among the Spanish Basques there is much equality of condition; the peasants usually living on their own freeholds or "courts," and only a few castles still belonging to the "elders" of the tribes. Scarcely any Basque towns are to be found. Their municipal institutions, which they preserved for so many centuries, are in part hereditary and in part popular. The people were governed by free assemblies, controlled by written charters, which assemblies always preserved a remarkable independence toward the Spanish kings.

Among their peculiar traits is a singular respect for

Singular traits.

the dead; and so strong at some periods have been the tokens of sorrow they have shown for the deceased that the Government has been obliged to control them by legislation.

They display the old Iberian * love for mining, and

* A very singular custom prevails among them, which is directly derived from the ancient Iberians, and which, according to Michel, has been observed among the Tâtârs. When a child is born, the mother, as soon as she is able, proceeds to the usual work of the household, while the husband is installed in bed with the infant, to receive the compliments of the neighbours! This custom existed also in Corsica.

are skilled in iron-work; they are good agriculturists, though the soil is poor. Urquhart relates that they still use an ancient instrument like a prong, for turning up the soil, instead of the spade or the plough. Their costume, amusements, and dances are all extremely ancient. The Basques are also brave sailors.

Though it is always unsafe to judge of the connections of race, alone from isolated mental peculiarities, yet we may fairly say that the propensity shown by the Basques to superstition, and their fondness for mining, give a certain weight to the evidence of language in establishing their relations to the Finnic races.

The whole population numbers over 784,000, of whom 130,000 are in France.

CHAPTER XXVII.

ARYAN RACES OF EUROPE.

I. The Slavonic Race.[1]

WITH one great family of Eastern Europe, the question of race is no longer a purely scientific or philosophic question, but becomes real and practical. Ethnology, to the Slavonian, is not a matter of philology or scholastic research, but belongs to the most stirring questions of politics, and is associated with the deepest national aspirations. Those mysterious ties of blood and common organization and common language, which elsewhere are only an interesting subject for the scholar, here agitate the heart of the people and direct the revolutions of nations. *Pan-Slavonism* is the expression of Race across the barriers of creeds, the diversities of dialects, and the separations of governments.

Pan-Slavonism.

Like the similar Anglo-American sentiment, it is a manifestation of a powerful national instinct, which alone is a pledge of the future of the race.

From the Adriatic to the mouth of the Amoor on the Pacific, from Poland to the borders of Persia, under countless varieties of climate and situation, this deep sentiment upholds a race, whose grand part is only beginning to be played in the drama of history Seventy or eighty millions of human beings are welded together by this mysterious instinct into an almost homogeneous mass, to act directly on surrounding peoples.

The Slavonian is the civilizer and governor of Asia, he protects commerce, he restrains the barbarous and roving Mongol and Turkish tribes from their bloody rapacities, he civilizes or extirpates the savage nomads of Northern Asia and his vigorous blood is poured into the worn-out races of Central Asia.

Russian influence.

On the side of Europe his influence is not felt, except in the vague dread which Russian barbaric power has caused; but, without doubt, the effete Turkish race—intruded into Europe and conferring few benefits on European civilization—is yet to give place to this race, which, though not young, has the tenacious vigour of a powerful and long-continuing manhood.

The Slavonian has thus far represented in Europe the principle of Despotism; this, however, seems a result rather of accidental circumstances and of the semi-civilized condition of the people. History shows that slavery never existed under his race in so oppressive a form, as under the Teutonic; and nowhere now does the unjust prejudice against race or colour, which disgraces the Anglo-German peoples, appear among the Russian.

The communal organization which, with characteristic *toughness*, the race has upheld for centuries against the oppression of their rulers, and the grand efforts which both people and government are making for the emancipation of the serfs, promise a better future. The Slavonian is naturally peaceful and inclined to agricultural pursuits. To him the Teuton probably owed the knowledge

Slavonic tenacity.

of the plough; and in the language of Gurowski (Russia, p. 248): "Agriculture—that aboriginal property of the Slavic race, now neglected and generally in the state of coarse empiricism—that inexhaustible source of wealth, that basis of national existence—agriculture will become an art and science, when the soil and the bondman tilling it, yoked together by oppression, but united in fraternal love—when both, in Russia as well as in the other Slavic regions, shall become disenthralled. This soil, ploughed by a freeman, sowed by a free hand, will yield more and better harvests than when scratched by the serf, than when the seeds thrown in, reach the furrow wrapped in the curse of a bent-down, oppressed creature."

The language, according to M. Müller, is characteristic of the civilization of the race, containing "powerful resources and flexible as Greek and Latin, yet all, as it were, without self-respect and self-dependence, always looking abroad and vainly decking itself with the tinsel of foreign countries, instead of gathering strength from within, and putting forth without shame the genuine fruits of its own not barren soil."

The Slavonic race divides itself into two great branches, distinguished by their dialects: I. the *Southeastern;* II. the *Western.*

Southeastern and Western Slavonians.

I. The southeastern is again divided into (1.) the Russian—including *Great Russian*, *Little Russian*, and *White Russian;* (2.) *Bulgarian;* (3.) the *Illyrian* (or *Serb*)—comprising the *Servians*, *Kroats*, and *Slovens.*

II. The Western includes (1.) the *Poles;* (2.) the *Bohemians* or *Tchechs*, comprising the *Slovaks*, and (3.) the *Wendians* or *Sorbians.*

All these various tribes, scattered over vast districts,

are, to a certain extent, mutually intelligible in language to one another: the Russians and Poles, for instance, conversing as easily as Italians and Spaniards.

The dialects of the minor tribes, however, are not so familiar to the others that they can be used by them in public proceedings, so that the great Slavonic Congress of 1848, in Prague, of Servians, Poles, and Illyrians, were obliged to employ the hated German language for their common tongue. The key of all the Slavonic languages is said to be the Russian, so that a Russian can make himself understood anywhere from the Elbe and the Adriatic to Siberia and the Pacific, wherever the Slavonic race is found.

Great Russian.

The leading branch of this race is the *Great Russian*, numbering according to Schafarik, 35,000,000, but, according to more recent enumerations, by no means so great a population. It forms the heart of Russia, and inhabits some twenty-five governments extending from the government of St. Petersburg, along the Volga, to the Ural and the Don.[2] A line drawn from Lake Peipus to the mouth of the Don, would mark the frontier of the Great Russians toward the Little and White Russians.[3] Their colonists extend over Siberia, Kamchatka, and the northwest of America. They form the centre of the intellectual activity and industry of the country; and their artisans and traders make up the great floating population in Russian cities of merchants, builders and manufacturers.

The language spoken by them—like the English in America—has no dialect, but is the same with the peasant as the scholar; the same in books as in common life; it is the official and literary language of Russia. The people are said to be grave in exterior, but with much gaiety and wit under the surface, and very fond of the song and the dance. They are very hospitable and polite to strangers, and shrewd and crafty in business. Their most prominent trait is their power of patient endurance—a quality which their race has always shown.

There are settlements of the Great Russians in various parts of Poland, and a few in the Turkish Empire, beyond the Danube.

The *Little Russians*, numbering 13,000,000, according to Schafarik, are scattered over the south of

Little Russian.

Russia, from Galicia to the Don ; holding the governments of Poltava, Kiev, Volhynia, Podolia, and others, as well as parts of Bessarabia, Taurida, Kherson, and other provinces, the country of the Cossacks of the Black Sea, and portions of Poland and Galicia and Hungary. The Rusniaks in these latter countries belong to this branch. Among the Little Russians, the original national character has maintained itself pure.[4] Their dialect is softer, and more poetic in expression, than that of the Great Russians, and the people have even a greater imaginative and musical feeling. The songs and ballads which they have produced, are remarkable for their poetic beauty.

The *White Russians* inhabit the governments of Mohilev and Minsk, and the greatest part of those of Vitepsk and Grodno. Their language is full of Polish expressions, as for several centuries they were under Polish dominion. The long-continued oppression is said to have degraded the White Russian, and to have extinguished much of his vitality and originality ;[5] he is the poorest and most dejected of the Russian peasants, and lives on the most unproductive soil in the country.

The numbers of the White Russians are given as 2,700,000, by Schafarik, though the census of 1857 would make them reach 8,000,000.

Cossacks.

The *Cossacks* are considered now by the best authorities to be Great Russian in race, though considerably mixed with Little Russian.

Bulgarians.

The *Bulgarians* are found almost entirely under the Turkish dominions, in the provinces south of the Danube —Bulgaria, Rumelia, and portions of Servia and Macedonia—a small number only, on the north of the Danube, being under Russia. Their name is derived from the Bulgars, a Finnic tribe from the Ural, who conquered them in the latter part of the seventh century, and whom they afterwards absorbed into themselves.

Their ancient language (of the ninth century), preserved in the translation of the Bible by Cyrillus, was the literary language of Russia till the fourteenth century, and is now the ecclesiastical language of the Greek Church in Russia, Servia, and Bulgaria.

The Bulgarians show the effects of the long-continued Turkish oppression, and are a weak and almost servile people, compared with most other Slavonic races. In physique they differ from the Servians, in having a smaller head, and one less square, and a longer face, with an aquiline nose. Their Turanian type has almost entirely yielded to the Slavonic.

Illyrians.

The *Illyrian* (Servian) branch is interesting as having been the especial object of the Slavonic aspirations for unity. And so far have these sympathies of race been carried out into practical reality, that within twenty years the Slavonic Illyrians have united their twenty different dialects in Styria, Dalmatia, Kroatia, Slavonia and Servia, into one national and cultivated language.

This branch, it will be remembered, includes the Servians, Kroatians and Slovenians. The word "Illyrian" has been used especially to denote the Roman Catholic portion of these Slavonic countries, and "Servian," the Greek—two parties bitterly opposed—so that the political unity of Slavonism is by no means accomplished.

The *Servians* hold the territory comprising the southern counties of Hungary, the whole of Slavonia, parts of Kroatia, Carniola, Istria, Dalmatia, the military frontier, and the principalities of Servia, Bosnia, Herzegovina and Montenegro. There are colonies also in Hungary and Russia.

The Servians are a high-spirited and heroic people, and one of the most vigorous of the Slavonic branches. They are more sober and grave than their neighbours, the Bulgarians.

The Slavonians of Turkey are said by an intelligent authority (M. Boué), to show something of the perseverance of the German, and the *fineness* of the Italian. "They possess more native genius than the Russians, and particularly than the Slovaks and Bohemians, and less *penchant* for pleasure and want of reflection than the Poles."

The *Slovens* are found in the district bounded by the Adriatic, the Upper Drave and Kroatia; they are also met with in Hungary.

The *Kroats* occupy the Comitats of Agram, Kreuz, and Warasdin, and portions of the western provinces of Hungary.

Western Slavonians.

The *Western Slavonians*. (1.) The *Poles* or *Lekhs*. This people occupy provinces on the western frontier of Russia, extending from the Baltic to the Carpathians, embracing a portion of Galicia and the ancient kingdom of Prussia.

The southern frontier runs past the towns of Sandec, Krosno, and Brozozow; the northwestern is formed by the Niemen. They number 9,300,000.

(2.) The *Bohemians* or *Tchechs*—the inhabitants of Bohemia and Moravia.

Within a few years a great impulse has been given to the Slavonic feeling of race in Bohemia, and to the cultivation of the Bohemian literature.

The Slavonians of Bohemia and Moravia are divided into five small groups: (a.) the *Horáks*, or Highlanders, who occupy the mountain plateau from Schildberg to Dacic; (b.) the *Hanaks*, inhabiting the rich territory included between the cities Wischau, Olmütz, Leipnik, and Kremsier; (c.) the *Slovaks*, holding the whole south-eastern part of Moravia, and extending over fifteen Comitats in Hungary, a degraded and depressed people; (d.) the *Wallachs* (to be distinguished from the Hungarian tribe of that name); and (e.) the *Water-Poles*.

Tchechs.

The *Tchechs* are reckoned by Schafarik at 7,200,000, though in this estimate must be included their colonies, and those who have emigrated from them.

Wends.

(3.) The *Wends* of Lusatia, numbering only about 150,000, occupy a small district around the towns Löbau, Neusalz, Spremberg, Lübben, and others. They are the remains of an ancient Slavonic population, left in the midst of the German, and which formerly extended beyond the Elbe to the Saale. Their language is also called the *Sorbian*, and possesses several written works.

The whole number of the Slavic populations is estimated by Gurowski at about eighty millions, of which Russia has fifty-seven or fifty-eight millions. The total population of Russia is given by the census of 1851, as 66,000,000.

Physical characteristics. The Slavonians vary greatly in physical type. The northern Russians are fair, with light hair; the southern or southeastern, as the Kroats and Servians, are dark, with black eyes and hair. The Slovaks, as the writer has observed, are powerful men, of moderate size, with long flaxen hair hanging over their faces, and coarse, strong features. The Poles, many of them, are of dark eyes and hair, and with tall, well-made figures. The race belongs physically to the *brachy-kephalic*, or short-headed; that is, to the class whose skulls are proportionally shorter from front to back than with most other European peoples.

Physical characteristics.

THE SLAVONIC RACES ARRANGED ACCORDING TO THEIR RELIGION.

(SCHAFARIK.)

	Greek or Eastern Church.	Greek, united with Rome	Roman Catholics.	Protestants.	Mohammedans.
Great Russians, or Muscovites	35,314,000	...	...	...	...
Little Russians, or Malorusses	10,154,000	2,990,000	...	...	...
White Russians	2,376,000	...	350,000	...	...
Bulgarians	3,287,000	...	50,000	...	250,000
Servians or Illyrians	2,880,000	...	1,864,000	...	550,000
Kroats	...	...	801,000	...	...
Carynthians	...	...	1,138,000	13,000	...
Poles	...	...	8,923,000	442,000	...
Bohemians and Moravians	...	...	4,270,000	144,000	...
Slovaks in the North of Hungary	...	...	1,953,000	800,000	...
Lusatians or Wends, Upper	...	...	10,000	88,000	...
Lusatians or Wends, Lower	...	...	...	44,000	...
Total	54,011,000	2,990,000	19,359,000	1,531,000	800,000

THE SLAVONIC RACES ARRANGED ACCORDING TO THEIR STATES.

(SCHAFARIK.)

	Russia.	Austria.	Prussia.	Turkey.	Rep. of Cracow.	Saxony.	Total.
Great Russians...	35,314,000	...	...	...	...	...	35,314,000
Little Russians...	10,370,000	2,774,000	...	...	...	...	13,144,000
White Russians..	2,726,000	...	...	..	...	...	2,726,000
Bulgarians	80,000	7,000	...	3,500,000	...	...	3,587,000
Servians and Illyrians......	100,000	2,594,000	...	2,600,000	...	...	5,294,000
Kroats	...	801,000	...	...	...	...	801,000
Carynthians	..	1,151,000	...	...	...	...	1,151,000
Poles	4,912,000	2,341,000	1,982,000	...	130,000	...	9,365,000
Bohemians and Moravians...	...	4,370,000	44,000	...	...	...	4,414,000
Slovaks (North Hungary) ...	...	2,753,000	...	...	...	...	2,753,000
Lusatians or Wends, Upp.	...	...	38,000	...	...	60,000	98,000
Lusatians or Wends, Low.	...	...	44,000	...	...	...	44,000
Total	53,502,000	16,791,000	2,108,000	6,100,000	130,000	60,000	78,691,000

CHAPTER XXVIII.

II. THE ALBANIANS.

ALBANIA, according to Mr. Leake, occupies almost the entire line of sea-coast on the east side of the Ionian and Adriatic seas, included between the 39th and 43rd degrees of latitude. Its extent inland is never more than 100 miles, and sometimes not more than 30. The northern boundaries are Montenegro and "the ridges which unite that mountainous province with Mount Scardus, and bound the plains of Scodra on the north." To the south, Albania reaches as far as Suli on the coast.

Probably descendants of ancient Illyrians.

Very interesting questions in ethnology have attached themselves to this comparatively insignignificant people, as their language contains words from various tongues, though the grammar is undoubtedly Aryan. After much discussion and investigation, the conclusion has been reached that this half-civilized people, now subject to the Turkish Empire, are the direct descendants of the ancient Illyrian race—the predecessors probably even of the Greeks in their peninsula—and a distinct branch of the great Aryan family. They are accordingly to be ranked, like the Kelts, Teutons, and Slavonians, as a separate member of this important family.

We quote from Leake's interesting remarks in his "Researches in Greece," page 237:—

"The Albanian must be considered as holding a distinct character in the midst of the languages by which it is surrounded, being in all probability the ancient Illyric, with some alterations of the same kind as Latin and Greek have undergone, from the Teutonic and Slavonian conquerors of Southern Europe.

"Through the whole course of Grecian history, from its earliest records to the fall of the Constantinopolitan Empire, we find a people distinct from the Greeks in race and language, inhabiting the north-western side of the country, and extending along the ridges which border the seacoast, or run parallel to it. They appear to have reached as far south as the Bay of Ambracia, for Scylax deems this gulf the northern boundary of Greece upon the west side, and Thucydides calls the Amphilochi, who inhabited the hills at the head of it, barbarians; by this word implying that they spoke a language different from the Greek. The same historian also applies the word barbarians to the people on the coast of Epirus, opposite to the island of Sybota, and Strabo informs us that the Epirotic tribes were mixed with the Illyrian and spoke two languages; meaning either that, like the greater part of the present Albanians, they used both the Greek and their own vernacular language, or that the Epirotic was distinct from the Illyrian tongue, and perhaps another dialect of the language which was spoken throughout Macedonia and the neighbouring countries, before the letters and civilization of Greece had spread over these provinces. It would appear that in Epirus and that part of Illyricum afterward called New Epirus, this change never took effect to so great a degree as it did in Thessaly and Macedonia; and that the lofty mountains and extreme ruggedness of this part of the country have in all ages afforded to the remains of the Aborigines a security against intruders. This supposition is in a great measure confirmed by those remnants of a distinct language which forms the basis of the modern Albanian dialect, and it is observable that all the words which resemble those of the same import in other modern languages may be accounted for by the revolutions which brought so many foreign nations into Albania or its vicinity; and that these extraneous words will be found to exist in the same proportion, as the impression made upon the country by several races of foreigners.

"Of the Greek words which occur in Albania, a few have internal marks, as having been adopted before the corruption of the language; a larger proportion afford the same evidence of having been taken from the Romaic Greek, and there are many also whose forms, being the same both in the ancient and modern Greek dialect, are of uncertain date.

Elements of language.

"Latin words are two or three times as numerous as Greek, but still much below the proportion in which they are found in the other modern languages of Europe. This may partly be accounted for by the secluded position and warlike habits of the mountaineers of Albania which, defending them from being ever completely subjugated by the Romans, preserved their language, like that of the Pyrenean and Cantabrian mountains, from ever receiving so large an admixture of Latin; and partly by the study of the Latin language, which has prevailed to so great an extent in civilized Europe, since the revival of letters.

"The few words of Gothic origin which exist in Albanian must have come into use in the fifth century, when the Goths of Alaric became complete masters of the greater part of the two Epirus provinces, especially the northern, where we afterward find some of their descendants settled in quiet possession of a part of the country.

"About the same period, another tribe of strangers, who proved to be the most numerous and the most formidable of any to the Greek emperors, began to make their appearance in the same part of the country. The Sclavonians, chiefly under the name of Bulgarians, continued their irruptions into the European provinces of the empire, during the seventh, eighth, and ninth centuries. In the tenth century the same race was settled at Nicopolis, the chief place of a Theme, which comprehended all Old Epirus, and it appears that about this time all the more accessible parts of Epirus were occupied by strangers of Sclavonian origin. Until the last periods of the Greek empire, the kings of Bulgaria and Servia continued to make occasional conquests and settlements in Greece, and even in the Morea; and they have to this day left traces of their long residence by the numerous names of places of Sclavonian derivation to be found in every part of the country. It was in these ages of Bulgarian prowess, that the remains of the Illyrian and Epirotic nations became finally included within the boundaries which they have ever since held. Many Sclavonian words then found their way into the Albanian language, and have been increased in number by the intercourse between Albania and the extensive regions of Servia and Bulgaria, which surround it on the north and east, and throughout which the Bulgarian dialect of Sclavonic is spoken. It may be thought surprising, perhaps, that under these circumstances the proportion of the Sclavonic words is not larger, and it may be considered as a proof that the strength of the Epirotic and Illyrian mountains and the spirit of their inhabitants were still equal, as in the time of the Romans, to protect them from being completely subdued."

Sclavonian mixture.

The Albanians, or *Skipetars* (rock-dwellers), as they call themselves, or *Arnauts*, as the Turks call them, are divided into four tribes, of which the most important are the Northern or *Geghian*, and the Southern or *Toskian*.

The country of the Northern tribe is level, and suited for cavalry, and has produced, says Leake, "a race combining the cruelty of the Albanian with the dulness of the Bulgarian."

The true character of the Albanian is to be sought in the barren mountainous southern districts. Here is to be found one of the poorest but most hardy and active peoples in the world; a race quarrelsome, selfish, eager, and avaricious, but with more honesty and fidelity than their neighbours, the Greeks.

The Albanian is a native soldier, and is the great mercenary of the East, serving with equal zest in Bagdad, Morocco, Naples, or Rome.

In physical structure he is thin, nervous, and muscular, with bony neck and very full breast; his eyes are light and small, eyebrows weak, forehead low, nose sharply cut, and head of a longish shape. There are Albanian colonies in Greece: they preserve their national dress, but are gradually losing their language. There are also descendants of Albanian colonies in Southern Italy and Sicily, who still speak their language.

Physique.

III. THE GREEKS.

One of the saddest spectacles which the earth affords, of the weakening and gradual extinction of the power of a race, is presented by the modern Greeks. It is more painful, even, than the degradation of the Romans; for the Greek stock, is, on the whole, purer and more directly descended from the ancient race. Amid the countless grafts of population from every nation of the earth, introduced by slavery into Italy, under all the successive layers of race deposited by so many conquests, who can say with confidence, that anywhere the old stock of heroic Rome buds forth among the people of modern Italy? But in Greece, no doubt, there are mountain-valleys and rural homes, where men till the ground and pasture sheep, with the same blood in their veins as those who fell at Thermopylæ; and it is not improbable that there may be petty politicians or traders now in Athens or Sparta, whose own ancestors were among those very men, who, in art or imagination, or pure intellect, have been the leaders and instructors of mankind.

Degeneracy of Greeks.

What singular influences those were in soil, or air, or sea, in the combination and natural selection of rare qualities of race, which produced that wonderful people of artists, and poets, and thinkers, and statesmen—who can say? And who, still more, can explain the mysterious causes which gradually broke the power and dwindled the genius, and changed the type of this gifted race? We know, indeed, that fatal political dissensions weakened the Græcian communities within, and that successive hordes of conquerors plundered and wasted the country, and expelled the inhabitants. We know that Roman, Slavonian, Teuton, Arab, and Turk, have either desolated Greece, or mingled their blood with that of its ancient race. We find still further, that these successive devastations have at length affected the climate and productions, and the Greece of modern days is not at all the woody, salubrious, well-watered, genial country, pictured as the Greece of old. The forests have been burned, or turned into sheep-pastures, and the encroaching desert-climate continually drives the woods higher up the mountains. On Parnassus the forest begins only at 2000 feet with the silver fir. These conditions, says Hettner, will be impossible to be changed, for the geographical limits of the elements which control the regular Flora, have been changed by the destruction of the luxuriant natural vegetation. "The want of wood on the arid and calcareous soil has increased the heat and dryness of the air; the springs have become scanty, and the parched earth draws no moisture from the atmosphere." The deficiency in wood and water has obstructed most kinds of manufacture and tillage, and this again has reacted on the people. Still, with all these obvious causes of the degeneracy of the Greeks, the astonishing change in the intellectual capacity of the race is not sufficiently accounted for, and perhaps from the subtile nature of the causes at work, never can be.

Climate of Greece changed.

The modern Greek is most of all remarkable for his

shrewdness and sharpness in business, and has anything but an enviable reputation for honesty; his especial direction seems to be toward commerce and trade. In general there is much equality of condition and personal independence among the Greeks, but a great want of discipline, and a tendency to jealousy and dissension—all characteristics of the masses of the old race.

Modern Greek.

Two races in Greece.

There are two prominent races now apparent in modern Greece—the Albanian and the Greek.

Of the Albanians, Mr. Finlay says:—

Albanian colonists now occupy all Attica and Megaris, with the exception of the towns of Athens and Megara, where they form only a portion of the population. They possess the greatest part of Bœotia, and a small portion of Locris. near Talanta. The southern part of Eubœa, and the northern part of Andros, the whole of Salamis, and a part of Egina, are peopled by Albanians. In the Peloponnesus they are still more numerous. They occupy the whole of Corinthia and Argolis, extending themselves into the northern part of Arcadia and the eastern part of Achaia. In Laconia, they inhabit the slopes of Taygetus, called Bardhunia, which extend to the plains of Helos, and, crossing the Eurotas, they occupy a large district around Monemvasia to the south of the Tzakonians, and to the north of a small Greek population which dwells near Cape Malia, in the district called Vatika. In the western part of the peninsula they occupied a considerable part of the mountains which extend from Lalla to the northeastern corner of Messenia, south of the Neda. Besides these large settlements, there are some smaller clusters of Albanian villages to the north of Karitena, and in the mountains between the Bay of Navarin and the Gulf of Coron. The islands of Hydra and Spezzia were entirely peopled by Albanians.

The extent of country occupied by the Albanian race is more clearly displayed in a coloured map, than by the most minute description. Marathon, Platæa, Leuctra, Salamis, Mantinea, Ira, and Olympia are now inhabited by Albanians, and not by Greeks. Even in the streets of Athens, though it has been for more than a quarter of a century the capital of a Greek kingdom, the Albanian language is still heard among the children playing in the streets, near the Temple of Theseus and the arch of Hadrian.

They can be distinguished by their thick body, round head, heavy face and badly-formed forehead, and by eyes rather quick than intelligent, while the pure Greeks in the rural districts are conspicuous for a fine oval face, well-arched forehead, intelligent eyes, straight nose and finely-cut features, and a form tall, supple and graceful. Their organization is dry, nervous and fine, like the climate. The Greeks of the cities, who are of a mixed race, do not show this fine type. M. de Pouqueville asserts that the models which inspired Apelles can be found now in the rural districts—especially among the women. According to him, the people are generally tall and well made, their eyes are full of fire, their mouths are admirably formed, and are furnished with the whitest teeth.

The Laconians are different from the Arcadians, both in appearance and temperament—the former showing their Spartan blood by their irritability and tendency to quarrel, while the latter are a quiet and pastoral people.

The national custom is to shave the beard, leaving only the moustache; those in mourning let the beard grow; another conspicuous fashion, even among the men, is to compress the waist to the utmost extent.

In Athens, there are two marked divisions—rather of society than of race—the *Phanariotes* and *Pallicares*.

The former were distinguished Greek families, who lived in the quarter *Phanar* of Constantinople, and occupied prominent official positions under the Turkish

Government. After the establishment of Greek independence, many of them returned to Greece and now form the leading families of the capital.

Pallicares.

The Pallicares, or *braves*, are mountain chiefs, who took a prominent part in the revolution, and now constitute the most original portion of the native population. They are very hospitable, and have many Turkish customs. Their language is largely sown with Turkish words.

There is, without doubt, a considerable Slavonic element in the modern Greek race, but in what exact proportion it is difficult to say.

Slavonic influences on Greece.

The Slavonians settled for a length of time in the interior districts, and were, as is usual with their race, devoted to agriculture, while the Greeks retired to the cities. For six centuries, from the ninth to the fifteenth, successive waves of Slavonic population swept over the peninsula, and yet they have by no means left the traces which might have been expected. The names of mountain-villages in Arcadia and of mountains, are the principal evidences of their ancient possession of the land. The Bulgarian language is still found in Southern Greece and on the western side of Macedonia, and in the eastern borders of the plains of Thessaly.

Beside the Slavonians, the Wallachs hold small districts in Greece—in the central parts of Mount Pindus. They are mostly migratory shepherds, but many of them have become merchants and artisans in the towns.

The modern Greek tongue is called the *Romaic*, and differs from the old Greek less than Italian from Latin, or, as some assert, less than many of the dialects of ancient Greece differed from one another. It is spoken most purely, according to some authorities, in Constantinople, near Mount Athos, and on the islands of Paros and Nicaria. In Cyprus much of the old Greek is preserved, though the accent is corrupted. The *Maniotes* from Sparta speak a very peculiar corruption of Greek.

The Maniotes.

The Greek inclines to Turkish idioms wherever Mussulmans are numerous, as in Macedonia, Egripo, Tripolitza and the towns of Southern Albania.

The Greeks number about 950,000; they occupy the new kingdom of Greece, and the whole northern coast of the Ægean, that is, the southern districts of Thrace and Macedonia, as well as all Thessaly and Epirus. They are bounded on the north, says Berghaus, by the Slavic Bulgarians and the Albanians. The islands of the Ægean are occupied by them, together with Cyprus and Candia. In Asia Minor, which they once possessed, they are to be met with principally in the towns and villages; the sea-coast is uniformly preferred by them to the interior. They live in Russia on the Sea of Azof, and in the Crimea, and a small settlement of them is found in Corsica.

CHAPTER XXIX.

IV. THE ROMANIC OR LATIN RACES.

(1.) *The Wallachs.*

Direct descendants of ancient Romans.

THIS people are direct descendants of the Latin stock, being in all probability the modern remains of the ancient Roman colonies in Dacia and Mœsia. Even a superficial acquaintance with their language shows to the student its intimate connection with the Latin and Italian, and the nation are proud to call themselves *Romàni.*

The classic sketches of the Dacians correspond wonderfully with the physical type now seen sometimes among the Hungarian Wallachs, as we have had, personally, the opportunity of observing. Their race is crossed, no doubt—as is their language—with Slavonic elements, and perhaps has something of the old Illyrian blood in it. Ages of inferiority and often of oppression have depressed the people, so that they now show little of the old vigour.

They are settled in Wallachia, Moldavia, and in parts of Hungary, Transylvania, and Bessarabia. They are also found in parts of Old Thrace, Macedonia, and Thessaly.

They are divided by language into two branches—the Northern, or *Daco-Romanic*, and the Southern, or *Macedo-Romanic.* The dialect of the former, says M. Müller, "is less mixed and has received a certain literary culture; the latter has borrowed a larger number of Albanian and Greek words, and has never been fixed grammatically."

The extent of the Wallach territory has diminished on the west since ancient times, under the encroachments of the Hungarians, while on the east it has increased and reaches as far as the Dniester. The condition of the mass of the people outside of Transylvania, is usually a miserable one. In Wallachia, they are divided into masters and serfs, and both morals and industry are at the lowest point.

Wallachia, according to Müller, has 2,056,000 inhabitants, of whom only 900,000 are Wallachs. Hungary contains about 3,000,000 Wallachs.

Wallachian language.

The Wallachian language derives about half its words direct from the Latin, while the rest are Gothic, Slavonic, Albanian, &c. It differs from the other modern languages of the Latin family in preserving one oblique case of the article so as to dispense with the preposition. Thus, says Müller in this expression: "*Io am vèndut vecinului miên gradina*"—"I have sold the garden to my neighbour," the article *lui* indicates the dative of the noun.

This language also puts the article after the noun—as, in Latin, *homo ille* was often used: it has beside employed auxiliaries, like most modern languages, to replace the old Latin tenses. The pronunciation is much softened.

(2.) *The Italians.*

Though Italy would seem to offer a field of extraordinary interest to the ethnologist, very few trustworthy observations have been made on the modern evidences of ancient race. The subject is yet open for some observing traveller.

The Teutonic blood—the Lombard—according to Mariotti, can be observed in the population of Piedmont, Lombardy, Parma, Modena, Bologna, Romagna, even as far as Ravenna and Rimini.

Teutonic mixture.

The *physique* is distinguished by light hair and fair complexion, elongated skull, large eyes, and by tall and portly, but seldom elegant forms. The temperament is sanguine, and in old age, lymphatic.

This race has always displayed especial talent in agriculture, commerce, and manufactures. They possess the German truth and constancy, as well as something of the German slowness and phlegm. Travellers describe them as a generous and hospitable people, with much simplicity and credulity. They send forth the best soldiers of Italy.

The *Genoese* show their descent from the ancient Ligurians, in their proud, independent characters, and hardy habits; they are an extremely enduring and indefatigable people, and produce the best sailors among the Italians. They are distinguished by their sharp but keen features, their small black eyes, and their short agile stature.

Genoese.

Above Genoa, along the whole chain of the Apennines, down to Abruzzo and Calabria, lives a primitive race, always hardy and independent, says the authority quoted above, too poor for taxation and too independent for conscription. From them, come the smugglers and banditti of Italy. They may be direct descendants of the ancient Italian tribes.

The physical type in *Venice* is a square, heavy frame, bulky and fleshy; head short and Slavonian in form; face rather oblong than oval, with full cheeks and heavy jaws; the nose is rarely arched.

In *Tuscany*, observers believe that many Etruscan

features may be clearly beheld, such as small eye, thick under-lip, pointed chin, and a long and narrow head with large forehead, and a sharp-pointed and arched nose, though no doubt Keltic elements, as well as Teutonic, are mingled in the people. The art and poetry of Italy have found their greatest impulse from the genius of this population. The ancient Etruscan valour is still shown by the inhabitants of the mountains, though those of the cities are much degenerated. The physical type is refined—the form being slender and graceful, and the features elegant and effeminate.

Etruscan traits.

The *Transteverini*, in Rome, are thought to have preserved the pure classic type. The common Roman type, still seen among the peasantry, according to Dr. Wiseman, is a large, flat head, a low wide forehead, a face broad and square, short thick neck, and a short broad figure, such as is found in many of the antique representations of the Roman soldier. The Sabinian shepherds are a model, now, for sculptors, when they would represent the ancient Romans. After a thousand years of priestly rule, says Gajani, the Romans are still the most warlike of Italian peoples.

The *Neapolitans* still manifest their early Greek origin in their levity and playfulness, their taste for sophisms and specious argument and their dances and festivals. A very intelligent observer, Signor Gajani, has informed us that he has visited districts in the Neapolitan States, where the peasants have preserved, in their costume, almost the exact ancient classic style. In both these and the Roman States, the mountaineers and the lower class of the cities are a purer race, as well as a superior one, in courage and capacity, to the upper class.

Greek blood in Naples.

The Neapolitan population has no doubt also received

large Semitic mixtures from early Phœnician and modern Arabian colonization and conquest. The Norman element seems to have been very slight.

Sicily, *Sardinia*, and *Corsica* show traces of the Moor, in the dark olive complexion, the pale bilious countenance, and guttural accent of the people. Almost all the races which in ancient times have passed over Europe, mingle in the inhabitants of these islands. They are described as showing the Semitic fanaticism and vindictiveness, with the Teutonic ambition; they are generally more given to mental than bodily exercise, and are fond of meditation and solitude.

Mingling of races.

On the whole, but little that is definite and satisfactory can be said of the ethnology of modern Italy. With the vast introduction of slaves by the Romans, and the successive waves of races that have passed over it, the mingling of blood and language has been complicated beyond all analysis.

Gajani's theory on this subject is deserving of mention and of more illustration than our space affords. According to this view, the great peculiarity of the Italian races from the most ancient times, is the attachment of the people to their cities and their municipal institutions. The earliest that we hear of the Etruscans is of their cities and of the civilization and art which distinguished them. These municipal institutions have been handed down from an immense antiquity in many parts of Italy, and still exist. Along with them, the populations have preserved their old race unmingled. The Teutonic invasions were *raids* or military occupations, rather than permanent settlements. The Teutons, from their differences of language and civilization, could not amalgamate with the Italians. The natives retreated to the mountains or remained

Gajani's theory.

isolated in their towns. The Germans brought feudal institutions with them, while the Italians retained their municipal. Even the Longobards did not mingle much with the North Italians, and one evidence is the comparatively little appearance now of their peculiar feature—the red beard. Out of the fifty different dialects in Italy, says this authority, not one is derived from the German, while many are older than the Latin. The Teutons, weakened by their intemperance and the luxuries of a more civilized race, gradually disappeared. Since Charlemagne, Italy has received no new accessions of race.

Venice he considers inhabited by the pure, original race. The vast introduction of slaves did not affect the blood of Italy, inasmuch as they were carried off again by the foreign invaders of the country.

Of this theory—which we have set forth very imperfectly from conversational notes—it is impossible to judge correctly without knowing more of the data on which it is formed. It is certainly possible that Italy may have retained her ancient race much more purely than is commonly supposed; but this view seems to us to make too little of the early Keltic conquests in North Italy, of the Teutonic invasions, and the immense introduction of foreign slaves.

Objections to it.

The subject is still open for the investigator.

(3.) *The Spaniards.*

Among all the nations who have been derived from a mixture of the Romans with the barbarian tribes, the Spanish, both in language and race, has probably the largest Latin element. Still with this, as with other Romanic peoples, various other races have mingled their blood. The Roman population, which was strongest in the cities and towns, combined at first with the Kelto-

Iberian tribes, driving back the pure Iberians—the Basques—to their mountains and inaccessible retreats, and gradually usurping with their language—a rural dialect of the Latin—the native dialects. When the Teutonic invasion swept over Spain, the Roman language, though the tongue of the conquered, prevailed early over the Gothic—and the present Spanish nation, with its Teutonic, Keltic, Iberian, and Roman mixtures of blood, may date back even to the sixth century.

Latin elements.

As the Spanish were the earliest Romanized nation, so their language contains the greatest number of Latin words, and probably the purest Latin sounds.

The changes of the various rural dialects of Latin into our modern European languages, lay in germ in these dialects, and were probably brought about by the natural tendency of the Teutonic and Keltic tribes to make their new language simpler and easier than the somewhat cumbrous and stiff classic or written Latin. Without dwelling on the details of the alterations, we may say that they consisted principally in dropping the declinations of nouns, using prepositions instead of case-endings, and substituting a more musical vocal termination for many of the terminations in rough consonants.

Formation of modern languages from Latin.

But before the present Spanish race was to be fully formed, there was to be mingled with it a slender current of Semitic blood, from the far east, in the Arabian conquest. From the earliest ages there had been, through Phœnician and Carthaginian colonies, slight mixtures of Semitic tribes with the Spanish. Though the Arabian empire in Spain lasted for centuries, it is doubtful if there was any deep and permanent union between the two families, so opposed in mental habits and religious faith. A certain degree of Moorish blood is still recognized in portions of the Spanish nation, and the influence of that race on the architecture and poetry, and language of their enemies will be for ever apparent; but that any melting together of the Semite and the Aryan took place here, such as history so often shows of the Roman and the Teuton, is not to be believed.

Moorish mixtures.

The very opposition to this hated race served to weld more completely together the Gothic and Keltic population, and to intensify the national and clan-feeling of a portion of the people. The Asturian, which was the dialect of the mountains whither the Gothic leaders took refuge from the Moor, is still distinguished from the Castilian, its descendant, by its freedom from Arabic words, and the "*blue blood*"—the designation of the blonde temperament of the Goth—is still used to describe the blood of the nobility, in distinction from the dark temperament of the classes more mingled with the Arabs.

The peculiar characteristics of the Spaniard can, with much apparent directness, be traced to his various ancestors. In his gallantry and courtesy, his stiffness of pride, his indomitable spirit of nationality, and his skill as a guerilla warrior, we behold the precise image of the ancient *Iberian*. In his fatal intolerance and bigotry—intensified, it is true, by centuries of warfare with the Mohammedan Arab—we see the *West-Goth*,* a race conspicuous beyond all other Teutonic branches for its bloody and bitter persecutions of those of a different faith. In his attachment to religious externalism and kingly power he is Roman;

Spanish traits traced to race.

* Montesquieu says that we owe all the principles and views of the present Inquisition to the West-Gothic kingdom, and that the monks only copied the laws of the West-Gothic bishops against the Jews.

in his tough individualism and the high respect always paid to woman, German; in his love of martial display and costume, Keltic. Yet with all these, and other elements of race, the Spanish race is one, and a new race among modern peoples.

There are three dialects of the language:—(1.) The *Castilian*, which was perfected after the conquest of the Moors, and which contains many Arabic words. (2.) The *Gallician*, in the northwest corner of the country, dating back before the Moorish invasion, and supposed to be derived from the Suevian language.

Portuguese.

The *Portuguese* are considered as the descendants of the people originally speaking this dialect. (3.) The *Catalan*, in the eastern provinces, a dialect of the Provençal, and derived from the language of the Frankish tribes.

The Spanish language is said by Clarus to contain $\frac{60}{100}$ words from the Latin, $\frac{10}{100}$ from the Greek, $\frac{10}{100}$ from the German, $\frac{10}{100}$ from the Semitic, and the remainder from Italian and other modern tongues. The terms for agriculture and science are Latin; for the church, Latin or Greek; for arms, riding, and war, Teutonic; for arts and plants in Southern Spain, Arabic. The geographical names in Northern Spain are Gothic or Suevic.

Of the modern evidences of race in the different provinces, travellers tell us that in Valencia the people

Modern evidences of race.

resemble both their Keltiberian and Carthaginian ancestors, being cunning, perfidious, vindictive, and sullen. The burning sun has tanned their skin dark, and aided to form in them an excitable and nervous temperament; they have, too, the superstitious tendencies that characterize the people of a hot climate. The costume is both Asiatic and antique.

The men wear sandals, and leave their legs naked, or cover them with leggings, such as were worn by the ancient Greeks. A many-coloured plaid is worn over the shoulders, and on the long red hair a silken band like a turban. The Valencian women are of fairer complexion than the men, and are conspicuous for their beauty of form. They wear the hair and the ornaments of the head after the old Roman style.

The *Andalusian*, with his lively and sparkling semi-Moorish temper, is a great contrast to the gravity and decorum of the Roman Castilian.

Catalan.

The *Catalan* is rude, active, and industrious, a good soldier, and fond of independence, resembling both Kelts and Iberians in his covetous, bold, cruel, and warlike character. The *Aragonese* are true children of the Goths in their force of will, their attachment to constitutional liberties, and their opposition to arbitrary power.

Mr. Borrow speaks of a cross of the Moors and the Goths, who are well known as the merchants of the country—the *Maragatos*. Their dress and customs are peculiar, and they never intermarry with the Spaniards. Their figures and faces are essentially Gothic; they are strong, athletic, heavy men, slow and plain of speech, using a much coarser pronunciation than do the other Spaniards. Like their Teutonic ancestors, they are very fond of spirituous liquors and rich meats.

As an instance, also, of the permanency of old oppositions of race, the same author relates that there are two villages now in Spain—Villa Seca and Vargas—the former of which is inhabited by a dark-complexioned people, of Moorish origin, and the latter by a fair race of Gothic blood, which are always in hostility with each other; the inhabitants refusing to intermarry, or even to speak to one another.

(4.) *The French.*

The difficulty which we have found in Italy in analyzing the modern remains of ancient races is almost equally great in France. The French are a new race, formed out of different tribes and races; and though presenting many of the peculiarities which belonged to each of the peoples that covered their soil, the several component parts of the nation are only with difficulty discovered.

The stock of the French people is probably Keltic, while on this have been grafted Roman and Teutonic growths, until it is impossible to say which race prevails. One of the rural dialects of the Roman Empire was the idiom of France in the eighth century, conquering the less-cultivated Keltic and Teutonic languages; and the modern language of France, though showing all the various influences of race which entered into its formation, places the people especially among the modern Romanic or Neo-Latin races.

Keltic the principal race.

The ruins and ancient edifices on the soil of France point distinctly to the various races who have formed its people:—(1.) the Keltic and Druidical remains, especially in Brittany; (2.) the Roman ruins found in the southern provinces and cities, as Nismes, Arles, and Vienne; and (3.) the Gothic or Mediæval cathedrals and edifices.

In character and genius the French show the evidences of the three powerful races who have constituted the nation—traits which sometimes seem contradictory, and which only those closely familiar with the French people can understand.

In their brilliant martial character, their love of display and *effect*, their sudden enthusiasm and as easy

Evidences of race.

discouragement, their readiness to be ruled by military leaders, their fondness for ornament and art, their gaiety, fickleness, and amorousness, they are thorough Kelts, such as their ancestors have been in all ages: but in the sober devoutness of a large mass of the people, in their seriousness, in their personal sensitiveness and personal independence, in their spirit of sceptical inquiry and the thoroughness of their scientific research, they are Teutons, while their wonderful talent for organization and their tendency to centralization are Roman. Still, with all this, and much more which might ingeniously be worked out of inherited qualities, one feels we no more describe the great French nation than a man of genius is described by picturing his forefathers. The French race, with its genius, its science, its grandeur, its faults which are the scorn of mankind, its misfortunes which afflict the world, its magnificent past, its uncertain present and mysterious future—is a unity—a new and living force entering into the life of mankind, and henceforth as distinct as any of the great races of antiquity.

French race new.

The provincial dialects in France give an evidence of the races that have mingled in the formation of the people. In Lorraine, says M. Maury, we see incontestable traces of both the Germanic and Latin elements: as Alsacia and the countries near the Rhine are approached, the Germanic element becomes more powerful, until, in German Lorraine, it finishes by prevailing entirely. As we go toward the north similar phenomena meet us; on one side the Flemish dialect spoken near Dunkerque and Hazebrouck, and on the other, the Picard and Wallon dialects; the latter being a compound of German and Latin. In Artois an intermediate patois of the two languages is found. The

Dialects.

termination *hem* in the names of places in some French provinces shows the ancient Flemish influence; *ange*, in Lorraine, is a corruption of the German *ingen;* while the endings, *fleur*, *bec*, *tot*, in Normandy, speak of the ancient occupation by the Northmen.

Ethnologists attempt to assign the physical traits of modern Frenchmen to their different origins. In the north of France, where Teutonic blood prevails, are to be found men of tall stature, blue eyes and light complexion. Like the Germans, they are somewhat phlegmatic, less communicative than other Frenchmen, but frank in disposition and very hospitable. They furnish the best soldiers of the French army and the most vigorous workmen.

Different physical types.

In the south where the Roman and Keltic blood is predominant, the men are smaller, with brown complexion, and dark hair, and, at the same time are more agile and active than the Teutonic French. They are remarkable for their promptness, gaiety, wit, and passion.

The west, which still contains the pure Keltic blood, has men of short and stocky frame, with dark complexion,* both these peculiarities showing the effects of climate, or of natural selection transmitted. The hair of the Bretons is dark and smooth.

Two Keltic types.

The two branches of the Kelts—the *Cymric* and *Gaelic*—are said to be represented by two physical types in France. The one—the Cymric—found in the north is distinguished by a long oval head, a high narrow forehead, nose curved downward and pointed, chin small, figure tall and spare. The other—the Gaelic—found in the centre and east,

* To this, however, there are many exceptions. (See Arndt.) Many Saxon colonies were settled on the coast of Brittany, which may have aided sometimes in preserving the blonde traits among the people.

has a flat head, forehead low and broad, face round and nearly square, chin prominent, nose small and short, or turning up, stature short, and figure thick.

The descendants of the old *Normans* have thin and curly hair. The *Béarnese* are of middle or small stature, with clear complexion, and remarkable for their spirited movements. The French Basque has a marked, brown face, and a most elastic, supple body.

Between the two extremes of north and south lie the great masses of the French peasantry, probably of Gallic and Roman origin, the most ignorant and apathetic of the people, the portion which has always opposed any movements of progress. Their distinctions of race cannot be certainly analyzed.

French physique.

The Frenchman is usually described as small in stature (the tallest men being found in Normandy and Upper Burgundy), robust but not possessing great strength; with no inclination to fat, and of great suppleness of body.

In picturing the different provinces, Brittany is spoken of[1] as containing a Keltic population, hard and unyielding as the soil; its character being that of blind, untameable resistance, producing such men as Descartes, Pelagius, Moreau, and Lamennáis.

The old Keltic spirit of submission to priests and nobles is still a trait of the Keltic French of Brittany, and La Vendée. Druidical remains are found in various parts of these provinces; but the Keltic language and the ancient customs are fast dying away.

Race in the provinces.

Gascony and Aquitaine contain the descendants of Iberians and Goths. Languedoc is a province remarkable for its strong and hard character, and a certain Teutonic earnestness—it is filled with the remains of Roman architecture and of Roman law, though the kernel of the population is

Teutonic; Guyenne for its quick wit, and Provence for hot-headed petulance. This province contains many Gothic and Burgundian elements, with probably some remains of the ancient Roman.

Dauphiny, Franche Comté, and Lorraine have a vigorous race, often of Teutonic blood, and have produced many distinguished analytic minds.

The population of such cities as Mâcon, Auxerre, Dijon, Besançon, Lyons, and of the surrounding country, is said by Arndt to be Burgundian by descent, and to show now many German characteristics. In Champagne, Picardy, and Artois, says the same authority, are plainly seen, in the dull forms and blue eyes of the people, the remains of the ancient Belgians.

Burgundy is the land of orators. Normandy, with the characteristic Scandinavian love of the sea of its Northmen, has laid the foundation for and sustained the French marine. The pure modern Kelts in France are said to number about 900,000; the Germans in Alsace, Lorraine, and in the department of Ardennes, 1,300,000; the Dutch about 178,000.

CHAPTER XXX.

THE KELTS.[1]

THIS great people have in general become absorbed into other nations throughout Europe, and have left but few distinct remains.

As has been previously mentioned, there are two great classes of the modern Kelts, separated according to dialects: the *Cymric*, embracing (1.) the Welsh, some of the inhabitants of Cornwall, and the *Bretons* of France; and (2.) the *Gaelic*, including the inhabitants of the Isle of Man, the Highlanders of Scotland, and the Irish. The latter, however, are much mingled with lowland Scotch in the north, and with Spanish colonists in the west.

Two branches of Kelts.

The Keltic element in England, except in Wales and Cornwall, has become merged in the Teutonic, and only leaves here and there the traces of itself in the names of places—as in those words ending in *ford*,[2] or *combe*, or *way* and *wye*.

The purest Kelts, says Latham, are the Gaels in Ireland. Scotland is Gaelic, but not so pure; there being much Scandinavian blood in the population of the Highlands and the Western Isles. Orkney and Shetland are Norse. The Isle of Man is Gaelic, but in part Norse. The distinct Keltic branch inhabiting Wales, speak a dialect unintelligible to the Gaels; while the Scotch and Irish Gaels can understand each other. The Kelts of Cumberland are Cymric. Enough has

U 2

been said of the characteristics of this race in the early part of this Treatise. Their prominent faults and virtues are as distinct in the most ancient European history, as at the present day. The vices and defects charged upon the Kelts (the Irish) in America are no doubt the effects, in a considerable degree, of the degraded condition of the race under English rule. It is highly probable that a new destiny will be opened to this people in their crossings with the Teutonic race — whether Anglo-American or pure German—on American soil. There is something in the Kelts' love of enjoyment, their light-heartedness and warmth of temperament, peculiarly fitting them for a union with the more grave, reserved, and cold Teutonic race.

Keltic mixtures with Teutonic.

There can be no doubt that a great change has taken place in the Keltic physique. In the time of the classical historians, the Kelts were described as tall, large-boned, fair, with red hair and blue eyes. The type now is a small frame, with dark hair, swarthy complexion, and darkish or black eyes; in some portions of the Keltic area, as Western Ireland, it is much degraded by unfavourable circumstances. A portion of the Highlanders of Scotland alone correspond to the ancient type.

This variation has undoubtedly been caused by the great changes which have arisen during many centuries in the climate and temperature of Europe and the mode of life of the people.

THE TEUTONIC FAMILY.

(1.) *Scandinavians.* (2.) *Germans.* (3.) *Dutch.* (4.) *English.*

(1.) The *Scandinavian* branch of the Teutons contains three different peoples—the *Danes*, *Swedes*, and *Nor-*

wegians. Of these, the latter preserve more of the ancient Teutonic vigour.

Scandinavian branch.

Their languages are three dialects of the ancient Norse, and the Danish and Swedish are now alone literary tongues. The Scandinavians are divided into two branches—the East and West Scandinavians—the former including the ancient Norwegians and Icelanders with their descendants, and the latter, the Swedes and Danes.

This people, at one period of their history, were the most vigorous race of Europe, and supplied the ruling class or family to Russia and England, as well as the maritime population of France. To them may be traced the most vigorous qualities of the English race, whether in Great Britain or America, and to them also some of the most unscrupulous and oppressive habits which have characterized both branches of this powerful family.

The Scandinavian physique is thoroughly Teutonic —frame large and sinewy, complexion fair, hair usually light, with blue eyes, nose large or aquiline, and temperament sanguine. The forehead is not so square and full as with the modern German.

(2.) The *Germans.* The languages of Germany belong mostly to the High-German class.* To the Low-

* The line which divides the High German from the Low German dialects is thus minutely drawn by Stricker. It leaves the French territory near Aix, and follows the Prussian frontier to the neighbourhood of Roermonde on the Maas, then turns to the west, and crosses the Rhine north of Düsseldorf, runs along its right bank near the stream to its mouth, then turns north of the river, and passes parallel to it on the mountains, and then north of the Edder to between Münden and Kassel. Here it passes to the Habicht Forest, the old frontier between the Franks and the Saxons, and meets the confluence of the Fulda and the Werra, passing then toward Hesse and Prussia, to the Lower Harz, and then north to the Elbe, between Barby and

German languages belong the *Friesic*, spoken on the Elbe and along the northern coast of Germany; the *Dutch* of Holland, and the *Flemish*. The *Plattdeutsch* is a Low-German language. Low German has ceased to be a literary language since Luther.

Among the great names of the Low-German branch are Luther, Flemming, Klopstock, Tieck, Handel, Beethoven, Leibnitz, Lessing, Kant, Fichte, and the Humboldts.

High-German great names.

In the High-German division may be mentioned among others, Göthe, Schiller, Hegel, Kepler, Schelling, Durer, Holbein, Gluck, and Mozart.

Early German area.

When Charlemagne began his wars with the Saxons, the boundary between the Saxons and Slavonians ran from the mouth of the Traave to the Elbe. After 804, it extended from Kiel to the Elbe, between Lauenburg and Hamburg. The Elbe and then the Saab became the separating line. Under the later emperors, this frontier was continually forced toward the east, and preserved by the formation of new bishoprics and earldoms, such as Brandenburg, Meissen, Austria, and others.

On the other side, the Slavic tongues had pressed into what is now Bohemia, Moravia, and Upper Silesia. The higher classes there are still German.

Among the Bohemian peasantry, the ancient Markomanns are said to have retained their Teutonic purity, even as the Basques their nationality in Spain, and to be still clearly recognized in their Teutonic customs and traits. They seldom intermarry with Slavonians.

Magdeburg. In the Harz is an island of High-German dialects. From Barby, the line goes to Wittemberg and the northern frontier of the Slavic Lausitz.

Among the descendants of the ancient German tribes, it is believed that the purest *Saxons* are found in Quedlenburg, Aschersleben, Magdeburg, and Soltwedel, down to the country of the Friesen and the Rhine; a long-bodied, long-armed, blue-eyed race, with fair hair, quiet in temperament, of firm, staunch, and genial character, holding inflexibly to old customs. They are thought to be less poetic and ideal than the descendants of the Alemanns and Goths. They spread originally to the west toward England, and on the east reconquered a portion of Germany, settling a portion of Eastern Holstein, Mecklenburg, Pomerania, Brandenburg, and Lausitz. Many of the Friesians, Hollanders, and Franks have mingled with them.

Saxons.

Around the Thuringian Forest are grouped the most joyful, pleasure-loving and musical people of Germany —the descendants of the *Thuringians* and *East Franks*. On the Elbe and in the Bohemian Forest, they are much mingled with Bohemians. They are a handsome race, more smooth in manner and less staunch than the Saxon.

The *Hessians* are considered to be the descendants of the ancient *Katti*, and of the purest German blood. They are of a firm, rough, indomitable character, little subject to changes—the most reserved and earnest people of Germany.

The *Austrians* in their mountains preserve many remains of ancient Keltic tribes and Roman colonists, which all the invasions of Roman, Chazar, Hunn, Magyar, and Turk, have not wholly obliterated. The masses of the population in Austria, Upper Bavaria, and the Tyrol are the descendants of the East Goths and the Rugians; and on the Danube and north of the Danube, probably the remains of the Burgundians, Hermunduri, and others.

Austrians.

Slavonians in Germany.

Many Slavonians are scattered about among the German populations of Austria, and are at once to be recognized by their dress and manners. In temperament, they are much more lively and uncontrolled than the Germans.

The *Alemanns* are believed to be found on the Moselle, the Upper Rhine, in Schwabia, and Switzerland.

The *Burgundians* make up also a portion of the Swiss people.

Two Slavonian islands are to be recognized in the German territory—one, the Upper Lausitz, where Bohemian is still spoken, and the other, the Prussian Lower Lausitz, where Polish is the popular language.

The population of pure Germans in the German States is reckoned at 17,600,000; of pure Germans over the world in seventy different countries, over 53,000,000.

Two very distinct types of physique can be seen now through Germany: one in the north—the old Teutonic type, marked by fair hair, blue or gray eyes, light complexion, and large bones and frame; the other, more frequently found in the south, though scattered through Germany, with dark hair and eyes, harsh or dark complexion, and smaller limbs and figures—the latter type in the lower classes being also frequently accompanied with defective physique. Whether the change from the old type is altogether due to the change of climate and modes of life, or somewhat to mixture with Keltic and Slavonic blood, is difficult to determine. We incline to the latter cause, from the remarkable purity of the Teutonic type in Scandinavia, where climate and habits of life must have also changed considerably, but where little foreign blood has been mingled with the people.

The old Teutonic character, as seen in the early German tribes and the Scandinavian peoples, is now best preserved, it seems to us, in the peculiarities, both bad and good, of their Anglican descendants on both sides of the ocean.

(3.) Another branch of the Teutonic race are the *Dutch*, belonging to the Low-German division. The northern provinces—those of Holland—are more purely Teutonic; while the southern—those of Belgium—have been mingled in blood with the Keltic and Roman populations. Dutch history presents the characteristics of each family as influencing the fortunes of their respective provinces. Mr. Motley well remarks, that in both of the great struggles between the inhabitants of the Dutch provinces and the Imperial power—in classic times against the Roman, and in modern against the Spaniard—the Keltic populations, inflammable, quarrelsome, and bold, were the first to assault and defy the royal authority; while the Teutonic inhabitants of the northern provinces were less ardent in the beginning, but were more enduring and steadfast. In both, he adds, the Southern Kelts fell away from the league, their courageous chiefs having been purchased by Imperial gold, but the Germans fought out the contest to the last. The northern provinces, with Batavian and Frisian blood, became one of the most celebrated Republics in history, while the southern, with Romanized Kelts, became the property of Roman, Spanish, and Austrian.

Teutonic and Keltic.

There are three dialects of the Low German still spoken in the Netherlands; the *Dutch*, between the Zuyderzee and the Meuse; the *Flemish*, at the south of the Meuse; and the *Frisic*, at the east of the Zuyderzee, whence it prolongs itself to Jutland.

Three dialects.

(4.) *The English Race.*

Like the other modern races of Europe, made up of many different elements, the English people is very difficult to analyze into its component parts.

Two thousand years and more of history passed on small islands, with successive inroads of various conquest and immigration, with incessant mixture and amalgamation of all the peoples that had settled or struggled on the soil, have finally, with slight exceptions, welded the English population into one compact and homogeneous whole—a race in many respects as distinct as any other in the world. We know, indeed, what families and nations have contributed their blood to this new variety of man; we are certain that the Kelts were its earliest historic progenitors; and that with these were united in very slight degree the Romans, and in much greater degree different tribes of Teutons, until the new people became almost entirely a Teutonic people. We have reason to believe, also, that a certain small proportion of Slavonic and Moorish blood mingles in the veins of this race, both from colonists of the north of Europe and from Roman legionaries. But, at the present time, to point out the exact traces of each of these various tribes and races; to say that here we have a Roman or Keltic feature, there a Teutonic; some trait or relic of Saxon, or Frisian, or Angle, or Dane, or Norwegian, or Romanized Northman; is very difficult to attempt. Still, without doubt, each of these peoples has left its peculiar stamp and its ineffaceable effect on the mind and the physique, the institutions, laws, and language of the English nation.

Great mixtures of blood.

What prominent peculiarities distinctive of race can be observed now in England, we propose to mention in the brief mode necessary for this Treatise.

Before detailing these, the reader must recall rapidly the ethnological history of England. Whether there were a primeval family on British soil, perhaps of Finnic origin, anterior to the Kelts, it is not necessary for our present purpose to inquire, nor farther, whether the ancient Picts were certainly Kelts or not. Historically, the Kelts were the earliest inhabitants of Britain, though without question there was a very early immigration of Teutonic tribes from the Continent. The Roman conquest and settlement followed. During several centuries succeeding—especially from the middle of the fifth to the middle of the sixth—there was a constant stream of German tribes from the western coasts of Germany between Holstein and the Rhine, to this fertile island—tribes known as Anglians, Jutes, Frisians, and Saxons, and representing two great branches of the Saxon family—the Friso-Saxon and the Anglo-Saxon. These were succeeded by another and more warlike branch of the Teutonic race—the Scandinavian Northmen, consisting of Danes and Norwegians. After these came yet other Northmen or Normans from France, who had been Romanized in language, and were no doubt intermingled with much Keltic and Frankic blood.

Ethnological history.

The main current in this mingling of so many streams of race is evidently Teutonic, and of it, the Anglian and the Norse seem the most important elements. The Roman blood has had little influence on the English race, and though the Keltic has had vastly more power, and has mingled to a much greater extent than many warm "Anglo-Saxons" would have us believe, still the two races and languages seem never to have united closely on British soil. The early Kelts were either exterminated by the Teutonic invaders, or driven to the mountains, where a portion of them

Keltic elements.

still survive, unmixed in blood and with their native dialect.

Of the Keltic element in our language, says Mr. Donaldson :—

The stoutest asserter of a pure Anglo-Saxon or Norman descent is convicted by the language of his daily life, of belonging to a race that partakes largely of Keltic blood. If he calls for his *coat** (Irish *cota*), or tells of the *basket* of fish he has caught (W. *basged*), or the *cart* he employs on his land (W. *cart* † from *càr*, a dray or sledge), or of the *pranks* of his youth or the prancing of his horse (W. *pranc*, a trick, *prancie*, to frolick), or declares that he is *happy* (W. *hap*, future, chance), or that his servant is *pert* (W. *pert*, spruce, dapper, insolent), or he affirms that such assertions are *balderdash* and a sham (W. *baldorddus*, idle prating, or *baldorz*, to prattle; *siom*, from *shom*, a deceit or sham), he is using the ancient language of our Keltic forefathers.

The Lancashire words *tackle*, "to set right," and "*griddle*," the last of which has passed to America, are Keltic—the one being from the Welsh "*taclu*," and the other from "*greidyl*" (bake-stone).

Still, with all this, a distinguished scholar, Mr. Marsh, has said :—

We may safely say that, though the primitive language of Britain has contributed to the English a few names of places, and of familiar material objects, yet it has, upon the whole, affected our vocabulary and our syntax far less than any other tongue, with which the Anglo-Saxon race has ever been brought widely into contact. I might go too far in saying that we have borrowed, numerically, more words from the followers of Mohammed, than from the aborigines of Britain; but it is very certain that the few we have derived from the

* It is curious that Stanihurst, some 300 years ago, should have mentioned this word—*coat*—as having been borrowed by the Irish from the English. See Marsh. Hist. and Origin, &c., p. 542.

† *Cart* may be of Gothic origin.

distant Arabic are infinitely more closely connected with us than the somewhat greater number which we have taken from the contiguous Keltic.

One of the most enduring traces of a race is in the names it gives to places; so that an ancient stream of population, flowing over a country, may utterly pass away, and yet leave relics more permanent than monuments, and more distinct than sculptured inscriptions, in the names it deposits of mountains, rivers, and towns.

The Keltic endings of *combe* (valley), *way* or *wye* (water), and *ford* (where it denotes a road or passage, and not an arm of the sea), are especially found in the western counties, though scattered here and there over various parts of England. The rivers bearing names in *exe*, *axe*, and *ouse*, are thought to show the Gaelic branch of the Kelts. The words *aber* and *inver*, used in compounds (as Aberdeen and Inverary), and meaning something like "confluence of waters," are Keltic. Numerous other Keltic endings and words are scattered over England and Scotland.

Geographical names in Keltic.

In general, of the Teutonic tribes it may be said, that the evidences of names show the occupancy of the northern and eastern counties of England by Angles, and of the southern and western by Saxons. In the south, the endings in *ton*, *ham*, *bury*, *forth*, and *worth* are Saxon; but even near the Thames, become mingled with Scandinavian, in *by*, *thorpe*, *thwaite*, *naes*, and *cy*. In the north, the endings in *toft*, *beck*, *with*, *tarn*, *dale*, *fell*, *force*, and *haugh* are Scandinavian. These latter are found more often on the coasts and along the rivers.

Teutonic names of places.

The Danish ending *by* ("place" or "town") is especially found in Lincolnshire, Leicestershire, Derbyshire, the East and North Ridings of Yorkshire, in Durham, Cumberland, Westmoreland, Lancashire, Cheshire, and Caernarvon.

It has been estimated by the curious, that Norfolk, Northamptonshire, and Lancashire have each about 50 places with names of Scandinavian origin; Leicestershire, about 90; Lincolnshire, about 300; Yorkshire, nearly 400; and Westmoreland and Cumberland, some 150. There are few Danish endings in the south; toward the north, they cease in Northumberland, and in the south-west part of Scotland and the Isle of Man. In this latter island, the Danish and Norwegian seem to meet, while the Norwegian element predominates over the Danish in the Orkneys, Shetland, the Hebrides, and Ireland.

Scandinavian names.

In the Lowlands of Scotland there are comparatively very few Scandinavian names, and these are found in the old border-land between the Cheviots and the Firths of Clyde and Forth, and in counties nearest to England.

To the evidence from names of places, it may be objected that they rather show the past history of a race, than the present ethnological analysis of a people. But they at least render it probable, that the ancient elements of race which were once prominent in a certain locality, still form a part of the mixture of blood in the modern race. Perhaps a more convincing evidence of race is to be found in the familiar words, customs, and superstitions of a population.

Evidence from dialects.

Judging from these, it seems probable that the Norman element is less strong in the north than in the south of England. Of Lancashire, Mr. Davies says, that *one-sixth* of the dialectic words in use by the people are Saxon; and that there is hardly the least trace of the Norman in the local names of the county, and only faint evidence of his race in the dialect.

In Suffolk, there is a Frisian relic in the Anglian usage of the vowel *o* for *a*—as *lond*, for land; *mon*, for man; *stond*, for stand.

An ancient difference in the use of vowels, supposed to have been noticed by Tacitus, between the Anglian and the Saxon, is still observed in England; the South-Saxon saying, *I geez*, and the East-Anglian, *I guiss*. The South-Saxon gives the full force to the *r*, while the East-Anglian drops it before a consonant; the former saying "*parrtridges*," and the latter, "*pattridges*,"—an Anglian pronunciation which has reached even to America. The South-Saxon retains the hard *g*, while the Angle gives us palatal sounds, as *aitchorn* for acorn, and *coksedge* for cocks' heads; and often like the Low German, the latter substitute *y* for *g*, or *h*, as *yowl* for howl, and *yate* for gate.

South-Saxon and Anglian words.

Yeou for you, and *tyeu* for two, which has been thought a pure Yankee pronunciation, is discovered to be North-Anglian. In the East Riding of Yorkshire are also found strong traces of the Frisian blood.

Of the glorious historic names in English history, the Anglians, it is claimed, have a stronger proportion than the Saxons: such men as Wycliffe, of Yorkshire, Isaac Newton, of Lincolnshire, Cromwell, Lord Bacon's family, Jeremy Taylor, Bently, Arkwright, and Stephenson, and even Shakespeare, are asserted by one able investigator (Donaldson), to belong to this branch.

Historical names.

Scandinavian relics are scattered over various parts of England. The *nix* or fairies, still feared by the North of England peasant boy, are the Norse spirits: the legends are the same: the superstitions the same;

the festivals are similar, such as the *Yule* festival and the burning of the Yule log. The Westmoreland boor still says *at think* and *at do*, for "to think" and "to do," as the Scandinavian pirates did; and the Yorkshireman speaks of a son "*braiding* on his father" (*i. e.* resembling, Swed. *braeas*, resembles), even as his Norse ancestors were in the habit of saying. The old English word *hustings* is a Scandinavian legacy.

Norse words.

Westmoreland, Cumberland, and the North of England contain a vast number of Scandinavian relics, both in language and customs. The bond which connects the north of England dialects and the Scotch is supposed to be the Scandinavian element in both.

In Westmoreland, the practice of combining several words into one, which is so common in the Norse languages, still exists; thus the "Scalthwaiterigggate" is "the road to the log-house on the cleared ground upon the ridge," as in Norway, *Viknesholmer* means "the islands in the bay beside the promontory."

Norse resemblances.

The names of berries, and trees, and plants—as Mr. Ferguson has so well shown—have a marked resemblance in this county and in Norway.

In Cumberland, where a large Norwegian population settled, land is still held in the same manner as in Norway, by a large number of small independent proprietors, which has had its natural effect in perpetuating the Norse sense of personal independence.

The coldness of manner, and the caution and shrewdness of the people, both in these counties and in Yorkshire, as well as their peculiar fondness for law-disputes, are genuine Scandinavian traits. It has always been observed that the northern counties of England, where the Norse invaders especially settled, are the most marked for their resolute spirit of independence, and their hatred of oppression.

Norse customs.

Among the Scandinavian customs transmitted is a dance at Christmas time, which has a strong resemblance to the ancient sword-dance; the old Norse wrestling matches are still kept up, and bear the ancient name—a word which has passed over to America, *russle* (N. *rusla*). The Norse oatmeal porridge, and the broad flat cakes of barley, so familiar to the traveller in Norway as "*flad brod,*" and called *scons* in England (N. *skán*, crust), are still in use among the people.

Scandinavian phrases.

Mr. Ferguson has given a great number of words and dialectic expressions in the north of England, which are Scandinavian, though many are also Saxon. Thus the change of *th* into *d*—as *fadder* for father, *smiddy* for smithy; and of *ch* and *sh* into *k*—as *kurn* for churn, *skift* for shift, *kirk* for church. (The same habit is noticed in Normandy, as *kien* for *chien.*) The change also of *f* to *p*, as *Jwosep* for Joseph (N. *lopt* for loft): all these are Norse practices; so the use of *drucken* (N. druckerin) for drunken, and of *timmer* for timber—*i. e.* forest—which last, in its application, has become an Americanism. A certain lengthening of the vowels—as *gy-ate* for gate, and *ny-ame* for name, is both Anglo-Saxon and Scandinavian. The fondness for *w*—as *worchit* for orchard, *cwuman* for come, *cworn* for corn, is especially Anglo-Saxon (as Wodin (S.) for Odin (N.); the use of thee and thou for you, in Westmoreland, Cumberland, Yorkshire, and the Orkneys, is Norse. The prepositions *fra* and *till* are probably from the same source, as well as the verb *mun* for must; the *at* for that, as "its time at he were here" is probably from the Danish conjunction *at*.

It is characteristic of the vigorous Northmen, that a

great number of almost slang words in the northern counties—many of which have crossed the ocean—meaning *beat*, are Norse; thus out of many, the words *baist*, *bang*, *lam*, *leather* or *lather*, *hide*, *dust*, &c., &c. To chaff—a Cumberland expression, is from the Scandinavian *káfa*, to banter; and *brass* (impudence) is no modern expression, but as old as the Vikings (*brasta*, to live in a dissolute manner). Even the luxurious *sofa* came in name from old Iceland or Norway (N. *sofa*, a sleeping-place); and the Americanisms, *bumble-bee* for humble-bee, *loft* for an upper room, and *muggy* (damp and foggy), and to *nab*, are all Scandinavian relics, left in the northern counties of England centuries ago.

Norse slang words.

Grimsby was almost the central Danish town, and a vestige of the famous Danish hero—Havelok—is still seen in the name of a street—*Havelok* Street; and, it may be, appears in the name of the modern hero of India.

In Scotland, the fishermen in the Nith use Norse words to this day—as *poknet* (Icelandic, *pokanet*), *lister* (I. *ljöster*), *haaving* (Nor. *haave*), or drawing small nets through the water.

Norse words in Scotland.

Yet with all these tokens of Scandinavian mixture, the Danish language never seems to have exerted any profound influence on the English or Anglo-Saxon. Its greatest peculiarity—the post-fix—its negative *ikke*, and its plural form of the substantive verb, as well as its numerals, have never been transferred to our language.

Of this evidence from the names of places, which can be gathered from the map of England, Mr. Ferguson beautifully says:—

The land is dotted over with little individual histories—rude and simple, it is true—yet such as was their life. Here, eight centuries ago, an Ulf or an Orme shouldered his axe, and strode into the forest, and hewed himself a home, nor deemed that his stalwart arm was marking the map of England. Here a wandering settler saw a blue lake gleaming among the trees, thought of his native land, and said "this shall be my home." Here, in the name of some mountain-dwelling, we have the story of him who, first in his Teutonic self-reliance, planted himself as an outpost in the solitude. Here he settled, and toiled, and lived, and died—it is all there is to tell. Here a Northman, faithful to Odin's command, set up the rude bauta to his departed friend. The stone is gone, and there is a busy town, but the memorial has borne his name far into an age which has outlived his life.

Of the English physical traits as distinctive of race, but little can be said with confidence. The various tribes have become so mingled, that but few bodily peculiarities can be discovered in their descendants, indicating their ancient origin. Mr. Worsaae, however, observes that the English of London and the south of England are distinguished by black hair, dark eyes, fine hooked nose, and long oval face; as if the Keltic and the Roman features predominated. As we proceed north, in Northumberland, he says, the form becomes broader, the cheek-bones project, the nose is flatter, the eyes and hair are lighter, and deep-red hair is more often seen. People are not very tall in stature, but are usually more compact and strongly built than in the south of England; perhaps indicating the Frisian and Scandinavian blood. The faces in Middle and North England, he remarks, are decidedly Norse.

Physical race-marks.

Bulwer also observes, that "the descendants of the Anglo-Danes in Cumberland and Yorkshire are taller and bonier than those of the Anglo-Saxons in Surrey and Sussex;" but the people of Cumberland, though compactly built, are less burly in form than those of

Yorkshire, and in this respect the former correspond to the Norwegians and the latter to the Danes, as they do also in many other particulars.

It is a work of ingenuity, rather than of solid, scientific or historic value, to speculate on the moral qualities transmitted by race, in such a composite people as the English. Yet one can see many characteristic qualities of their forefathers in both the English and American progeny.

English qualities of blood.

The boundless spirit of individual enterprise; the personal pride; the love of the perils of the sea (which the Saxons never showed); the recklessness of life; the shrewdness and skill in technical law; the fondness for wassail and wine; the respect for woman, and, above all, the tendency to associated self-government, are Norse peculiarities. From the Friso-Anglian have come especially the patient industry, the sound practical sense, the solid courage, the love of constitutional freedom and the spirit of industrial enterprise, which form the other side of the English character, and which equally distinguish the Frisian of Holland.

The immeasurable contempt and prejudice against the inferior race, which characterize all branches of the English race, whether the British masters ruling Hindoo servants, or English landlords with Irish Kelts, or Anglo-Americans among Indian tribes, or Southern slaveholders toward slaves, or "Yankees" toward negroes, is an unfortunate but legitimate inheritance from Teutonic ancestors.

Even the most ancient traditions of the Teutons—the Norse-sagas—show the deep prejudice of the blonde race against dark colour, and the ancient Germans were exceedingly oppressive to the inferior races.

One of the most natural feelings in surveying the

ethnological condition of England is of wonder at the little impress which the great conquering race of antiquity—the Roman—made upon the language, the geographical names, or the physique of the British races with which they were thrown in contact.

They ploughed the island with lines of defence, with military works and roads, but the evidence of language and of history agrees that their blood and that of our forefathers scarce ever mingled; and Providence seems to have designed that the new and powerful Race of modern times was to have in its composition hardly a drop of the worn-out blood from that haughty Italian people who had once ruled the world. And with the exclusion of the Roman race is linked a long chain of exclusions of priestcraft and tyranny and centralized government, whose good effect has not yet ceased to be felt.

Slight Roman influence.

CHAPTER XXXI.

WANDERING RACES.

The Gypsies.

EXCEPTING the Jews, no people have ever shown such tenacity of race as the Gypsies. A Hindu tribe of Aryan race originally, perhaps of nomadic and plundering habits in their provinces on the Indus, and forced out into Europe and Asia in the early part of the fifteenth century, they have encamped or settled in almost every country of Europe, without scarcely ever changing the pure current of their Hindu blood. Whether in the mountain-villages of Norway, or on the pusztas of Hungary, or in rural England, or among the wild mountains of Spain, whether under the burning heat of Africa, or on the plateaus of Asia, in Egypt, Persia, or India, the Gypsy is substantially the same; with a similar physique, with the same language only dialectically different, and with the ineradicable habits of the plundering nomad in him. Sometimes enslaved, always scorned, the victim of legislation through more than three hundred years, driven from country to country, incessantly urged by the influences of civilization and by the ministers of religion—yet always, in all countries and for four centuries, the same—a vagrant, a jockey, a cheat, and a heathen and stranger to each people and country. The civilization, the science, and the Christianity

Hindu in race.

Low morality.

of modern times, have done almost nothing for him. A few exceptions to this general character of the race are found in Russia, where individual Gypsies have become wealthy; but in most countries, they seldom engage in any pursuit of mechanics or agriculture. The only mechanical branch in which they are ever proficient is the smith's; and in Persia, they have become celebrated as workers in gold and silver.

Tenacity of race.

While other races become absorbed in the powerful races, or mingle in endless variety with the peoples in contact with them, or die out and pass away—this Indian tribe keeps itself unmingled and preserves its savage vitality. Such a tenacity, both of race and of barbarian habits, seems hardly characteristic of the Aryan family, and would remind one more of the peculiar traits of the Semites. In many countries they have been supposed to be Egyptians, and their name in English, French, Spanish, and Hungarian, points to this belief. Most other nations have given them a name in some way connected with that of a Hindu robber-tribe on the Indus, from whom they are supposed to be descended—*Tschingani.**

M. de Gobineau, who has examined the condition of the Gypsies of Persia, concludes that the whole race are the descendants of the ancient peoples of Bactriana and Aria, and that at length, driven out from their territories, they have settled in Persia, among the numerous nomad races of that country.

These and all the other theories in regard to them, do not seem, however, sufficiently well based to overbalance the evidence of language, which places them

* The name *Zincali*, *Zingari*, or *Zigeuner*, is also derived by some from *Zingáneh*, a Kurdish tribe of Gypsies. (See Zeit. f. Alg. Erd., p. 82, 1857.)

among the Aryan tribes of India, and their dialect among the modern Sanskrit dialects.

Physique.

In physique, the Gypsies are almost universally alike —tawny in complexion, with black hair, quick black eyes, high cheek-bones, slightly-projecting lower jaw, narrow mouth, with fine white teeth, and a figure remarkably lithe and agile. In general, they are decidedly ugly in appearance, but the writer has seen faces in Hungary which were very pretty, and in Spain, they are said to show female countenances and figures of wonderful beauty. In all countries and climates, they have a peculiar preference for red as a colour of costume.

The Gypsies, from their constant change of residence and their close intermarriage, show little effect of climate on bodily traits. They present, however, in the mountains of Antiochia, the blue eyes, which for some unknown reason seem usually a feature of the inhabitants of mountainous regions.

In mental and moral characteristics, this tribe are notorious for almost every vice and meanness: the exceptions in their favour being their faithfulness to one another, and in some countries, their personal chastity, even while acting as panders for others. They accept with indifference the religion of every country in which they happen to be, where its profession will bring them profit. Their language is said to contain no words for God or Immortality—though for the former a word has been adopted.

Language.

The Gypsy tongue shows phonetic elements identical with those of the *Devanagari;* it has no neuter gender nor dual number. There is no alphabet to the language; and the only literature are some wild songs, repeated from mouth to mouth.

The number of Gypsies in Europe was estimated in 1830 as about 700,000. The whole number of the tribe has been supposed to be 5,000,000. It is believed that one small party only of this singular people has ever reached America.

PART EIGHTH.

GENERAL QUESTIONS IN ETHNOLOGY.

CHAPTER XXXII.

THE ANTIQUITY OF MAN.[1]

THE object of this Treatise, it should be remembered, has not been so much to investigate the origin of races as to trace them as they appear in human history. Still, in considering the subjects of the Unity or Diversity of races, of the Formation of Varieties, and of the historical course or the different families of man, the question of *Time* comes necessarily in view.

How long has the human family been upon this earth?—is the inquiry that constantly forces itself on every student of Ethnology. And yet the search for human origins, or the earliest historic and scientific evidences of man on the earth, is but a groping in the dark.

We turn to the Hebrew and the inspired records; but we soon discover, that, though containing a picture unequalled for simplicity and dignity, of the earliest experiences of the present family of man, they are by no means a monument or relic of the most remote period, but belong to a comparatively modern date, and that the question of *Time* is not at all directly treated in them.

We visit the region where poetry, and myth, and tradition have placed a most ancient civilization—Egypt, the Black-Land, the Land of the Nile: we search its royal sepulchres, its manifold history written in funereal records, in kingly genealogies, in inscriptions, and in the thousand relics preserved of domestic life, whether in picture, sculpture, or the embalmed remains of the dead; and we find ourselves thrown back to a date far beyond any received date of history, and still we have before us a ripened Civilization, an Art which could not belong to the childhood of a race, a language which (so far as we can judge) must have needed centuries for its development, and the divisions of human races, all as distinct as they are at the present day.

We traverse the regions to which both the comparison of languages and the Biblical records assign the original birthplace of the leading races of men—the country of the Euphrates and the plateau of Eastern Asia. Buried kingdoms are revealed to us; the shadowy outlines of magnificent cities appear which flourished and fell before recorded human history, and of which even Herodotus never heard; Art and Science are unfolded, reaching far back into the past; the signs of luxury and splendour are uncovered from the ruin of ages: but, remote as is the date of these Hamitic and Semitic empires, almost equalling that of the Flood in the ordinary system of Chronology, they cannot be near the origin of things, and a long process of development must have passed ere they reached the maturity in which they are revealed to us.

The Chinese records give us an antiquity and an acknowledged date before the time of Abraham (if we follow the received chronology), and even then their language must have been, as it is now, distinct and solidified, betraying to the scholar no certain affinity with any other family of language. The Indian history, so long boasted of for its immense antiquity, is without doubt the most modern of the ancient records, and offers no certain date beyond 1800 B.C.

In Europe the earliest evidences of man disclosed by our investigations are even more vague and shadowy. Without, probably, antedating in time these historical records of Asia, they reach back to a more primitive and barbarous era. The earliest history of Europe is not studied from inscription or manuscript, or even monument; it is not, like the Asiatic, a conscious work of a people leaving a memorial of itself to a future age. It is rather like the geological history, an unconscious gradual deposit left by the remains of extinct and unknown races in the soil of the fields or under the sediment of the waters. The earliest European barbarian, as he burned his canoe from a log, or fabricated his necklace from a bone, or worked out his knife from a flint, was in reality writing a history of his race for distant days.

In tracing the various indications of man at an early age in Europe, we find one of the first to be in the *Peat Deposits in Denmark*. These deposits, formed in hollows in the northern drift, are from ten to thirty feet in thickness. From the remains of trees found around them, and at various depths in them, as well as from the human implements preserved by the bog, Danish antiquaries and naturalists have discovered that there were three periods of vegetation, which in part corresponded with the human eras, previously mentioned. The early vegetation, long before the historical period, was that of the Scotch fir; this was followed by the oak, and this by the forests of beech which covered the

Danish islands in the classical period. The "Age of Stone" corresponded with that of the fir, and in part of the oak; the "Age of Bronze," mostly with the oak; and that of Iron, with the beech. Eighteen centuries have made but little change in the beech-woods. How much time was needed for the destruction and growth of each of these new kinds of vegetation cannot be certainly estimated; but the minimum of time required for the formation of the peat, say some authorities, is 4000 years, and "there is nothing," says Sir Charles Lyell, "in the observed rate of the growth of peat, opposed to the conclusion that the number of centuries may not have been four times as great." (Antiquity of Man, p. 17.)

Another indication of their antiquity is found in the changes which must have occurred during the Stone period in the physical geography of the Baltic. The shells found in the heaps to be presently described show that the oyster existed then in its full size, in places where now it is excluded, owing to the want of saltness of the water, and that various marine univalves and bivalves were of their ordinary dimensions, when in the ocean—the same shells being now dwarfed by the quantity of fresh water poured by rivers into the Baltic. The inference, of course, is that the ocean had at that day more free access into this inland sea than at present—perhaps communicating through the Peninsula of Jutland. (Ant. of Man, p. 13.) Still here again, the time necessary for these physical changes, as well as for those of the forest-growths of the country, is entirely uncertain.

Still another evidence for human antiquity is furnished by the *Kjoeekken moedding* (Kitchen leavings).

For a long time, great heaps of sea-shells had been observed on the Danish shores, which were thought to show an ancient sea-level; but on closer examination it was perceived that they bore marks of artificial stratification. With farther research, the bones of various wild animals were discovered in them, some of extinct species; then flint implements were found, with rough pottery, charcoal and cinders. There was never, even in the largest heaps, the slightest trace of metal, whether iron or bronze, nor were bones seen of any domestic animal, except the dog. It finally became clear that these were the "leavings" (or "*middings*," as the Yorkshiremen yet say) of primeval oyster-suppers on the fiords and bays of the Baltic and North Sea, where some ancient people, living by fishing and hunting, had held their feasts and left their implements, and, during the course of ages, had deposited these immense heaps of refuse.

They evidently dated back to that remote period when even bronze was unknown in Northern Europe, and their interest lay in the fact that they had remained undisturbed for so many centuries, and thus furnished true museums of antiquity containing specimens of the most ancient human implements, and of an early fauna and flora.

These heaps, or *Kitchen-middings*, were found principally in Seeland, along the Isefiord, the islands of Fyen, Moen, and Samsoe, and in Jutland. Similar remains, no doubt from the same people, have been discovered in Scania, Sweden, and now are beginning to be met with in North Italy, especially on the borders of the Gulf of Genoa.

No human bones have been discovered in these mounds. The pottery is of the coarsest nature, made by hand; the flint implements are very rude, and different from those ordinarily found in ancient European mounds, more like, says Mr. Worsaae, the implements which have been found in Abbéville, and near Amiens, France. Bones, carved and worked, are frequently picked up, and bones broken for marrow, for which savage tribes have so remarkable a fondness.

The only clue to the date of these refuse-heaps is furnished by the remains of vegetation discovered in them, which places them contemporaneously with the fir epoch, and the older part of the peat deposit described above—or probably at least 4000 years since.

The Lake-dwellings of Switzerland.

Some eight years ago a remarkable dryness of the waters in the Lake of Zurich laid bare a portion of its bottom, which was speedily secured for agricultural purposes by means of dykes, and by mud thrown up in dredging. In building the embankments and dredging the shallow water various remains were found which plainly indicated the existence of a village in the lake, at some ancient date. It was discovered that some early tribes had constructed their village on piles in the water, as, according to Herodotus, did the Pæonians of Thrace, or as the Papuas of New Guinea and other barbarous tribes do now. These discoveries aroused the eager attention of learned men, and the lakes of Italy, the French Jura, Savoy, and Switzerland, were carefully searched for similar relics.

Pile-villages.

In Switzerland, alone, the remains of over 150 villages were discovered beneath the waters. These early Europeans seem to have resorted to this very natural method to escape the wild beasts or hostile tribes, securing a safe refuge in these artificial islands, whose only communication with the land must have been by boat or bridge.

A mere glance of the eye, says an interesting writer in the *Rev. des Deux Mondes* (transl. in Smithson. Rep., 1861), through the transparent water, enables us to perceive piles in parallel rows, or planted, it may be, without order. The charred beams which are seen between the posts, recall the platform once solidly constructed at a height of some feet above the waves. The interlaced boughs, the fragments of clay hardened by fire, evidently belonged to circular walls, and the conic roofs are represented by some layers or beds of reeds, straw, and bark. The stones of the fireplace have fallen just below the place which they formerly occupied. The vessels of clay, the heaps of leaves and of moss which served as beds for repose, the arms, the trophies of the chase, the large stag-horns and skulls of wild bulls which adorned the walls—all these different objects, mingled together in the mind, are nothing else but the ancient furniture of the habitations. By the side of the piles we can still distinguish remains of the hollowed trunks of trees which served for canoes, and a range of posts indicates the pristine existence of a bridge, which led from the threshold of the lacustrian dwelling to the neighbouring shore. Not only are we enabled to determine from the number of piles what were the dimensions of the largest aquatic villages, composed generally of two or three hundred cabins; we can even measure, in some cases, the diameter of the huts constructed so many ages ago. The fragments of the coat of clay which lined them on the inside, show on their convex face the marks of the interlaced boughs of the wall, while their concave side is rounded into the arc of a circle; by calculating the radius of this arc, we find that the size of the habitations varied from three to five metres (10 to 16 or 17 feet), dimensions quite sufficient for a family which seeks in its dwelling a simple shelter.

Athwart an interval of thirty or forty centuries, we can conceive how picturesque an effect must have been produced by this agglomeration of small huts, closely compacted together in the midst of the waters. The shore was uninhabited; a few domestic animals alone fed in the grassy clearings; great trees spread their masses of verdure over all the slopes; a deep silence brooded in the forest. Upon the waters, on the contrary, all was movement and clamour; the smoke curled above the roofs; the populace bustled upon the platforms; the canoes passed and repassed from one group of dwellings to another, and from the village to the shore; in the distance floated the boats which served for fishing or for war. The water seemed then the real domain of man.

It is in German Switzerland that the oldest of these lake-dwellings are found. Western and Northern Switzerland shows populous villages in Lakes Neufchatel, Zurich, and Constance. M. Troyon, by measuring the dimensions of each hut, and calculating the number which could probably be sheltered in it, has estimated the population of fifty-one of the oldest villages—those of the Age of Stone—at 31,875 persons. In a single village, Wangen, 40,000 piles are used.

Population.

These Swiss savages, simply using flint stones, stone hatchets, bone implements, and the firebrand, felled the largest oaks, split them into flooring and stakes, which were driven deep within the mud; constructed canoes; trenched the main land to protect their domestic animals; reared *tumuli* and monuments; hunted, fished, and carried on war; and even cultivated the ground. Among the relics discovered are immense numbers of stone hatchets, flint arrow-heads, blades of silex, edged or toothed, serving as knives and saws, stone hammers and anvils, bows of yew, awls and needles of bone, and fragments of pottery, made by hand. Beside these, mats of hemp and flax, and real cloth, with cords and cables made of fibres and bark, fishing-nets, as well as small baskets. Ornaments, too, are found, hair pins of bone, bone rings and bracelets, toys and quoits of stone.

They were a hunting people, as is shown by the partly-devoured bones of the urus, the bison, the deer, the elk, the roe, the chamois, and wild birds. They ate, also, the nuts of the pine and the beech, the walnut, and the raspberry. They were pastoral and agricultural, rearing cattle, sheep, goats, and swine, and using the dog; manufacturing cheese, cultivating the apple, the pear, and the plum, and storing their fruit for the winter; sowing barley and wheat, and making bread. They either carried on a certain kind of commerce, or they obtained foreign articles by plunder, such as silex from Gaul and Germany, yellow amber from the Baltic, and nephrite from Asia.

In a large number of these villages no trace of metal has been met with, and they are accordingly assigned to the "Stone Age." From the evidences furnished by the remains, it is supposed that a succeeding tribe, or collection of tribes, using implements of bronze, attacked these lake-dwellers, and in some cases burned their huts and occupied their dwellings.

No metals found.

With regard to the date of the earliest Swiss Lake-peoples, all is dark. M. Troyon has resorted to the following method of determining it:—

Under the alluvial strata deposited by the torrents which discharge themselves into the Lakes of Geneva and Neuchatel, there have been discovered numerous groups of piles, dating evidently from the age of stone. An ancient Lacustrian site of this epoch is found near Villeneuve, at more than four hundred and fifty metres from the present shore of Lake Leman. There have been, also, recognized traces of villages of the same age, on different points of the alluvial deposits of the Neuchatel basin; at the mouths of the Mantua and the Reuse; in the midst of the marsh of the Thiele; and chiefly in the marshy valley of the Orbe, which stretches to the south of the town of Yverdun. In order to know the age of these piles buried under the deposits of alluvium, it suffices to measure the distance which separates the present bank from the ancient one, and to find between these two concentric lines a given point, of which the age is known, and which may furnish an approximate estimate of the rate of progress of the alluvium. This point exists in the valley of the Orbe: it is the site of the ruins of the ancient Gallo-Roman city of Eburodunum. Between the down on which they rest and the lake, on the space partly occupied by the town of Yverdun, there is found no vestige of Roman antiquities; and we may thence conclude that at the commencement of our era, the shore of the lake approached much more nearly to the foot of the down. Admitting that its waters bathed the walls of the *castrum Eburodunense*, it would have required at least fifteen centuries for the formation of the zone of eight hundred metres in extent, which lies between the ruins and the shore; but it is highly probable that the retreat of the waters has not been so rapid, for the Celtic name of Eburodunum testifies in favour of a more ancient establishment than that of the Romans. However, if we accept, as a point of comparison, this datum of fifteen centuries (evidently too little), we perceive that another period of eighteen centuries must have been necessary for the filling up of the space of one thousand metres, which separates the down from the ancient piles situated to the south, at the base of the hillock of Chamblon; thus we are carried back to the fifteenth century before our era. At the latest, it was at this epoch, and, perhaps, long before, that the Lacustrian village of Chamblon, invaded by the turf and the alluvium of the Orbe, must have been abandoned by its inhabitants. In order to arrive at the epoch of the foundation, it is still necessary to ascend the course of ages, and to add some centuries for the filling up of the strait which separated the village from the ancient shore, still easily recognizable at the foot of the isolated little hill. While acknowledging that these figures establish nothing absolutely, M. Troyon is led to fix the construction of the Lacustrian habitations of Chamblon, by the primitive colonists of Helvetia, at two thousand years before the Christian era. It might, perhaps, be objected that the level of the lake may have sunk considerably during the historic ages, and have left dry the marshy plain of Yverdun; but the ancient shore is situated at exactly the same height with the present shore. The level of the lake has, therefore, remained the same during the last forty centuries of history. (Des Habitations Lacustres. M. Troyon.)

Of another lake-village and its antiquity Sir Charles Lyell says:—

The piles in question occur at the Pont de Thiéle, between the Lakes of Bienne and Neufchatel. The old convent of St. Jean, founded seven hundred and fifty years ago, and built originally on the margin of the Lake of Bienne, is now at a considerable distance from the shore, and affords a measure of the rate of the gain of land in seven centuries and a half. Assuming that a similar rate of the conversion of water into marshy land prevailed antecedently, we should require an addition of sixty centuries for the growth of the morass intervening between the convent and the aquatic dwelling of Pont de Thiéle, in all 6750 years. (Ant. of Man, p. 29.)

Still another method of ascertaining the antiquity of these early Swiss lake-tribes is through an examination of the fauna and flora discovered under the "palisade-buildings." Two species of cattle, belonging to the diluvial or drift era, are found—the *Bos primigenius* and *B. trochoceros*, both tamed. Bones of eight species of our domestic animals are met with: the dog, the hog, the horse, ass, goat, sheep, and two bovine species; of ten of fishes, three of reptiles, seventeen of birds, and thirty-six of mammals. No bones of chickens or cats are seen. The dog, the horse, and the donkey seem to have been but little used. The same wild animals which inhabit Switzerland now furnished game to the hunter then; the bear, the badger, the stone-marten, the tree-marten, the pole-cat, the ermine, the otter, the wolf, the wildcat, the hedgehog, the squirrel, and the woodmouse; besides these, the auerochs, the bison, the elk, the chamois, and the ibex. The fox was one-third smaller then than he is now; the rat had not then infested Europe. Three races of swine existed at that day: the wild hog (*Sus scrofa ferus*) being much larger than the present wild breeds. The

Fauna and flora.

gigantic stag (*Cervus elephas*) was the favourite food and game of those early hunters. This animal, with the auerochs (*Bos primigenius*), had been contemporaries with the rhinoceros of Europe, and the latter with the gigantic mammoth (*Elephas antiquus*) who wandered through the forests of Germany and France. Both the rhinoceros and the mammoth had disappeared from the neighbourhood of the Swiss lakes before these palisade-builders laid their piles and founded their huts.

The *flora* of those remote ages is not materially different from that of our own time. Wheat was evidently their oldest cereal, and the grains are smaller than those of the modern. Oats and rye have not been discovered. The dwarf pine (*P. maghus*) grew then in the lowlands, though it is found now alone in elevated Alpine regions. A few aquatic plants have, since that age, retreated to the mountains.

The few human bones and skulls found throw but little light on the race or antiquity of the pile-builders. The fauna shows most of the species which belonged to the post-tertiary epoch, which commenced with the mammoth, the rhinoceros, the cave bear, and the fossil hyena. Human bones.

Some of the larger ones, says Mr. Lubbock, have since fallen away in the struggle for existence, and others are becoming rarer and rarer every year, while some maintain themselves even now, thanks only to the inaccessibility and inclemency of the mountainous regions which they inhabit. The gradual process of extermination, which has continued ever since, had, however, even then begun. (Nat. Hist. Rev., p. 43. Jan., 1862.)

This fauna is distinguished, then, from the present "by the possession of the urus, the bison, the elk, the stag, and the wild boar, as well as by the more wide distribution of the beaver, the bear, the wolf, the ibex, the roe, &c.;" and differs from that of the drift era, "by the absence of the mammoth, the rhinoceros, the cave bear, and the cave hyena."

Era of pile-builders.

The pile-builders must have arrived in Europe since the glacier era, which probably gradually forced the elephant and the rhinoceros into warmer climates; and "drove the marmot and the reindeer into the Swiss lowlands" (Rütimeyer). They are later, too, than the long period of inundations, which will be hereafter described—the diluvial age. They belong to the received eras in human history, and very probably, as Troyon supposes, may date back, at least, 2000 years before the birth of Christ.

Improbability of the fossil man.

Such, until recently, were the historic and scientific evidences with regard to the antiquity of man. His most venerable records, his most ancient dates of historic chronology were but of yesterday, when compared with the age of existing species of plants and animals, or with the opening of the present geologic era. Every new scientific investigation seemed, from its negative evidence, to render more improbable the existence of the "Fossil Man." It is true that in various parts of the world, during the past few years, human bones have been discovered in connection with the bones of the fossil mammalia; but they were generally found in caves or in lime-deposits, where they might have been dropped, or swept in by currents of water, or inserted in more modern periods, and yet covered with the same deposit as the more ancient relics. Geologists have uniformly reasoned on the *à priori* improbability of these being fossil bones, and have somewhat strained the evidence—as some distinguished *savans* * now believe—against the

* Pictet and Lyell.

theory of a great human antiquity. And yet the "negative evidence" against the existence of the Fossil Man was open to many doubts. The records of geology are notoriously imperfect. We probably read but a few leaves of a mighty library of volumes. Moreover, the last ages preceding the present period were witnesses of a series of changes and slowly-acting agencies of destruction, from which man may have in general escaped. We have reason to believe that during long periods of time, the land was gradually elevated and subject to oscillations, so that the courses of rivers and the beds of lakes were disturbed and even the bottom of the ocean was raised. The results were the inundation of some countries, and the pouring of great currents of water over others, wearing down the hills and depositing in the course of ages the regular layers of gravel, sand, and marl, which now cover so large a part of Europe.* This was still further followed by a period in which the temperature of the earth was lowered, and ice and glaciers had perhaps a part in forming the present surface of the northern

Drift period.

* The following is, in a condensed form, the succession of the changes (according to Lyell) in physical geography, just preceding the present order of things, in England and the adjacent areas. (1.) A *Continental Period*, when the land was, at least, 500 feet above its present level, perhaps much higher, filling up the English channels and much of the ocean near by. (2.) A *Period of submergence* and of floating ice, by which the land north of the Thames and the Bristol Channel and that of Ireland was gradually reduced to an archipelago. (3.) A *second Continental Period*, when the bed of the glacial sea, with its marine shells and erratic blocks, was laid dry, and when the quantity of land equalled that of the first period. During this period, glaciers in some parts of Europe were in action. Near the close of this period, was probably the first appearance of man, who ranged from all parts of the continent into the British area, at the same time with the woolly rhinoceros and the Mammoth. (4.) The last change comprised the breaking up of the land of the British area into numerous islands, ending in the present order of things.

hemisphere. During this period the "Post-Pliocene or Diluvian Period,"* the mighty animals lived whose bones are now found in caverns, or under the slowly-deposited sediment of the waters, or preserved in bog—the mammoth, and rhinoceros, and elk, and bear, and elephant, as well as many others of extinct species.

Man probably escaping.

We may suppose that, if man did exist during these convulsions and inundations, his superior intelligence would enable him to escape the fate of the animals that were submerged; or that, if his few burial-places were invaded by the waters, his remains are now completely covered by marine deposits under the ocean. If, however, in his barbarian condition, he had fashioned implements of any hard material, and especially if, as do the savages of the present family of man, he had accidentally deposited them, or had buried them with the dead in mighty mounds, the invading waters might well sweep them together from their place and deposit them almost in mass, in situations where the eddies should leave their gravel and sand.†

Such seems in reality to have been the case; though

* We should bear in mind that the Quaternary or Diluvian Period, however ancient in point of time, has no clearly distinguishing line of separation from the present period. The great difference lies in the extinction of certain species of animals, which lived then, whose destruction may be due both to gradual changes of climate and to man. —Pictet.

† Sir C. Lyell, in his remarks before the British Association in 1859, said upon the discovery alluded to here: "I am reminded of a large Indian mound which I saw in St. Simon's Island, in Georgia, a mound ten acres in area, and having an average height of five feet, chiefly composed of cast-away oyster shells, throughout which, arrow heads, stone axes, and Indian pottery were dispersed. If the neighbouring river, the Altamaha, or the sea which is at hand, should invade, sweep away, and stratify the contents of this mound, it might produce a very analogous accumulation of human implements, unmixed, perhaps, with human bones."—*Athenæum*, September 24, 1859.

in regard to so important a fact in the history of the world, much caution must be exercised in accepting the evidence. We will state briefly the proofs, as they now appear, of the existence of a race of human beings on this earth in a remote antiquity.

Flints in France.

A French gentleman, M. Boucher de Perthes, has for thirty-four years been devoting his time and his fortune, with rare perseverance, to the investigation of certain antiquities in the later geological deposits in the north of France. His first work, "Les Antiquités Celtiques et Antédiluviennes," published in 1847, was received with much incredulity and opposition; a second, under the same title, in 1857, met with a scarce better reception, and it was with the greatest difficulty that he could induce even the *savans* of his own country, to look at the mass of evidence he had collected on this subject.

Geological description.

He made the extraordinary claim to have discovered a great quantity of rough implements of flint, fashioned by art, in the undisturbed beds of clay, gravel, and sand, known as *drift*, near Abbéville and Amiens. These beds vary in thickness, from ten to twenty feet, and cover the chalk hills in the vicinity; in portions of them, upon the hills, often in company with the flints, are discovered numerous bones of the extinct mammalia, such as the mammoth, the fossil rhinoceros, tiger, bear, hyæna, stag, ox, horse, and others.

The flint implements are found in the lowest beds of gravel, just above the chalk, while above them are sands with delicate fresh-water shells and beds of brick-earth —all this, be it remembered, on table-lands 200 feet above the level of the sea, in a country whose level and face have remained unaltered during any historical period with which we are acquainted.

It must have required, says Sir Charles Lyell, a long period for the wearing down of the chalk which supplied the broken flints (stones) for the formation of so much gravel at various heights, sometimes 100 feet above the level of the Somme, for the deposition of fine sediment, including entire shells, both terrestrial and aquatic, and also for the denudation which the entire mass of stratified drift has undergone, portions having been swept away) so that what remains of it often terminates abruptly in old river-cliffs. besides being covered by a newer unstratified drift. To explain these changes, I should infer considerable oscillations in the level of the land in that part of France, slow movements of upheaval and subsidence. deranging, but not wholly displacing the course of ancient rivers.

The President of the British Association, in his opening speech at the meeting of 1860, affirms the immense antiquity of these flint implements, and remarks :—

At Menchecourt, in the suburbs of Abbéville, a nearly entire skeleton of the Siberian rhinoceros is said to have been taken out about forty years ago—a fact affording an answer to the question often raised, as to whether the bones of the extinct mammalia could have been washed out of an older alluvium into a newer one, and so re-deposited and mingled with the relics of human workmanship. Farfetched as was this hypothesis, I am informed that it would not, if granted, have seriously shaken the proof of the high antiquity of human productions; for that proof is independent of organic evidence or fossil remains, and is based on physical data. As was stated to us last year by Sir Charles Lyell, we should still have to allow time for great denudation of the chalk, and the removal from place to place, and the spreading out over the length and breadth of a large valley, of heaps of chalk-flints in beds from ten to fifteen feet in thickness, covered by loam and sands of equal thickness, these last often tranquilly deposited—all of which operations would require the supposition of a great lapse of time.

Or, in Lyell's own words :—

Yet we by no means need the evidence of the ancient fossil

fauna to establish the antiquity of man in this part of France. The mere volume of the drift at various heights would alone suffice to demonstrate a vast lapse of time, during which such heaps of shingle, derived both from the Eocene and the cretaceous rocks, were thrown down in a succession of river channels. We observe thousands of rounded and half-rounded flints, and a vast number of angular ones, with rounded pieces of white chalk of various sizes, testifying to a prodigious amount of mechanical action accompanying the repeated widening and deepening of the valley, before it became the receptacle of peat; and the position of many of the flint tools leaves no doubt on the mind of the geologist that their fabrication preceded all this reiterated denudation. (P. 144.)

An independent proof of the age of these gravel-beds and the associated loam, containing fossil remains, is derived by the same authority from the large deposits of peat in the valley of the Somme, which contain not only monuments of the Roman, but also those of an older, Stone period, the Finnic period; yet, says Lord Wrottesley, "distinguished geologists are of opinion that the growth of all the vegetable matter, and even the original scooping out of the hollows containing it, are events long posterior in date to the gravel with flint implements—nay, posterior even to the formation of the uppermost of the layers of the loam with fresh-water shells overlaying the gravel."

Peat deposits.

The number of the flint implements is computed at above fourteen hundred, in an area of fourteen miles in length and half a mile in breadth. They are of the rudest nature, as if formed by a people in the most degraded state of barbarism. Some are mere flakes of flint, apparently used for knives or arrow-heads; some are pointed, and with hollowed bases, as if for spear-heads, varying from four to nine inches in length; some are almond-shaped, with a cut-

Flint implements.

ting edge, from two to nine inches in length. Others, again, are fashioned into coarse representations of animals, such as the whale, saurian, boar, eagle, fish, and even the human profile; others have representations of foliage upon them; others are either drilled with holes or are cut with reference to natural holes, so as to serve as stones for slings, or for amulets, or for ornaments. The edges, in many cases, seem formed by a great number of small artificial *tips*, or blows, and do not at all resemble edges made by a great natural fracture. Very few are found with polished surfaces like the modern remains in flint; and the whole workmanship differs from that of flint arrow-heads in other parts of Europe, as well as from the later Finnish (or so-called Keltic) remains, discovered in such quantities in France.* The only relics that have been found resembling them are, according to Mr. Worsaae, some flint arrow-heads and spear-points discovered at great depths in the bogs of Denmark. A few bone knives and necklaces of bone have been met with in these deposits, but, thus far, no human bones. The people who fabricated these instruments seemed to be a hunting and fishing people, living in some such condition as the present savages of Australia.

An hypothesis is advanced by Sir Charles Lyell (page 141) that the flints were used by a succession of savage tribes for centuries in cutting holes in the ice of the river and fishing, and falling into these holes, they were

* "It is a remarkable fact," says Wilson, "that the stone axe of the South Sea Islander of the eighteenth century, presents a closer resemblance to that of the British or Gaulish fabrication of the first or earliest centuries, and the modern flint lance, or arrow-head of the Red Indian can scarcely be distinguished from that found in the most ancient British graves, while no such correspondence is traceable between the latter and the still older manufactured weapons in the underlying drift." (Pre-Historic Man, vol. i. p. 265.)

swept away with the gravel on the breaking-up of the ice in the spring.

These discoveries of M. de Perthes at length aroused the attention of English men of science, and during 1859 a number of eminent gentlemen—among them Sir Charles Lyell, Mr. Prestwich, Dr. Falconer, and others—visited M. Perthes' collection, and saw the flints *in situ*. They have avowed their conviction of the genuineness and antiquity of these relics.

The objections that would naturally be made to this evidence are, that the flints are purely natural formations, and not works of man,—the deposit is alluvial and modern, rather than of the ancient drift,—or that these implements had been dropped into crevices, or sunk from above, in later periods.

Objections.

The testimony of disinterested observers seems to be sufficient as to the human contrivance manifest in these flints; and the concurrence of various scientific men hardly leaves room for doubt that these deposits are of great antiquity, preceding the time in which the surface of France took its present form, and dating back to the Post-Pliocene period. Their horizontal position, and the great depth at which the hatchets are found, together with their number, and the peculiar incrustation and discoloration of each one, as well as their being in company with the bones of the extinct mammalia, make it certain that they could not have been dropped into fissures, or sunk there in modern times. In regard to the absence of human bones, it should be remembered that no bones are easily preserved, unless they are buried in sediment or in bog; and furthermore, that the extent of the researches in these formations is very small indeed. Besides, the country where above all we should expect the most of human

Absence of human bones.

remains in the drift deposits, as being probably the most ancient abode of man—Asia—has been the least explored for such purposes.

We must also remember, in the words of Lyell, that—

> Instead of its being part of the plan of nature to store up enduring records of a large number of the individual plants and animals which have lived on the surface, it seems to be her chief care to provide the means of disencumbering the habitable areas lying above and below the waters, of those myriads of solid skeletons of animals, and those massive trunks of trees, which would otherwise soon choke up every river, and fill every valley. To prevent this inconvenience, she employs the heat and moisture of the sun and atmosphere, the dissolving power of carbonic and other acids, the grinding teeth and gastric juices of quadrupeds, birds, reptiles, and fish, and the agency of many of the invertebrata. We are all familiar with the efficacy of these and other causes on the land; and, as to the bottoms of seas, we have only to read the published reports of Mr. McAndrew, the late Edward Forbes, and other experienced dredgers, who, while they failed utterly in drawing up from the deep a single human bone, declared that they scarcely ever met with a work of art even after counting tens of thousands of shells and zoophytes, collected on a coast line of several hundred miles in extent, where they often approached within less than half a mile of a land peopled by millions of human beings. (P. 146.)

Only few bones of animals found.

It should be borne in mind also, that it was not till 1855 that the bones of one animal, which must have been very widely dispersed, the musk buffalo, were found in the fossiliferous gravel of the Thames, and not till 1860 that it was proved to have co-existed in France with the mammoth.

So (as is mentioned by Lyell) on the old bottom of the Lake of Haarlem, now dry land—a tract containing over 45,000 square acres—in the innumerable trenches dug there, as well as in the great canal, some thirty miles long, not a single human bone was found. Yet hundreds of Dutch and Spanish sailors had been drowned in the old lake, and a population of 30,000 or 40,000 had lived on its borders.

On this topic, Mr. Lubbock calls attention (Nat. Hist. Rev., July, 1862) to the small number of human bones found in the Danish "Refuse heaps," where a thousand times more worked flints are discovered than in the French gravel deposits. In the water villages of the Swiss Lakes, M. Troyon estimates the population in the "Stone Age" at 32,000; in the "Bronze Age" at 42,000. In four lakes, the remains of seventy villages were discovered, yet, except a few bones of children, only *five skeletons* have been found. At Concise, Lake Neufchatel, 24,000 flints were found, and not one skeleton.

It is also to be noticed, says Mr. Lubbock, that in the drift at St. Acheul, no trace has ever been found of *any animal as small as man;* even the small bones of large animals having all disappeared.

The chain of evidence in regard to this important question seems to be filled out by a recent discovery* of M. Edouard Lartet in Aurignac, in the south of France, on the head-waters of the Garonne. The weak point in M. de Perthes' discoveries was the absence of human bones in the deposits investigated, though this might have been accounted for by the withdrawal of human beings from the floods of the period. M. Lartet's investigations have fortunately been conducted in a spot which was above the reach of the ordinary inundations of the Drift Period, and whither human beings might have fled for refuge, or where they might have lived securely during long spaces of time.

M. Lartet's discoveries.

Some ten years since in Aurignac (Haute Garonne),

* Ann. des Sc. Nat. 4me Série, tome xv. Nat. Hist. Rev., Jan. 1862.

in the *Arrondissement* of St. Gaudens, near the Pyrenees, a cavern was discovered in the nummulitic rock. It had been concealed by a heap of fragments of rock and vegetable soil, gradually detached and accumulated probably by atmospheric agency. In it were found the human remains, it was estimated, of seventeen individuals, which were afterward buried formally by the order of the mayor of Aurignac, though, unfortunately, they were not examined by any scientific person, and no conclusions could be derived from them as to their race or development. Along with the bones were discovered the teeth of mammals, both carnivora and herbivora; also certain small perforated corals, such as were used by many ancient peoples as beads, and similar to those gathered in the deposits of Abbéville. The cave had apparently served as a place of sacrifice and of burial. In 1860, M. Lartet visited the spot. In the layer of loose earth at the bottom of the cave he found flint implements, worked portions of a reindeer's horn, mammal bones, and human bones in a remarkable state of preservation. In a lower layer of charcoal and ashes, indicating the presence of man and some ancient fireplace or hearth, the bones of the animals were scratched and indented as though by implements employed to remove the flesh; almost every bone was broken, as if to extract the marrow, as is done by many modern tribes of savages.

In this deposit, M. Lartet picked up many human implements, such as bone knives, flattened circular stones, supposed to have been used for sharpening flint knives, perforated sling-stones, many arrow-heads and spear-heads, flint knives, a bodkin made of a roebuck's horn, various implements of reindeer's horn, and teeth beads, from the teeth of the great fossil bear (*Ursus spelæus*). Remains were also found

Animal remains.

of nine different species of carnivora, such as the fossil bear, the hyæna, cat, wolf, fox, and others, and of twelve of herbivora, such as the fossil elephant, the rhinoceros, the great stag (*Cervus elephas*), the European bison (aurochs), horse and others. The most common were the aurochs, the reindeer, and the fox. How savages, armed only with flint implements, could have captured these gigantic animals, is somewhat mysterious; but, as M. Lartet suggests, they may have snared many of them, or have overwhelmed single monsters with innumerable arrows and spears, as Livingstone describes the slaying of the elephant by the negroes at the present day.

With reference to the mode in which these remains were brought to this place, M. Lartet remarks:—

> The fragmentary condition of the bones of certain animals, the mode in which they are broken, the marks of the teeth of the hyæna on bones, necessarily broken in their recent condition, even the distribution of the bones and their significant consecration, lead to the conclusion that the presence of these animals and the deposit of all these remains are due solely to human agency. Neither the inclination of the ground nor the surrounding hydrographical conditions allow us to suppose that the remains could have been brought where they are found by natural causes.

The conclusion, then, in palæontology, which would be drawn from these facts, is, that man must have existed in Europe at the same time with the fossil elephant and rhinoceros, the gigantic hyæna, the aurochs, and the elk, and even the cave-bear. This latter animal is thought by many to have disappeared in the very opening of the Post-Pliocene Period; so that this cave would—judging from the remains of that animal—have been *prior* to the long period of inundations in which the drift-

Man in the drift-period.

deposits of Abbéville and Amiens were made. The drift which fills the valleys of the Pyrenees has not, it is evident, touched this elevated spot in Aurignac.

In chronology, all that is proved by these discoveries of M. Lartet, is, that the fossil animals mentioned above and man were contemporaries on the earth. The age of each must be determined inferentially by comparing the age of strata in which these animals are usually found, with the age in which the most ancient traces of man are discovered—such as the deposits already described in the north of France.

Of the moral conclusions to be derived from these facts, Lyell beautifully says:—

> If the fossil memorials have been correctly interpreted—if we have here before us at the northern base of the Pyrenees, a sepulchral vault with skeletons of human beings, consigned by friends and relatives to their last resting-place—if we have also at the portal of the tomb the relics of funeral feasts, and within it indications of viands destined for the use of the departed on their way to a land of spirits; while among the funeral gifts are weapons wherewith in other fields to chase the gigantic deer, the cave-lion, the cave-bear, and woolly rhinoceros—we have at last succeeded in tracing back the sacred rites of burial, and, more interesting still, a belief in a future state, to times long anterior to those of history and tradition. (P. 192.)

M. Delanoue, in a pamphlet addressed to the Minister of Public Instruction (Feb. 1862), describes minutely the geological deposits at St. Acheul (near Amiens), in which large numbers of these flint implements have been found along with the bones of fossil animals. They are evidently even more than those of Abbéville, removed beyond the suspicion of modern deposit or the possibility of disturbance by interference. The objects found are in the very bottom of the drift, beneath at least three separate deposits, the

Acheul deposits.

fresh-water gravel (*gravier lacustre*), with delicate shells, the reddish drift (*diluvium rougeâtre*), with fragments of rounded silex, and the *loess* or brick earth, with the modern vegetable soil above.*

Similar discoveries on a smaller scale are recorded by Mr. Prestwich in Suffolk, England, and in Devonshire. Professor Pictet, the celebrated geologist, who also gives his adhesion to the discoveries of M. de Perthes, states that the cave evidence has by no means been sufficiently valued by geologists. Under the impulse of the new discoveries, the caves have been more closely searched in different countries, and the following are some of the most important results as detailed by Lyell.

Cave evidence.

In a cavern at *Arcy sur Yonne*, a series of deposits have been discovered by the Marquis de Vibraye, with human bones and remains of quadrupeds of extinct and recent species, such as the mammoth, the rhinoceros, the cave-bear and others.

In *Long Hole*, South Wales, in 1861, the remains of two species of fossil rhinoceros were found in an undisturbed deposit, in the lower part of which were well-shaped flint knives, showing clearly that man must have been coeval with these animals.

In a *Liège cavern* near the Meuse, Sir Charles Lyell and Prof. Malone found the bones and teeth of the cave-bear, and afterwards the latter gentleman excavated from a depth of two feet below a crust of stalagmite, three fragments of a human skull, and two perfect

* M. Delanoue mentions that in 1860, M. Alb. Gaudry found nine of these flint weapons *in situ*. M. Elie Petit discovered an elephant's tooth and a flint hatchet in the drift deposit at *Précy sur Oise*. M. Buvignier has made a similar discovery at Giory, M. Gosse at Grenelle, and MM. Lartet and Collomb at Chichy.

lower jaws with the teeth, all associated with bones of fossil mammalia, in such a manner as to leave no doubt that man was contemporaneous with them.

Neanderthal skull. A very remarkable skull with a portion of the skeleton has been found in a cave in Neanderthal, near Düsseldorf. Though it is probably of very great antiquity, yet the evidence is not decisive. It is the most ape-like skull ever discovered, and belongs to a man of very low brain-development and immense strength of bodily frame. As but a single skull of this extraordinary type has been found it may have been an abnormal instance—the skull of a crétin or an idiot. To disturb any confident conclusions as to "progressive development," during the vast period since these deposits, another skull discovered by Dr. Schmerling, in a Liège cavern, imbedded with the remains of the elephant, rhinoceros, bear, hyæna, and other extinct quadrupeds, and probably more ancient still, is of a high Aryan type.

Brixham cave. The following were the deposits: (1.) At the top a layer of stalagmite, varying in thickness from one to fifteen inches, and which sometimes contained bones, such as reindeer's horns, and an entire humerus of the cave-bear. (2.) Loam or bone-earth, of an ochreous or red colour, from one to fifteen feet thick. (3.) At the bottom, gravel, with many rounded pebbles, probed as far as twenty feet. The bones at the top were those of the mammoth, rhinoceros, hyæna, cave-lion, reindeer, and others. No human bones were found there, but many flint knives chiefly from the lowest part of the bone-earth—in one instance with a bone of the cave-bear in the overlying stalagmite, and another entire left hind-leg in close proximity to a perfect flint tool. It is clear, says Sir C. Lyell (page

101), that the bear lived after the flint tools were manufactured; or in other words, that man in this district preceded the cave-bear.

Other instances might be given of human bones and implements found in ancient deposits, but these are the strongest and are sufficient for the purpose. For a more full and scientific statement of the subject, we refer the reader to the recent valuable work of that most careful and philosophical geologist, Sir CHARLES LYELL.

The conclusion from all these discoveries—the most important scientific discoveries relating to human history, of modern times—is, that ages ago, in the period of the extinct mammoth and the fossil bear, perhaps before the Channel separated England from France, a race of barbarian human beings lived on the soil of Europe, capable of fabricating rough implements. The evidence has been carefully weighed by impartial and experienced men, and thus far it seems complete.

Conclusion.

The mind is lost in astonishment, in looking back at such a vast antiquity of human beings. A tribe of men in existence hundreds of thousands of years before any of the received dates of Creation! savages who hunted, with their flint-headed arrows, the gigantic elk of Ireland and the buffalo of Germany, or who fled from the fierce tiger of France, or who trapped the immense clumsy mammoth of Northern Europe. Who were they? we ask ourselves in wonder. Was there with man, as with other forms of animal life, a long and gradual progression from the lowest condition to a higher, till at length the world was made ready for a more-developed human being, and the Creator placed the first of the present family of man upon the earth?

Were those European barbarians of the Drift Period a primeval race, destroyed before the creation of our own race, and lower and more barbarian than the lowest of the present inhabitants of the world? or, as seems more probable, were these mysterious beings—the hunters of the mammoth and the aurochs—the earliest progenitors of our own family, the childish fathers of the human race?

The subject hardly yet admits of an exact and scientific answer. We can merely here state the probability of a vast antiquity to human beings, and of the existence of the FOSSIL OR PRE-ADAMITIC MAN.*

As says Sir Thomas Browne:—

> The greater part must be content to be as though they had not been: to be found in the register of God, not in the records of men. The number of the dead long exceedeth all that shall live. The Night of Time far surpasseth the Day, and who knoweth the Equinox?

* A portion of the above Chapter was published by the author in the December "Atlantic," 1862.

CHAPTER XXXIII.

UNITY OR DIVERSITY OF ORIGIN.

In considering the great question of a Treatise of Ethnology—that of the *Unity of Origin* of the different races of men—it is important to disentangle from it any irrelevant matters. The inferiority or superiority of a given race, the questions of justice to the weak, and of Human Brotherhood, have no connection whatever with the scientific problem of Origin. The strong are equally bound to be merciful to the weak: men are equally under obligations to follow the Law of Love, and Slavery is equally wicked and damnable, whether mankind have one parent or twenty parents. The moral Brotherhood of man does not depend on community of descent, but on a common nature, a similar destiny, and a like relation to their common Father—God. The subject is purely scientific.

Irrelevant topics.

Nor is it well, in discussing it, to dispute on the term, *Species*. Whatever be the idea attached to this much-debated word, we can still consider separately the fact, or the presumption, of many origins or of one origin to mankind.

It must be remembered also, that this question cannot be settled by absolute demonstration on one side or the other. Like all similar subjects, it must be determined by a nice balancing or a gradual accumulation of probabilities. So far forth as the peculiar source of evidence is concerned, which has been examined in this Treatise—Language—there is no doubt that *it has not proved Unity of Origin, though pointing toward it.** Classification by language, though the best that can be made, is still far from perfect. Many tribes of men speak tongues that are scarcely known; many languages have never been thoroughly and scholastically investigated; and study and experience are yearly improving the methods of investigation for those that are known.

Language not proving unity.

As to the gaps between languages, Lyell has well remarked:—

We must remember that it is not part of the plan of any people to preserve memorials of their forms of speech expressly for the edification of posterity. Their MSS. and inscriptions serve some present purpose, are occasional and imperfect from the first, and are rendered more fragmentary in the course of time, some being intentionally destroyed, others lost by the decay of the perishable materials on which they are written; so that to question the theory of all known

* The great advocate of diversity of origin in Languages, M. Renan, admits (L'Origine des Langues, p. 212) that "the soft and impressionable constitution of the infant-man permitted combinations become impossible since human nature has contracted, in growing old, a sort of stiffness.

"The question of the original independence of different groups of languages is not then as simple as it appeared at first. It admits degrees: families of language, apparently isolated, have been able to have fruitful contacts at an epoch when they were yet susceptible of re-forming themselves. One cannot too carefully distinguish, when there is a question of languages, the embryonic state, during which accidents, indifferent to the mature age, could have had a capital importance, from the perfect state where they are fixed, so to speak, into a definite mould. The embryonic state of languages could have lasted very little time, but it has existed, and at that moment, in which was formed the individuality of races, human nature, still flexible, ought to have received for eternity, profound traces."

languages being derivative on the ground that we can rarely trace a passage from the ancient to the modern through all the dialects which must have flourished. one after the other, in the intermediate ages, implies a want of reflection on the laws which govern the recording as well as the obliterating processes. (P. 461.)

Still farther he remarks :—

But another important question still remains to be considered, namely, whether the trifling changes that can alone be witnessed by a single generation, can possibly represent the working of that machinery which, in the course of many centuries, has given rise to such mighty revolutions in the forms of speech throughout the world. Every one may have noticed in his own lifetime the stealing in of some slight alterations of accent, pronunciation, or spelling, or the introduction of some words borrowed from a foreign language to express ideas of which no native term precisely conveyed the import. He may also remember hearing for the first time some cant terms or slang phrases, which have since forced their way into common use, in spite of the efforts of the purist. But he may still contend that, "within the range of his experience," his language has continued unchanged, and he may believe in its immutability in spite of minor variations. The real question, however, at issue is, whether there are any limits to this variability. He will find, on further investigation, that new technical terms are coined almost daily in various arts, sciences, professions, and trades, that new names must be found for new inventions, that many of these acquire a metaphorical sense, and then make their way into general circulation, as "stereotyped," for instance, which would have been as meaningless to the men of the seventeenth century as would the new terms and images derived from steamboat and railway travelling to the men of the eighteenth. (Ant. of Man, p. 462.)

With regard to the borrowing of words, he adds :—

Proofs also of borrowing are discernible, letters being retained in the spelling of some words which have no longer any meaning as they are now pronounced, no connection with any corresponding sounds. Such redundant or silent letters, once useful in the parent speech, have been aptly compared, by Mr. Darwin, to rudimentary organs in living beings, which, as he interprets them, have at some former period been more fully developed, having had their proper functions to perform in the organization of a remote progenitor. (P. 465.)

In the two great families of language, the Semitic and Indo-European, and in the more comprehensive group, the Turanian, as well as in the Chinese and monosyllabic family, there is no absolute proof established, as yet, of their common source; yet there are indications—gradations and links of connection which would make the hypothesis of one origin for all, not improbable, provided there were more of these gradations hereafter discovered. Adopting the theory that languages gradually develope from the monosyllabic condition to the agglutinative, and then to the inflectional, there are links of connection believed to be discovered between the families representing these various stages of growth.

Links of connection between languages.

In Chinese, says Müller (Sc. of Lang.), and particularly in Chinese dialects, we find rudimentary traces of agglutination The *li* which I mentioned before as the sign of the locative, has dwindled down to a mere post-position, and a modern Chinese is no more aware that *li* meant, originally, interior, than the Turanian is of the origin of his case-terminations. In the spoken dialects of Chinese, agglutinative forms are of more frequent occurrence. . . . . M. Stanislas Julian remarks that the numerous compounds which occur in Chinese prove the wide-spread influence of the principle of agglutination in that language.* (P. 329, Amer. Edit.)

* If Lepsius's theory should be verified that Chinese was originally a polysyllabic language, since degraded to a monosyllabic, this instance adduced by Müller would be undoubtedly weakened in its force. Lepsius, however, admits the probability of a growth from monosyllabism to the agglutinative stage in human language. (See Abhand. d. Kön. Akad., Berlin, 1860.) Lepsius, &c.

One agglutinative language—the Mandchu—has scarcely a richer Grammar than the Chinese, and presents many words without distinctive termination which can be used as various parts of speech. The condition of the Mongol language may be looked upon as a living evidence of the growth of a tongue from a low condition, approaching monosyllabism, to one of agglutination.

Instance of growth in Mongol.

Castrèn states—as we have mentioned before—that while the literary language shows no pronominal affixes, whether subjective or predicative, that feature has just begun to appear in the spoken dialects.

The hypothesis that Chinese was arrested by some unknown influence and fixed in a primitive state, from which its sister tongues escaped, is not an incredible one.

The change or gradation from the agglutinative to the inflectional is believed to be seen in various languages. Thus, says Müller, "Such has been the advance that the Turkish has made toward inflectional forms, that Professor Ewald claims for it the title of a synthetic language, a title which he gives to the Aryan and Semitic dialects, after they have left the agglutinative stage and entered into a process of phonetic corruption and dissolution. 'Many of the component parts,' he says, 'though they were originally, no doubt, as in every language, independent words, have been reduced to mere vowels or have been lost altogether.' . . . . Nay, he goes so far as to admit some formal elements which Turkish shares in common with the Aryan family, and which could therefore only date from a period when both were in their agglutinative infancy."

Change from agglutinative.

Castrèn states that the language of the *Samoieds*,

shows such a great development of the principle of agglutination, as to approach the flexion of the Aryan tongues, and possibly to form the link of connection between the one family and the other.

There is every reason to believe that eventually the *roots* of the Semitic and the Aryan languages will be demonstrated to be from one source, while there are already discovered many remarkable coincidences between the Turanian roots and those of these two families.

The question is thus carefully summed up by Müller.

Müller's summing up.

> (I.) Nothing necessitates the admission of different independent beginnings for the *material* elements of the Turanian, Semitic, and Aryan branches;—nay, it is possible even now to point out radicals, which, under various changes and disguises, have been current in these three branches, ever since their first separation. (II.) Nothing necessitates the admission of different beginnings for the *formal* elements of the Turanian, Semitic, and Aryan branches of speech; and though it is impossible to derive the Aryan system of grammar from the Semitic, or the Semitic from the Aryan, we can perfectly understand how, either through individual influences or by the wear and tear of speech in its own continuous working, the different systems of grammar of Asia and Europe may have been produced. (Sc. of Lang., p. 340.)

Indirectly, Language, as running its line of evidence for community of descent right across the lines of physiological divisions, has done very much to render unity of origin probable.

We believe that under the new lights furnished by science during the last few years, this question can be investigated to far better advantage and with more probability of a conclusion than ever before.

There are two great facts, or laws, applying to all

organic nature, which must be thoughtfully considered in the very outset of this investigation—one, the *Law of Inheritance*, or the principle that the offspring shall inherit the characteristics of the parent, which lies at the basis of the permanence of type and of many other important facts in nature; and the other, the *Law of Variation*, or the tendency in the offspring to differ from the parents and from one another, whether as an effect of external influences, or from some power in the organism itself.* The latter secures idiosyncrasy and variety in nature, as the former gives stability and order. It should be remembered that though we cannot give an explanation of Variation in every particular instance, it is none the less an effect of laws, and is far removed from accident or chance.

Principles of Inheritance and Variation.

Thus far, at least, we can see, that the offspring, combining to a degree the qualities of both its parents, must present a result different from either; if we add to this the influence of external circumstances which must, for every newly-organized being, be somewhat different than for its parent, we shall see some cause for each generation presenting a slightly new combination of characteristics. When Variation has once begun, and the offspring is produced with a slightly different peculiarity (why, we may not be able to tell), *its* offspring again is acted upon through the principle of Inheritance, by what we may figuratively describe as two forces—one, the tendency to resemble its own pa-

* Compare Isidore St. Hilaire, Hist. des Règnes organiques, vol. ii. p. 431.

"Dans ce dernier cas (*i. e.* a change of surrounding circumstances,) les caractères nouveaux de l'espèce, sont, pour ainsi dire, la *resultante* de deux forces contraires : l'une, *modificatrice*, est l'influence des nouvelles circonstances ambiantes ; l'autre, *conservatrice* du type, est la tendance héréditaire à reproduire des mêmes caractères de génération en génération."

Two forces acting on each life-germ.

rent, and the other, that to resemble all its ancestors. M. Vilmorin[1] has well called this latter, "an aggregation of forces, composed of the individual attraction of a series of ancestors," which is the attraction of the type of the species, and generally determines the result. But the attractions to its own immediate parent, though less powerful than that to its ancestry, is more close, and tends to give the offspring all the parental characteristics. So, says Dr. A. Gray, "when the parent has no salient individual characteristics, both the longer and shorter lines of force are parallel, and combine to produce the same result. But whenever the immediate parent deviates from the type, its influence upon its offspring is no longer parallel with that of the ancestry; so the tendency of the offspring to vary no longer radiates around the type of the species, as its centre, but around some point upon the line, which represents the amount of its deviation from the type."[2]

Natural selection.

The variations—though we may not be able to explain their origin, whether from external influences on the germ-cell, on the fœtus, or the growing organism—are perpetuated according as they are of advantage to the possessor, enabling it to gain more nourishment or to resist better destructive influences, while those destitute of these advantages perish.

It will be seen, from these brief statements, why, at a certain period, there may be numerous variations in a given stock, and, afterward, these varieties become (historically) permanent.

Phenomenon of sporting.

It is well known that with plants, a new variety tends to *sport*, or as it were to play off into new deviations. It is "loosed, as it were, from the ancestral influence, which no longer acts upon a straight and continuous line, but upon one broken and interrupted by the opposing action of the immediate parents and grandparents."[3]

Now, in nature, suppose a family of animals removed by some accident to a different climate and feeding-ground than those to which they are accustomed: as, for instance, a flock of sheep from Europe to South America. Some of the lambs are born, we know not why, with a little hair instead of wool. In other countries this variety would have had no more chance for surviving than any other variety; perhaps less, as it would be more exposed to the cold. But here, the slight advantage of the hair may give the lamb a better power of enduring the heat, and so this variety be perpetuated, and its descendants, being "loosed from the attraction" towards its ancestors, may show various singular deviations, until, at last, a new type is formed—still a sheep, according to the Law of Inheritance, but a new variety of sheep—fitted the best to procure food and to resist destructive agencies in its new circumstances.

Formation of a new variety.

So, again, suppose swine introduced from Europe to South America. If turned out to become wild, the pigs, which from some chance are born with a slight peculiarity—as longer teeth, or more erect ear, or more solid hoof, or blacker colour—which peculiarity may be an advantage in escaping the hunters, or in rooting for food, or destroying their enemies, will naturally have the best chance of living and propagating, and their offspring again, so far as they possess these advantages, will be perpetuated, and these singularly-marked hogs, with tusks, or erect ears, or solid hoofs, or black colour, may become varieties (or even species). They may deviate even more singularly, having once begun to vary from their ancestors, and the only limits may be in the force of the Law of Inheritance, and in the adaptation of the new varieties to their new circumstances.

It will be possible, also, that these wild hogs, if, after a long course of time, re-transplanted to other countries and climates, may still show their acquired properties as permanent characteristics, for the Law of Inheritance will then be in favour of their preserving their new type, as all their more recent ancestors have belonged to this type. But then, again, in the still new circumstances (if sufficient time be given), yet another new type may be formed.

We need not say that these instances are, in the main, not supposed cases, but facts.

Our argument, then, as applied to man, will be: (I.) that, *à priori*, we should expect man to vary; (II.) that he presents no greater varieties than do animals who are known to be of one origin; (III.) that the members of a well-marked race of men differ among themselves as much as some of the various races differ from one another; (IV.) that the phenomena of acclimation and of crossing of races are in favour of the presumption of unity; and (V.) that under the principles already stated, of Inheritance and Variation, with the element of *sufficient Time* added, we can more satisfactorily account for the present varieties of man, on the hypothesis of a common origin than on any other hypothesis.

Statement of the argument.

I. Without being able to account for the fact that the offspring differs from its parent, we can have no doubt that external influences act upon the living principle of the germ, and this again reacts upon its circumstances. If, farther, we suppose this germ, when developed, to be inspired with a living power exceedingly sensitive to every kind of influ-

Probability of human variation.

ence and able again to work back upon the structure and organs which it employs, we might well expect the developed organism to be wonderfully modified.

Man is such a being, not merely exposed to the usual unexplained variations of all animals, but possessing a soul which is affected by everything surrounding it, and which is constantly moulding or influencing its bodily structure.

We should expect man to show more varied offspring than any other creature, and the only wonder is that he does not present more varieties or races. In mental peculiarities, we may at least claim for him greater variation, or, in other words, greater individuality—than for any other animal.

Animals vary as much as men.

II. In point of fact, however, animals show as great variation, even when of one common stock, as do the different races of men. The facts collected in support of this point by Isidore St. Hilaire, Roulin, Prichard, De Salles, and others, are so numerous that it will be difficult to condense them within the space required.

The principal seat of variation in animals is the epidermic or horny tissue, showing the variety in horns, hoofs, and skin, and it corresponds to the extra-cutaneous texture in man which manifests the changes in colour and hair.

Of the change in *swine*, when transported to South America, we have already spoken. Some have acquired erect ears, vaulted foreheads, and heads much larger than were found on the original breed. With some, the colour becomes black, and with others the skin acquires a thick fur, beneath which is a species of wool; some, again, are red; others have solid hoofs.[4] One breed is found in Quebaya, with toes half a span in length, long white ears, pendant belly and long tusks, crooked, like the horns of oxen.[5]

The hogs* in the West Indies, when left out wild, become in time the wild boars. It is an evidence that variations in animals are not confined to superficial changes, but are sometimes to a degree structural, that the number of the caudal, sacral, lumbar and dorsal vertebræ vary in the hog; and that the wild hog has six incisor teeth in his upper jaw and six in the lower, while the tame animal is reduced to three.[6]

Instances of variations.

Sheep,[7] under different circumstances, have produced great varieties. Among those introduced into South America, a hairy breed has grown up. A breed has been formed with monstrous tails; others are found with projecting lips and pendent ears. Sheep, says De Salles, have been seen among the Kirghis with mere masses of hairless fat for tails, and these same sheep when transported to another country lose their fatty appendages. The sheep of Yemen, introduced into Egypt, have acquired a straight rude

* "It is perfectly demonstrated," says Dr. Hollard, "that all our races of domestic pigs, with their difference of size, form, skin, colour, proceed from the wild animal, thick and short, low upon the legs, with large head, stiff ears, armed with triangular defences, which project from the mouth, covered with hard bristles, longer upon the back, and under which is hidden a little hair, and, in a word, whose natural colour is a blackish grey. Restored to liberty, the domestic pig retakes, after a few generations, the characteristics of the wild type; the bristles become stiff, a sort of woolly skin developes itself under them, the natural colour reappears, the defences lengthen and increase; the skull itself, which, in the domestic state, is remarkably straight, retakes this lower line of profile, and the more massive jaws which distinguish the head of the wild boar. Nothing is more variable, on the contrary, than the races of this species submitted to the influence of man; their disposition to be modified is most marked." (De l'Homme, p. 242.)

hair, with a fine down at the roots. Some of the merino sheep are covered with wool and others with hair, quite differing in structure, and sometimes the same individual under new circumstances shows the changes from wool to hair.[8]

Our readers are abundantly familiar with the short-legged breed of "Otter sheep," originated by accident in Massachusetts, and transmitted by inter-breeding.

The *Goat*, since its introduction into South America, has formed a variety more agile and slender, with better-formed heads, smaller horns and smaller teats, than the original stock.[9]

Cattle, exported from Europe to the Antilles and to South America, have formed a hairy breed; others are hornless, and still others become hairless, and transmit this property to their descendants. When wild, the cow loses her large dugs.[10]

With increased food in domestication, the ox and sheep have their abdominal viscera enlarged; to suit the increased size of the stomach and the intestinal canal, the trunk becomes larger in all its dimensions; the respiratory organs change, and with them the form of the chest; the limbs are shorter and farther apart, and the body being nearer the ground, the neck becomes shorter. Various muscles from disuse diminish, and the tendency to obesity increases. Thus a new form and new habits are acquired and are transmitted.[11]

M. de Filippi reports the existence of a race of cattle in Piacentino, which have fourteen pairs of ribs instead of thirteen. (Quatrefages, p. 128.)

The horses, according to M. Roulin, transported to South America, have formed a race with fur, instead of hair, and have changed to an almost uniform bay colour.

Of two colts of the same race, says Carpenter, born

in Lorraine, for instance, and transported, one to Flanders, and the other to Normandy—after three years the one will be the light elegant carriage-horse, and the other an enormous animal, fitted only for the heaviest work, and almost incapable of a trot. Here food is probably the especial cause of variation. Horses, when transported to North India, are said to acquire wool instead of hair.

De Salles relates that the asses on the Cordilleras become hairy as bears; and the wild ass is well known to change its rough tubercular skin into a smooth skin, under domestication.

Of *cats* and *dogs* St. Hilaire says that the former have their alimentary canal lengthened, and the latter their front brain enlarged by domestication. Both mewing and barking seem to be lost by these animals in their wild state. Dogs carried to North India acquire wool instead of hair, while others in Africa become hairless. The European dog, if left wild on the coast of Africa, gradually comes to look like a jackal; his hair becomes red, tail branchy, ears stiff, and his voice changes to a howl.[12] The Dingo dog, in Australia, has the appearance of a wolf.[13]

It is related,[14] as an instance of the change which may be brought about in a breed, that English greyhounds exported to the mountain-plateaus of Mexico—some 9000 feet above the level of the sea—and employed to hunt hares, could never catch them, but fell down gasping for breath, so unaccustomed were they to the rarity of the atmosphere. They produced pups, however, that became adapted in their lungs to the atmosphere, and caught the hares easily.

In exporting *fowls* to South America, the first experience with the geese, for instance, was that half of the young died, but gradually some survived who were a little more adapted to the climate, until a permanent variety was formed, suited to its new circumstances. A breed of hens has been originated by the influence of climate in South America, which are nearly naked; another in Nicaragua, which are black.[15]

All are aware that the Dorking breed was preserved by fanciers, from an (apparently) accidental variety, with five toes and some other peculiarities. With geese and ducks, when the eggs of the wild birds are obtained and the young are supplied with abundant food, the intestines and abdomen become enlarged, so that the bird nearly loses the power of flight, and her wings become unserviceable, and she produces young as helpless as herself.[16]

Variations from food.

Among birds, the bullfinch, according to St. Hilaire, becomes *black* when fed on exciting food, especially hemp seed.

The great importance of these facts, which might be multiplied indefinitely, is that they all relate to animals, whose origin we *know*.

It cannot be replied in regard to the phenomena of variation, observed, for instance, in sheep and swine in South America, that each well-marked breed had its own separate parent there, who was created in that country, with all his peculiarities. We know that all these various races—woolly and hairy—short-legged and long-legged—black and white—with all their other peculiarities, came from one common stock. It must be remembered that the changes from the original breed, which these animals manifest, are not merely external and superficial, but often deviations in structure and functions.

Variations in animals of one origin.

Similar instances might be increased to an indefinite extent, from animals who are generally supposed by naturalists to belong to the same species and to be of one origin, but who have now deviated widely. But as the case seems sufficiently strong with these facts in regard to animals, whose common origin is certain, we refrain from treading on ground in any way disputed.

If, without a knowledge of the variations in animals, we were to see for the first time a Guinea negro of low type and a Circassian of high type placed side by side, we might naturally doubt whether they could have originated from the same ancestor. But when we discovered on the one side a succession of types, rising by almost imperceptible gradations from the low Congo type to the highest black Nubian type, and to the brown Tawàrek or Berber, so that an experienced observer in Africa—M. d'Abbadie*—could declare that, after thirteen years' observation, it was impossible for him to say where the black type ended and the brown began; on the other side, when we found the highest Circassian type descending by a series of slight changes to the brown, so that from physical evidence it was impossible to decide where one race terminated, and the other commenced, we may well imagine ourselves hesitating in our objections as to their community of descent. But, if still farther, we examined the different varieties of animals, confessedly of one stock, and found that their differences were greater, both in kind and degree, than those between these various human races, we might still farther hesitate.

Gradations in human varieties.

In human variation, perhaps the greatest apparent change is in the *colour*. This was formerly supposed to arise, in the dark races, from the presence of a membrane, which is wanting in the white races, while the occasional change of hue in the latter, was supposed to depend merely on causes which worked upon the scarf-skin or cuticle.

Colour.

* The same remark is made by D'Escayrac (1855).

But more minute microscopic investigations have shown that there is no organic difference in this respect between the skin of the negro and the white; that the colour in both is contained in pigment-cells, not membranes; and that the discolourations in the white, such as the *areola mammarum* of women, the summer freckles and moles, and the brown spots which occasionally appear on the skin, all depend on the presence of cells filled with pigment, similar to those which produce the colour of the negro.

These discolourations correspond also to the blackening of the skin produced by the disease called *melanosis*.[17]

Dr. Bachman's views of this subject are worth quoting in full. He says:—

> Microscopic anatomy has recently very satisfactorily proved that the colour of the skin exists in the epidermis only, and that it is the result of the admixture of pigment cells with the ordinary epidermic cells. The office of these pigment cells appears to be the withdrawing from the blood and elaborating in their own cavities, colouring matters of various shades; and all the different hues which are exhibited by the eleven races of men, depend on the relative quantity of those cells, and the colour of the pigment deposited in them. The *rete mucosum*, which was once described as a separate colouring layer underneath the epidermis, is simply the new soft layer of epidermis. If we examine the skin of the negro anatomically, we shall find no structure peculiar to it, for the very same dark cells are found in the fairest of mankind. (Quoted in Smyth's Unity, et cæt., p. 257.)

Explanation of colour.

The following are the views of a distinguished physiologist, Dr. Draper, on this subject:—

> If I am not mistaken, darkness of the skin and a prognathous form of skull may be dependent in the dark tribes on the same circumstance. Functionally, the liver is in connection with the calorifacient apparatus; its secretion, the bile,

coinciding in habitudes with a hydrocarbon. Much of it is therefore re-absorbed, and eventually devoted for the support of a high temperature. But besides this combustible material, the bile likewise contains a colouring matter, which is in all respects an effete body, and useless to the system. This pigment is derived from the blood-discs, or rather from their hæmatin, as is proved by the fact that it occurs in the meconium of the new-born infant, and likewise, like hæmatin, it is rich in iron. Its source is, therefore, not immediately from the food. To remove this useless material is thus one of the primary functions of the liver.

Now, there is no organ which is more quickly disturbed in its duty by a high temperature than the liver. Whether such a high temperature produces its effect through a disturbance of the action of the lungs, or through an impression on the skin, is quite immaterial. If the organ be in any manner enfeebled in its duty, and no other avenue is open, through which the degenerating hæmatin may escape, it must accumulate in the circulation, and be deposited here and there in suitable places. Under such circumstances, there arises a tendency for its accumulation in a temporary manner in the lower and more spherical cells of the cuticle, from which it is removed by their gradual exuviation and destruction as they become superficial. The temporary deposit of the colouring matter in this situation imparts to the skin a shade more or less deep. It may amount to a perfect blackness; for the origin of the black pigment of the negro is the same as that of the black pigment of the eye in all races, and the predominating percentage of iron it presents plainly betrays that it arises from a degenerating hæmatin, in which the same metal abounds.

I believe, therefore, that the colouration of the skin, whatever the particular tint may be, tawny-yellow, olive-red, or black, is connected with the manner in which the liver is discharging its function. That deposits of black pigment can normally arise in the way of a true secretion by cell action, is satisfactorily proved by their occurrence in angular and ramified patches in the skin of such animals as the frog; and that hæmatin, in its degeneration, may give rise to many different tints, is substantiated by the colours exhibited by echymoses.

Having thus traced the colouration of the skin to existing

peculiarities of hepatic action, I may repeat the remark already made, that it is not improbable that, in the most degraded negro type, the prognathous form of the skull may be attributed to the same cause. (Draper's Physiology, p. 588.)

Change of colour.

The process of a decided change of colour is witnessed even at the present day. M. d'Abbadie states that the Abyssinians have a word to express "the growing black," which is a change greater than the mere tanning of the skin. M. Lefebvre (according to Hollard) also notices a change of colour and skin in men and animals in Abyssinia, according to the seasons—the olive-brown complexion of the natives becoming pale, and like the European in the rainy season, while a removal of habitation from the mountains to the sea-shore, and exposure to greater heat, produces a dark-brown colour, almost black.

Similar changes are noticed with animals, especially in sheep.

Portuguese colonists in Cachaux, West Africa, according to Durand, have become very black mulattoes; and according to other authorities, on the Cape Verd Islands, the coast of Guinea, in Batavia and Bombay, and in Floers and Timor, they are almost black, though of pure blood.[17 a]

The lower classes of Spain and Portugal are so much like Indians in colour, that St. Hilaire felt it necessary to account for the colour of Indians solely by climate and uncleanness!

Hair.

The variation in *hair*, in a scientific view, is a more marked distinction, even, than that of colour. The hair of the negro was formerly considered to be wool, but the late investigations, as recorded by Prichard, show that it is not at all wool, and does not differ from the hair of the white races, except in being more crisped, and more filled with colouring matter;

the two latter peculiarities perhaps depending on one another.

From the facts before presented in regard to animals, it will be seen that those of similar origin present even greater varieties in colour and skin than the races of men.

The changes from the tubercular skin of the wild ass to the smooth skin of the tame; from the woolly sheep of England to the hairy sheep of South America; from the light swine of Europe to the black variety of the same when exported; from the hairy dog of France to the naked dog of Africa; from the tame hog to the wild boar, are certainly quite equal to any supposed changes in the human races.

In *size* and *structure*, the differences between the races of men are very slight indeed: two feet is probably the average difference between the height of the tallest and shortest races; though if the "Doko" tribe, of whom Krapf heard reports in Eastern Africa, are the pigmies they are described, this difference would be slightly increased. This, of course, is no greater than can be seen often in animals of the same stock. The differences in the human skull of different races are also comparatively small.

Dr. Bachman concludes from the measurements of Dr. Tiedemann and Dr. Morton, that the negro skull, though less than the European, is within one inch as large as the Persian and the Armenian, and three square inches larger than the Hindoo and Egyptian.*

Variations in skull.

The difference between the average English and Irish skull is nine cubic inches, and

* The scale is thus given by Dr. Morton: European skull, 87 cubic inches; Malay, 85; Negro, 83; Mongol, 82; Ancient Egyptian, 80; American, 79. The ancient Peruvians and Mexicans, who constructed so elaborate a civilization, show a capacity only of from 75 to 79 inches.

only four between the average African and the Irish. The largest African skull in his collection measured ninety-nine inches, and the largest Irish, ninety-seven inches. "Were we to give," he says, "white colour and straight hair to some negro skulls, the most practised anatomist would be deceived." Still other observations by Huschki make the average capacity of the skull of Europeans, 40·88 oz.; of Americans, 39·13; of Mongols, 38·39; of Negroes, 37·57; of Malays, 36·41.

There is nothing in the structure, either of the brain or the skeleton, in the different races, which would indicate a separate origin. Of the brain of the negro Tiedemann says: (1.) Its weight is equal to the average European. (2.) In the capacity of its cavity, it is not smaller than the average European races. (3.) The form and structure of the spinal cord do not differ from those of other races, except as resulting from the different size of the body. (4.) The cerebellum in outward form, fissures, and lobes, is exactly similar to the European. (5.) The cerebrum has for the most part the same form as in other races. (6.) The internal structure of the brain shows the same substance; and (7.) The brain is equal to the average European in size, and the nerves are not thicker than those of other races. It is true that the skull of the negro is usually somewhat thicker than the European skull, but this peculiarity is not distinctive of the African. The New Hollanders have the same; and the natives of Van Diemen's Land are said to break wood over their own heads without injury. The Indians of South America, and those of Cuba and Haiti, were reported by the Spanish authorities to present the same feature—even the Kelts of Brittany are marked by it, as were the ancient inhabitants of France, judging from the skulls which have been discovered.

Thickness of skull.

In a similar manner, negro features, such as the projecting teeth, the deficient calf of the leg, and the length of the fore-arm, are shared by other races. Of the latter, Jarrold has proved that the forearm of the Scot is the medium between that of the negro and the Englishman, and that his hand is lengthened proportionally.

The peculiarly flexible use of the toes by the negroes was once thought to separate them from other races, but it is found that the New Hollanders have a similar power, as well as the Malays and many tribes of South American Indians, some of the latter using their toes to pick up pieces of money.

Human variations.

The pelvis of the female negro, differing in form slightly from that of the European, the heavier skeleton of the male, the somewhat different curvature of the legs and the heels, the thicker skull, and the less development of the fingers in some of the black tribes, are differences by no means so great as are seen in many animals of the same stock.

Animal.

The solid hoof of one variety of hogs; the five toes of the Dorking fowl; the contrast between the wild boar and the tame hog, between the tailless breeds of poultry and sheep and those with tails, are more suggestive of difference of origin, than any human peculiarities.

The fatty appendages (*steatopyge*) upon some of the female Bushmen, Caffres, and Somaulis, as well as on the Asiatic Kurds,* are only an addition of what is found normally in other races, while the changes in animals of the same breed involve often an absolute change in structure.†

* Dr. Rigler.

† Of the changes wrought by man in the vegetable world, says Sir Charles Lyell: "the crab has been transposed into the apple; the aloe

III. Our third point is, that the members of a race often differ among themselves, as much as the various races differ from one another.

It is almost universally admitted now, by scholars, that the Aryan or Indo-European family of nations is of one origin; yet they include physical types as diverse as the dark Hindoo, the blonde Norwegian, the classic Greek, and the depressed Irish. Colour, size, features, and shape of the head, are all exceedingly different in these various types. We see not what the supporters of the Diversity of Origin can do with such extreme variations in a family acknowledgedly from one source.

Variations in Indo-Europeans.

This Treatise has been full of instances of corresponding variations in recognized races. Thus, what greater apparent contrast could there be than between the blonde Jew of Eastern Germany, and the black Arab of the banks of the Jordan—both now reckoned of one origin; or between the brown Jew of Abyssinia and the black Jew of Cochin-China or the Great Desert?

In a single small race, we often find marked differences, as between the brown Afghans of East Afghanistan and the light Afghans of the west with blue eyes and red hair; between the dark Hindoos of the Dekkan, Malabar, and Ceylon, and the blonde Hindoos of the Himalaya; the olive and blonde Arabs of Armenia and Syria, and the brown of Yemen, and the black of the Jordan; the olive Tuariks of the southern slope of

into the plum; flowers have changed their colour and become double; and these new characters can be perpetuated by seed. A bitter plant with wavy sea-green leaves has been taken from the sea-side, where it grew like wild charlock, has been transplanted into the garden, lost its saltness, and has been metamorphosed into two distinct vegetables as unlike each other as is each to the parent plant—the red cabbage and the cauliflower." (Prin. of Geol., vol. ii. p. 32.)

the Atlas, and the black of interior Africa; the white Chinese of the north, with rosy complexion, and the brown of the south.

The *Guebres*, or descendants of the ancient Persians, are said by De Salles to be badly made and ugly in person, with brown complexions, while depressed under the Persian Government; while with those in Bombay, who are favoured by the English Government, and have become wealthy, the physique is noble and beautiful; the men are large and strong, and the women are elegant, with large eyes and arched brows, and a white complexion, just gilded in tint.[18]

The *Magyars* present, perhaps, the most beautiful physical type of any people of Europe, and yet their nearest relatives, undoubtedly of the same origin, are the Finns and Laps, the most ugly and ill-formed race in Europe.

Of the shape of the skull, as distinctive of different origin, Professor M. J. Weber has said, "there is no proper mark of a definite race form of the cranium, so firmly attached that it may not be found in some other race." The same measures of skull, the same types, whether of classic purity and beauty, or of savage degradation, appear in individuals of all races. Tiedemann has met with Germans, whose skulls bore all the characters of the negro races; and an inhabitant of Nukahiwa, according to Silesius and Blumenbach, agreed exactly in his proportions with the Apollo Belvidere.

Among Chinese, Japanese, and Siamese, persons are sometimes seen, says Perthes, of unmixed native blood, who precisely resemble Europeans in features and complexion.

Many of the New Zealanders have skulls like Europeans, while their faces resemble North American

Indians. The Hottentots, in complexion, shape of the skull, and form of the face, are like the Mongols, though there is not the least evidence that they are related to them. The Georgians and Circassians show a perfect Greek type of feature, though they belong to an entirely distinct family.

Travellers tell us that blue or brown eyes, and light hair and complexion, are occasionally seen in all races, even among the blacks, where there could be no suspicion of mixture of blood. (See Waiz.)

Dr. Meigs is quoted by Wilson (Pre-Historic Man, p. 245), as giving his conclusion in the observations of 1125 different human crania, "that there is a marked tendency of these forms to graduate into one another, more or less insensibly. None of these forms can be said to belong exclusively to any race or tribe. None of them, therefore, can be regarded as strictly typical; for a character of form, to be typical, should be exclusive and constant." Wilson himself (p. 285) gives it as his conclusion from a great variety of data, in regard to an American type of skull, that "it seems scarcely possible to evade the conclusion that the ideal American typical head has no existence in nature." . . . . . . "The form of the human skull is just as little constant among the different tribes or races of the New World as of the Old."

No fixed type.

Prof. Huxley, in a note to Lyell's recent work on Antiquity (p. 87), gives the various measurements of two fossil skulls (the "Engis" and the "Neanderthal") and a number of Australian, and then compares them with an English skull, which is described in the Hunterian museum as "typically Caucasian." The differences are incredibly small, and justify Huxley's conclusion that "cranial measurements alone afford no safe indication of race."

Physical Degeneration produces types in small numbers from a given nation, which correspond to the types of degraded races elsewhere. The *crétin* differs more from the European, favoured by physical circumstances, than the Australian differs from him.[19] He recalls under various stages of his degeneration, some of the race-types; as the brown races in his brown complexion; the Kalmucks and Oceanicans in his large ears; the Congo-negroes in his thick lips, large mouth, and flat nose; the Australians in his slender limbs.

Degeneration.

Mayhew in his "London Labour, &c.," speaking of the vagabond poor, says (vol. i. p. 2), "According as they partake more or less of the purely vagabond nature, doing nothing for their living, but moving from place to place, preying on the earnings of the more industrious portion of the community, so will the attributes of the nomadic races be found more or less marked on them; and they are all more or less distinguished for their high cheek-bones and protruding jaws."

The following is the description of physical degeneracy among the Portuguese, quoted by Morel in his *Traité des Dégénérescences*, p. 413. It is a terrible picture of human degradation, and the effect can be traced in great degree to moral causes.

Malacca, says Dr. Yvan, has about 30,000 inhabitants. This population is composed of Portuguese, Dutch, English, Malays, and Chinese. Among the inhabitants of European origin, the Portuguese are the most numerous. They are, for the most part, descendants of the ancient conquerors of Malaisia. Their fathers were the companions of Vasco di Gama and Albuquerque, but, like the monuments that their ancestors raised, and which cover the soil of their ruins, they also have been injured by degradation and age. In the midst of the Malayan population with which they have been for a very long time allied the 3000 descendants of the ancient Portuguese are physically the ugliest, and morally the most degraded. They must not be confounded with the Malays of pure origin. They have not in appearance, or in attitude, the wild energy of these men. One would say, rather, that they have borrowed the character which distinguishes them from the Ethiopian races. Their features have something of the animal; in a word, they bear upon their contracted and oily brow the sign of a moral fall. The poor people have no idea of their glorious ancestors. Tradition, that consolatory remembrance of fallen races, is effaced from the memory of the people. The majority bear illustrious names, and they are ignorant who were their fathers, and what ray of the past pierces their obscurity.*

* "It is truly dreadful," says Dr. Yvan, "to adjust the balance of the losses that these men have made. In the space of half a century, perhaps, religion, morals, tradition, written transmission of thought, are effaced from their remembrance. The most hideous idleness and absence of all wants, are substituted for enjoyments acquired by labour. This degradation presents itself under its characteristic forms: stunted growth, physical ugliness, want of life among children, obtuse intelligence, perverted instincts, progressive successions of sickly transformations, reaching, as a final result, to the extreme limits of imbecility." This last degenerative form appears strikingly in the descriptions of Dr. Yvan, and we cite his own words. "There exists," says Dr. Y., "in the environs of Malacca, in the direction of Mount Ophir, a little hamlet situated in the midst of the jungles. The inhabitants of this hamlet are in a frightful state of destitution; they do not cultivate, they live outside of all social laws, having neither priest to marry them, nor cadi, nor judge, nor mayor, to regulate their differences. Their dwellings are a kind of cabins made of reeds covered with leaves of the palm-tree, and their only industry consists in going into the woods to search for the wax produced by wild bees, in washing sand, and in gathering the resin which runs down the trees.

"I had often heard of this population; during one of our suspensions at Malacca, a priest of the foreign missions proposed to me to go to visit them. We set out on horseback, and after a march of five hours through rice-fields, rushes, and vast lands covered with sacchariferous plants, we arrived at the foot of a little elevation, upon which the village is established. Nothing announced the neighbourhood of an

In the plains of the Argentine Republic, near Cordova and San Luis, the Spaniards are as inactive and backward as the natives themselves, while the German and Scottish colonies south of Buenos Ayres, present a most blooming condition.

In Sertajo and Goyaz, according to Waiz, the Portuguese have become almost savages.

Degeneracy of Europeans.

On one of the Fernando Islands, says Webster (Narr. of Voy. to S. Sea, 1834), is a Portuguese penal colony. The men have become so degenerated that they have abandoned agriculture, and do not even possess a boat—a depth of misery which the lowest South Sea Islanders have not reached.

The same is true of the Portuguese on the coasts of Eastern Africa; they have become as lazy and barbarous there as the lowest native negroes, and yet they

inhabited place; none of the accustomed sounds interrupted the silence of the solitudes; one neither heard the joyous cries of children, nor the crow of the cock.

"Even the signs by which one is aware of the presence of man, did not exist in this wild place. No trace of cultivation was s n. Not even were those spiral lines of smoke perceived among the trees, which point out ordinarily the humblest dwelling. The beaten paths which wound through the forest, resembled rather the prints left upon the soil by fallow beasts than paths frequented by men. For the rest, what I call pompously a village, was a collection of dilapidated huts of the most miserable aspect; these were all open to the first arrival; it was seen that the inhabitants concealed nothing from their neighbours, but it was easily understood that if they had all in common, they enjoyed little but common misery. When we arrived, the women were squatted down around the huts, some chewing betel without doing anything, others holding suspended to their sinking breasts some feeble abortions.

"The three or four men that we found in the hamlet, were lying down aside, smoking coarse maize cigarettes, and chewing the *siri* like the women. Every one was naked or wore very little clothing. The complexion of the children was almost white; that of the men and were once one of the leading maritime peoples of Europe.

It is said, also, that in Equador, in the province of Loxa, there are wild, barbarous Spaniards, of entirely unmixed blood, who have lost every trace of historic tradition (Tschudi).

The Arabians were once the most powerful of the Semitic races, and stamped their influence on the civilization of the globe; yet in Socotra, they are said to have become so degraded and inactive, as not even to possess a boat. In Nubia, they are thought to be more lazy, and less capable of invention and enterprise than negroes (Waiz), and they live in the greatest misery.

In Ireland, in Sligo and Northern Mayo, two centuries of degradation and hardship are said to have produced physical effects on a population once vigour-

women, soot-colour. They had thick lips, large black eyes, straight projecting nose, and rough long hair. They were all small and thin. One would have said that this population passed without transition from infancy to the decline of manhood; youth seemed not to exist for these unhappy people; their eyes were hollow, and their skin withered.

"Our guides, who were Malays, addressed some of the women, asking them how they named their village, where were their husbands, &c. But after having heard their replies, they declared to us that they could not comprehend perfectly what they said, on account of a great many words that were not Malayan. The priest who accompanied me, descended from his horse, approached them, and discovered that the language they spoke was a simple mixture of Malay and Portuguese.

"This language itself was the most real expression of the sad mental state of these unhappy people. They knew neither who they were nor whence they came. The names by which they were called represented no family recollection, for they lived rather promiscuously. The idea of time was above their weak conception, and most of them made themselves remarked by such brutishness that their visitors could obtain no reasonable reply even to the most simple questions."

ous and well-formed, which would liken them to the appearance of some of the lowest African and Oceanican tribes. "They are remarkable for open, projecting mouths, with prominent teeth and exposed gums, and their advancing cheek-bones and depressed noses, bear barbarism on their very front." Others are described as "five feet two inches on an average, pot-bellied, bow-legged, and abortively featured." [20]

Features affected by civilization.

It cannot be questioned that the degree of civilization or barbarism, affects all the features of the body and face. Thus, among a thousand instances which might be selected, Mrs. Norton observes that the free-born negro children in Sierra Leone have more intelligent eyes, freer bearing, and a more agreeable form than their emancipated parents. Day says that the higher is the position of a negro in the West Indies, the more his type is found different from the low (Congo) negro type, and approaching the European, or at least the Jewish features. It is generally admitted that the low, barbarous type of one tribe of negroes found in the Northern United States and the West Indies—that of the coast negro of Guinea—has been much improved, merely by contact with whites and by a state of freedom. The testimony from missions in South Africa (according to Philip) and from the Philippines (see Mallat), is, that in the third generation the shape of head of the children begins to change.

Change of type.

Rèzius—the great advocate of the theory that the shape of the skull is the only distinctive mark of race—admits that the skulls of town and country people in Sweden, differ in size, owing to their different mode of life; and Wilson states that the skulls of the ancient barbarian Scots are smaller than those of the modern civilized people.

So again the *Bushmen*, living in the districts northeast of Lake Ngami, have much better forms than those in the extreme south, owing to their better nourishment. In *New Holland*, the appearance of the natives varies according to their position and their opportunities for acquiring food; and in New South Wales, even the hair varies to a great degree among people apparently of the same origin, some having it smooth, some curly, and some crisp. (See *Waiz.*) Hale notices very great contrasts in the inhabitants of South and North Kingsmill Islands (Micronesia), though of the same race—differences to be traced entirely to external causes.

Differences in same race.

These examples could be multiplied to any extent.

We are not contesting in these statements the existence of physical types, which are distinct, and are transmitted among men; but we would only urge that this diversity among races confessedly of the same origin, and this likeness among races who are by many classified as distinct, cannot be accounted for on the theory that the present physical differences of mankind spring from a Diversity of Origin.

IV. It is well known in regard to animals, that a process of *Acclimation* occurs. A certain race, for instance, changes its climate and soil and physical circumstances; the first offspring are in part, weakly, or they in part, die out; at length, a slight variation occurs in the internal or external structure, which enables its possessors better to resist the destructive agencies around it and finally to survive. These peculiarities are transmitted and increased, inasmuch as they are beneficial to those who possess them, until finally the race becomes accustomed to its new circumstances.

Acclimation.

The same thing takes place with men. All races of men, so far as we know, are capable in time of becoming acclimated to any new country or climate; as witness the Jews living from the heats of tropical Asia and Africa to the cold of Russia, or the Aryan descendants, surviving and transmitting vigorous offspring, whether in India or Iceland. It is true that after centuries or ages of residence on a given soil and under a given climate, a new physical type is formed, fitted for its circumstances, which may not be easily and at once transplanted; any more, for instance, than the tame duck or goose with his changed organs, would be fitted to live at once in the wild state. A habit of climate has sprung up, which may need long spaces of time and new circumstances to change. Thus Dr. Clark reports that in Dominique, in 1793–'96, the epidemic struck all the negroes just imported from Africa, while those long on the island, escaped. In some cases, this acclimation may occur rapidly; as, for instance, it is said the pure negroes in this country, of the third generation from African parents, cannot return with impunity to the malarious coasts of Africa, though their fathers lived there in complete health.

In general, too, acclimation is in part dependent on moral causes: the power in any given race intelligently to adapt its habits to new circumstances, and above all, the capacity of *self-control*, so that the vices and indulgences of a strange country and climate may be resisted.[20] Very much of the effects attributed to climate, is due to human vices; and it will generally be found that the races most gifted with self-control—those of most moral principle—are those which endure foreign climates best. Who can doubt that the lamentable picture given above,

Acclimation dependent on moral causes.

of Portuguese degeneracy in the East Indies, is due in great measure to moral causes? as is the like degeneracy in our own southern continent.

The lower, the more ignorant and degraded a people is, the less fitted is it to change its climate, and the more sure to perish under the change.

Probably, no race endures diversities of climate so well as the great Teutonic race, and it will be found that their various branches, transplanted to tropical or warm countries—as the Dutch in Africa and East India, the English in India, and the Americans in the Southern States of North America—owe their vigour and their health more to moral causes than physical; for, of all great families of men, we may assert that this in the highest degree is gifted with self-control. We may sometimes see a people under process of acclimation; as, for instance, the Anglo-Americans and Germans in North America, whose physical type is gradually changing from the original German or English type and adapting itself to its new circumstances, though it is impossible to say how far intermarriage may have part in this change of type. The first effects of this process will, no doubt, appear unfavourable; the weaker and those unsuited to our climate must perish, while the stronger will gradually survive and transmit their descendants, until a new type is formed, adapted to the country and climate.*

Endurance of Teutonic race.

* It is a great error of many writers on Ethnology, to suppose that the American physique has degenerated from the English type. If it were within the field of this Treatise, the contrary could be easily proved from innumerable data. We would only call attention to some notorious evidences in favour of our vitality and power. It is well-known by manufacturers and employers in this country, that for labours requiring the utmost physical endurance and muscular power, such as "iron-puddling," "lumbering," in the forests and on

The grand fact that various races can thus accustom themselves to all climates seems to us a presumption in favour of their common origin.

Hybridity.[21] The strongest evidence to the minds of men of science in favour of unity of origin has been usually held to be the fact that all races are fruitful with one another.

All races fruitful together.

There is no exception to this; and the few instances looking in the other direction have all yielded before more minute investigations.* [22]

All races of men, of all countries, are fertile with one another. Still, it is claimed that, even if this be the

the streams, and pioneer-work, foreigners are never so suitable as the native Americans.

The reports of the examining surgeons for volunteers—such as that of Dr. W. H. Thompson to the Surgeon-General, in 1862, who examined 9000 men—show a far higher average of physique in the Americans examined, than in the English, Germans, or Irish.

The immense physical achievements of the Anglo-American race in clearing and improving the surface of this Continent, are alone proofs of great vitality and physical power

It is a fact well-known to our life insurance companies that the average length of life here is greater than that of the English tables.

The effect of the climate is indeed to produce a somewhat spare, nervous and muscular type—quite different from the English—though to this there are vast numbers of exceptions; but the average of health, of muscular strength, and power of sustained endurance, we believe to be greater here than in England or in any civilized country.

* The statement at one time urged, that the native females or "gins" of New Holland, after producing children with the English, became barren with their own males, is found to be incorrect. This statement was originally made by Count Strzlecki, and has been repeated over and over, till the world has believed it. It is contradicted most clearly and carefully by the best authority—Dr. Thompson—a gentleman personally familiar with the Island. See his article in Journ. of Ethnol. Soc., vol. 3, p. 243.

case, the offspring of very different races—as, for instance, the Congo negro and the white European—are weakly and sterile, and finally die out.

Facts in regard to this important subject are extremely difficult to obtain. The general impression in our Southern States is, that mulattoes do not perpetuate themselves for many generations. **Sterility of Mulattoes.** But, on the other hand, in the Middle States, every one knows mulatto families who are apparently vigorous and healthy for several generations. As it is generally understood that a considerable part of the slaves at the South are of mixed blood, and as the rate of increase of the slaves is known to be large, the conclusion would seem probable that mulattoes do perpetuate themselves freely, even in America. Still, we have, as yet, no trustworthy statistics on this very interesting question. The author has been able, after much investigation, only to collect a few facts bearing upon it. It is to be hoped that scientific men and statisticians will keep in mind this disputed point in reporting statistics of population.

Fortunately, thorough reports since 1774 are preserved of the numbers of the mulatto population in Cuba. The following are the tables given by M. de la Sagra. We have purposely left out of view the statistics relating to the mulattoes in slavery, inasmuch as the severities of that system might modify the natural increase of the population.

Men.		Year.	Women.	
White.	Free Mulattoes.		White.	Free Mulattoes.
55,576	10,201	1774	40,864	9,006
72,299	15,845	1792	61,260	18,041
130,519	30,512	1817	109,311	29,170
168,653	28,053	1827	142,398	29,456
227,144	43,658	1841	191,147	44,396

From these it appears that during the sixty-seven years before 1841 the white males of Cuba increased 4·08+ times, while the mulatto males increased 4·28+ times; and the white females 4·67+ times, but the mulattoes of the same sex 4·92+ times. This certainly looks very little like a want of power in the cross of perpetuating itself.

Still farther, according to the same author, the excess of births over deaths in the island in 1827 was,—for free negroes, 11·5 in every 100; for slave negroes, 45·3; for slave mulattoes, 44·3; for whites, 48·7; and for free mulattoes, 57·7.

Facts from Cuba.

This plainly indicates no inferiority in vital power in the mulatto.

Humboldt gives for 1793 the relative numbers of different races in the city of Mexico over 50 years of age.

The proportion of mixed races over 50 years was 6 in every 100; of the Indian, 6$\frac{4}{5}$ per cent.; of the Spaniard, 8; and the mulatto, 7 per cent; a fact showing that the cross between the negro and the white there is more long-lived than the cross between the Indian and the white, and even more than the native stock itself.

Mulattoes in Mexico.

In St. Miguel, Brazil, the following was the state of the population in 1816:—Out of 1,942 whites, there were 21 over 70 years, and 3 over 85, and none over 95; while, from 3,010 free mulattoes, there were 107 over 70 years, and 32 over 85, and 1 over 100 years; of 1,112 free negroes, there were only 5 over 70 years; and of Indians, none.

The results among the Pitcairn Islanders are equally convincing that the Polynesian and Teutonic races can unite with the same results as in kindred races.

In 1790 the population of the island consisted of only

30 persons—namely, 4 European sailors, 10 Polynesian women, and their children. In 1825 they numbered 66; in 1856, 187, without any foreign immigration.

The children of the New Zealanders and the English (according to Waiz) are a healthy and muscular race; those of the Philippine Islanders and the Europeans are more beautiful than the Europeans themselves.

That the offspring of the same grade of mixture in different races are fruitful with one another is proved by the careful names which are given in South America to the various crosses.*

There are some apparent exceptions found, it is true, to the permanent fruitfulness of different races, but they are usually to be accounted for by local causes. Thus, the offspring of the Hollanders and Malays on

* The following vocabulary is from M. de Larenandière's History of Mexico (quoted by Quatrefages), indicating the different degrees of the mixture effected between the three races, white, black, and red :—

Mestisa—product of a Spaniard and an Indian woman.
Castisa—of a Mongrel woman and a Spaniard.
Espagnola—of a Castiso and a Spanish woman.
Mulâtre—of a Spanish woman and a Negro.
Morisque—of a Mulatto woman and a Spaniard.
Albino—of a Morisque and a Spanish woman.
Tornatras—of an Albino and a Spanish woman.
Tentinelaire—of a Tornatras and a Spanish woman.
Lovo—of an Indian woman and a Negro.
Caribujo—of an Indian woman and a Lovo.
Barsino—of a Coyote and an Indian woman.
Grifo—of a Negress and a Lovo.
Canisa—of a Mongrel woman and an Indian.
Albarazado—of a Coyote and an Indian woman.
Mechino—of a Lovo and a Coyote.

Some of these terms have, in other places besides Mexico, a different signification; several are replaced by other expressions.

Fitzroy [states (Journ. of Ethnol. Soc., 1862) that twenty-three human varieties are enumerated by *savans*, in Lima, from the mingling of the Peruvian, the Negro, and the Spaniard.

Apparent exceptions.

the Island of Java are said not to survive beyond the third generation; but, on the other side, those of pure whites die out in the second, so that this result seems fairly attributable to climate.

The immense increase and the physical beauty (in many instances) of the various mixtures of colours and races in South America favour the view that all races can transmit permanent and healthy offspring.

We quote from Quatrefages, p. 322 :—

During the four years that I passed in Brazil, Chili, and Peru, says M. Hombron, I was amused to observe the singular mixture of negroes with the aborigines; I even made an exact note of the number of children that resulted in a great number of households from the alliance of a white man with a negro woman; of a white with an American woman; of a negro with a woman of Chili or Peru; of an American with his countrywoman; and, finally, of a negro woman with a negro.

I can affirm that the unions of whites with Americans have presented me with the most elevated average; then come the negro and negro woman; and, lastly, the negro and American. In our colonies, the negro women and the whites offer a middling fruitfulness; the mulatto women and the whites are extremely prolific, as well as the mulattoes and mulatto women.

The offspring of the white Turk and the negro woman, according to Dr. Rigler, is a vigorous and intelligent race; and such marriages are peculiarly prolific.

Professor Wilson, in his "Pre-historic Man," has collected some very valuable facts in regard to the extensive population of half-breeds on the Red River and the Canadian frontier. "In the Red River settlement," he states (vol. ii. p. 348), "where there are about 6,500 with Indian blood, the families descended from mixed parentage are larger

Half-breeds in America.

than those from white parents." Archdeacon Hunter, a Catholic clergyman, familiar for a long time with the Indian population of British America, in reply to the question, "In what respects do the half-breed Indians differ from the pure Indians as to habits of life, courage, increase, &c., &c.?" says, "They are superior in every respect, both mentally and physically." The mixed offspring, says Wilson, does not fail but generally, by intermarriages, it becomes very difficult to determine whether they are pure whites or half-breeds. Mr. J. S. Dawson, of the Red River exploring expedition, describes the half-breeds as a hardy, vigorous race of men, and frequently with large and healthy families. "I know," says Wilson, "from my own observation, that the French half-breeds at Red River are a gigantic race, as compared with the French Canadians of Lower Canada."

"There are many independent tribes of half-breeds," he states, "partaking of the characteristics of both their parents."

Rev. J. Marault speaks highly of the physical and mental qualities of the *Abenakis* (mostly half-breeds), and says that they are "superior in intelligence to the Canadians."

The *Hurons*, on the St. Charles River, have been mingling with the whites for nearly two centuries, so that they have nearly lost their language. They are the most advanced in civilization of all the Canadian tribes. It is ascertained by the Indian census of 1844 that their numbers have very considerably increased.

"Statistics show," says Dr. Wilson, farther (p. 390), "that in Upper and Lower Canada the intermixture of red and white blood, though there carried out under unfavourable circumstances, does not lead to degeneracy, sterility, or extinction, but has created an extensive population of half-bloods, totally apart from those of mixed blood, who are re-absorbed into the native tribes."

African Bastards.

In South Africa, a cross between the Hottentots and the Dutch—the *Bastards*—have perpetuated themselves, and a portion of them—the *Griquas*—become a permanent tribe, quite as vigorous as either of their parents. Still, there are not yet facts sufficient from which to obtain an absolute scientific conclusion on the matter.

And we would say, *à priori*, we should expect, on the theory which we shall soon state, that there would be a difficulty in two very diverse types crossing at first with permanent fertility. Their mutual differences and varying constitutions would naturally render the surviving of the first offspring somewhat doubtful. Take the matter of acclimation alone. Each parent is adapted to a different and peculiar condition of temperature, soil, and climate. The offspring, if it shares these adaptations equally, must be in so far unadapted to its climate and circumstances. That is, a half-blood mulatto in our Northern States, in so far as he has a negro constitution, is unfitted for our climate; in the Southern he is equally unadapted, from his white blood, to the climate there, and it may be several centuries before he becomes suited to either.

Probability of mulattoes being weakly.

We may suppose, too, that the different tendencies to disease in such different races might make the constitution weaker; and, farther, in this country there may be moral causes of which we are not sufficiently aware. In every mulatto there is something of the pride and the sensitiveness of the ruling race, while his mixture with black blood exposes him continually to the vulgar prejudice and base insult which our populace heap on this oppressed race.

Explanation of weak races dying out.

He may die out, as the Indian dies out, from the wear and contact with a different and grasping race.* There may be, too, a physical cause, in the fact that mulattoes, who are naturally a small population, intermarry much with one another, and thus, from the accumulation of like tendencies to disease, their children are weakly and do not survive.†

There is nothing in the gradual diminution and destruction of a savage or inferior race in contact with a more civilized and powerful which is "mysterious," as is frequently said, or which has anything to do with the subject of hybridity. The first gifts of civilization are naturally fatal to a barbarous people, from the fact that their constitutions and habits have been formed under entirely different circumstances, and it requires time to adapt them to the new conditions. Thus it is related that the Sandwich Islanders first began to take cold after wearing clothes. Then, a savage race are always inclined to the destructive stimulants of civilized races, as alcohol, tobacco, and opium, without having the intelligence to guard against

No mystery.

* This must not be understood to be a poetic or sentimental statement, It is a scientific consideration now, in explaining the diminution of any barbarous or inferior race in presence of a more powerful one—the effect on the spirits or temperament which the contrast of a different and more fortunate people causes. No doubt with the North American Indian, *melancholy* is to be set down in the driest statistical list of the causes of his decline.

† "We suspect that this (*i. e.*, the lessening of vigour and fertility by close interbreeding) is not an ultimate fact, but a natural consequence of inheritance—the inheritance of disease or tendency to disease, which close interbreeding perpetuates and acccumulates, but wide breeding may neutralize or eliminate." (Dr. A. Gray, Rev. of Darwin's Theory, &c., p. 15.) This most ingenious suggestion, we believe, is original with Dr. Gray, to whose investigations and clear reasonings on the subject of the formation of varieties, every student of races is under such great obligations.

their ill-effects. So with the diseases of civilization; and even the food of a house-dwelling people is sometimes entirely unsuited to an outdoor and active people. Morbid appetites for new food arise, as it is said that the *Maori* of New Zealand have been diminishing since 1830, principally from the disorders brought on by eating *putrid corn* imported by Europeans.

A barbarous people in contact with a higher people is frequently diminished or exterminated from the *destruction of game* caused by the superior skill of the other. Thus the Indian Commission, according to Wilson, reported in 1858 of the *Montagnars*, on the Lower St. Lawrence, that "they were diminishing rapidly; upwards of 300 have died within ten years, one half of whom have fallen victims to starvation," owing to the fish and game having been so much diminished by the whites.

Causes of extinction.

One of the greatest causes, however, is often neglected by investigators, that is, *intermarriage*. It is evident from Dr. Wilson's statistics that large numbers of the Indians in British America and the United States have intermarried with whites, and have become gradually absorbed in the superior race, and are no longer distinguishable from it; each new marriage of the mixed progeny being naturally with the ruling race.*

It does not necessarily follow that the civilized race exterminates the savage. Sometimes the inferior has the most vigour, and the cultivated people becomes degraded and dwindles away, as the Portuguese already described in contact with the Malays; or the Spaniards in South America, where the mixed races seem destined to have the preponderance. Sometimes, two races of

* Of the famous Mohawks, says Wilson, only *two* are found on the Bay of Quinte, unmixed with white blood.

very different origin can live side by side for centuries, each fulfilling its separate office, as the brown and light Brahmanic Aryans of India with the Turanian blacks; or they can intermarry, as the uncivilized Kelts and Teutons with the cultured Romans, or the Turks with the Greeks. There is every reason to believe that in this country, in the warm districts, the negro and white can live side by side without the former diminishing, as do the American Indians in contact with the whites. It is only in the cold latitudes here that the negro race dwindles away.* Two races in contact.

Nor is it necessarily true that mixed races are inferior physically; thus, the offspring of the Turks and the Moors are more beautiful than either of their parents. The Arabs and Abyssinians produce a healthy and handsome race. The much-mingled Indian population in Paraguay and Cochabamba are more beautiful after some generations than the pure Spaniards. In Peru, the *Chotos*, a cross of the Mestizo and Indian, exceed in bodily activity and capacities all other races on the soil. The Fejees, which are supposed to be a mixture of the Polynesians with the "Oriental negroes," are a remarkably powerful race. The facts already mentioned in regard to the American half-breeds are to the same effect. Vigour of mixed races.

V. The most favourite objections made to unity of origin are, that in the remotest human antiquity, at least 2,500 years before Christ, and near the received date of the Flood, we find the different human types as

* The increase of the total black population, both free and slave, of the Southern States from 1840–50, was 27·40 per cent.; while that of the whites from 1830–40, was only 26·54 per cent.

In the Northern States, New York is about the northern limit for the free black population—beyond this, the climate acting fatally.

distinctly pictured on the monuments of Egypt as they exist now. The low negro type, the brown Turanian, the Semitic, and the white Aryan, are perfectly represented there. If human physical types are utterly unchanged for a period of 4000 or 4500 years, they ask, is there any reason to suppose that they changed during the 2000 or 4000 years preceding? The negro had his black skin, his thick lips, protruding jaw, and curved legs; the Semite his bent nose; the Egyptian his bronze complexion and voluptuous lips; the Aryan his white skin and noble features before the time of the Pharaohs: why is it to be thought that in the few thousand years preceding they had any different traits?

Objections to unity from Egyptian monuments.

Who ever sees, they triumphantly inquire, a race-type changing? When has the Ethiopian changed his skin? When did a European ever become a negro? Where has man seen an American Indian pass into a white? Where, even, has a Jew, without crossing with other races, acquired a Greek or English form of features? Who ever hears of Englishmen or Frenchmen becoming black under the tropics? Where does straight hair change into frizzled, or thin lips to negro-lips? Where is the process going on which shall convert one race to another?

These we conceive to be the strongest objections that can be made against the unity of origin, and we have stated them fully.

We are ready to admit that, under the received chronology, it is very difficult to account for such a variety as the negro. But, before reconsidering the subject of the formation of varieties and our explanation, the reader must familiarize his mind with the possibility of a very extended duration of the human race. The Egyptian discoveries render probable a greater human antiquity; many indications over the world point toward it, and now these recent geological discoveries, which we have described above, as carefully interpreted by impartial men of thorough science, may be said to present a very strong proof of it. We cannot say what the duration of man has been on this earth; we do not attempt even a theory or estimate of the number of centuries or chiliads that must be added to human annals. We only rest on the probability of a *much longer time* for the existence of man on this earth than is commonly supposed.

Antiquity of man.

Referring back, now, to the principles already laid down of variation and inheritance, we find that plants and animals, when once they have begun to vary, may for a time vary exceedingly, or "sport," until a permanent variety or type is formed. The same thing is undoubtedly true of man.

Suppose, in some very remote age of the past, long before the received commencement of human annals, an Asiatic tribe, of some intermediate type, between all the present races of men, had emigrated to an entirely new country and climate, say to the east of Africa. All the external influences on the physique of this tribe are changed; the soil (for soil is found to have an important effect on human constitutions*), the water, the temperature, the scenery, the miasmatic influence, the electrical, the moral influences, in their different pursuits and means of livelihood, all are different from what they have been. From these, or from some cause with which we are unacquainted, a slight variety appears in the offspring; it may, possibly,

Formation of a black race.

* See Morel's discussion of *Cretinism* in his *Traité sur les Dégénérescences.*

be some change of internal structure, fitting the possessors to resist better the destructive influences of the new climate and soil; this change may be accompanied, as "a correlating feature," with a slightly-darker shade of colour, or a minute change in the hair, or the outward structure of the body. Those children who, from unknown causes, have acquired this almost imperceptible advantage are, of course, more likely to survive. *Their* children again, on the principle of inheritance, will, in the first place, tend to be like their immediate parents, but they will also tend in a less degree to be like all their parents; so that the "attractions" of resemblance will, in some cases, be compounded of the closer and stronger attraction toward the variety, and that toward all the ancestors, or the type of the species. The resultant will naturally be some new variety of colour or structure. In this way we can understand how, for a given time, there might be started many varieties of man, after once the variation had begun. This would go on for a certain period, perhaps during many centuries, and there would be only two limits to the new varieties; one would be the principle of *inheritance*, which would always make the children like their long line of ancestors, and thus keep the type of the species, and preserve the child from changing into anything but a MAN; and the other, the advantage of the variations to their possessors.

Natural selection.

Principle of inheritance.

In the case supposed we have imagined a slightly-darker shade of colour, the correlating feature to some imperceptible advantage of structure or function. This is not an improbable supposition. There are many correlating features which accompany changes of structure and function; why, we cannot tell. We know not why blue eyes and light colour

Correlating features.

should be connected with a sanguine temperament; why the feathered feet and skin between the toes of young pigeons should have anything to do with their future colour; why a female cat is more likely to have the tortoise-shell fur; why a cock with a large "top-knot" has usually a smaller comb; why a deformity in one part of the human frame has often a corresponding deformity in another part.[23]

We do see certain cases where the internal functions have a direct effect on the complexion, as the condition of the liver. Without, then, explaining it, we merely suppose that slight variations have arisen, which are of benefit to those who possess them. Their offspring, again, in so far as these variations are adapted to their new circumstances, will be more likely to live and transmit descendants; and these variations will increase according as they are of profit, and continue to increase and deviate from the parent stock until they have reached the utmost point in which these peculiar features are beneficial. Those destitute of these advantages will be more likely, on a broad scale, to perish, and in the process of ages only those will remain who have them; and with them, when the time comes that the extreme variations are not profitable, or are of positive loss, those having them will be less likely to live than those with less extreme variations, and so the last profitable variation will continue and become permanent because adapted to its circumstances.

Natural selection.

If the supposed tribe were, like most of the early tribes of men, nomadic, the variations we have imagined would be the more likely to occur; each variety either arising or perpetuating itself, according as it was adapted to the new climates and countries which the tribe visited.

We see no difficulty on this supposition, on the Darwinian theory of an imperceptible accumulation of profitable changes through long periods of time, which few will question in regard to man, of accounting for the origin of the negro from the white man, or from the brown, or from some other race.*

Darwinian theory.

It may be thought that on this view we do not make enough of the direct effect of *climate* in forming a race. We are quite ready to admit the immense influence of climate on the physique of man. The facts in this treatise, especially those presented in the account of the African races, go to show that elevation and coolness of temperature are usually associated either with a race of lighter complexion or with a lighter branch of the same race. Still, there are many exceptions to this in Africa, and especially in Australasia; and though it is ungracious to pick a flaw in the teachings of the great master of the science of ethnology, PRICHARD, we conceive that the weakness of his argument for unity was in laying too exclusive stress on the effects of climate. Such is the power of race, or of the principle of inheritance, that we are not surprised at finding the probable descendants of the ancient Vandals in North Africa still blonde with blue eyes, and the North American negro as black as his Congo ancestor 200 years ago.

Climate not sole cause of variation.

* "So long as physiologists continued to believe that man had not existed on the earth above six thousand years, they might, with good reason, withhold their assent from the doctrine of a unity of origin of so many distinct races; but the difficulty becomes less and less, exactly in proportion as we enlarge our ideas of the lapse of time, during which different communities may have spread slowly and become isolated, each exposed for ages to a peculiar set of conditions, whether of temperature, or food, or danger, or ways of living." (Lyell, Ant. of Man, p. 386.)

So, again, we find the Mexicans in their comparatively cool districts, darker than the native races of the hottest countries of South America, and the Guiacas at the sources of the Orinoco whiter than the Indians in precisely the same latitude and circumstances. (Waiz, *Anthropologie.*) Neither does height, as has been intimated, always necessarily cause a lighter complexion, as witness some tribes on the mountains around the Gulf of Guinea and the inhabitants of the mountains of New Guinea and the Philippines, as well as of many other islands in Oceanica, who are as black as the blackest negroes that dwell on the plains. The Malayan race has the same complexion, stature, and features on the Equator and twenty degrees away from it; in mountainous islands as in level islands. The colour of the Malays under the Equator is nearly the same with that of the Esquimaux of the Arctic Circle. "At the same distance from the Equator," says Crawfurd, "we find fair Europeans, yellow Chinese, red Americans, and black Australians."

Exceptions to climatic influence.

We do not call in climate alone, but all external influences and internal mental powers reacting on the bodily, as an explanation of variation; and, taking all the analogies of the animal world, we say that we cannot fairly explain the laws by which Nature forms varieties: nor are we forced to by our argument.

Variation unexplainable.

On the theory we have stated, there would be a period in human history, just as there is in the history of plants, when numerous varieties of man would appear. After a long course of time, each variety becomes adapted to its country, and climate, and pursuits; and all the spaces for human varieties are filled up. Then, the principle of inheritance comes in to make the variety permanent, inasmuch as the attraction of resemblance would be toward a long line of ancestors who had already varied from the original stock; and, as time passed on, this attraction would become the stronger, and it would be the more difficult to break away from the line; thus, at length, the varieties, after long courses of time, would become *permanent types*. In this view, the fact of the negro presenting his pure type 4,000 years ago, unchanged, is what we should expect. Neither in these few centuries or chiliads should we expect to see his type changing into that of the white. We should be prepared to see *permanent human varieties*, unchanged in the historic period, each with its own features, its habits, its peculiar diseases, and its separate exposure to disease, even each with its own parasites and its own odours.*

Permanent varieties.

Then a degree of correspondence of the man with the *fauna* and *flora* of given latitudes[24]† would be the

* In regard to this, M. Huc says that though the Chinese did not penetrate their disguise, the dogs always smelt them and barked at them. He states that he learned to distinguish the different odors of Negroes, Tartars, Thibetans, Hindoos, Arab, and Chinese. The North American Indians are said by Galton to have an entirely peculiar odor, as probably do many tribes of negroes. Humboldt states similar facts of Mexicans and negroes. Reugger observes (according to Waiz) that acclimatized Europeans in Paraguay acquire an unpleasant odor to their skin, and in consequence, are less troubled with mosquitoes and insects. Of parasites, Dr. Bachman, according to Smyth, states that there are twenty-one species, infesting different parts of the human system, and that they trouble equally the white and black races. There is a species of lice, infesting the negro, darker than that found on the white, while the mulatto has one of an intermediate shade—the colouring matter probably being supplied from beneath the human skin. It passes, however, from the black nurse to the white child indifferently. (Smyth, p. 162.) The tape-worms of human beings are said by Owen to be different in the different nations of Europe. The tame swine has a different species of parasite from that found on the wild.

† Prof. Agassiz's view, as set forth in Gliddon and Nott's "Types."

natural effect of a variety grown up after ages of trial in adaptation to its circumstances, and precisely what we should expect.

We should also, on this theory, count upon an *imperceptible gradation* of the varieties of men, every shade of colour and physical type running into one another; we should expect that all varieties would *breed fruitfully* with one another: we should be prepared for given groups of a remote common origin, *embracing very diverse physical types;* we should sometimes, though rarely, expect *to see changes of type*, and we should expect to find an utter *community of constitution and nature* among men.

Restatement of argument.

All these things are discovered as facts, and of the last Dr. Smyth has thus well summed up:—

Men are essentially the same, he says, in their location, food, employments, and character; in their embryonic condition and transformations; in the number, variety, and composition of their tissues; in the number, character, and purpose of those large and distinctly-limited cavities destined for the lodgment of certain organs, such as the brains, lungs, &c.; in the well-defined and compact form of the organs lodged in these cavities; in the process by which the food is elaborated and digested; in the peculiar organs which give the sensation of sight, hearing, smell, taste, and touch; in the structure and position of the eye, ear, and nose; in that perception, memory, and reasoning which constitute intelligence;* in the entire skeleton, which is an

Unity of man.

We need not say that the whole course of ethnological investigation has been against his classification of "realms of men," as indicating separate origin or local creation. This Treatise itself has been a continual statement on the other side. Still we would not doubt that there is a certain correspondence, in certain cases, between the human beings and the animal and vegetable kingdoms.

The alleged incapacity for rapid progress in learning of negro children, after they have reached fourteen or fifteen years, is not peculiar to them, but is manifested by Sandwich Island, Nubian, and Egyptian children. (Waiz.)

essential test of species; in the functions of digestion, circulation, secretion, and respiration; in their teeth, their hearts, their skin, their glands; in all the peculiarities of the two sexes; in ovulation; in the gradation of more and more complicated adaptation by which they are distinguished; in the same general appearance; and in all those transformations which precede or which succeed birth.

Now, if these are facts, on what hypothesis can they be explained so naturally and philosophically as on that of a community of descent of all the tribes of mankind from one pair? It is unphilosophical to suppose more causes than are sufficient to explain the facts. One pair, one source, will account for all these results; why need we suppose several pairs?

Descent from one pair.

Still farther, the supposition of a separate creation of each human variety will not meet all the conditions of the case. Under that theory, we could not account for all the facts stated above.

The conclusion to which we have thus come on philosophical grounds—of the greatly overbalancing probabilities in favour of the descent of mankind from one pair—will explain some of the apparent defects in the Science of Ethnology, and the causes which have led to this Treatise. Man being of but one species and one origin, it is to be expected that the varieties which spring from the original stock would be distinguished from one another with great difficulty, and that a definite race-mark would be a thing not easily found. Accordingly, we may understand why almost every new writer on Human Races has a classification of his own. Scarcely any marks of a human variety are permanent. They continually shade into one another, or are changed or pass away. Whether the distinctive feature be the shape of the skull, or the

Causes of defects of classification.

nature of the hair, or the colour, or the facial outline, or any other physical peculiarity, we find that it does not belong exclusively to any one nation or race, or to all its individuals. This is what we should expect on the hypothesis of Unity of Origin (for which we have been arguing); and one natural effect is, that little agreement can be reached among investigators in their classification of races. One divides the human family into three races, another into five, another into eleven, and another into sixty-three.

Superiority of classification by Language.

The same objection may equally be urged against the classification followed in this Treatise—that by Language. Its superiority to the division by physical traits lies in the facts that the distinctions on which it rests are more permanent and less affected by outward circumstances than the physiological marks of race, and that the groups which it unites by similar characteristics, indicative of community of descent, and the groups which it separates from others by these same features, include every variety of physical peculiarities usually thought distinctive of human races. When once an objector to this classification has admitted the Aryan or Indo-European class of peoples, as a group of races connected by the bonds of a common descent, he has admitted a new principle of arrangement of human varieties, and has tacitly allowed that a very extreme divergence of physical features is consistent with a community of origin.

We would not by this deny the existence of distinct physical types among men, transmitted and long preserved. We only urge that these are not so permanent or distinctive, or so characteristic of the common origin of given groups, as types of language. We trust that this has been fairly proved by the facts brought forward in this work.

Naturally, as was before said, against this principle of arrangement, there lie similar objections to those urged against the physiological division. Related languages absorb one another, or fuse together; in some cases a language entirely disappears in contact with another of very different character; similar peculiarities of structure are found in tongues, separated by immense spaces. With regard to a portion of the Turanian races, it is still a matter of dispute whether their linguistic resemblances are a mark of community of descent, or only of a like stage of progress and development.

Objections to classification by Language.

These also are what we should expect from a universal community of descent of mankind. Even the clearest test of a human variety would be exposed to doubt. Still, these apparent objections can be fairly answered. We have only claimed, and attempted by facts to support, that *Languages are the best evidence of Race**—not a perfect and exclusive test. We have

* We quote from a note in Lewis's "Romance Languages":—

The pertinacious adherence of mankind to their mother-tongue (says Mr. Anderson, in his work on the Irish language), might be verified by a number of remarkable proofs. "It is a curious fact," says a writer in the *Statistical Account of Scotland*, vol. xx. p. 490, "that the hills of King's Seal and Craigy Barns, which form the lower boundary of Dowally (parish in Perthshire), have been *for centuries* the separatory barrier of the English and Gaelic. In the first house below them, the English is and has been spoken, and the Gaelic in the first house, not above a mile distant above them." In different parts of Ireland something similar to this will be found. It is said, that on crossing the river Barrow, a very striking difference is observable; on the eastern bank, English is spoken and Irish scarcely known; a little way interior it is quite the reverse (p. 48).

Lyell also remarks:—

"We may compare the persistency of languages, or the tendency of each generation to adopt without change the vocabulary of its predecessor, to the force of inheritance in the organic world, which causes the offspring to resemble its parents. The inventive power which coins attempted to show that when related languages fuse, the different elements are still manifest to the eye of the scholar. We have resorted to history, to popular dialects, and to the nomenclature of local objects, for the purpose of filling out the defective evidence in the spoken or written languages. No proof has been afforded us of the absolute disappearance of a tongue of any one of the three great families, in contact with another, while a sufficient number of the race survived to form a community. Apparent exceptions to this may indeed occur, where small numbers of individuals are gradually transported to a foreign country, their language becoming absorbed into that of the superior race—as with the Africans in the West Indies and the United States.

Language best mark of race, not the only one.

Apparent exceptions.

Such instances are happily rare. But even with them, History on the one side, and a close linguistic study on the other, could easily demonstrate the mixture of tongues, and the foreign origin of the inferior race and speech.*

new words or modifies old ones, and adapts them to new wants and conditions as often as these arise, answers to the variety-making power in the animate creation." (Ant. of Man, p. 467).

* Creole French, says a writer in the March "Atlantic," 1863, was created by the negroes (of San Domingo), who put into it very few words of their native dialects, but something of the native construction and certain euphonic peculiarities. It is interesting to trace their love of alliteration and a concord of sounds in this mongrel French, which became a new colonial language. The bright and sparkling French appears as if submitted to great heat, and just on the point of running together. There is a great family of African dialects, in which a principal sound, or the chief sound of a leading word, appears in all the words of a sentence, from no grammatical reason at all, but to satisfy a sweetish ear. It is like the charming gabble of children, who love to follow the first key that the tongue strikes. . . . . These characteristics appear in the formation of the Creole French, in connection with another childlike habit of the negro, who loves to put

The migrations of whole tribes or nations seldom cause an entire or immediate change of language. With respect to the similar features of language in nations at a vast distance—of which so much is made by the learned Prof. Pott, in his arguments against

Pott's objections.

this theory—though they may in some cases be merely marks of a similar stage of deve-

himself in the objective case, and to say *me* instead of *I*, as if he knew that he had to be a chattel.

The article *un*, *une*, could not have been pronounced by a negro; it became in his mouth *nion*. The personal pronouns *je*, *tu*, *il*, were converted into *mo*, *to*, *ly*, and the possessive *mon*, *ton*, *son*, into *à moue*, *à toue*, *à ly*, and were placed after the noun, which negro dialects generally start their sentences with. Possessive pronouns had the unmeaning syllable *quien* before them, as *Nous gagné quien à nous*, for *Nous avons les nôtres;* and demonstrative pronouns were changed in this way: *Mo voir z'animaux là yo*, for *J'ai vu ces animaux*, and *Ci la yo qui té vivre*, for *Ceux qui ont vécu.* A few more examples will suffice to make other changes clear. A negro was asked to lend his horse; he replied, *Mouchée* (Monsieur) *mo pas gagné choual, mais mo connais qui gagné ly, si ly pas gagné ly, ly faut mo gagné ly, pour vous gagné:* "Massa me not got horse, but me know who got um; if him not got um, him get me um for you." *Quelquechose* becomes *quichou; zozo = oiseau; gourneé = combattre; gueté = voir; zombi = revenant; bougé = demeurer; helé = appeler;* et cet. Here is a verse of Creole song, written in imitation of the negro dialect:—

Dipi mo perdi Lissette
Mo pas souchié Calinda,
Mo quitté bram-bram sonette
Mo pas batte bamboula
Quand mo contré l'aut negresse,
Mo pas gagné z'yeu pour ly,
Mo pas souchié travail pièce,
Tou qui chose a moué mouri.

The French of which is as follows:—

Mes pas, loin de ma Lissette,
S'éloignent du Calinda;
Et ma ceinture à sonnette
Languit sur mon bamboula.

lopment, it may in many others be more philosophical to regard them as the effects of very distant migrations of certain tribes, and thus evidences of community of origin. And even if sustained, these objections only hold against the Turanian class, not against this general classification by language.

CONCLUSION.

It will be seen from the views presented in this Treatise, that we do not regard the Races of men now

Mon œil de toute autre belle
N'aperçoit plus le souris ;
Le travail en vain m'appelle,
Mes sens sont anéantis.

We quote again from a note in Lewis's " Romance Languages " :—

Ainsi nous voyons encore aujourd'hui des gens du peuple transportés dans un pays étranger, se faire avec ceux dont ils ont besoin, un patois de convention qui n'est le leur, ni celui de leurs hôtes, mais que tous deux comprennent, et qui empêche tous deux d'arriver, à la langue de l'un ou de l'autre. Ainsi dans les bagnes de l'Afrique et de Constantinople des esclaves Chrétiens de toutes les parties de l'Europe mêlés avec les Maures, n'ont point enseigné à ceux-ci leur langage, et n'ont point appris, celui des Maures ; mais ils se recontrent avec eux dans un jargon barbare qu'on nomme *langue franque ;* il est composé des mots romans les plus nécéssaires à la vie commune dépouillés des terminaisons qui marquent les temps et les cas, et unis ensemble sans syntaxe. Ainsi dans des colonies d'Amérique, les planteurs s'entendaient avec les nègres dans la langue Créole, qui est de même le Français mis à la portée d'un peuple barbare, en le depouillant de tout ce qui donne de la précision, de la force, ou de la souplesse. (*Littérature du Midi*, vol. i. p. 19, and compare p. 33). " The Moravians have translated the Bible and a book of hymns into the Talkee-talkee or negro language, of which they have also composed a grammar. It is curious that this patois of the blacks, though it includes many African words, should have for its basis the English language, *pared of inflections*, and softened by a multitude of vowel terminations. (Bolingbroke, *Voyage to Demarary*, cited in the *Quarterly Review*, vol. xliii. p. 553, where specimens are given of a similar negro corruption of the Dutch language, in which the inflexions are also obscured." p. 22.)

Races not permanent.

existing as permanent. Their lines converge into one another in the past, and they may meet again in the future or they may cease altogether. They are long successions of human beings, bound to one another by the tie of blood, whose similar qualities and powers enable us to consider each race as an individual. Like individuals, each group has its peculiar office and duty in the world's development, and manifests on a broad scale the divine ideas which it is the province of human history to unfold. Like them, too, a Race may die young, or it may live a weakly life, or it may grow to a vigorous maturity, or it may wear out from luxury and vicious indulgence. The same grand retributive laws, whether physical or moral, that govern individuals, govern races.

The destiny of man.

In a work upon Man, it is not inappropriate to speak, in conclusion, of his moral destiny, especially as connected with the question of Race.

The great design of the Creator, in the world, we reverently believe to be, the development of each human being into "the perfect man in Christ Jesus," and the building up of an organic "*Kingdom of God.*" And as God hath been once especially manifested in Humanity that He might draw all things to Himself, and as all human history is henceforth only the course of the slow working of this Divine Life among men, may we not hope that, after the long lapse of ages, the spirit of Christ shall so fill the individual men that at length a Race shall be born, who shall embody and transmit divine ideas and inspirations, and thus an organic "Kingdom of God" be formed among nations, and so the goal of Humanity be reached?

Then shall the mysterious property of Inheritance—the centre of so many theological problems—which had transmitted the effects of the first violation of conscience and the first indulgence of a selfish will, through innumerable generations with constantly-increasing power, at last be turned to the side of goodness and purity, and Truth and Holiness be equally inherited and embodied among men.

THE END.

NOTES.

CHAPTER II.

([1]) *Arya* in later Sanskrit, means "a lord," or "of good family." The Zend-avesta, the Vedic hymns, the kuneiform inscriptions, and the traditions reported by Herodotus, show that this name was applied by the Hindoos, the Persians, and Medes to their own race. Some connect it with the root AR (to plough); Aryans then meaning the agricultural tribes. See M. Müller's Sc. of Lang. ([2]) ([3]) ([4]) ([5]) Max Müller. Bunsen, p. 237. *Turanians.* The Hindoos called the heretical countries outside of Aryâ (the Honourable Land) "*Târyâ,*" or "outside of Aryâ," or "the dishonourable." The Persians also called the misbelieving lands to the north and east, inhabited by those who did not worship the sun, "*Tûran,*" or "beyond Irân." Touran indicates, perhaps, geographically Turkistan and the Turks, as the type of the class of nations included under the term Turanians, which, as a name, is certainly equally appropriate with the name "Indo-European," given to the Aryan races. See Gliddon and Nott's Indig. Races. Quotation from Bergmann. Müller makes the essential meaning of Turanians (*Tura*) refer to the "swiftness of the horse," thus describing the nomadic races in distinction from the agricultural. (Sc. of Lang., p. 238.) ([6]) Herodotus alludes to the Scythian element everywhere in Western Asia. Berosus, a priest of Bel in Babylon, who wrote down the Babylonian traditions in Greek, about 280 B.C., and Justin, plainly speak of this empire. ([7]) ([8]) Rawlinson's Herodotus, vol. i. p. 434, p. 648. ([9]) In modern times, in Persian, Arabic, and Turkish. See Oppert's Exped. Scien. ([10]) Rawlinson's Herodotus, vol. i. p. 426. ([11]) Renan, Knobel, and Max Müller. Lang. at the Seat of War, p. 23. ([12]) Bunsen's Philos. of Hist., vol. i. p. 185. ([13]) Pliny states that the inhabitants of the banks of the Nile were not Ethiopians but Arabs. According to Herodotus, the current opinion did not place Egypt as a geographical part of Africa. ([14]) Rawl. Herod., i. p. 650. Knobel's

Völkertafel. ([15]) Pliny (3 Proem) speaks of the Nile as the boundary of Asia. Strabo, i. pp. 48–51. ([16]) The Somauli language, the language of the Danakil, Adaiel, and Ashantis show Hamitic or Cushite traces. (Renan. Les Langues Semitiques.)

CHAPTER III.

([1]) Authorities consulted,—Brugsch. Boeckh. Bunsen. Lepsius, Königsbuch der alten Egypter. 1858. Nolan. Poole. Scyffarth. Uhlemann. ([2]) Bunsen's Egypt, v. 336. ([3]) Herod., i. 443. ([4]) Herod., i. 319. Oppert. Dr. Brandis. Herzog's Real Encyclopædie (Ninive). Knobel's Völkertafel. Renan (Les. Lang. Sem.). C. Niebuhr, Gesch. Assurs. Gutschmidt. Chowlson's Ueberreste d. Alt. Bab. Lit. Oppert's Exped. Sc. ([5]) The arrow-headed writing is divided into three classes :—(a) *The old Persian* (or Aryan), employed in monumental inscriptions by the Persian kings, from Cyrus to Artaxerxes III., as an alphabet of an Aryan language. It closes with the Achæmenides. This is the simplest class; the figures representing letters, and there being only sixty signs. (b) *The Turanian* (or Scythic), used to express Turanian dialects. (c) *The Semitic.* This last is the most difficult and confused, each figure representing a syllable. The *Assyrian* arrow-headed inscriptions are nearly the same with the last, and even more difficult. Most common words are interpreted in them, but proper names are exceedingly doubtful. They contain more than 500 signs; the figures represent syllables. The arrow-head reaches as far west as Cyprus and Beirut, and east to Bactria. The Susian, Armenian, and Chaldee inscriptions are classed by Oppert under the Turanian, or second class, but not so intimately connected with it as Rawlinson intimates.

CHAPTER IV.

([1]) Max Müller, Lang. at Seat of War. ([2]) Gesenius and H. Hadley. ([3]) Rawlinson. ([4]) Max Müller.

CHAPTER V.

([1]) Bunsen. M. Müller. Lassen. ([2]) Mommsen. ([3]) Dr. Haug's Vêndidâd. Bunsen. ([4]) ([5]) Rawlinson's Herod.

CHAPTER VI.

([1]) ([2]) Duncker, Gesch. d. Alth. Movers. ([3]) Ezekiel, 27, 10, 20. Isaiah, 60, 5, 9. ([4]) ([5]) Rawlinson. Duncker. Kruger. ([6]) ([7]) Rawlinson. ([8]) Rawlinson's Herod. Dict. of Gr. and Rom. Geog. Niebuhr. ([9]) Curtius' Grec. Gesch. Merivale. Thirlwall. Niebuhr. Grote. Rawlinson. Duncker. Mommsen. Prichard.

CHAPTER VII.

(1) Gobineau. Weinhold. Schafarik. Leonzon le Duc. Rühs. Rezius, et alii. (2) M. de Troyon. Gobineau. Rawlinson. See Owen's Brit. Foss. Mamm., and Wilson's Pre-Historic Annals. (3) In Lorraine (v. Gobineau). They are also found in Denmark, according to Worsaae. (4) Dict. Gr. and Rom. Geog. Niebuhr, et alii. (5) Arnold. (6) Prichard. Latham. Bunsen. Aufrecht. M. Müller. (7) Worsaae. Wilson, et alii.

CHAPTER VIII.

THE KELTS.

(1) *Kelts* rather than *Celts* is in harmony with Greek analogy, and is coming now into general use, even by English writers. (2) Authorities consulted :—Prichard's East. Orig. of Keltic Nat. Latham's Ethnol. Thierry's Hist. des Gaul. Dr. C. Meyer (Bunsen). M. Müller. Niebuhr. Mommsen's Rom. Gesch. Dict. of Greek and Rom. Geog. Encyc. Brit. Gobineau. Parke Godwin. Mone. (3) Dr. C. Meyer and others. (4) M. Müller. Dr. Meyer. (5) Mommsen. Niebuhr. Arnold. Bunsen. Steubb. (6) Mommsen.

CHAPTER IX.

(1) Keferstein. Dr. Wirth. Prichard. Zeuss. Ersch und Gruber. Tacitus (Latham's). (2) Wirth. Gesch. d. D. Staaten. Dict. of Gr. and Rom. Geog. (3) (4) (5) De Gobineau. Staats Lexikon (D. Stämme). Dr. Wittmann. Link. Zoepfl. Scherr. Parke Godwin.

CHAPTER X.

(1) Schafarik. Zeuss. Keferstein. De Gobineau. Prichard. Gurowski. Talvi, et alii. (1 a) Many writers make the *Wendes* a third division, but Jornandes' classification seems the more probable. He says :—"Winidorum natio populosa consedit. Quorum nomina licet nunc per varias familias et loca mutentur, principaliter tamen *Sclaveni* et *Antes* nominantur (c. 5). (2) Max Müller. (3) Schafarik. (4) M. Müller.

CHAPTER XI.

(1) Dict. of Gr. and Rom. Geog. Zeuss. Koeppen. Vivien de St. Martin. (2) Latham. (3) Prichard claims them as Turkic, but the evidence produced by Viv. de St. Martin in his monogram on the Khazars seems to establish their Finnic origin.

CHAPTER XII.

SEMITES.

(1) Koeppen. Gibbon. Dr. W. H. Thompson on Pre-Islamitic Arabs.

THE TURANIANS.

(2) Stritter, Memor. pop. e script. Byzant. Ritter. Prichard. De Guignes. Viv. de St. Martin. M. Müller. Koeppen.

THE MONGOLS.

(1) Prichard. Koeppen. Gibbon. M. Müller. D'Ohsson fils. De Guignes. Plath. Ritter. Von Hammer—Purgstall. (2) M. Müller.

CHAPTER XIII.

(1) Lassen. Max Müller. Prichard. Journ. Asiat. Soc., 1852. (Capt. S. C. Macpherson. L. Gen. Briggs.) Amer. Orient. Soc. Journ., 1854. J. R. Logan. E. Behm. (Petermann's Geo. Mitt. (1857).) (1 2) J. R. Logan. (2) Lassen. (3) M. Müller. (4) Mr. Hodgson. Journ. As. Soc. of Bengal, 1849. (5) Prichard. (6) Amer. Or. Soc. Journ. Brit. Assoc., 1850. Abor. Tribes of India. J. Briggs. R. Caldwell. E. Webb. (7) M. Müller in Bunsen's Phil. of Univers. Hist. Prichard.

CHAPTER XIV.

CHINESE.

(1 Prichard. M. Müller. (Amer. Or. Soc. Journ.) W. Whitney. E. Biot (Journ. Asiat.). Williams. Huc. Chinese Repertory. Kaeuffer, Gesch. Ost Asien. Maury. (La Terre, et cet.) Humboldt-Kawisprach. Klaproth. (2) J. R. Logan. (3) (4) Rev. S. R. Brown. (5) Chinese Repertory, 1845. (6) Kaeuffer. (7) Prichard.

JAPAN.

(8) Ersch. u. Gruber. Kaeuffer, et alii. (9) (10) Amer. Expedit. Ethnog. of Lew Chew Islands. (11) Prichard. Encyc. Brit. Klaproth. Pott. D. M. Z.

CHAPTER XV.

TIBETANS.

(1) Cunningham's Ladak. Prichard. Müller. Huc. (2) Bunsen's Phil. of Hist. (3) Cunningham. (4) Prichard.

TUNGUSIANS.

(5) (6) M. Müller. (7) William's China. (8) Castrén and Castrén's Tung. Spr. (1856).

MONGOLS.

(9) Huc's Tartary. Atkinson's Siberia. Prichard. Latham. Elphinstone's Cabul. Rémusat's Lang. Tart. Castrén, Buriat. Spr. (1856). (10) Williams' China. (11) Rémusat. (12) Elphinstone.

SAMOIEDES.

(1) Castrén. Latham. Prichard.

CHAPTER XVI.

TURKS.

(1) M. Müller. Latham. Prichard. Atkinson. Petermann's Geog., &c., Dec., 1858. (2) Prichard. (3) (4) Lang. at Seat of War. (5) (6) Latham. (7) Müller. (8) Prichard.

CHAPTER XVII.

(1) Prichard. Latham. Müller. Elphinstone. Vigne. Capt. Prostans in Eth. Soc. Journ. Amer. Or. Soc. Journ., vol. i. Kund. d. Morg. Ges. (2) (8) Prichard. (3) (6) Latham. (4) M. Müller. Capt. Raverty. (7) Amer. Or. Journ. For. Miss. Journ. Müller. Gobineau. Pott. Rödiger. Zeit. f. Morg. Ges. v. 12, 1857. (8) Dr. Blau. (9) Layard. Badger. Dr. Grant. W. F. Ainsworth. Trans. of Ethnol. Soc., 1861. (10) Perkins. Badger. Grant. Rich. Bib. Repos., 1841-42. (Dr. Robinson and Rev. Mr. Homes.).

CHAPTER XVIII.

(1) Prichard. Latham. Dwight and Smith. Haxthausen. Müller. Klaproth. De St. Martin. Ad. Berger (Die Berg-Völker des Caucasus. v. 1860. Peterm. Mitth.).

CHAPTER XIX.

POLYNESIA.

William von Humboldt, Die Kawi Sprache. Crawfurd's History of Ind. Archip. Essays of Crawfurd. G. W. Earl (Ind. Archip.). Ethnol. Library (1853). Journ. of Ethnol. Soc. Swainson's N. Zealand. Lang. Rev. R. Taylor. Wilkes' Ex. Expedit., and Hale's Ethnog. Strzelecki. Müller. Prichard. Ellis' Polyn. Research. Philolog. Rev. vol. i. Tasmanian Rev. Rev. Wm. Ridley (Journ. Ethnol. Soc.). Dr. T. R. Thomson. Fiji and Fijians, by Williams and Calvert. Gust d'Eichthal. North Brit. Rev., May, 1861 (Austr. Ethnol.). Prof. Owen on the Osteology and Dentition of the Andaman Islands. (Athenæum, Sept. 21, 1861.) Die Melanesischen Sprachen, et cet. H. C. von der Gabelentz, Leipzig, 1860.

CHAPTER XX.

THE BERBERS AND HAUSSA.

(1) Dr. Barth. Renan, Les Lang. Sem. Exploration Scient. de l'Algerie. Movers, Die Phœnizer. Knobel, Vöelkertafel. F. W. Newman. Prichard. E. Norris. Koelle. (3) Exped. Scient. de l'Algerie.

ABYSSINIANS AND SOMAULI.

(1) Renan. Parkyn's Life, &c. Voy. en Abys., M. Lefebvre. Voy. dans le Roy. de Choa, d'Hericourt. Rev. S. Gobat's Abys. Docum. sur l'Afr. Or. par ordre du Govt., Guillain. Burton's E. Africa. Bulletin de Geog. (M. d'Abbadie). De Lauture. M. Peney. Viv. de St. Martin. Waiz. Krapf.

CHAPTER XXI.

KOPTS, FELLAHS, AND EASTERN NUBIANS.

(1) Lepsius' Discoveries. L'Univers. Egypte Mod. Bayle St. John. Wm. H. Yates. Lane. (2) M. Gisquet. Gliddon's Indig. Races. (3) Prichard.

THE GALLAS.

(1) D'Hericourt, Voyage, &c. (2) Rev. S. Gobat. Renan. Johnston. Von. Klöden. Ewald. Krapf. Burton.

THE NUBIANS.

(1) Wilkinson. Lepsius. L'Univers, Nubie. Combe. Yates. (2) Lepsius.

CHAPTER XXII.

FELLATAH AND MANDINGOES.

(1) D'Eichthal. Raffenel. Dr. Barth. Esquisses Senegalaises, Boilat. Dr. Wilson. F. Carriére. Prichard. Wm. B. Hodgson.

(2) (4) (6) D'Eichthal. (3) Idem and Hodgson. (5) (7) Wilson.

CHAPTER XXIII.

SOUTH GUINEA.

(1) Wilson. Bowen. W. F. Daniell. Forbes. Poole. Zeit. d. mor. Ges., vol. 8. Livingstone.

CHAPTER XXIV.

THE DAMARAS AND OVAMPOS.

(1) Anderson. Rev. F. N. Kolbe (Ethnol. Soc. 1854). Latham. Petermann's Mitth. (2) Kolbe. (3) Latham. Ladislaus Magyar.

(4) THE BECHUANAS.

Or. Soc. Journ. Anderson. Petermann. Livingstone.

KAFFIRS.

([1]) Rev. F. Fleming. Petermann's Mitth. Ethnol. Soc. Journ. Or. Soc. Journ. ([2]) ([3]) ([4]) Petermann's Mitth. ([5]) Petermann's Mitth. and L. Grout. Krapf. W. W. Greenough (Or. Soc. Journ. vol. 1).

CHAPTER XXV.

HOTTENTOTS.

([1]) Petermann's Mitth. E. Norris. Waiz. ([2]) Livingstone. Anderson. Moffatt. ([3]) ([4]) ([5]) Petermann's Mitth. ([6]) Bulletin de Geog., 1859.

CHAPTER XXVI.

THE FINNIC AND TURKIC RACES.

([1]) M. Müller. Latham. Prof. Munck. Müller's Ugrischer Volkstamm. Brace's Hungary and Norse-Folk. Léonzon le Duc. Norst. Maenedskrift, 1st Hefte. H. D. Seymour. Ubicini. ([2]) ([3]) Bouie's. Turquie d'Europe.

THE BASQUES.

([1]) Balbi. Berghaus. Dict. de la Conversation. Stephens. Michel. Wm. Von Humboldt. Graslin. Amer. Encyc. Erro. Labastide Encyc. des Gens du Monde. Arndt.

CHAPTER XXVII.

THE SLAVONIANS.

([1]) Schafarik. Latham. Gurowski. Kubalski. Mickiewicz. Geog. Mitt., 1855. Müller. ([2]) ([4]) ([5]) Gurowski. ([3]) M. Müller.

CHAPTER XXVIII.

THE ALBANIANS AND GREEKS.

Wm. M. Leake. Curzon. Finlay. About. Arndt's Europ. Spr. Buchon. M. Müller. E. Curtius. Hettner. Henry Skeene (Ethnol. Journ., 1850). F. Thiersch. Hahn's Alban. Studien.

CHAPTER XXIX.

WALLACHS.

Paget. Von Czoernig.

ITALIANS.

L. Mariotti. Edwards and Dr. Wiseman (quoted by Gliddon). Gajani.

SPANIARDS.

L. Lemcke. Ticknor. L. Clarus. De Jonnès. Murray's Handbook. Borrow.

FRENCH.

Michelet. De Courzon. J. Janin. Maury.

CHAPTER XXX.

KELTS.

(1) Müller. (2) Vaughan and Prichard.

ENGLISH.

Kemble's Saxons. Worsaae's Danes in England. Ferguson's Northmen in Cumberland, &c. Donaldson's English Ethnology. Cambridge Essays, 1850. Proceed. of Philog. Soc. (Eng.). Latham's Ethnol. of British Islands.

CHAPTER XXXI.

GYPSIES.

Pott's Zigeuner. Spengler. Borrow. Zeit. f. D. Morg. G., 3rd, 8th and 11th vols. Casca. Paspati.

CHAPTER XXXII.

ANTIQUITY OF MAN.

(1) Boucher de Perthes, Les Antiquités Celtiques. Evans' Report (Athenæum, June 11, 1859). Sir C. Lyell (Athenæum, Sept. 24, 1859). J. J. A. Worsaae. Athen., No. 1679. Wilson's Archæology, &c. Poole's Genesis of Earth and Man. Les Comptes Rendus, 1859, t. 49, pp. 463, 465, 581, 634, &c., and t. 23, 24, 25, and 46. Pictet, L'Homme Fossile, Bib. Univ. de Genève. Lord Wrottesley, British Assoc., in Athenæum, June 30, 1860. Blackwood, Oct., 1860. Lartet, Ann. des Sc. J. D. Dana. Prof. Owen. Delanoue. Lyell's Antiq. of Man. J. Lubbock, Nat. Hist. Rev. M. Troyon, Des Habitations Lacustres. Smithson. Reports, 1861. Rütimeyer. Wilson's Pre-Historic Man.

CHAPTER XXXIII.

UNITY OR DIVERSITY OF ORIGIN.

(1) (2) (3) Silliman's Journal, 1859, p. 441, cited by Dr. A. Gray. (4) (5) (7) (9) (10) (11) (15) Prichard. Roulin, d. Sc. Nat., t. 16, 1829. (6) Smyth. (8) (12) (13) (16) (20) De Salles. (14) (18) Carpenter, (17a) Waiz. (17) Dr. Draper. Tiedemann. Prichard. Hollard, Smyth. De Salles. Waiz, et alii. (19) (20) Morel. Hist. de Dégénérescences. (21) See Dana on Species, in Sill. Journ., Nov., 1857. Darwin's Origin of Species. (22) Ethnol. Journ., vol. 3. (23) See Darwin, St. Hilaire, and Quatrefages. (24) Agassiz.

LIST OF AUTHORITIES.

Abbadie d'.—Bulletin de la Soc. de Géographie.

About, E.—La Grèce Contemporaine. Paris, 1855.

Agassiz, L.—Essay on Classification. London, 1859.

Ainsworth, F. W.—Yezidis. Trans. of Ethnol. Soc. London, 1861, vol. i.

American Cyclopædia.

American Oriental Society Journal.

Anderson, C. J.—Lake Ngami. London, 1856.

Annuaire de la Soc. Impériale des Antiquaires, &c.

Archives für Wissenschaftliche Kunde von Russland. Berlin, 1841.

Arndt, C. G. von.—Frankfurt, 1818. Ueber den Ursprung und die verschiedenartige Verwandtschaft de Europ. Sprachen.

Arndt, C. W.—Leipzig, 1843. Versuch in vergleichender Völkergeschichte.

Atkinson, T. W.—London, 1858. Oriental and Western Siberia.

Balbi, A.—Atlas Ethnographique du Globe. Paris, 1826.

Bartlett, J. R.—Progress of Ethnology. New York, 1848.

Barth, Dr. H.—Reisen und Endeckungen in Nord und Central Afrika. Gotha, 1857.

Baudrimont, A.—Histoire des Basques, &c.

Berger, A.—Die Berg Völker des Kaukasus. 1860.

Berghaus, Dr. H.—Die Völker des Erdballs. Leipzig, 1847.

Berghaus, Dr. H.—8te Abtheilung Atlas.

Berteiul, A.—L'Algerie Française. Paris, 1856.

Biblical Repository—1841-42 (Dr. Robinson and Rev. Mr. Homes).

Biot, E.—Journal Asiatic Society.

Boeckh, A.—Manetho und die Hundstern Periode. Berlin, 1845.

Bode, Baron de (Bokhara). London, 1845.

Bodenstedt, F.—Die Völker des Kaukasus. Frankfurt, 1849.

Burton, R. F.—The Lake Regions of Central Africa. New York, 1860.

Burton, R. F.—First Footsteps in East Africa. London, 1856.

Bunsen, C. C. J.—Outlines of the Philos. of Univ. Hist. London, 1854.
Bunsen, C. C. J.—Egypt's Place in Univ. Hist. London, 1848-58.
Boilat, Abbé—Esquisses Sénégalaises. 1853.
Bulletin de la Société de Géographie. Paris.
Boudin, M. J. C.—Traité de Géographie et des Statisques Médicales. Paris, 1757.
Borrow, George—The Zincali. New York, 1842.
Borrow, George—Bible in Spain. Philadelphia, 1843.
Bowen, T. J.—Central Africa. New York, 1857.
Bowring, Sir J.—A Visit to the Philippine Islands. London, 1859.
Bouchon, J. A.—La Grèce Continentale. Paris, 1843.
Brace, C. L.—Hungary in 1851.
Brace, C. L.—Norse-Folk.
Brandis, Dr. J.—Ueber den Historischen Gewinn, aus der Entzifferung der Assyrischen Inschriften. Berlin, 1856.
Breggs, J.—British Assoc., 1850. Aborig. Tribes of India.
Brugsch, H.—Uebersichtliche Erklärung der Egyptischen Denkmäler. Berlin, 1850.
Boué Ami—La Turquie d'Europe. Paris, 1840.

Cambridge Essays—Donaldson on English Ethnology. London, 1856.
Carpenter, W. B.—Zoology. London, 1857.
Carrère, Fred.—De la Sénégambie Française.
Curzon, R.—Monasteries of the Levant. New York, 1849.
Casca, Fr. von—Skizze Einer Geschichte de Zigeuner. Stuttgart, 1840.
Castrén, M. A.—Ethnol. Vorlesungen über die altäischen Völker. St. Petersburg, 1857.
Castrén, M. A.—Buriat, Spr.
Charencey, M. de—1858. Langue Japanaise. Annales de la Philosophie Chrétienne, Tome 18.
Charencey, M. de—Recherches sur les Origines de la Langue Basque. Annales de la Philosophie, et cet. Juillet, 1859.
Chinese Repertory—1845.
Chowlson's Uebereste der Alt. Bab. Literatur.
Churchill, H.—Mt. Lebanon, &c. London, 1853.
Clarus, L.—Darstellung der Spanischen Literatur. Mainz, 1846.
Combe, E.—Voyage en Egypte, et Nubie. Paris, 1846.
Cooley, W. D.—Negroland of the Arabs, et cet. London, 1841.
Crawfurd, J.—History of Indian Archipelago. Edinboro', 1820.
Crawfurd's Essays.
Cunningham, A.—Ladak, et cet. London, 1824.
Curtius, E.—Peloponnesus, et cet. Gotha, 1851.
Czoernig, K. von—Ethnol. der Oestereichischen Monarchie. Wien, 1857.

Dana, J. D. on Species, American Journal of Science, Nov., 1847.
Daniells, W. F.—Journal of Ethnographical Society, 1856, vol. 4. Ethnography of Gold Coast.
Darwin, C.—Origin of Species. London, 1859.
De Courzon, A.—Histoire des Peuples Bretons. Paris, 1846.
De Gobineau, A.—Essai sur l'Inégalité des Races Humaines. Paris, 1853.
De Guignes, J.—Histoire générale des Huns, Turcs, Mongols, et autres Tartares Occidentaux. Paris, 1756–58.
Delanoue, M. J.—De l'Ancienneté de l'Espèce Humaine. Valenciennes, 1862.
De Salles, E. Fr.—Histoire Générale des Races Humaines. Paris, 1849.
D'Halloy, J. J. D.—Des Races Humaines. Paris, 1859.
Dictionnaire de la Conversation. (Basques.)
Dictionary of Greek and Roman Geography.
Diefenbach, L. von—Origines Europææ. Frankfurt am M. 1861.
Draper, Dr. J. W.—Human Physiology. New York, 1856.
Duncker, M.—Geschichte des Alterthums. Berlin, 1855.
Dwight and Smith—Missionary Researches in Armenia. London, 1834.

Earl, G. W.—Native Races of the Indian Archipelago. London, 1853.
Eichthal, d' Gustave—Memoires de la Société Ethnologique. Vol. 1.
Ellis, W.—Polynesian Researches. London, 1852.
Elphinstone, M.—An Account of the Kingdom of Cabul and its Dependencies. London, 1842.
Encyclopédie des Gens du Monde.
Encyclopædia Britannica.
Erro, Don Juan de—El Mundo Primitivo, t. 10. Madrid, 1815.
Ersch und Gruber—Encyklopädie Allgemeine. Leipzig, 1818.
Ethnological Library, 1853.
Ethnological Journal.
Evans, J. W.—(Flints.) Report to Society of Antiquarians. (Athenæum, June 11, 1859.)
Exploration Scientifique de l'Algerie. Paris, 1848 et 1853.

Ferguson, Robert—The Northmen in Cumberland and Westmoreland. London, 1856.
Ferrier, S. P.—Voyages en Perse, et cet. Paris, 1860.
Finlay, G.—Greece under the Romans. Edinburgh, 1844.
Fleming, Rev. F.—Caffraria and its Inhabitants. London, 1853.
Forbes, Fred. E.—Dahomey and the Dahomans. London, 1851.

Forbiger, A.—Handbuch der Alten Geographie, aus den Quellen bearbeitet. Leipzig, 1842-48.

Gabelentz, H. C. von der—Die Melanesischen Sprachen, et cet. Leipzig, 1860.

Gerard, P. A. F.—Histoire des Races Humaines d'Europe. Bruxelles, 1849.

Gibbon, E.—The History of the Decline and Fall of the Roman Empire. London, 1806.

Giullain—Documents sur l'Afrique Orientale, publiés par l'ordre du Gouvernment.

Gisquet, M.—L'Egypte, les Turcs et les Arabes. Paris.

Gobat, Rev. S.—Three years' Residence in Abyssinia. New York, 1850.

Godwin, Parke—The History of France. New York, 1860.

Grant, Dr. A.—The Nestorians or Lost Tribes. New York, 1853.

Graslin, L. H.—De l'Ibérie ou Essai critique sur l'Origine des premières Populations de l'Espagne. Paris, 1838.

Greenough, W. W.—Journal of Oriental Society. Vol. 1st (Kaffirs).

Grout, L.—Journal of Oriental Society (Kaffirs).

Gutschmid, A. von—Beiträge zur Ges. d. Alt. Orient. Leipzig, 1858.

Gurowski, A.—Russia as it is. New York, 1854.

Hahn, T. G. von.—Alban. Studien. Jenae, 1854.

Hammer, Purgstall J. von—Histoire de l'Empire Ottoman. Paris, 1836.

Haxthausen, Baron de—Etudes sur la Situation, &c., de la Russie. 1847.

Haxthausen, Baron de—Transcaucasia, &c. London, 1854.

Haxthausen, Baron de—Tribes of the Caucasus. London, 1855.

Herodotus, History of—Rawlinson, G.—London, 1858-60.

Hettner, H.—Athens and the Peloponnese. Edinburgh, 1854.

Herzog's Real Enclopædie.

Hodgson, W. B.—Notes on North Africa.

Hodgson, B. H.—Selections from the Records of the Government of Bengal. Papers relative to the Himalaya Mountains and Népál.

Hodgson, B. H.—1860. Continuation of the Grammatical Analysis, et cet.

Hodgson, B. H.—1857. Comparative Vocabulary of the Languages of the Broken Tribes of Népál.

Hodgson, B. H.—Aborigines of the Nilgiris, and of Eastern Ghat.

Hodgson, B. H.—Aborigines of the Nilgiris, with Remarks on their Affinities.

Hodgson, B. H.—On the Aborigines of the Eastern Frontier.
Hodgson, B. H.—On the Chepang and Busunda Tribes of Népál.
Hodgson, B. H.—1850. Aborigines of the North-east Frontier.
Hodgson, B. H.—Aborigines of Ceylon.
Hodgson, B. H.—Calcutta, 1849. Aborigines of Southern India.
Hodgson, B. H.—Route from Báthmándú, the Capital of Népál, et cet. interspersed with Remarks on the People and Country.
Hodgson, B. H.—1853. On the Indo-Chinese Borderers.
Hodgson, B. H.—Calcutta, 1847. On the Aborigines of India.
Hoffman—Die Iberer.
Hollard, H.—De l'Homme, &c. Paris, 1853.
Huc, M.—Journey through the Chinese Empire. New York, 1856.
Huc, M.—Journey through Tartary, Thibet, and China. New York, 1852.
Humboldt, Wm. von—Prufung, &c., über die Urbewohner Hispaniens, &c. Berlin, 1821.
Humboldt, Wm. von—Ueber die Kawi Sprache auf der Insel Java, &c. Berlin, 1836.

Janin, Jules—La Normandie. Paris, ——
Johnston, C.—Travels in Southern Abyssinia, through the Country of Adel to the Kingdom of Shoa. London, 1844.
Jornandes.—De Getarum sive Gothorum origine. 1597.
Journal Oriental Society.
Journal Royal Asiatic Society.
Journal Asiatic Society, 1852. (Capt. S. C. Macpherson, L. Gen. Briggs).
Journal Asiatic Society of Bengal.

Kæuffer, J. G. R.—Geschichte von Ost-Asien. Leipzig, 1858.
Kaffirs—Proceedings of the Committee to inquire into the State of. Parts 4 and 5. Natal, 1853.
Kemble, A. M.—Die Sachsen in England. 1853.
Klaproth, J. von—Vocabulaire et Grammaire de la Langue Géorgienne. Paris, 1827.
Klaproth, J. von—Mémoires relatifs à l'Asie, et cet. Paris, 1824.
Knobel, A.—Die Völkertafel, et cet. Giessen, 1850.
Kœppen, A. L.—The World in the Middle Ages. New York, 1854.
Kolbe, Rev. F. N.—Journal of Ethnological Society. 1854.
Kolbe, Rev. F. N.—An Account of Damara Country.
Krapf, J. L.—Vocabulary of the Galla Language. 1842.
Kubalski, N. A.—Recherches Slavoniques et Historiques, et cet. Tours, 1852.

Kurd de Schloezer—Les premiers Inhabitants de la Russia. Paris, 1846.

Labastide, C. de—Dissertation sur les Basques. Paris, 1786.
Lane, E. W.—Account of the Manners and Customs of the Modern Egyptians. London, 1842.
Lang, J. D.—View of the Origin and Migration of the Polynesian Nation. London, 1834.
Lartet, M.—Sur l'Ancienneté Geologique de l'Espèce humaine dans l'Europe Occidentale.
Layard—Nineveh and its Remains. London, 1849.
Leake, Wm. M.—Researches in Greece. London, 1814.
Lemcke, von E.—Handbuch der Spanischen Literatur. Leipzig, 1855.
Lefebure, T.—Voyage en Abyssinie executée pendant les Années 1839–43. Relation historique et cet. Paris, 1845.
Leo, Vorlesungen über die Geschichte des Deutschen Volkes. 1854.
Léouzon le Duc—La Finlande. Paris, 1845.
Lewis, Sir G. C.—Origin and Formation of the Romance Languages. London, 1862.
Livingstone's Travels in Africa. New York, 1858.
Logan, J. R.
Lottner, Dr. C.—Transactions of Philog. Society. 1860–61. Sister Families of Language.
Lücken, H.—Die Einheit des Mensch. Geschlechts. Hanover, 1845.
L'Univers (Egypte Moderne).
L'Univers (Nubie).
Lepsius—Königsbuch der alten Egypter. 1858.
Lepsius, R.—Das Todtenbuch der Egypter, nach dem Papyrus in Turin. Leipzig, 1842.
Lepsius, R.—Die Chronologie der Egypter. Einleitung und Erster Theil. Kritik der Quellen. Berlin, 1849.
Lepsius, R.—Discoveries in Egypt, Ethiopia, and the Peninsula of Sinai, in the years 1842–45. Edited by K. R. H. McKenzie. London, 1853
Link, H. F.—Die Urwelt und das Alterthum. Erster Theil. Berlin, 1834.
Lubbock, J.—Natural History Review.
Les Comptes Rendus.
Lyell, Sir C.—Reports of British Association.
Lyell, Sir C.—Flint Implements in Drift. Athenæum (1665) 1859.
Lyell, Sir C.—Antiquity of Man. London, 1863.
Latham, R. G.—The Ethnology of the British Islands. London, 1852.
Latham, R. G.—Ethnology of the British Colonies and Dependencies. London, 1851.

Latham, R. G.—Man and his Migrations. London, 1851.
Latham, R. G.—Native Races of the Russian Empire. London, 1854.
Latham, R. G.—Descriptive Ethnology. London, 1859.

Magyar, Ladislaus—Reisen in Süd-Afrika.
Mariotti, L.—Italy, Past and Present. London, 1849.
Marsh, G. P.—Origin of the English Language, &c. New York, 1862.
Maury, A.—Questions rélatives à l'Ancienne Ethnologie de la France.
Maury, A.—La Terre et l'Homme. Paris, 1857.
Maury, A.—Bulletin de la Soc. de Géographie. Les Populations Primitives du Nord de l'Hindoustan. Avril, 1854.
Mazure, M.—Béarn et le Pays Basque.
Michel, F.—Histoire des Races Maudites de la France, et de l'Espagne. Paris, 1847.
Michel, F.—Le Pays Basque. Paris, 1857.
Michelet, J.—Histoire de France. Bruxelles, 1834.
Mickiewicz, A.—Les Pays Slaves et la Pologne. Paris, 1849.
Moul, B. A.—Traité des Dégénérescences, et cet., de l'Espèce Humaine, &c. Paris, 1857.
Motley, J. L.—Rise, &c., of Dutch Republic. New York, 1856.
Movers, F. C.—Das Phoenizische Alterthum, Erster Theil. Politische Geschichte und Staatsverfassung; Zweiter Theil, Geschichte der Colonien. Berlin, 1849.
Moreau de Jonnés, Alex.—Statistique de l'Espagne. Paris, 1834.
Moreau de Jonnés, Alex.—Ethnogénie Caucasienne. Paris, 1861.
Mommsen, T.—Römische Geschichte. Berlin, 1856–59.
Moffat, R.—Missionary Labours and Scenes in South Africa. New York, 1843.
Müller, F. H. Dr.—Ugrischer Volkstamm. Berlin, 1837.
Müller, M.—(Bunsen's Phil. of Universal History.)
Müller, M.—Science of Language. New York, 1862.
Müller, M.—Languages at the Seat of War. London, 1855.
Münch. Nord. German. Volk. (1853.)
Münch, Prof.—Norst Mainidskrift. 1st Hefte.
Murray's Handbook for Spain. London, 1847.

Nestemont, M. A.—Histoire de la Conquête d'Algerie. Paris, 1856.
Niebuhr, M.—Geschichte Assur's und Babel's. Berlin, 1857.
North British Review, May, 1859.—Australasian Ethnology.
Nott, E. and Gliddon, J. R.—Types of Mankind, etc. Philadelphia, 1854.
Nott, E. and Gliddon J. R.—Indigenous Races, et cet. Philadelphia, 1857.

Oppert, J.—Zeit der Morgenl. Ges. 10, 288-802.

Oppert, Jules.—Expedit. Scientif. en Mésopotamie, et cet. Paris, 1858-59.

Owen, Prof.—Athenæum, Sept. 21st, 1861. Osteology and Dentition of the Natives of the Andaman Islands.

Owen, R.—Palæontology. Edinburgh, 1860.

Ohsson, fils, d' M. C.—Histoire des Mongols.

Pott, A. F.—Zigeuner, Zeit. d. M. Ges. Vol. 3, 8, 11.

Pott, A. F.—Zigeuner in Europa und Asien. Halle, 1844.

Pott, A. F.—Ungleichheit Menschlicher Racen. Lemgo, 1856.

Parkyn—Life in Abyssinia. 1853.

Paget, J.—Hungary and Transylvania. Philadelphia, 1850.

Proceedings of Philological Society.

Postans, Capt.—In Ethnol. Soc. Jour. Vol. 1.

Prichard, J. C.—Eastern Origin of Celtic Nations, et cet. London, 1831.

Prichard, J. C.—Researches into the Physical History of Mankind. London, 1841.

Prichard, J. C.—Natural History of Man. London, 1848.

Poole, T. E.—Life, et cet., in Sierra Leone, &c. London, 1850.

Philological Review.

Plath, J. H.—Geschichte des östlichen Asiens. Göttingen, 1830.

Perthes, Boucher de—Les Antiquités Celtiques, et cet. Paris, 1847.

Pictet, F. G.—Bibliothéque Universelle. De la Question de l'Homme Fossile. Genève, 1860.

Pulszky, F.—The Tricolour on the Atlas. London, 1855.

Poole, R. S.—The Genesis of Earth and of Man. Edinburgh, 1856.

Petermann, Dr.—Geographische Mittheilungen, 1857. No. 9, 1859. Die Englische Expedition unter Burton und Speke nach Inner Africa.

Petermann, Dr.—No. 5. Süd-Africa in 1858. E. Behm.

Petermann, Dr.—Die Hottentotten Stämme, 2, 1858.

Petermann, Dr.—Die Völker in Öst Africa, 10, 1858.

Peney's Soudan.

Quatrefages, A. de—Unité de l'Espèce Humaine. Paris, 1861.

Ritter—Die Erdkunde von Asien. 1832.

Rich, A.—Narration of a Journey to the site of Babylon, et cet. London, 1839.

Renan, E.—Histoire Générale des Langues Semitiques. Paris, 1855.

Ridley, Rev. Wm.—Polynesia. (Journal Ethnological Society.)

Rémusat, J. P. A.—Recherches sur le Langues Tartares. Paris, 1820.
Rütimeyer, Prof.
Revue de l'Orient, 1858. Place de l'Armenien.
Revue Archéologique, November, 1845.
Raverty, Capt. H. G.—A Grammar of the Pushtu, or Language of the Afghans. London, 1859.
Renan, E.—La Litérature Nabath. Rev. Germanique, 1860.
Ridley, Rev. Wm.—Journal Ethnological Society.
Rafenel, A.—Nouveaux Voyages dans le Pays des Négres, 1806.
Rafenel, A.—Voyage dans l'Afrique Occidentale, 1842.
Rigler, Dr. von L.—Die Türkic und derem Bewohner. Wien, 1852.
Roulin—Des Sciences Naturelles, Tome 16, 1829.
Robinson, Mrs.—Language and Lit. of Slavic Nations. New York, 1850.
Rochet d'Hericourt, C. E.—Voyage, et cet., dans le Royaume de Choa. Paris, 1852.

St. Hilaire, J. G.—Histoire Générale et Particulière des Anomalies. Bruxelles, 1837.
St. Hilaire, J. G.—Histoire Naturelle des Regnes Organiques. Vol. 2. Paris, 1859.
Schafarik, P. J. Slavische Alterthümer. Leipzig, 1843.
Seymour, H. D., M.P.—Russia on the Black Sea. London, 1855.
Spengler, Fr. R.—Dissertatio de Cinganis. Lugd. Bat., 1839.
Scudder, Rev. D. C.—Bib. Sac., Vol. 17, No. 68. Aborigines of India, 1860.
Stricker, W.—Die Verbreitung des Deutschen Volkes, et cet. Leipzig, 1845.
Stephens, E. B.—The Basque Provinces. London, 1837.
Strzelecki, P. E. de—Physical Description of N. S. Wales and Van Diemen's Land. London, 1845.
St. Martin, Viv. de—Bulletin de la Soc. de Géographie (White Nile).
Schlatter, G. F.—Die Unwahrscheinlichkeit der Abstammung des Menschengeschlechts von einem gemeinschaftlichen Urpaare. Mannheim, 1861.
Seyffarth, Gust.—Chronologia Sacra. Leipzig, 1861.
Silliman's Journal, 1859.
Smyth, Thomas—The Unity of the Human Races. Edinburgh, 1851.
Smithsonian Reports. 1861.
Silliman's Journal, Vol. 39. African Languages.
St. John, Bayle—Village Life in Egypt. 1853.
Stritter—Memor. pop. e. Script. Byzant. Petropoli, 1771.
Schleicher, Alg. Monatsch. für Wissen. Sept., 1853. Staats Lexikon.

Troyon, M. F.—Habitations Lacustres de Concise dans le Canton de Vaud. Rev. Arch. 1861. Ditto, en Suisse.
Thiersch, F.—De l'Etat actuel de la Grèce. Leipzig, 1833.
Tiedemann, Dr. F.—Das Hirn des Negers. Heidelberg, 1837.
Ticknor, G.—History of Spanish Literature. New York, 1849.
Tacitus—Notes by Latham. London, 1851.
Tasmanian Review.

Urquhart, D.—The Pillars of Hercules, &c. London, 1850.
Ubicini, M. F.—Lettres sur la Turquie. Paris, 1853.
Uhlemann, Fr.—Die Israeliten und Hyksos in Aegypten. Leipzig, 1856.
United States' Exploring Expedition. Ethnography of Lew Chew Islands. Philadelphia, 1846.

Von Köppen, Peter—Petermann's Geographische Mittheilungen, 1855.
Von Klöden, G. A.—Das Stromsystem des Oberen Niles. Berlin, 1856.
Vulliemin, L.—Bib. Univ., Aug. 1861. Des Habitations Lacustres en Suisse.

Wagner, Dr. A.—Geschichte der Urwelt. Leipzig, 1857.
Weber, A.—Ind. Studien. Berlin, 1849.
Wilson, Rev. J. L.—West Africa, 1856.
Webb, Rev. E.—Jour. Amer. Or. Soc., Vol. 7, 1862. Evidences of the Scythian Affinities of the Dravidian Language, from Rev. R. Caldwell's Dravidian Grammar.
Wilson, D.—The Archæology and Pre-Annals of Scotland. Edinburgh, 1857.
Wilson, D.—Pre-Historic Man. Edinburgh, 1863.
Worsaae, J. J. A.—Letter in Athenæum, No. 1679, 1859. (Lake Maribo.)
Weber, Dr. M. J.—Die Lehre von den Ur u. Racenformen, et cet. Düsseldorf, 1830.
Wales, N. A.—The Picturesque Antiquities of Spain. London, 1846.
Wilkinson, J. G.—Modern Egypt and Thebes. London, 1843.
Williams and Calvert—Fiji and the Fijians. 1859.
Wirth, J. G. A.—Geschichte der Deutsch. Staaten in der Urzeit, Emmishoffen, 1840.
Whitney, W.—American Oriental Society Journal and New Englander.
Wittmann, Dr.—Abhandlungen der Baier. Acad. 1853.
Waiz, Dr. T.—Anthropologie der Naturvölker. 1, Leipzig, 1859; 2, Leipzig, 1860.

Worsaae, J. J. A.—Account of Danes, et cet., in England. London, 1852.

Worsaae, J. J. A.—Athenæum. Dan. Antiquities. 1679.

Wrottesley, Lord—British Association. Athenæum, June 30, 1860.

Wilkes's Exploring Expedition and Hale's Ethnography. Phil. 1848.

Williams, S. W.—Middle Kingdom, Survey of Chinese Empire. New York, 1848.

Yates, William H.—Modern History and Condition of Egypt. 1843.

Zimmermann, Dr. F. A.—Le Monde avant la Création de l'Homme. Paris, 1857.

Zoepfl, Dr. H.—Alth. des Deutschen Reichs und Rechts. Leipzig, 1860.

Zeuss, K.—Die Deutschen, &c. München, 1837.

Zeitscrift für die Kunde des Morgenlandes.

Zeitscrift für die vergleichende Sprachforschung.

Zeitscrift für die Wissenchaft d. Sprache.

Zeitscrift für d. Deutsche Morg. Gesellschaft.

Zeitscrift für allg. Erdkunde.

INDEX.